BN 6485698

VEDA
PUBLISHING HOUSE OF THE SLOVAK ACADEMY OF SCIENCES

SLOVAK ACADEMY OF SCIENCES

DEPARTMENT OF ORIENTAL STUDIES

CHIEF EDITOR

IVAN DOLEŽAL

EXECUTIVE EDITOR

JOZEF GENZOR

EDITORIAL BOARD

JOZEF BLAŠKOVIČ

ANNA DOLEŽALOVÁ

LADISLAV DROZDÍK

MARIÁN GÁLIK

VIKTOR KRUPA

JÁN MÚČKA

ANNA RÁCOVÁ

ASIAN AND AFRICAN

STUDIES

DEPARTMENT OF ORIENTAL STUDIES
OF THE SLOVAK ACADEMY OF SCIENCES BRATISLAVA

XVI

1980

1980

VEDA, PUBLISHING HOUSE
OF THE SLOVAK ACADEMY OF SCIENCES ● BRATISLAVA

CURZON PRESS ● LONDON

PUBLISHED OUTSIDE THE SOCIALIST COUNTRIES
SOLELY BY CURZON PRESS LTD ● LONDON AND DUBLIN
ISBN 0 7007 0137 0
ISSN 0571 2742

CONTENTS

ZUM SIEBZIGSTEN GEBURTSTAG VON JOZEF BLAŠKOVIČ

Auch wenn man nicht sagen kann, daß die Orientalistik in der Slowakei zu den weit entwickelten wissenschaftlichen Bereichen gehören würde, darf sie doch auf eine lange Tradition zurückblicken. Das Hauptaugenmerk wurde in der Vergangenheit vor allem auf das Studium des Hebräischen und in kleinerem Maße auch dem Türkischen gewidmet. Die Bedeutung des Türkischen entsprang der Tatsache, daß das Gebiet der jetzigen Slowakei das Grenzgebiet des Osmanischen Reiches und ein Teil des Gebietes im 16. und 17. Jahrhundert direkt unter osmanischer Herrschaft war. Aus praktischen Gründen beherrschten zu jener Zeit, aber auch später mehrere Leute das Türkische, ob schon um dolmetschen zu können oder gar aus wissenschaftlichem Interesse.

In der Mitte des 17. Jahrhunderts führte Ján Hrabský aus Radvaň, der schon früher den Rektor des evangelischen Kollegiums in Prešov J. Matthaeides mit einem türkischen Gedicht ehrte, an der Wittenberger Universität ein Disput zum Thema *Exercitatio Philologica Generalis de Utilitate et Necessitate Linguarum Orientalium*. Während seines Aufenthalts in Deutschland korrigierte er die türkischen Ausgaben der Bibel, die in Leipzig erschienen, und zu Hause wirkte er dann als Dolmetscher des Türkischen.

Ein bedeutender Wissenschaftler slowakischer Herkunft František A. Kollár, gebürtig aus Terchová (1718), der als Direktor der Kaiserlichen Bibliothek in Wien tätig war, machte sich um die Turkologie durch die zweite Ausgabe von Meninskis *Institutiones linguae Turcicae* (1756) verdient, und zwei Defters, die später in Göttingen hinterlegt wurden, blieben aus seiner Sammlung erhalten.

Der slowakische Geograph Ján M. Korabinský (1740—1811) trug zur Kenntnis des Türkischen in der Slowakei mit einem kleinen mehrsprachigen Wörterbuch *Versuch eines kleines Tuerkischen Woerterbuchs mit beygesessten deutsch-ungarisch und boehmisch Bedeutungen und einer kurzgefassten tuerkischen Sprachlehre von... Pressburg 1788 bei.*

Die Kenntnis des Türkischen in der Slowakei im 18. Jahrhundert war vor allem unter den balkanischen orthodoxen Kaufleuten, Bürgern des Osmanischen Reiches verbreitet. Noch vom Ende des 18. Jahrhunderts besitzen wir den Beweis über einen türkischen Dolmetscher in Bratislava.

Unter den Turkologen, die im ehemaligen Ungarn berühmt wurden, muß auch Ján Repický, gebürtig aus Nový Tekov (23. 4. 1817) erwähnt werden, der nach seiner Reifeprüfung am Lyzeum zu Bratislava das Hebräische, Arabische, Türkische und Persische an den Universitäten in Tübingen und Wien studierte. Neben seiner umfangreichen orientalistischen Arbeit (Grammatiken des Türkischen und Persischen, orientalische Literaturen) sammelte er einen Band ungarischer Übersetzungen türkischer Schriftstücke aus der Zeit der osmanischen Herrschaft in Ungarn.

Dieser kurze Überblick des Interesses für das Türkische in der Slowakei, bzw. über die Arbeit von Turkologen slowakischer Herkunft wollte aufweisen, daß das Interesse für diese Problematik tiefe Wurzeln hat, die turkologische Forschung sich jedoch mit Hinblick auf die ungünstigen politischen und kulturellen Verhältnisse erst nach der Befreiung in vollem Ausmaße realisieren konnte.

Das größte Verdienst um die Veröffentlichung der osmanischen Quellen zur Geschichte der Slowakei hat zweifelsohne unser Jubilar Jozef Blaškovič, der diesem Werk drei Jahrzehnte seiner Tätigkeit gewidmet hat. Wie bei der Mehrzahl der älteren Orientalisten, war auch sein Weg zur Turkologie nicht geradlinig.

Jozef Blaškovič wurde am 12. Juni 1910 in Imeľ, Kreis Komárno, in der Familie eines Dorfschmiedes geboren. In den schweren Jahren des ersten Weltkrieges besuchte er die Schule zuerst in seiner Geburtsgemeinde und später das Gymnasium in Komárno (1921—1929). Hier legte er seine Reifeprüfung ab und studierte weiter an der Lehreranstalt in Bratislava (1930—1931). In der Zwischenzeit wirkte er als Hilfslehrkraft in Topoľníky (1929—1930). Nach Beendigung seines Militärdienstes war er längere Zeit als Lehrer an der Bürgerschule in Galanta (1938—1946) tätig. Zu dieser Zeit beendete er im Fernstudium das Studienfach Mathematik-Physik an der Pädagogischen Hochschule in Szeged (1943). Noch während des zweiten Weltkrieges begann Blaškovič turkologische Vorlesungen an der Budapester Universität zu besuchen, wo J. Németh und L. Fekete zu seinen Lehrern gehörten.

Nach dem Krieg unterrichtete er an der Mittelschule in Bratislava-Prievoz und für eine bestimmte Zeit arbeitete er bei der Katalogisierung orientalischer Handschriften in der Universitätsbibliothek in Bratislava. Gleichzeitig setzte er sein Studium des Türkischen bei Professor J. Rypka an der Karls-Universität in Prag fort. Im Jahre 1950 erwarb er den Doktorgrad in Philosophie auf Grund der erfolgreich verteidigten Dissertation (Nr. 5), in der er 47 osmanische Urkunden, wichtig für das Erfassen der Politik der Hohen Pforte zu Siebenbürgen und Teilen der nordöstlichen Slowakei in der zweiten Hälfte des 17. Jahrhunderts behandelte. Es geht um die Bearbeitung eines Teils der Urkunden aus der, einst in Göttingen aufbewahrten, im 2. Weltkrieg vernichteten Handschrift Turc. 29.

Seit dem Beginn des Wintersemesters 1950 war Dr. Blaškovič als Fachassistent an der Philosophischen Fakultät der Karls-Universität tätig, wo er praktische Übungen im Türkischen und Ungarischen leitete. Es war sein Verdienst, da das traditionsgebundene, islamistisch orientierte Studium des Türkischen später um Vorlesungen aus der allgemeinen Turkologie, aus der Geschichte der modernen türkischen Literatur und aus der älteren Geschichte der Türkenvölker erweitert wurde. Für Studenten des Türkischen verfaßte er das Skriptum Geschichte der neuen türkischen Literatur (Nr. 25), das auch ins Bulgarische übersetzt wurde.

Dr. Blaškovičs wissenschaftliche Tätigkeit war vor allem auf die Erforschung der türkischen Quellen zur Geschichte der osmanischen Herrschaft in Ungarn und Slowakei in heimischen sowie ausländischen Archiven gerichtet. In seiner Habilitationsschrift bearbeitete er die Sammlung türkischer Urkunden aus Rimavská Sobota, die wertvolle Dokumente über die wirtschaftliche Stellung dieses kleinen Städtchens unter der osmanischen Herrschaft im 17. Jh. darstellen (Nr. 120). Von ähnlichem Charakter sind auch die türkischen Urkunden aus Miskolc, die Blaškovič als Kandidatendissertation bearbeitete (Nr. 50). Im Jahre 1962 wurde er zum ordentlichen Dozenten der Turkologie an der Philosophischen Fakultät der Karls-Universität in Prag ernannt.

In der darauf folgenden Zeit verfaßte er eine große Anzahl von Studien und Artikeln, die unbekanntes türkisches Material zur Geschichte der osmanischen Herrschaft in der Slowakei behandeln (Nr. 44, 52, 56, 71, 75, 78, 84, 85, 86, 92, 96, 99, 102, 103, 106). Seine Aufmerksamkeit widmete der Jubilar auch den Traditionen der turkologischen Forschung in der Slowakei, deren neuen Aufgaben und informierte in ausländischen Fachzeitschriften über den Stand der turkologischen Forschung in der Tschechoslowakei (Nr. 53, 57, 73, 76, 87, 122).

Ein anderes Gebiet des wissenschaftlichen Interesses von J. Blaškovič war die Erforschung der Turzismen im Tschechischen und Slowakischen, onomastische Probleme, besonders Ortsnamen altturksprachigen Ursprungs in der Slowakei, sowie weitere linguistische Fragen (Nr. 54, 81, 82, 91, 111, 114, 116). Für die Studenten verfaßte Blaškovič ein Lehrbuch des Türkischen, das in zwei Auflagen erschien (Nr. 80, 104).

Wir haben bereits erwähnt, daß der Jubilar kurz nach Beginn seiner Tätigkeit an der Philosophischen Fakultät die Geschichte der neuen türkischen Literatur verfaßte. Da er Vorlesungen über die moderne türkische Literatur hielt, widmete er sich auch weiterhin dieser Problematik. Für das Werk Geschichte der Weltliteratur verfaßte er eine kurze Übersicht der türkischen Literatur (Nr. 74). In Skripten für Studenten der Orientalistik bearbeitete er die turkmenische Literatur (Nr. 68) und für PEN-Club eine Übersicht über die Nachforschungen und Übersetzungen aus der türkischen Literatur in der Tschechoslowakei (Nr. 70). Der neuen türkischen Literatur widmete er einen selbständigen Artikel, in dem er sich mit den Erfolgen dieser Literatur in der Welt in den 50er und 60er Jahren befaßte. Wenn wir schon über die Arbeiten des Jubilars auf dem Gebiet der Literatur berichten, können wir auch seine Beiträge für Literaturwörterbücher nicht unbeachtet lassen (Nr. 93, 128). Mit der literarischen Arbeit hängt auch die übersetzerische Tätigkeit des Jubilars eng zusammen. Er übersetzte aus dem Türkischen beinahe zehn Bücher ins Slowakische, Tschechische und Ungarische, vor allem aus dem Schaffen Nazım Hikmets, Sabahattin Alis und Aziz Nesins. Er übersetzte hauptsächlich für Zeitschriften jedoch auch türkische Volksliteratur, kasachische, aserbaidschanische und tatarische Autoren. Auch die Propagierung der türkischen Literatur in kleineren, populärwissenschaftlichen Zeitschriften, wie Nový Orient, Kultúrny život, Nedeľa, Život, Új Szó, usw. muß erwähnt werden.

In seinen Arbeiten aus der Folkloristik widmete Blaškovič seine Aufmerksamkeit der Folklore der Dobrudscha- und Krim-Tataren. Dem verbreiteten Motiv der türkischen Kriege in der mährischen und slowakischen Folklore widmete er eine selbständige Studie.

Die Ergebnisse seiner Katalogisierungsarbeit an der Sammlung islamischer Handschriften in der Universitätsbibliothek in Bratislava publizierte er im Katalog *Arabische, türkische und persische Handschriften der Universitäts-Bibliothek in Bratislava* (Nr. 59). Diese, im Jahre 1924 von Savfet Beg Bašagić angekaufte Sammlung stellt eine der bedeutendsten aus Bosnien und Herzegowina stammender Sammlungen islamischer Handschriften dar. Dr. Blaškovič war als Redakteur der Publikation tätig, und bearbeitete die türkischen Handschriften.

Seit dem Beginn der 60er Jahre widmete sich J. Blaškovič intensiv der Vorbereitung der Herausgabe türkischer Urkunden aus Rimavská Sobota. Er bereitete zuerst die deutsche Version, und nachher die slowakische Übersetzung dieser Urkunden mit einer umfangreichen Einleitung und diplomatischer Analyse vor, die unter dem Titel *Rimavská Sobota v čase osmanskotureckého panstva* (Nr. 120) erschien. Aus den osmanischen, in Rimavská Sobota und Miskolc aufbewahrten Urkunden gehen auch weitere Studien des Autors hervor, die nicht nur einige Probleme der Stellung dieser Städte unter der osmanischen Herrschaft lösen, sondern auch zu breiteren Fragen der osmanischen Geschichte einen Beitrag leisten.

Ein weiteres großes Thema des Jubilars war die Arbeit an den osmanischen Verzeichnissen des *Eyalet* Nové Zámky. Es war vor allem der *Defter-i mufassal-ı eyalet-i Uyvar* aus dem Jahre 1664, der mehr als 700 Gemeinden in der südlichen und westlichen Slowakei, die von der osmanischen Finanzverwaltung besteuert wurden, festhält. Teile dieses Verzeichnisses gab Blaškovič in kurzen Artikeln mit Fotokopien, einer Transkription ins Lateinische und einer Übersetzung heraus (Nr. 124, 127, 130, 107). Auf ähnliche Weise veröffentlichte er auch ein Verzeichnis der Vaqfe des Großwesirs Köprülüzade Ahmed Pascha im Eyalet Nové Zámky (Nr. 112, 117). Der Autor hat gegenwärtig weitere Studien auf Grund dieses Materials vorbereitet und er bereitet dessen vollständige Ausgabe vor.

Das Bild der wissenschaftlichen Tätigkeit des Jubilars wäre nicht vollständig, würden wir nicht zumindest kurz dessen Arbeit auf dem Gebiet der Hungaristik erwähnen. In tschechischer Sprache verfaßte er Lehrbücher des Ungarischen von praktischen Handbüchern bis zur normativen Grammatik, Wörterbüchern und Konversationshandbüchern, die mehrere Auflagen erreichten.

Während seiner Tätigkeit an der Philosophischen Fakultät nahm Jozef Blaškovič an mehreren Kongressen der Türk Dil Kurumu, Türk Kurumu, am Internationalen orientalistischen Kongreß in Moskau (1960), an Sitzungen der PIAC, sowie an Vortragsaufenthalten in der Türkei, Ungarn und Rumänien teil. Für seine Verdienste um die Turkologie wurde er zum korrespondierenden Ehrenmitglied der Türk Dil Kurumu gewählt (1957) und mit dem Ehrendiplom der Türkischen Republik ausgezeichnet (1975).

Der Jubilar ist Mitglied des Redaktionsrates unseres Jahrbuchs seit dessen Gründung, und er war der Herausgeber des ersten Jahrganges. Im Namen der Mitarbeiter und seiner Schüler möchten wir dem Jubilar gute Gesundheit und viel Kraft für seine weitere Arbeit wünschen, die zur Bereichung unserer Kenntnisse über die osmanische Expansion in der Slowakei und über die Kontakte unserer Vorfahren mit den Türkenvölkern beitragen wird.

Vojtech Kopčan

AUSGEWÄHLTE BIBLIOGRAPHIE VON JOZEF BLAŠKOVIC AUS DEN JAHREN 1931—1979

Abkürzungen der Zeitschriften:

AAS — Asian and African Studies, Bratislava
AOH — Acta Orientalia Academiae
    Scientiarum Hungaricae, Budapest
ArOr — Archív orientální, Praha
HŠ — Historické štúdie, Bratislava
KŽ — Kultúrny život, Bratislava

NO — Nový Orient, Praha
NOB — New Orient Bimonthly, Praha
PaS — Príroda a spoločnosť, Bratislava
TFA — Türk Folklor Araştırmaları, Istanbul
TT — Természet és társadalom, Bratislava
ÚSz — Új Szó, Bratislava
VJ — Voprosy jazykoznanija, Moskva

Der Verfasser hat seine Beiträge unter den Namen József Blaskovics, Jozef Blažkovič, Jozef Blaškovič, Josef Blaskovics, Yusuf Blaşkoviç und Josef Kováč veröffentlicht.

1. Tevfik Fikret: *A reggeli ima* (Allah akbar). Magyar Néplap, *5*, 1931, Nr. 32 (9. 8.), S. 2.
2. Sinaszi: *A róka és a szamár* (Eşek ile tilki). Magyar Néplap, *8*, 1934, Nr. 11 (2. 9.), S. 7—8.
3. *Vtáčia reč* (Kuşların dili). Nedeľa, *1*, Bratislava 1948, Nr. 16 (17. 10.), S. 16.
4. *Malý pastier* (Küçük çoban). Nedeľa, *1*, 1948, Nr. 19 (7. 11.), S. 14.
5. *Listiny Vysokej Porty vo veci obsadenia Košíc, košickej a sedmohradskej dane v rokoch 1644—1672* (Die Urkunde der Hohen Pforte in Sachen der Besetzung Kaschaus, der Kaschauer und Siebenbürgener Steuer aus den Jahren 1644—1672). Bratislava 1949. 212 S. (Handschrift.)
6. Ferit Celât Güven: *Strapec hrozna* (Bir salkım üzüm). Nedeľa, *2*, 1949, Nr. 5 (6. 2.), S. 7—8.
7. *Hriešnici v žalári* (Die Schuldigen im Kerker). Nedeľa, *2*, 1949, Nr. 10 (13. 3.), S. 18.
8. *Figliar kováč* (Schelmischer Schmied). Nedeľa, *2*, 1949, Nr. 11 (20. 3.), S. 18.
9. Hikmet Noyan: *Vtáci v zajatí* (Esir Kuşlar). Nedeľa, *2*, 1949, Nr. 12 (27. 3.), S. 7.
10. *Prísny padišah a múdry rybár* (Der strenge Padischah und der weise Fischer). Nedeľa, *2*, 1949, Nr. 13 (3. 4.), S. 6.
11. *Prečo nie Parkán?* (Warum nicht Parkán?) Nedeľa, *2*, 1949, Nr. 19 (15. 5.), S. 8.
12. *Šibalstvá Nasreddina hodžu* (Die Streiche des Hodscha Nasreddin). Nedeľa, *2*, 1949, Nr. 37 (25. 9.), S. 8.
13. *Islamské rukopisy v Knižnici Slovenskej univerzity* (Islamische Handschriften in der Bibliothek der Slowakischen Universität). In: Z bratislavských knižníc. Bratislava 1950, S. 77—85.
14. Ferit Celâl Güven: (Die Überflutung). Nedeľa, *3*, 1950, Nr. 32 (13. 8.), S. 8.
15. Názim Hikmet: *Industrialisace, Smuteční vrba, Svatý břich* (Industrialisation, Trauerweide, Heiliger Bauch). NO, *6*, 1951, Nr. 1, S. 1. (Mit V. Kubíčková).
16. Názim Hikmet: *XX. století* (XX. Asır). NO, *6*, 1951, Nr. 4, S. 82. (Mit V. Kubíčková.)
17. Sabahattin Ali: *Chinín* (Kinin). Život, *1*, 1951, Nr. 20 (18. 5.), S. 14—15.
18. *Názim Hikmet bojovník za právo a spravedlnost* (N. H. Kämpfer für Recht und Gerechtigkeit). NO, *6*, 1951, Nr. 7, S. 141—142.

19. *Názim Hikmet — tribún mieru a slobody* (N. H. — der Tribun des Friedens und der Freiheit). KŽ, *6*, 1951, Nr. 29 (22. 7.), S. 5.

20. Sabahattin Ali: *Dve manželky* (Zwei Gattinen). Život, *1*, 1951, Nr. 33 (17. 8.), S. 15.

21. Názim Hikmet: *Bojujúce srdce* (Das kämpfende Herz). Výber z poézie v prebásnení P. Horova. Bratislava, Slovenský spisovateľ 1951. 104 S.

22. *Bojovník za mier Názim Hikmet* (N. H., Kämpfer für Frieden). KŽ, *6*, 1951, Nr. 47 (25. 11.), S. 5.

23. Ferit Celâl Güven: *Hrozen vína* (Bir salkım üzüm). NO, *7*, 1952, Nr. 4, S. 67.

24. Sabahattin Ali: *Ayran*. Bratislava, Slovenský spisovateľ 1952. 128 S.

25. *Dějiny nové turecké literatury* (Geschichte der neuen türkischen Literatur). Praha, SPN 1953. 216 S.

26. Baren Boszu: *Zsoldosok* (Die Söldner). Bratislava, SVKL 1953. 180 S.

27. Sabahattin Ali: *Mocsárláz* (Schüttelfrost). Bratislava, SVKL 1953. 182 S.

28. *Anatolské příběhy* (Anatolische Geschichten). Praha, SNKL 1953. 176 S.

29. Názim Hikmet: *Orchestr* (Orkestra). NO, *8*, 1953, Nr. 2, S. 29. (Mit V. Kubíčková.)

30. Sabahattin Ali: *Ayran*. NO, *8*, 1953, Nr. 3, S. 49—51.

31. *K pátému výročí smrti Sabahattina Aliho* (Zum fünften Todestag von Sabahattin Ali). NO, *8*, 1953, Nr. 4, S. 66.

32. Sabahattin Ali: *Vražda* (Der Mord). NO, *8*, 1953, Nr. 4, S. 66.

33. Sabahattin Ali: *Přednáška o družstevnictví* (Vortrag über das Genossenschaftswesen). NO, *8*, 1953, Nr. 7, S. 114.

34. Názim Hikmet: *Petrograd 1917*. ÚSz, *6*, 1953, Nr. 310 (7. 11.), S. 1.

35. *Zivatar* (Das Gewitter). Bratislava, SVKL 1953. 134 S.

36. *Učebnice maďarštiny pro začátečníky* (Lehrbuch der ungarischen Sprache für Anfänger). Praha, SPN 1954. 358 S.

37. Názim Hikmet: *Szívem* (Mein Herz). Bratislava, SVKL 1954. 120 S. (Mit T. Tóth.)

38. Džambul Džabajev: *Píseň léta* (Sommerlied). NO, *9*, 1954, Nr. 7, S. 102. (Mit E. Herold.)

39. *Názim Hikmet bojovník za spravodlivosť* (N. H. Kämpfer für Gerechtigkeit). In: Bulletin Národného divadla v Bratislave, 15. 1. 1955. Mit Gedicht O nohaviciach (Über die Hosen).

40. Mirsej Emir: *Ospalost děda Möstäkyjma* (Die Schläfrigkeit des Großvaters Möstäkyjm). NO, *10*, 1955, Nr. 2, S. 28—29.

41. *Učebnice maďarštiny. I. Úvod do maďarštiny* (Lehrbuch der ungarischen Sprache. I. Einführung in die ungarische Sprache). Praha, SPN 1955. 262 S.

42. Džambul Džabajev: *Stalingradci* (Die Stalingrader). NO, *10*, 1955, Nr. 4, S. 54.

43. *Učebnice maďarštiny. I. Úvod do maďarštiny* (Lehrbuch der ungarischen Sprache. I. Einführung in die ungarische Sprache). 2. umgearb. Ausgabe. Praha, SPN 1956. 262 S.

44. *Ein Schreiben des Ofener Defterdār Muṣṭafā an der Hatvaner Mauteinnehmer Dervīš Baša*. In: Charisteria orientalia. Praha 1956, S. 60—71.

45. *Istorija na novata turska literatura*. Sofia 1957. 200 S. Vgl. Nr. 25.

46. *Učebnice maďarštiny* (Lehrbuch der ungarischen Sprache). Praha, SPN 1957. 356 S.

47. *Učebnice maďarštiny. II. Normativní gramatika* (Lehrbuch der ungarischen Sprache. II. Die normative Grammatik). Praha, SPN 1957. 374 S.

48. *Cvičebnice maďarštiny* (Übungsbuch der ungarischen Sprache). Praha, SPN 1958. 416 S.

49. *Malá učebnice maďarštiny* (Kleines Lehrbuch der ungarischen Sprache). Praha, Magyar Kultúra 1958. 125 S.

50. *Turecké historické listiny v Miškolci z r. 1591—1684* (Türkische historische Urkunden in Miskolc aus den Jahren 1591—1684). Praha 1959. 353 S. 45 Abb. (Handschrift.)

51. *Arabské, turecké a perzské rukopisy Univerzitnej knižnice* (Arabische, türkische und persische Handschriften der Univeristätsbibliothek). Univerzitná knižnica v Bratislave 1914—1919—1959. Martin, Matica slovenská 1959. S. 125—145. (Mit K. Petráček.)

52. *Some Notes on the Turkish Occupation of Slovakia.* In : Acta Universitatis Carolinae. Philologica I. Orientalia Pragensia I. Praha 1960, S. 41—57.

53. *Çekoslovak Türkolojisinin şimdiki durumu ve ilerideki vazifeleri.* In: 8. Türk Dil Kurumu Kurultayında okunan bilimsel bildiriler 1957. Ankara, TDK 1960. S. 19—23.

54. *Çek Dilinde Türkçe kelimeler.* Ibidem, S. 87—112.

55. *Malá učebnice maďarštiny* (Kleines Lehrbuch der ungarischen Sprache). Praha, Magyar Kultúra 1960. 125 S.

56. *Beiträge zur Lebensgeschichte des Köprülü Mehmed.* AOH, 11, f. 1—3, S. 51—55.

57. *Les buts, l'organisation et l'activité de l'école orientaliste tschécoslovaque.* In : Studia et acta orientalia, 2, Bucarest 1960, S. 61—69.

58. *Transkripce tureckých textů* (Die Transkription der türkischen Texte). In : Zprávy čs. orientalistické společnosti, 3, Praha 1961, Nr. 2, S. 98—105.

59. *Arabische, türkische und persische Handschriften der Universitäts-Bibliothek in Bratislava.* Unter der Redaktion J. Blaškovič... Bratislava, Universitätsbibliothek 1961. S. 5—28 (Einführung), S. 277—371 (Türkischen Handschriften).

60. Aziz Nesin: *Psí ohony* (Die Hundeschwänze). NO, *16*, 1961, Nr. 3, S. 53.

61. Sabahattin Ali: *Šťastný pes.* (Der glückliche Hund). Praha, SNDK 1961. 96 S.

62. *Dobruca Tatarları folkloruna ait notlar.* TFA, 1961, Nr. 145, S. 2467—2469; Nr. 146, S. 2498—2501.

63. *Cvičebnice maďarštiny* (Übungsbuch der ungarischen Sprache). Praha, SPN 1961. 416 S. 2. Aufl.

64. Aziz Nesin: *Naštěstí nejsem žena* (Zum Glück bin ich keine Frau). NO, *17*, 1962, Nr. 1, S. 18—19.

65. Aziz Nesin: *Dog Tails.* In: NOB, *2*, 1962, Nr. 1, S. 20—22.

66. *Dobruca Tatarlarının Halk Türküleri.* In : Németh Armağanı. Ankara, TDK 1962. S. 69—78.

67. *Světový tlumočník 26 řečí. Turečtina* (Weltdolmetscher der 26 Sprachen. Türkisch). Praha 1962, S. 448—505.

68. *Turkmenská literatura* (Turkmenische Literatur). In: Z dějin literatur Asie a Afriky. III. Praha 1963, S. 145—155.

69. Aziz Nesin: *Udělej něco, Mete!* (Bir şey yap, Met!). Praha, Dilia 1963. 81 S.

70. *Turkish Literature. Literatures of the Near East in Czechoslovakia 1945—1963.* Prague, PEN 1963, S. 56—66.

71. *Dél-Szlovákia a török uralom alatt* (Die Südslowakei unter türkischer Herrschaft). TT, *3*, 1963, Nr. 4, S. 26—32.

72. *Maďarština pro samouky* (Ungarisch für Autodidakten). Praha, SPN 1963. 200, XII, 112 S.

73. *Sovremennoje sostojanije i perspektivy razvitija tjurkologii v Čechoslovakii.* VJ, 1963, Nr. 5, S. 104—108.

74. *Turecká literatúra* (Türkische Literatur). In : Dejiny svetovej literatúry. I. Red. M. Pišút. Bratislava 1963, S. 65—74.

75. *K dejinám tureckej okupácie na Slovensku* (Zur Geschichte der türkischen Okkupation in der Slowakei). HŠ, *8*, 1963, S. 95—116.

76. *Tradice a úkoly turkologie na Slovensku* (Die Tradition und die Aufgaben der Turkologie in der Slowakei). In : Orientalistický sborník SAV. Bratislava 1963, S. 53—61.

77. *Nasrettin Hoca.* Dost, *11*, Istanbul 1963, Nr. 30, S. 11.

78. *Padli Turci na Poniky...* (Es fielen die Türken in Poniky ein...). PaS, *12*, 1963, Nr. 12, S. 36—43.

79. *Česko-maďarské rozhovory* (Tschechisch-ungarische Gespräche). Praha, SPN 1964. 228 S. (Mit I. Sipos und L. Hradský.)

80. *Učebnice turečtiny. Úvod do turečtiny* (Lehrbuch der türkischen Sprache. Einführung in die türkische Sprache). Praha, SPN 1964. 350 S.

16

81. *„R" sessizin söylenişi.* In: 10. Türk Dil Kurultayında okunan bilimsel bildiriler 1963. Ankara, TKD 1964. S. 5—10.

82. *Gönül — Güğül.* In: AAS, *1*, 1965, S. 49—52.

83. *Sovietico-Turcica. Beiträge zur Bibliographie der türkischen Sprachwissenschaft in russischer Sprache in der Sowjetunion 1917—1957.* Unter der Redaktion von G. Hazai. Budapest, Akadémiai Kiadó 1960. 320 S. In: AAS, *1*, 1965, S. 203—204.

84. *Dolgozó népunk sorsa a török uralom alatt* (Das Schicksal des arbeitenden Volkes unter der Türkenherrschaft). ÚSz, *18*, 1965, Nr. 9 (10. 1.), S. 11.

85. *Mit írt egy jancsár költő Érsekújvár elfoglalásakor?* (Was hat ein Janitscharen-Dichter in der Zeit der Eroberung von Neuhäusel geschrieben?). ÚSz, *18*, 1965, Nr. 50 (20. 2.), S. 6.

86. *Mit és menyit termelt Tardoskedd a török hódoltság alatt?* (Was und wieviel erzeugte Tvrdošovce unter der Türkenherrschaft?). ÚSz, *18*, 1965, Nr. 112 (24. 4.), S. 6.

87. *Die Tradition und die Aufgaben der Turkologie in der Slowakei.* In: Studia semitica philologica necnon philosophica I. Bakoš dicata. Bratislava, VSAV 1965, S. 55—68.

88. *Nasrettin Hoca ve tesir alanı.* TFA, 1965, Nr. 192, S. 3795—3796.

89. *Maďarština pro samouky* (Ungarisch für Autodidakten). 2. Aufl. Praha, SPN 1965. 204, 112 S. (Mit L. Hradský.)

90. *Entwicklung und Erfolge der gegenwärtigen türkischen Literatur.* In: Acta Universitatis Carolinae. Philologica 2. Orientalia Pragensia 4. Praha 1965, S. 5—18.

91. *Çekoslovakya topraklarında eski Türklerin izleri.* In: Reşit Rahmeti Arat Armağanı. Ankara 1966, S. 341—351.

92. *Einige Dokumente über die Verpflegung der türkischen Armee vor der Festung Nové Zámky im Jahre 1663.* In: AAS, *2*, 1966, S. 103—127.

93. *Slovník spisovatelů SSSR* (Wörterbuch der Schriftsteller der UdSSR). Praha, Svět sovětů 1966.

94. *Učebnice maďarštiny* (Lehrbuch der ungarischen Sprache). 3. Aufl. Praha, SPN 1966. 458 S.

95. *Studia et acta orientalia 2.* Bucarest 1960. 360 S. ArOr, *34*, 1966, Nr. 2, S. 270—271; AAS, *2*, 1966, S. 172—174.

96. *Köprülü Mehmed Paşanın Macarca bir ahdnamesi.* Türkiyat Mecmuası, *15*, 1968 (1969), S. 37—46.

97. *Die Protokolbücher des Kadiamtes Sofia.* Hrsg. von G. Galabov und H. Duda. München, Oldenbourg 1960. 462 S. ArOr, *34*, 1966, Nr. 4, S. 639.

98. *Kapesní česko-maďarský slovník* (Tschechisch-ungarisches Taschenwörterbuch). Praha, SPN 1968. 426 S.

99. *Rimavská Sobota pod osmansko-tureckým panstvom* (Rimavská Sobota unter der osmanisch-türkischen Herrschaft). In: Kapitoly z dejín a prírody okresu Rimavská Sobota. Bratislava 1968, S. 23—70. Auch ungarisch erschienen.

100. *Çek folklorunda Türkler.* In: 11. Türk Dil Kurultayında okunan bilimsel bildiriler. Ankara 1968, S. 189—207.

101. *Einige tatarische Volkslieder aus der Dobrudscha.* In: Les études balkaniques tchécoslovaques 3. Praha 1968, S. 125—139.

102. *Peniaze, miery a váhy používané na území Slovenska okupovanom Turkami v 17. stor.* (Geld, Maße und Waagen in der Slowakei unter der türkischen Okkupation im 17. Jh.). HŠ, *14*, 1969, S. 210—216.

103. *Néhány mátyusföldi falunév érdekes multja* (Die interessante Vergangenheit einiger Dorfnamen von Mathiasland). Népművelés, *14*, 1969, Nr. 8, S. 5—6; Nr. 9, S. 18—19.

104. *Učebnice turečtiny* (Lehrbuch der türkischen Sprache). 2. Aufl. Praha, SPN 1970. 354 S.

105. *Turistická maďarština* (Ungarische Sprache für Touristen). Praha, Čs. rozhlas 1970. 164 S. (Mit L. Hradský.)

17

106. *Türkische Quellen das Wort Kuruc betreffend.* In: Studia Turcica. Budapest, Akadémiai Kiadó 1971, S. 73—88.

107. *Turecký daňový súpis nitrianskej župy z r. 1664* (Türkische Steuerkonskription des Neutra-Komitates aus dem J. 1664). Agrikultúra, *10*, Bratislava 1971, S. 29—37.

108. *Česko-maďarské rozhovory* (Tschechisch-ungarische Gespräche). 2. Aufl. Praha, SPN 1971. 228 S. (Mit I. Sipos.)

109. *Turecké historické listiny z Gemera* (Türkische historische Urkunden aus Gemer). In: Vlastivedné štúdie z Gemera. I. Bratislava 1972, S. 9—25.

110. *Türkische historische Urkunden aus Gemer.* In: AAS, *8*, 1972, S. 71—89.

111. *Toponimy starotjurskogo proischoždenija na territorii Slovakii.* VJ, 1972, Nr. 6, S. 62—75.

112. *Vakfy v novozámockom a nitrianskom okrese* (Vakfe in den Bezirken Nitra und Nové Zámky). HŠ, *18*, 1973, S. 265—275.

113. *Verzeichnis der orientalischen Handschriften in Deutschland XIII:* 1. Flemming, B.: *Türkische Handschriften 1.*; Götz, M.: *Türkische Handschriften 2.* Wiesbaden 1968. Orientalistische Literaturzeitung, *68*, 1973, Nr. 3—4, Kol. 165—173.

114. *Some Toponyms of Turkic Origin in Slovakia.* In: AOH, *27*, 1973, S. 191—199.

115. *Osmanlılar Hâkimiyeti devrinde Slovakya'da vergi sistemi hakkında.* In: Türk Araştırmaları Dergisi, 7, 1969 (1973), Nr. 12—13. S. 191—199.

116. *Régi török nyelvi eredetű helynévek Szlovákiában.* In: Hungarian Past 3, Sydney 1974, Nr. 1, S. 1—14. Vgl. Nr. 114.

117. *Das Sultansdekret (Sünurname) über das Vakf in Bezirk Nové Zámky.* In: ArOr, *42*, 1974, Nr. 3, S. 300—309+ IV.

118. *Das Osmanisch-Türkische in Donauraum im 17. Jahrhundert.* In: Schriften zur Geschichte und Kultur der altaischen Völker. Berlin, Akademie-Verlag 1974, S. 125—138.

119. *Dva tureckich dokumenta k istorii Transil'vanii.* In: Vostočnyje istočniki po istorii narodov Jugo-Vostočnoj i Central'noj Jevropy. III. Moskva 1974, S. 150—160.

120. *Rimavská Sobota v čase osmanskotureckého panstva* (Rimavská Sobota in der Zeit der osmanisch-türkischen Oberherrschaft). Bratislava, Obzor 1974. 363 S.

121. *Slovakya'da eski Türkçe yeradları.* In: 12. Türk Dil Kurultayında sunulan bilimsel bildiriler. Ankara, TDK 1975. S. 295—298.

122. *Tjurkologičeskije issledovanija v Čechoslovakii.* VJ, 1975, Nr. 1, S. 122—126.

123. Hazai, G.: *Das Osmanisch-Türkische im XVII. Jh.* Budapest 1973. 498 S. In: AAS, *10*, 1974 (1975), S. 231—233.

124. *Ziemie lenne (ḫāṣṣ) namiestnika Nowych Zamków w latach 1664—1685* (Die Ḫāṣṣ-Länder des Statthalters von Nové Zámky in den Jahren 1664—1685). In: Rocznik Orientalistyczny, *38*, 1976, S. 83—91.

125. *Zwei türkische Lieder über die Eroberung von Nové Zámky aus dem Jahre 1663.* In: AAS, *12*, 1976, S. 63—69.

126. *Research in Altaic Languages.* Budapest 1975. 338 S. In: AAS, *12*, 1976, S. 274—276.

127. *Ein türkisches Steuerverzeichnis aus dem Bezirk von Žabokreky aus dem Jahre 1664.* In: ArOr, *46*, 1977, Nr. 3, S. 201—210.

128. *Slovník spisovateľů. Sovětský svaz. I—II.* (Wörterbuch der Schriftsteller. UdSSR. I—II). Praha 1977: altaische, tschuwaschische, baschkirische, tatarische und tuwinische Schriftsteller.

129. *Slovenská jména v tureckých daňových soupisech r. 1664* (Slowakische Namen in den türkischen Steuerkonskriptionen des Jahres 1664). In: Zpravodaj místopisné komise ČSAV, *19*, 1978, Nr. 1—2, S. 13—25.

130. *Turecký daňový súpis Žabokreckého okresu z roku 1664.* Agrikultúra, *15*, 1978, S. 65—76. Vgl. Nr. 127.

ARTICLES

LES CAPITULATIONS ET LES VILLES OTTOMANES

ZDENKA VESELÁ-PŘENOSILOVÁ, Prague

Cette étude analyse les conséquences des capitulations pour la structure sociale des villes ottomanes. Celles-ci, dépendant de l'administration d'Etat, ne jouaient qu'un rôle subalterne dans la vie politique du pays. Par contre, le système des *millets* (communauté religieuse) présentait un facteur important divisant la structure de la bourgeoisie. Au dernier siècle, les chrétiens de l'Empire Ottoman pouvaient aussi jouir des capitulations. Ainsi, les capitulations, tout en soutenant la bourgeoisie chrétienne, obligeaient la bourgeoisie turque à garder une position secondaire et de cette façon, représentaient un facteur retardataire dans l'evolution des villes ottomanes vers une vie sociale du pays sur son chemin historique vers le capitalisme.

Les capitulations, accomodements entre le gouvernement ottoman et les représentants des Etats étrangers concernant les droits de leurs ressortissants au pays, connaissaient dans la région de la Méditerranée de l'Est une longue tradition antécédente à l'époque, où le sultan Süleyman le Magnifique signa les privilèges accordés aux sujets du roi de France. Pour l'Empire Ottoman, les capitulation offertes à la France formaient un geste comportant une possibilité de présenter sa puissance et grandeur. Quant à la France, c'était pour elle une nouvelle possibilité de pénétrer sur les territoires que les Européens avaient été obligés de quitter après l'échec des Croisades, une possibilité qui s'ouvrait pour elle avec ces relations nouvelles. Bien que cet aspect de la politique internationale se reflétât aussi dans les autres capitulations conclues successivement par les Ottomans avec la plupart des Etats européens, les privilèges y confirmés ne perdaient pas le caractère d'un facteur facilitant le commerce international.[1]

Tout d'abord, nous nous permettons de présenter ici un petit tableau des idées principales des conventions en question. Les sujets «qui n'appartiennent pas à l'Etat elevé (L'Empire Ottoman)» et «les sujets et les commerçants de l'Etat mentionné qui viennent dans ces regions» ne sont obligés de payer les impôts qu'au consulat.

---

[1] Nebioglu, Osman: *Die Auswirkungen der Kapitulationen auf die türkische Wirtschaft*, Jena 1941, pp. 14, 15; Sousa, N.: *The capitulary régime of Turkey. Its history, origin and nature*, Baltimore 1933; Lehman, W.: *Die Kapitulationen*, Weimar 1917; von Overbeck, A. A.: *Die Kapitulationen des Osmanischen Reiches*, Breslau 1917; Pélissié du Rausas, G.: *Le Régime des Capitulations dans l'Empire Ottoman*, Paris 1902—1905 (2 vols.); Taner, T.: *Kapitülasyonlar nasıl ilga edildi?* (Comment furent abolies les capitulations?), İkt. Yürüyüş, 21—22 (391—394), 1960—1961 etc. — Le texte turc de l'ahdnâme pour la reine d'Angleterre, presque identique avec celui des autres capitulations — d'après M. T. Gökbilgin en İA, VI, 838 — est publié à *Münşeâti Ferîdûn*, t. II, pp. 473—477.

Les fonctionnaires ottomans n'avaient pas le droit de donner le permis d'entrée et de sortie aux bâteaux ne possédant pas le certificat (*tezkere*) du consul. De l'autre côté, personne n'avait le droit de déranger les serviteurs du consul, de même que les autres sujets étrangers, par une demande des rentes, des droits de boucheries et d'autres impôts (*rüsum*) et des impôts coutumiers (*tekâlîfi örfiye*), par une demande de la douane (*resmi gümrük*), ni de la douane de transition (*bâç*). Les sujets étrangers avaient le droit d'aller où ils désiraient et personne n'avait le droit ni de les déranger, ni de se mêler dans leurs affaires, ni de s'occuper de leurs marchandises et animaux etc. Si l'étranger portait les armes sur les lieux dangereux, personne ne devait s'y mêler. Les capitulations garantissaient de même la sécurité de la vie des sujets des Etats européens.[2]

Jusqu'aux années quarante du XIXe siècle, ce n'étaient que les commerçants étrangers qui jouissaient des privilèges mentionnés. A côté de ceux-ci, c'était un pourcentage insignifiant de ceux qui avaient le droit de jouir des privilèges offerts par le sultan Mehmed Fatih après la conquête de Galata et Pera, devenues plus tard des quartiers d'Istanbul, aux commerçants de Venise et de Gênes. Mais, avec l'offensive du colonialisme contre l'Empire Ottoman, augmentait aussi le nombre de ceux qui réssissaient à gagner, outre la nationalité ottomane, encore la nationalité d'un Etat européen qui avait conclu avec le gouvernement du sultan ottoman la convention des capitulations. Dans ce cas, n'importe quel citoyen de l'Empire Ottoman pouvait jouir des privilèges garantis par les capitulations et contribuer par son activité au développement du commerce non seulement international, mais aussi du commerce intérieur et il avait de même la possibilité d'influencer l'industrie et enfin de contribuer à l'évolution des rapports et des forces productrices dépassant et décomposant l'ordre féodal de la société. Dans la société féodale d'un type européen, on pourrait s'attendre à ce que les changements sociaux pouvant s'y réaliser, auraient probablement trouvé leur reflet aussi sur l'évolution de la structure sociale des villes. Mais, dans la situation ottomane, où le régime suivant le système des timars et où les villes différaient de la cité européenne, l'influence des privilèges des capitulations se réalisait d'une toute autre façon.

Les villes de l'Empire Ottoman ne formaient pas, même dans la deuxième moitié de notre millénaire, une agglomération organisée avec une auto-administration plus ou moins grande, telle que la réalisaient les villes sur la plupart des territoires européens.[3] Les villes de l'Empire Ottoman, ce qui vaut tant pour *şehir* que pour *varoş* (la ville ouverte), n'étaient qu'une agglomération d'habitants plus ou moins grande ou bien une agglomération de petites communes.[4] L'état juridique de ces

---

[2] Suivant notre édition, *Le décret impérial (nişânı hümâyûn) délivré pour le consul général de l'Autriche-Hongrie à Alexandrie*, Archiv orientální, *37*, 1969, pp. 12—18.

[3] Sur la ville ottomane voir par ex. une des dernières études: Me jer, M. S.: *K charakteristike ekonomičeskoj žizni gorodov Osmanskoj imperii v XVIII veke* (A propos de la vie économique des villes en Empire Ottoman au XVIIIe s.), in: *Problemy genezisa kapitalizma*, Moscou 1978, pp. 242—275.

villes ne différait pas de celui des communes plus petites. A la tête de l'administration des villes se trouvaient les fonctionnaires d'Etat. Par l'intermédiaire de ceux-ci, l'Etat contrôlait tous les domaines de la vie économique et sociale. La personne principale était le *kadi* (juge), choisi et nommé par l'administration d'Etat d'une liste de candidats ayant terminé l'étude juridique et possédant encore d'autres aptitudes de travail. Le *kadi* n'avait le plus souvent aucune relation avec les habitants de la ville, où il exerçait sa fonction, en ce qui concerne sa provenance ou son siège stable. Il était originaire d'une autre part du pays et il ne resta sur la place plus de deux ou quatre ans. Ce n'était donc qu'une exception, quand le *kadi* avait ses propres intérêts liés aux intérêts des citoyens les plus riches de la ville. Les *kadis* appartenaient à la bureaucratie ottomane, à la couche sociale dispersée sur tout le territoire de l'Empire et restant en même temps au-dessus des intérêts locaux.[5]

Les corps de métier, surtout leurs chefs, jouaient certainement un rôle bien important dans l'organisation de la vie économique des villes. Mais, il n'y existait pas d'organe dirigeant composé de représentants des corporations avec le droit de décider d'une façon indépendante des questions économiques et d'autres. Les représentants des corporations prenaient part à la concrétisation des décisions en divers problèmes, mais leurs opinions ne dépassaient pas les limites données par les ordres de l'administration gouvernementale, représentée par le *kadi*.[6]

Bien que le représentant d'*ayanlık* ait été chargé de tous les devoirs du *kadi* auquel il succédait dans la fonction dès le XVIIIe s., et pour cela, on ne devrait pas prêter une attention à ce changement en administration urbaine, il nous faut prendre compte de la position sociale des personnes exerçant ces deux fonctions, dont l'une succédait à l'autre. Cela signifie que d'un côté, il y avait le *kadi* qui appartenait aux *ulemâ* (les intellectuels musulmans) et à la bureaucratie, et de l'autre côté, l'*ayanlık* qui était choisi parmi les *âyâns* (féodataires-fermiers, bénéficiants ou bien aristocratie urbaine). La fondation de la fonction de l'*ayanlık*, dont les fonctionnaires furent ainsi rangés parmi les bureaucrates bien qu'ils provinssent d'une autre couche sociale, encouragea la participation à l'administration d'Etat, exercée par les couches sociales restant jadis hors de la bureaucratie.

Toutefois, même ici, il ne faut pas exagérer ces faits historiques, tant que les bénéficiants, les féodataires furent dans le système militaire-administratif (le système de *timars*) chargés aussi de quelques devoirs de l'administration. C'est pourquoi le choix des personnages dirigeant la ville parmi les bénéficiants représentait plutôt une manifestation du changement dans le caractère du féodalisme

---

[4] Notre article: *Quelques remarques sur l'évolution de l'organisation urbaine en Empire Ottoman,* ArOr, *42,* 1974, pp. 200—224.

[5] Karpat, Kemal H.: *Structural Change, Historical Stages of Modernization, and the Role of Social Groups in Turkish Politics,* in: *Social Change and Politics in Turkey, A Structural-Historical Analysis,* Leiden 1973, pp. 40 sq.

[6] Notre article: *Quelques remarques...* et la littérature y mentionnée.

ottoman à l'époque mentionnée, qu'un fait très important pour l'évolution urbaine.

Laissant de côté des faits plutôt exceptionnels comme, par exemple, celui où le chef des corporations à Saray Bosna (Sarajevo)[7] devint pour un certain temps la tête de l'administration urbaine, nous ne trouvons pas jusqu'aus réformes du XIXe s. de changements plus radicaux dans la structure urbaine telle quelle s'est formée pendant le XVIe s. Il ne faut pas oublier dans ce contexte que la société urbaine ottomane était d'un caractère professionnel, les habitants étant membres des corps de métier, ce qui la rendait différente des villes du Monde Musulman de l'époque classique du Khalifat et des Etats qui lui succédaient.[8]

Nous avons mentionné le caractère de la ville ottomane pour pouvoir expliquer quel était le groupe social auquel les capitulations tournaient avant tout. En plus, il y avait encore une autre réalité bien importante pour le caractère de la société ottomane, c'est-à-dire le fait qu'à côté de la division «*horizontale*» de la société basée sur la structure des classes, il y existait une division «*verticale*», qui était très souvent plus importante : c'était la division suivant l'appartenance religieuse. Celle-ci partageait toute la société de la classe féodale jusqu'aux couches sociales les plus populaires. C'était donc le système des *millets*, des groupes socio-religieux, qui formait la seule division des habitants de l'Empire Ottoman appuyée sur la loi. Chaque citoyen était membre d'un *millet* d'après son appartenance religieuse. Chaque *millet* contenait une structure sociale complète, bien qu'il faut remarquer que le rangement de cette structure différait selon les *millets*. Cette différence tenait non seulement de la position préférant les musulmans dans l'Etat théocratique basé sur l'islam, comme l'était l'Empire Ottoman, mais aussi de la tradition de l'évolution historique des territoires ayant formé l'Empire du sultan. Cela signifie donc que les musulmans, tenant une position préférée dans l'administration et dans l'armée, formaient presque toute la classe féodale du pays, tandis qu'au contraire, une grande partie des citadins appartenait aux *millets* non-musulmans, surtout aux chrétiens orientaux soumis au patriarche de Constantinople. Le système des *millets* contribuait ici à la conservation des minorités religieuses dont plusieurs évoluèrent plus tard vers les minorités nationales, éventuellement vers les nations en sens contemporain.[9]

Maintenant, nous voilà arrivés au moment ayant une importance spéciale pour l'existence ainsi que pour la réalisation des capitulations. Nous avons déjà mentionné l'ancienne tradition des privilèges offerts aux étrangers par les gouvernements de

---

[7] C'était en 1791 à Saray Bosna (Sarajevo) le *şehir kethodası — gradski ćegaha,* — Sućeska, A.: *Ajani,* Sarajevo 1965, p. 138 sq.

[8] Par ex. Cahen, C.: *Y a-t-il eu des corporations professionnelles dans le monde musulman classique ?* in: *The Islamic City,* Oxford (1970), pp. 51—63.

[9] Filipović, N.: *A Contribution to the Problem of Islamization in the Balkan under the Ottoman Rule,* in: *Ottoman Rule in Middle Europe and Balkan in the 16th and 17th Centuries,* Dissertationes Orientales, vol. 40, Prague 1978, pp. 305—358.

la Méditerranée de l'Est à l'époque pré-ottomane. Le sultan Mehmed Fatih pouvait prolonger les traditions des Empereurs de Byzance très facilement en signant de différents privilèges aux Vénitiens et aux Génois, un tel acte étant tout à fait d'accord avec la conception musulmane acceptant les chrétiens pour les citoyens protégés (*zimmî*), éventuellement «*musta'mîn*» — ne restant sur le territoire musulman qu'un temps abrégé. Les derniers, après un séjour de plus d'une année, devenaient «*protégés*». Ils possédaient donc le droit de prolonger les privilèges. Dans ce sens, les Français obtenaient le droit du commerce libre sur le territoire gouverné par le sultan Bayezid II et leurs privilèges furent précisés par les documents émis en leur faveur par Süleyman le Magnifique (*Kânûnî*).[10]

Même les autres Etats, en affirmant plus tard les accomodements des capitulations — et il n'y manquait aucun pays important européen — gagnaient les mêmes privilèges pour leurs sujets. On caractérise, avec raison, ces capitulations entre l'Etat puissant des Ottomans et ses partenaires commerciaux, comme les ententes égales en droit. Dans le temps en question, ces capitulations cachaient déjá l'effort des puissances européennes de pénétrer en Empire Ottoman, surtout sur les marchés de la Méditerranée de l'Est, mais elles ne sapaient pas encore la puissance ottomane, ni économique ni politique. On n'en doute pas qu'elles ne soutinssent avec le commerce aussi la couche commerciale pré-bourgeoise, mais ils ne s'agissait pas ici d'une influence troublante. Elles s'orientaient avec leur commerce vers les territoires littoraux avec la majorité des membres des *millets* chrétiens en les tenant pour partenaires ottomans.

C'était probablement dans la première moitié du XIXe s., que ces relations ont changé. Malheureusement, nous ne connaissons pas le moment, à partir duquel on date d'état juridique spécial des double-nationalités des citoyens de l'Empire Ottoman.[11]

Avec la pénétration du capital européen dans l'économie ottomane, surtout après l'emission du *Hattı Hümâyûn* de 1856, il se passait toujours plus souvent que les citoyens ottomans acceptaient aussi la nationalité d'un Etat européen. Il s'agissait évidemment des membres des *millets* chrétiens qui de cette façon entrèrent sous la protection juridique du souverain de leur patrie récemment adoptée. Nous éviterons en ces relations le problème bien connu de la «*protection des chrétiens oppressés*» formant une partie importante de la propagande et du programme politique surtout des puissances européennes. Par ces paroles, elles justifiaient leur politique expansive envers l'Empire Ottoman et soutenaient leur thèse démagogiques de la «*question orientale*». Dans cette phase historique du combat entre le Monde musulman-orien-

---

[10] Sousa, N.: op. cit., p. 38; Arslan: *Sovremennaja Turcija*, Moscou 1923, p. 7.

[11] Quant aux Arméniens, voir le livre de Krikorian Mesrob, K. (*Armenians in the Service of the Ottoman Empire 1860—1908*, London — Boston (1978)), appellant la situation de ceux-ci «*established status of a favoured Christian ‹ Millet ›*» (p. VII).

tal et chrétien-européen, se réalisant à l'époque du capitalisme offensif européen et du féodalisme défensif ottoman, les capitulations jouaient un rôle bien important. Nous éviterons ici de traiter la manière, dont les privilèges des capitulations aidaient le capital étranger de changer les pays ottomans en semi-colonies, mais nous essayerons de suivre la façon dont ces privilèges exerçaient leur influence sur la structure sociale des villes ottomanes.

Sans posséder les données exactes en ce qui concerne l'obtention de la double-nationalité, on peut cependant supposer qu'elle fût pratiquée en grand vers la fin des années cinquante du siècle passé. C'était donc l'époque où le gouvernement ottoman avait commencé à émettre les ordres ayant pour but d'empêcher la réalisation de cette double-nationalité. Ainsi, le 21 avril 1858, l'édit impérial abrogea le droit de l'héritage sur les terres pour celui des citoyens ottomans qui avait accepté une autre nationalité.[12]

Mais plus tard, le 18 janvier 1867, cette loi fut pratiquement annulée, les étrangers ayant de nouveau obtenu le droit, justifié par un *irade impérial*, de posséder des immeubles. C'est pourquoi le gouvernement ottoman avait répété son effort d'empêcher à ses sujets l'obtention d'une nationalité d'un Etat étranger et le 19 janvier 1869, il avait émis un autre *irade impérial*, par lequel il avait défendu la naturalisation sous un gouvernement étranger, ainsi que le *paragraphe V* y avait strictement défendu l'expatriation des citoyens de l'Empire Ottoman qui n'avaient pas obtenu une autorisation spéciale du gouvernement ottoman. Ces efforts restèrent, naturellement, sans succès. Les seuls résultats, c'étaient les négociations compliquées avec les diplomates représentant les Etats européens.[13]

La pratique de double-nationalité était trop avantageuse pour les cercles intéressés pour qu'on pût empêcher sa réalisation. Ainsi, un certain nombre de commerçants chrétiens — avant tout — arriva aux positions des sujets des Etats européens, dont les citoyens jouissaient des privilèges garantis par les capitulations. Ces privilèges libérèrent les «étrangers» de plusieurs impôts, du payement de la douane et de diverses taxes, en leur apportant aussi de différents privilèges d'un caractère économique. Tous cela influença d'une manière positive la situation économique des personnes en question. Quant à une telle réalité, nous en avons la preuve dans plusieurs publications traitant de l'influence du système des capitulations sur l'économie de l'Empire Ottoman non seulement en ce qui concerne les territoires de la Turquie elle-même, mais aussi les pays se trouvant près de la frontière, par exemple, la Bosnie. Les commerçants serbes sont devenus bien riches, surtout dès la moitié du XIXe s., grâce à l'intensification des relation commerciales avec le marché autrichien.

A l'époque dont nous possédons quelques données sur l'évolution économique des citoyens des villes ottomanes en quelques régions, des citoyens provenant des

---

[12] Sousa, N.: op. cit., p. 110.

[13] Ibidem, p. 105; Talat, A.: *La Construction turque du 20 avril 1924*, Chambéry 1935, p. 6.

couches privilégiées de la société féodale, par exemple, des janissaires, ces groupes sociaux devenaient les partenaires des commerçants étrangers. Cette situation se réalisa par exemple, quand le capital ragusien collaborait avec ces couches féodales ottomanes. Il n'y a pas lieu d'exagérer l'importance de ce processus, mais en tout cas, on doit y marquer la possibilité de la société féodale ottomane d'évoluer au capitalisme. Il s'agissait d'un processus historique troublé par l'impact des forces coloniales et enfin aussi par les capitulations.[14]

L'Empire Ottoman se changea an semi-colonie et le changement vers la manière capitaliste de production de son économie se passait sous des conditions très aggravées. A cette époque de transition, il y avait encore le système de *millets* facilitant la division des personnes appartenant aux divers *millets* qui pourraient éventuellement se changer d'entreprises industrielles. Ainsi, les *millets* contribuèrent à une évolution isolée surtout de la bourgeoisie commerciale des chrétiens. Si l'on voulait considérer la durée de la fonction des *millets* du point de vue de l'évolution nationale de quelques nations, comme étaient par exemple les Arméniens et les Grecs, on devrait bien l'apprécier en soulignant sa contribution à la formation de la nation moderne. Mais, il y restait toujours une circonstance défavorable, à savoir, que cette bourgeoisie nouvelle des nations évoluantes était dans une grande mesure partagée quant à son territoire et qu'elle n'avait pas de possibilité de se faire valoir dans la vie politique de l'Empire.

Et cela nous amène à un fait de grande importance pour l'évolution de la structure urbaine. Nous avons traité de l'influence positive des privilèges garantis par les capitulations exercée sur l'économie, surtout sur le commerce extérieur, avec lequel le commerce intérieur ottoman s'était lié. C'étaient avant tout les membres des communautés religieuses chrétiennes qui avaient pris part au commerce de l'Empire Ottoman déjà avant les influences du colonialisme, surtout grâce à leur participation aux avantages des capitulations, leur position dans la vie économique de l'Empire devint toujours plus forte.

Le fait que «*la bourgeoisie turque jouait pendant une époque de longue durée dans la vie économique du pays un rôle de deuxième rang en comparaison avec la bourgeoisie des autres nations*»,[15] a été constaté déjà par plusieurs historiens. D'autre part, il n'est pas nécessaire de répéter les idées traitant de la façon dont les capitulations facilitèrent les actions commerciales grâce aux privilèges y garantis. Ayant parlé du texte des capitulations, il nous convient de faire ici une petite remarque. C'ést avec l'accroissement du capital européen qui avait pénétré sur le territoire de l'Empire du sultan pendant le siècle précédent que s'élargissait même la sphère des capitulations. Ce point est à souligner non seulement à cause de la

---

[14] Filipović, N.: op. cit., p. 327; Ekmečić, M.: *Ustanak u Bosni* (La révolte en Bosnie), 1875—1878, Sarajevo 1960.

[15] Indžikjan, O. G.: *Buržuazija osmanskoj imperii* (La bourgeoisie de l'Empire Ottoman), Erevan 1977, p. 15.

possibilité dont jouissaient les étrangers, d'acheter et de posséder des terres, ce qui avait été légalisé déjà par le *Hattı Hümâyûn* de 1856, mais surtout à cause de l'institution des tribunaux mixtes.

Les privilèges des douanes et des impôts rendaient même au marché les marchandises apportées et vendues par les étrangers — les étrangers vrais et les «étrangers» nominaux — plus attractives et ainsi, ces privilèges se mêlaient à la sphère économique. Les tribunaux mixtes affranchirent une partie des citoyens de la jurisdiction des tribunaux ottomans, les mettant ainsi dans une position d'exterritorialité. De cette manière, ils portèrent atteinte directement à l'autorité juridique et administrative de l'Etat ottoman. Par rapport aux sujets privilégiés, les capitulations se présentaient comme un facteur rendant ces citoyens dans une position plus avantageuse même au sens politique. Ceux-ci devinrent ainsi en fait insaisissables à cause d'une activité dépassant éventuellement la loi ottomane. Ce côté pouvait leur offrir la possibilité d'une activité politique. Mais nous ne voulons plus en traiter ni y attribuer une grande importance, connaissant plusieurs événements où la réalité historique apparaissait un peu différente. Ainsi, par exemple, envers le mouvement burgeois des Dachnaktsuthyuns arméniens, le gouvernement ottoman se servait d'autres moyens pour sa défense et ne se sentait pas restreint par les prescriptions de la loi.[16]

En tout cas, les capitulations et les privilèges s'étant tournés encore plus tard en faveur des étrangers et des citoyens chrétiens de l'Empire Ottoman, soutenaient les citadins non-musulmans. Nous pouvons encore mentionner que l'évolution du commerce et l'augmentation des possibilités d'exporter les marchandises menaient surtout pendant le XIXe siècle vers l'agrandissement des grandes propriétés foncières, dont la production agricole était orientée vers la vente. Tandis que parmi les Turcs c'étaient des anciens féodataires qui changèrent leurs villages de différentes manières en grandes propriétés foncières du caractère féodal,[17] en Anatolie augmentait le nombre de grandes propriétés foncières dont les possesseurs étaient les Arméniens. Ces grands propriétaires fonciers de nationalité arménienne ne provenaient pas, naturellement, de la classe des féodataires, mais c'étaient déjà des bourgeois, membres de la bourgeoisie naissante, qui avaient commencé à placer les investissements dans la sphère économique la plus avantageuse de l'époque — dans l'agriculture.[18] Ici, nous revenons de nouveau au fait que les capitulations aidaient le renforcement de la bourgeoisie non-musulman.

---

[16] *Genocid Armjan v Osmanskoj imperii. Sbornik dokumentov i materialov.* Pod red. prof. M. G. Nersisjana (La génocide des Arméniens dans l'Empire Ottoman. Recueil des documents et des matériaux. Sous la réd. de M. G. Narsisjan), Erevan 1966.

[17] Sur les grandes propriétés foncières, voir par ex. Pop-Georgiev, D.: *Sopstvenosta vrz čiflicite i čifligarskite agrarno-pravni odnosi vo Makedonija do balkanskata vojna 1912*, Skopje 1956.

[18] Koljubakin, A. N.: *Materialy dlja vojenno-istoričeskogo obozrenija Aziatskoj Turcii*, Tiflis 1888, t. I, pp. 119, 220 — cité d'après Indžikjan, O. G., op. cit., p. 83.

Le fait que de cette façon on avait renforcé la partie bourgeoise de la société ottomane pourrait nous amener à l'appréciation positive de l'influence des capitulations. Mais, il faut nous rappeler la situation historique : même dans la deuxième moitié du XIXe s., ce n'étaient pas les non-musulmans qui avaient la possibilité de jouer un rôle important dans la vie politique du pays et de l'influencer de cette façon. Le soutien de la partie chrétienne de la bourgeoisie contribuait au contraire à l'agrandissement des divergences existant déjà dans la structure sociale des villes ottomanes. Nous avons prêté attention au système des *millets* apportant une autre division qui dans le régime théocratique ottoman plaçait les habitants non-musulmans dans une position secondaire. C'est pourquoi le support économique des membres des *millets* chrétiens aidait justement la partie bourgeoise qui ne possédait ni les droits politiques ni la possibilité de se présenter sur la scène politique. Cette partie menait son combat surtout dans la sphère économique, le dirigeant contre ses rivaux plutôt que contre les liens féodaux. Nous possédons donc les preuves de la collaboration de la bourgeoisie chrétienne avec la bourgeoisie turque, par exemple les Dachnaktsuthyuns arméniens soutenaient la lutte des Nouveaux Ottomans (dits Jeunes Turcs) pour le Parlement, mais dans la sphère politique et économique, même ces deux partis de la bourgeoisie ottomane n'étaient que des ennemis.

Dans cette concurrence, les commerçants et les entrepreneurs chrétiens gardaient leur positions traditionnellement avantageuses et les renforçaient justement grâce aux privilèges des capitulations et à leur collaboration plus étroite avec le capital étranger. Et il ne faut pas oublier de mentionner que le capital étranger exerçait le rôle du facteur soumettant et changeant l'Empire Ottoman en une semi-colonie. L'intérêt de ces forces pro-coloniales et coloniales était également de maintenir la situation sociale, de ne pas changer le caractère féodal de la société ottomane en général. Ces forces ne demandaient que quelques changements insignifiants, comme l'élimination des douanes locales, l'amélioration du transport, le déplacement plus facile des habitants etc., donc quelques-unes des libertés bourgeoises.

En suivant la sphère d'influence des capitulations et le renforcement des positions des grands capitalistes, nous arrivons à la question : quel était le résultat de l'influence approfondissante de la bourgeoisie non-musulmane dans l'évolution urbaine et dans la position de la bourgeoisie en général, dans la société. Et ici, il y a lieu de répondre que les capitulations n'y exerçaient qu'une influence peu importante ; ou bien, on peut caractériser cette influence comme un fait dirigé vers le chemin improductif.

La bourgeoisie turque, de même que la bourgeoisie des autres nations de l'Empire, évoluait et éveillait sa conscience politique plus tard que la bourgeoisie des nations chrétiennes. Dans leur structure économique aussi bien que sociale, les villes ottomanes passaient par un changement très peu remarquable jusqu'au bout du XIXe s. Elles n'arrivèrent pas à la situation, dans laquelle pourrait naître une bourgeoisie nationale bien établie et capable de présenter les demandes politiques.

Les citadins plus évolués dans le sens mentionné ne se trouvaient que dans quelques villes, où un plus grand nombre de janissaires avait déjà auparavant pénétré parmi les bourgeois et s'était mis en accord avec leurs intérêts.[19] Bien qu'il s'agît d'événements rares, on peut les tenir pour une preuve des changements qui commencèrent à apparaître dans la société féodale ottomane.

Dans la structure sociale ottomane, compliquée par la division théocratique en *millets* et en plus par la pénétration du capital étranger, le soutien des parties sociales imperspectives exerçait son influence retardatrice sur l'évolution sociale et contribuait ainsi à une complication plus grande du chemin historique de la société ottomane.

On peut dire avec raison que le renforcement de la partie apolitique, au lieu du soutien de la partie turque-musulmane bourgeoisie qui en ce temps-là devenait relativement de plus en plus faible, fonctionnait comme un facteur retardateur dans toute l'évolution historique de l'Empire Ottoman. Ainsi, les capitulations affaiblissaient justement cette partie de la bourgeoisie qui avait la possibilité de se réaliser au point de vue politique, qui avait pris part à la direction politique et administrative de l'Etat et qui — ce qui était le plus important — avait son propre intérêt au changement du régime féodal. En prononçant cette thèse, nous nous appuyons par exemple sur les réformes de l'époque du Tanzimat dans lesquelles surtout les paragraphes demandant l'égalité de tous les citoyens de l'Empire, sans égard pour la religion, furent accueillis avec un consentement énorme par la propagande européenne, mais en même temps, ils n'éveillaient que très peu d'enthousiasme justement chez les citoyens ottomans touchés par les paragraphes en question.[20] C'est pourquoi nous ne trouvons trace de l'effort de garantir une position vraiment égale à tous les citoyens qui viserait à éliminer la division basée sur le système des *millets*.

Au temps où la bourgeoisie de la nation la plus nombreuse des régions centrales de l'Empire, les Turcs, entrait sur la scène historique, les capitulations influençaient donc d'une façon tardive, surtout l'évolution des villes. Si nous examinons la situation économique de plusieurs villes de la région, non seulement les grande ports comme Saloniki, Izmir, Istanbul, mais aussi de quelques villes anatoliennes comme Trabzon, Sivas, Adana, nous voyons une évolution économique relativement grande se réalisent dans la deuxième moitié du dernier siècle.[21] Par leur potential économique, ces villes entraient dans une position d'une communauté socio-économique pouvant déjà exercer une grande influence sur l'évolution de tout le pays. En effet, il

---

[19] On y mentionne par ex. quelques villes en Yougoslavie d'aujourd'hui. Voir *Historija naroda Jugoslavije*, t. II, les œuvres de H. Kreševljaković et d'autres y citées.

[20] Inalcik, H.: *Application of the Tamzimat and its Social Effects*, PdR Press Publications in Ottoman Social History, 1, p. 13.

[21] Indžikjan, O. G., op. cit., p. 147 sq.

y avait des conditions préalables pour l'entrée plus énergique de la jeune bourgeoisie dans la sphère politique.

Mais, à cause de la situation sociale compliquée, dont nous avons déjà fait mention, la bourgeoisie de ces villes n'avait pas la possibilité de prendre sa place ni dans le gouvernement des villes elles-mêmes, ni plus tard, dans la vie politique du pays. En même temps, un noveau fait historique commençait à se réaliser: la bourgeoisie turque, bien que plus faible au point de vue économique et en outre, affaiblie aussi par les capitulations, commençait à se faire prévaloir dans l'économie de l'Empire. A côté des entreprises en agriculture, dans lesquelles surtout les grands propriétaires fonciers de provenance féodale s'étaient fait valoir, aussi les entrepreneur turcs étaient actifs dans les investissements du capital étranger. Nous attirons ici l'attention aux constructions de chemins-de-fer, des routes, des ports et d'autres grandes entreprises, dans lesquelles la collaboration de l'Etat ottoman avec les sujets des pays européens prédominait. L'Etat ottoman y était représenté surtout par le profit des capitalistes turcs provenant des rangs de l'armée et de la bureaucratie. Dans cette collaboration, les entrepreneurs et les sociétés de l'Allemagne et de l'Autriche-Hongrie se trouvaient au premier plan. Ceux-ci s'étaient orientés déjà auparavant vers les Turcs, tandis que les autres puissances européennes se dirigeaient vers les minorités des autres nations.[22]

En connexion avec ces faits, nous ne voulons pas suivre plus profondément l'influence et la pénétration de diverses puissances européenes dans les catégories des habitants de l'Empire Ottoman, la façon par laquelle ces Etats pénétraient dans ses sphères de leurs intérêts quant aux combats et contradictions en liaison avec «la question orientale». Cette division des intérês se montrait encore plus tard, pendant la première guerre mondiale et vers sa fin, comme le facteur décisif dans la lutte des classes entre la bourgeoisie des différentes nations. A l'époque mentionnée, c'étaient justement les capitulations qui devenaient un moyen de ce combat; c'était donc l'effort d'abolir ces privilèges qui est devenu la demande d'une grande importance.

Les capitulations ne favorisaient donc qu'une partie de la bourgeoisie, celle qui ne pouvait pas changer la vie politique. Elles ne soutenaient pas la bourgeoisie de la nation la plus forte et ainsi, elles n'aidaient pas l'évolution sociale en dérangeant la possibilité de réaliser l'effort commun contre le gouvernement féodal exercé par la bourgeoisie de l'Empire sans différence.[23] Les capitulations représentaient un obstacle pareil à celui représenté par le système des *millets*. La bourgeoisie turque le

---

[22] Hassinger, H.: *Die erste Wiener Handelskompagnie (1667—1683)*, Vierteljahrschrift für Sozial- und Wirtschaftsgeschichte, Jhrg. 35, H. 1, 1942.

[23] Gasanova, E. Ju.: *Ideologija buržuaznogo nacionalizma v Turcii* (Idéologie du nationalisme bourgeois en Turquie), Baku 1966, p. 43; sur la collaboration de différents millets au siècle passé, voir Petrosjan, Ju. A.: *Mladotureckoje dviženije* (Le mouvement des Jeunes Turcs), Moscou 1971, p. 209.

savait très bien, comme nous avons la preuve dans les actions entreprises aussitôt qu'elle eut réussi à gagner une position assez puissante dans l'Etat.

Même la bourgeoisie turque n'était pas homogène, en se divisant en bourgeoisie provenant des cercles féodaux-bureaucrates qui était liée avec le sultanat au point de vue politique et économique, surtout après avoir pris le gouvernement entre ses mains après la révolution de 1908 — et en bourgeoisie sortant avant tout des villes anatoliennes pendant la première guerre mondiale, qui devenait plus tard hégémone de la lutte de la libération nationale. Les processus historiques compliqués s'y sont présentés de nouveau par le fait qu'une des raisons contribuant à l'incorporation des territoires intérieurs de l'Anatolie dans la sphère économique la plus avancée des régions de l'Ouest du pays, était justement l'abolition des privilèges des capitulations et l'élimination de la concurrence de la bourgeoisie chrétienne qui lui succédait. L'Allemagne avec l'Autriche-Hongrie, collaborant dès longtemps avec les Turcs et avec la bourgeoisie régnante des Turcs, réussirent d'une manière relativement facile à réaliser l'entrée de l'Empire Ottoman en guerre mondiale à leur côté. Par ce fait, l'Empire Ottoman se trouva tout à coup dans la position d'ennemi envers ses partenaires commerciaux traditionnels, et il en profita toute de suite pour abolir les capitulations. Son partenaire au combat, l'Allemand, lui avait fait les avances : l'Allemagne de Wilhelm a révoqué volontier ses capitulations en renonçant aussi à tous les privilèges pour tous ses sujets. Après le 1er octobre 1914, le gouvernement ottoman abolit la validité de tous les privilèges des capitulations en général.[24] Les protestations du côté de l'Angleterre, de la France et des autres pays de l'Entente se sont avérées vaines par le fait même que ces pays se trouvaient en état de guerre avec l'Empire Ottoman et leurs sujets ne pouvaient donc pas jouir de la protection du sultan. De cette façon, les capitulations étaient abolies *de facto* déjà avant que cet acte eût obtenu une forme juridique légale dans la convention de la paix signée à Lausanne.

L'abolition des capitulations, c'était l'acte que toutes les parties de la bourgeoisie turque approuvaient. Ce fait même porte preuve de l'importance attaché antérieurement aux capitulations. La première guerre mondiale apportait de grands changements dans la structure économique et sociale de la Turquie.[25] Ces changements «*ont ouvert l'Anatolie à l'activité historique*». Brièvement : l'économie anatolienne fut liée avec les marchés ottomans et mondiaux, une évolution rapide se présentait chez la bourgoisie nationale turque des villes de l'Asie Mineure et par cela, la bourgeoisie nationale turque entrait sur la scène politique. La lutte de la libération nationale

---

[24] M i l l e r, A. F.: *Očerki novejšej istorii Turcii* (Résumé de l'histoire contemporaine de la Turquie), Moscou—Leningrad 1948, p. 41 ; M a z a r d, J. A.: *Le Régime des Capitulations en Turquie pendant la Guerre de 1914*, Alger 1923, pp. 54—55, 75 etc.

[25] N o v i č e v, A. D.: *Ekonomika Turcii v period mirovoj vojny* (L'économie de la Turquie pendant la première guerre mondiale), Leningrad—Moscou 1935.

turque, dont la jeune bourgeoisie nationale turque est devenue hégémone, reste aujourd'hui hors du plan de nos lignes.

Mais ici même, nous pouvons observer que l'abolition *de facto* des capitulations a rapidement affaibli la position privilégiée de la bourgeoisie non-musulmane. La bourgeoisie turque s'est fait pleinement valoir à la tête de l'Etat à l'époque suivante. Les villes turques ont contribué à l'édification de l'économie capitaliste et de la société capitaliste en général. Seulement, cette édification se réalisait sous une forme un peu différente de celle qu'on aurait pu supposer en tenant pour base l'analyse du système ottoman à l'époque du féodalisme avancé. On n'en doute pas qu'il n'y ait un grand nombre de facteurs exerçant leur influence, mais les capitulations avec leurs privilèges formaient en tout cas un facteur ralentissant causant la retardation de l'évolution politique et sociale des villes ottomanes.

DIE OSMANISCHE EXPANSION UND DIE SLOWAKEI

(*Ergebnisse und Perspektiven*)

VOJTECH KOPČAN, Bratislava

Der Autor faßt die bisherigen Ergebnisse der Forschung über die osmanische Expansion auf dem Gebiete der jetzigen Slowakei samt bibliographischer Angaben zusammen und umreißt die Perspektiven der weiteren Erforschung dieser Problematik.

Die Erforschung der osmanischen Expansion in der Slowakei reicht in die zweite Hälfte des 19. Jahrhunderts, als Herausgaben von Urkunden über „türkische Kriege" oder Bearbeitungen einiger Probleme in den ersten slowakischen Zeitschriften erschienen. Es waren vor allem P. Križko und F. V. Sasinek, die in den Zeitschriften Sokol, Letopis Matice slovenskej und Slovenský letopis die von Türken herausgegebene Briefe und Schriftstücke, oder Urkunden über türkische Kriege aus Archiven slowakischer Städte oder anderen Institutionen veröffentlichten.[1]

F. V. Sasinek ist auch der Autor der ersten Bearbeitung der osmanischen Expansion in der Slowakei, die er unter dem Titel *Turci na Slovensku* (Türken in der Slowakei) in der Zeitschrift Slovenský letopis herausgegeben hat.[2] Im wesentlichen ist dies eine Übersicht von Ereignissen aus ungarischen Chroniken, besonders der von Istvánffy, zusammengestellt und mit Dokumenten, welche er direkt im Text zitierte, vervollständigt.

Auch die, aus der Feder von A. Trenkus,[3] J. Ľ. Holuby[4] oder P. Križko[5] stammen-

---

[1] Über P. Križkos Editionstätigkeit informiert D. Lehotská im Buch *Z dejín banských miest na Slovensku* (Aus der Geschichte der Bergstädte in der Slowakei). Bratislava 1964, S. 51—52 und 76—78. Über F. V. Sasinek siehe O. Pekáriková-Hvizdošová: Edičná činnosť Františka Víťazoslava Sasinka (Die Editionstätigkeit František Víťazoslav Sasineks). Historické štúdie, *4*, 1958, S. 285—286.

[2] SL, *2*, 1877, S. 55—65, 107—121, 241—246, 273—275; *3*, 1878, S. 14—17, 197—200.

[3] *Národ slovenský tekovského Pohronia r. 1647—1652* (Die slowakische Bevölkerung des Tekover Grantals in den Jahren 1647—52). Letopis Matice slovenskej, *6*, 1869, Nr. 2, S. 19—31 beschreibt die türkischen Einfälle in das Grantal und die Schlacht bei Veľké Vozokany im Jahre 1652 auf Grund der Quellen des Gespanarchivs des Komitats Tekov.

[4] *Stopy tureckého hospodárenia v Trenčiansku v XVI. a XVII. storočí* (Spuren der türkischen Witschaftsführung im Gebiet von Trenčín im XVI. und XVII. Jahrhundert). In: Slovenské pohľady, *14*, 1894, S. 653—674, 697—711. Der Autor geht vorwiegend aus den Matrikeln der Seniorate der evangelischen Kirche hervor und bringt eine Anzahl von Belegen über Schicksale von Menschen, die im Jahre 1663 in die türkische Gefangenschaft verschleppt wurden.

[5] *Hrozná noc pukanská* (Die grauenvolle Nacht von Pukanec). Slovenské pohľady, *15*, 1895, S. 129—138. Auf Grund von Quellen aus mittelalterlichen Bergstädten wird der Überfall der Stadt durch

den Artikel sind nichts anderes, als eine Interpretation einzelner Begebenheiten oder Zeitabschnitte aus den türkischen Kriegen auf Grund neuen Archivmaterials.

Eine ablehnende Einstellung zur osmanischen Expansion präsentierte den slowakischen Lesern der russische Professor V. Lamanskij, die Ansichten russischer Slawophilen repräsentierend.[6]

In den Werken slowakischer Autoren kommt deren national-aufklärerische Sendung klar zum Vorschein, indem sie auf die Rolle der Slowaken in den gegentürkischen Kämpfen hinweisen wollen.

Ein bedeutendes Stück Arbeit bei der Erforschung der osmanischen Expansion in der Slowakei leistete Michal Matunák (1866—1932), der seit dem Ende des vorigen Jahrhunderts in lokalen Wochenblättern, aber auch in ungarischen historischen Zeitschriften und nachher auch in der Zeitschrift Slovenské pohľady Artikel über verschiedene Fragen der türkischen Herrschaft in der Slowakei veröffentlichte. Seine bedeutendsten Arbeiten betrafen die Gründung von Nové Zámky[7] und dessen Rolle als Zentrums der osmanischen Provinz in den Jahren 1663—1685,[8] die osmanische Expansion im Gebiet der Bergstädte[9] und im Gau von Hont.[10]

Matunák schrieb im Geiste der offiziellen ungarischen Ideologie. Er hob die Rolle der einheimischen Verteidiger hervor, während er die vom Wiener Hof entsandten Söldnerabteile als „schlechte Soldaten, die kein Mitgefühl mit dem Land und dem Volk, zu deren Verteidigung sie entsandt wurden, aufweisen; deren Feigheit nur noch die Tyrannei gegenüber dem verlassenen Volk überbietet, so daß dieses von ihnen mehr zu leiden hatte, als von den expansiven Türken" bezeichnete.[11] Er hob die Rolle des ungarischen Adels, vor allem des Landadels, darunter auch der Slowaken, im Kampf gegen die Türken hervor. Die Bewertung des Angreifers ist eindeutig: „Noch niemals hat irgendjemand Ungarn so viel Schaden zugefügt, wie die Türken in den anderthalb Jahrhunderten ihrer Herrschaft."[12] Matunák baute Türken im Jahre 1635 beschrieben.

[6] Moc Turkov-Osmanov v Európe 1396—1739 (Die Macht der Türken-Osmanen in Europa 1396—1739). Slovenské pohľady, 2, 1882, S. 1—16.

[7] Érsekújvár alapítási éve (1545). Századok, 30, 1896, S. 338—341; Érsekújvár második alapítása (1581). Hadtörténelmi Közlemények, 10, 1897, S. 102—109.

[8] Nové Zámky pod tureckým panstvom 1663—1685 (Nové Zámky unter der türkischen Herrschaft 1663—1685). Slovenské pohľady, 18, 1898, S. 129—132, 231—236, 486—496, 554—561, 569—578, 668—676. In ungarischer Sprache, Nitra 1901, 132 S.

[9] Turecko-uhorské boje v severozápadnom Uhorsku (Türkisch-ungarische Kämpfe in Nordwestungarn). Slovenské pohľady, 17, 1897, S. 505—531, 568—591, 632—651, 697—705. Vígľašský zámok (Das Schloß Vígľaš). Zvolen 1960. 88 S.; Z dejín slobodného a hlavného banského mesta Kremnice (Aus der Geschichte der Frei- und Hauptbergstadt Kremnica). Kremnica 1928. 541 S.

[10] Drégely és Palánk, katonai szerepe a törökök alatt 1552—1593. Krupina 1901. 70 S.; Korpona várkapitányai. Krupina 1901. 89 S.; Adatok az 1552-iki Honti hadjárat történetéhez. In: Történelmi Tár, 29, 1907, S. 452—477.

[11] Turecko-uhorské boje (Türkisch-ungarische Kämpfe), S. 511.

[12] Ibid., S. 597.

seine Arbeiten vor allem auf Archivmaterialien aus den mittelslowakischen Bergstädten auf, er kannte jedoch gut auch weitere publizierte Quellen und die Literatur. Insofern er osmanische Quellen benutzte, waren dies hauptsächlich ungarische Übersetzungen osmanischer Defters aus Ungarn, sowie Thúrys und Karácsons Übersetzungen osmanischer Chroniken.

Es waren jedoch nicht nur slowakische Geschichtsschreiber, sondern auch die ungarischen Historiker und Archivare Ö. Kárffy, A. Komáromy, L. Merényi, K. Tagányi und später N. von Relković,[13] die große Mengen an Materialien zur osmanischen Expansion in der Slowakei herausgaben, wobei wir die Publikationen gesamtungarischer Bedeutung nicht erwähnen.

Nach der Gründung der Tschechoslowakischen Republik traten ins Interesse der Historiker politisch bedeutende Themen aus der jüngsten, sowie auch aus der älteren Vergangenheit in den Vordergrund. So war die erste bedeutende Arbeit aus der Problematik der osmanischen Expansion in der Slowakei die Veröffentlichung der türkischen Urkunden aus Dolný Kamenec durch J. Rypka.[14] Es war eine mustergültige Bearbeitung von vier türkischen Dokumenten aus der zweiten Hälfte des 17. Jahrhunderts, die in der Gemeinde Dolný Kamenec im Gebiet der oberen Nitra erhalten blieben, mit einem Umriß des historischen Hintergrunds, auf dem die Urkunden entstanden sind (Köprülüzade Ahmed Paschas Kriegszug gegen Nové Zámky im Jahre 1663 und die Entstehung des Eyalet Nové Zámky), und einem Aufruf zur weiteren Suche nach türkischen Materialien in der Slowakei.

Die Artikel von E. Tejnil richteten die Aufmerksamkeit auf das Vorfinden von türkischem Urkundenmaterial in der Slowakei und wiesen praktisch auf Möglichkeiten der Benützung osmanischer Quellen für die Geschichte der Slowakei hin.[15] Tejnil ging in seinen Arbeiten aus älteren ungarischen Übersetzungen türkischer Quellen hervor.

Von den, sich an heimische Quellen anlehnende Arbeit müssen Matunáks Geschichte der Stadt Kremnica und V. Bakers Artikel erwähnt werden, in denen er einige Dokumente zur osmanischen Expansion veröffentlichte und die gegentürkische Verteidigung von Banská Štiavnica bearbeitete.[16]

Zu einem ausdrucksvollen Aufschwung der Erforschung der osmanischen Expan-

---

[13] Kopčan, V.: *Bibliografia slovenskej turkológie a osmanskej expanzie na Slovensku* (Die Bibliographie der slowakischen Turkologie und der osmanischen Expansion in der Slowakei). Bratislava 1977. S. 25—30.

[14] Čtyři turecké listiny z Dolného Kamence na Slovensku (Vier türkische Urkunden aus Dolný Kamenec in der Slowakei). Prúdy, *11*, 1927, Nr. 6, S. 335—365, Nr. 8, S. 471—482, sowie ein Separat 24 S.

[15] Příspěvky k dějinám tureckého panství na Slovensku (Beiträge zur Geschichte der türkischen Herrschaft in der Slowakei). Český časopis historický, *41*, 1935, S. 373—381. Derselbe: Miscelanea z Uher a ze Slovenska v době tureckého panství (Miscelanea aus Ungarn und aus der Slowakei in der Zeit der türkischen Herrschaft). In: Sborník Matice slovenskej, *15*, 1937 — Jazyk, S. 131—139.

[16] Schemnitz zur Zeit der Türkenherrschaft. In: Karpathenland, *4*, 1931, S. 106—122.

sion in der Slowakei kam es erst in der zweiten Hälfte der 50er Jahre. Es war dies zweifelsohne eine Folge des quantitativen und qualitativen Aufschwungs der tschechoslowakischen historischen Wissenschaft nach der Befreiung. J. Kabrda[17] unterstrich das berechtigte Interesse der tschechoslowakischen Geschichtsschreibung an einer gründlichen Erforschung des Zeitabschnittes der türkischen Herrschaft in unserem Lande. Er machte auf eine weitere osmanische Quelle zur slowakischen Geschichte, *Kanunname-i eyalet-i Uyvar* aus dem Jahre 1664 aufmerksam, brachte deren inhaltliche Analyse und verglich sie mit dem umfangreichen osmanischem Material vor allem vom Balkan.

Im selben Jahr publizierte J. Blaškovič ein türkisches Schriftstück aus dem Städtischen Museum in Rimavská Sobota aus dem Jahre 1654, das den Handel der Einwohnerschaft von Rimavská Sobota auf türkischem Gebiet betrifft.[18] Der Defterdas von Buda schreibt an seinen Unterordneten in Hatvan, er solle vom Händler aus Rimavská Sobota die Gebühr nicht zweimal einholen und ihn schikanieren. Blaškovič führt auch detailliertere Angaben über den Inhalt der türkischen Schriftstücke aus Rimavská Sobota an.

Ein umfangreiches Material zur Geschichte des Sandschaks Fiľakovo (1554—1593) wurde von E. Tejnil gesammelt.[19] Er befaßte sich mit der Eroberung von Fiľakovo durch das osmanische Heer, mit der Verwaltung des Sandschaks, sowie dessen nachfolgender Geschichte bis zur Wiedereroberung durch die kaiserlichen Heere und knapp noch bis zum Ende des 17. Jahrhunderts. Tejnil lehnte sich vor allem an zeitgenössische ungarische Chroniken, Quelleneditionen und Literatur an, in den Teilen über die osmanische Verwaltung, die militärische Organisation und das Steuersystem jedoch geht er aus den ungarischen Übersetzungen der von A. Velics herausgegebenen Defters hervor.

Ein bedeutender Beitrag zur Erkenntnis der wirtschaftlich-gesellschaftlichen Lage in den, von der osmanischen Expansion bedrohten Gebieten war die Studie von J. Vlachovič.[20] Der Autor äußerte seine Meinung, daß der türkische Vormarsch gegen die mittelslowakischen Bergstädte nicht so sehr als Ausdruck der militärischen Kraft türkischer Grenzgarnisonen zu betrachten ist, der Hauptgrund ist vielmehr im wachsenden wirtschaftlichen und gesellschaftlichen Verfall dieses

---

[17] Turecké pramene vzťahujúce sa na dejiny tureckého panstva na Slovensku (Türkische, auf die Geschichte der Türkenherrschaft in der Slowakei sich beziehende Quellen). Historický časopis, 4, 1956, Nr. 2, S. 156—169. Auch französisch Les sources turques relatives à l'histoire de la domination ottoman en Slovaquie. Archiv orientální, 24, 1956, S. 568—580.

[18] Ein Schreiben des Ofener Defterdār Muṣṭafā an den Hatvaner Mauteinnehmer Derviš Baša. In: Charisteria orientalia. Praha 1956, S. 60—71.

[19] K dejinám tureckého panstva na Slovensku. I, II. Dejiny fiľakovského sandžaku (Zur Geschichte der türkischen Herrschaft in der Slowakei. I, II. Die Geschichte des Sandschaks Fiľakovo). Historické štúdie, 4, 1958, S. 181—221; 5, 1959, S. 149—220.

[20] Príspevok k problematike prenikania tureckej moci na Slovensko (Beitrag zur Problematik des Vordringens der türkischen Macht in die Slowakei). Historický časopis, 7, 1959, Nr. 2, S. 234—265.

Gebietes zu suchen. Vlachovič bringt viele neue Belege über die Verschlechterung der wirtschaftlichen Stellung der Bergstädte nach der Bildung der nordungarischen Sandschaks, über den Handel mit Kupfer in Richtung zur türkischen Seite hin und über den Versuch der Bergleute aus den mittelslowakischen Bergstädten unter dem Einfluß der schwierigen wirtschaftlichen Lage auf die türkische Seite arbeiten zu gehen. Ein unbestrittenes Positivum dieser Studie ist auch die Tatsache, daß der Autor bei seinen Schlußfolgerungen größtenteils aus dem Studium von Archivmaterial hervorging.

Eine erste Übersicht über osmanische Quellen zur Geschichte der osmanischen Expansion in der Slowakei wurde von J. Blaškovič zusammengestellt.[21] Der Autor teilte das türkische Material zu dieser Frage in drei Gruppen ein. 1. Schriftstücke, wo er die Sammlung aus Rimavská Sobota kurz charakterisiert, türkische Schriftstücke aus Miskolc und die Handschriften Turc. 29 und 30 aus Göttingen. 2. *Kanunname, Defters* und *Ruznamçe* — hier weist er hauptsächlich auf die Verzeichnisse des Eyalet Nové Zámky Nr. 115 und 653 aus dem Başvekâlet Arşivi in Istanbul und auf die Verzeichnisse in der Nationalbibliothek in Wien hin. 3. Historische Werke und anderes — hier zählt der Autor einige osmanische Chroniken zur slowakischen Geschichte auf. Als Beilage bringt er die Transkription und die Übersetzung von vier türkischen Schriftstücken aus Miskolc.

Die Herausgabe der osmanischen Quellen zur slowakischen Geschichte sezten in den folgenden Jahren J. Kabrda, J. Blaškovič und Z. Veselá fort.

J. Kabrda veröffentlichte, mit einem detaillierten Kommentar versehen, *Kanunname-i eyâlet-i Uyvar* aus dem Jahre 1664 in lateinischer Transkription und mit tschechischer Übersetzung,[22] sowie das Gesetzbuch des Sandschaks Szécsény aus der Mitte des 16. Jahrhunderts.[23] Nebst neuem Material brachten Kabrdas Editionen ein reichhaltiges Vergleichsmaterial aus den Gesetzbüchern weiterer ungarischer und balkanischer Sandschaks.

Im Laufe der Bearbeitung verschiedener Probleme der osmanischen Expansion in der Slowakei und in Ungarn veröffentlichte J. Blaškovič eine große Anzahl türkischer Schriftstücke aus Rimavská Sobota und Miskolc.[24]

---

[21] Some Notes on the History of the Turkish Occupation of Slovakia. In: Acta Universitatis Carolinae. Philologica I. Orientalia Pragensia I. Praha 1960, S. 41—57. Eine erweiterte Übersetzung dieses Artikels erschien in slowakischer Sprache unter dem Titel K dejinám tureckej okupácie na Slovensku (Zur Geschichte der türkischen Okkupation in der Slowakei). Historické štúdie, *8*, 1963, S. 95—116 samt einer Übersetzung von 8 türkischen Urkunden aus Rimavská Sobota.

[22] Kánúnnáme novozámeckého ejáletu (Kanunname des Eyalets Nové Zámky). Historický časopis, *12*, 1964, Nr. 2, S. 186—214.

[23] Kánúnnáme szécsényských rájů (Kanunname der Rajas von Szécsény). Slovenská archivistika, *2*, 1967, Nr. 1, S. 48—62.

[24] Die Tradition und die Aufgaben der Turkologie in der Slowakei. In: Studia semitica philologica necnon philosophica I. Bakoš dicata. Bratislava 1965, S. 55—68. Einige Dokumente über die Verpflegung der türkischen Armee vor der Festung Nové Zámky im Jahre 1663. In: Asian and African Studies, *2*,

Aus der, einst in Göttingen hinterlegten Handschrift Turc. 30 veröffentlichte Z. Veselá zwölf Schriftstücke, die die Hohe Pforte an I. Thököly in den Jahren 1682—1684 sandte.[25]

Später publizierte V. Kopčan drei türkische Schriftstücke aus den Archiven in Banská Bystrica. Es war eine, in Gemlik herausgegebene Entlassungsurkunde für einen Sklaven slowakischer Herkunft, Yusuf, und zwei, die Auszahlung des Soldes betreffende Schriftstücke.[26]

Mit Fragen des Studiums der osmanischen Expansion in der Slowakei befaßte sich programmatisch J. Kabrda bei der 5. Orientalistischen Konferenz in Smolenice im Jahre 1961.[27] Er konstatierte, daß im Vergleich zu den Balkanländern das ungarische Donauland eine kürzere Zeit unter osmanischer Herrschaft lebte, dies sei jedoch gerade die Zeit der Wendung in der Geschichte des Osmanischen Reiches gewesen. Die Aufgaben der Turkologie bei der Erforschung der osmanischen Expansion in der Slowakei stellte er wie folgt: „Gerade hier kann unsere Turkologie einen bedeutenden Beitrag leisten durch eine verläßliche Herausgabe und gründliche Analyse der betreffenden türkischen Quellen. Es ist selbstverständlich, daß die Nachforschung über die Geschichte der türkischen Herrschaft nicht in einem engen regionalen Rahmen geführt werden kann... Das bedeutet, daß es notwendig ist die Verhältnisse in diesem Rahmen im Zusammenhang mit jener Situation zu erforschen, wie sie damals auf dem übrigen Gebiet des türkischen Ungarns war. Dadurch erweitert sich die Studien- und Quellengrundlage wesentlich. Aber auch das reicht noch nicht aus. Beim Studium der Verhältnisse im ungarischen Donauland müssen auch jene wirtschaftlichen, sozialen und rechtlichen Umstände berücksichtigt

---

1966, S. 103—127. Türkische historische Urkunden aus Gemer. In: Asian and African Studies, *8*, 1972, S. 71—94. Beiträge zur Lebensgeschichte des Köprülü Mehmed. In: Acta orientalia ASH, *11*, 1960, S. 51—55. Köprülü Mehmed Paşanın Macarca bir Ahdnamesi. In: Türkiyat Mecmuası, *15*, 1968, S. 37—46. Rimavská Sobota pod osmansko-tureckým panstvom (Rimavská Sobota unter der osmanisch-türkischen Herrschaft). In: Vlastivedné poľady z okresu Rimavská Sobota, *10*, 1968, S. 23—70. Türkische Quellen, das Wort Kuruc betreffend. In: Studia Turcica. Ed. by L. Ligeti. Budapest 1971, S. 73—88.

[25] Quelques chartes turques concernant la correspondance de la Porte Sublime avec Imre Thököly. Archív orientální, *29*, 1961, S. 546—574. In abgekürzter Form erschien dieser Beitrag auch auf tschechisch Příspěvek ke vztahům Imricha Thökölyho k Osmanské říši. Historický časopis, *10*, 1962, Nr. 4, S. 569—577.

[26] Tri turecké listiny zo slovenských archívov (Drei türkische Urkunden aus slowakischen Archiven). Historické štúdie, *18*, 1973, S. 247—263.

[27] K problematice studia tureckého feudalismu na Balkáně a v uherském Podunají (Zur Problematik des Studiums des türkischen Feudalismus auf dem Balkan und im ungarischen Donauland). In: Orientalistický sborník. Bratislava 1963, S. 86—91. Mit technischen Fragen der Bearbeitung und der Herausgabe osmanischer Quellen befaßte sich J. Kabrda beim 25. Internationalen Kongreß der Orientalisten in Moskau im Jahre 1960, Quelques problèmes de l'étude de l'histoire des peuples balkaniques et Danubien à l'époque de la domination ottomane. In: Trudy 25-go meždunarodnogo kongressa vostokovedov. T. II. Moskva 1963, S. 490—493.

werden, wie sie sich schon früher in der nahen Nachbarschaft — am türkischen Balkan — entwickelt hatten. Das ganze donauländisch-balkanische Gebiet war doch im 16. und 17. Jahrhundert ein integrierender Teil des Osmanischen Reiches" (S. 87).

Für diese Arbeit forderte Kabrda zuerst die Bearbeitung der grundlegenden Bibliographie der türkischen Okkupation in Südosteuropa und das Schaffen einer kritischen Übersicht der Quellen und der Literatur über den türkischen Feudalismus.[28]

Als weitere Aufgabe stellte er die systematische heuristische Erforschung des türkischen Quellenmaterials. Nach der erfolgreichen Durchführung der angeführten Erforschung sollte dieses Material in wissenschaftlichen Herausgaben von Archivquellen benützt werden. Ebenfalls im Rahmen seines Referats verlangte Kabrda eine Feststellung und Charakterisierung der ortsbedingten Unterschiede im feudalen Regime am Balkan und im ungarischen Donauland. Andere wichtige, der turkologischen Forschung von Kabrda auferlegte Aufgaben, wie das Studium der feudalen Grundrente, die Zusammensetzung der Gesellschaft, die Erforschung der Fragen des Klassenkampfes, des Rechtswesens und weitere, hatten einen eher allgemeinen Charakter.

Nach der Gründung des Kabinetts für Orientalistik der Slowakischen Akademie der Wissenschaften im Jahre 1960 wurde in dessen Forschungsprogramm auch das Studium der osmanischen Expansion in der Slowakei eingereiht. Nach Bratislava wurde eine Sitzung von Turkologen einberufen, bei der der bedeutende ungarische Turkologe L. Fekete einen Vortrag über die Auswahl und Herausgabe osmanischer Quellen hielt.[29] L. Fekete konstatierte in seinem Vortrag einleitend, daß die slowakische historische Forschung nur teilweise auf türkische Quellen angewiesen sei, da sich lediglich ein Teil der Slowakei unter türkischer Herrschaft befunden hätte. Daher könnte sich die slowakische Geschichtsschreibung auch auf anderssprachige Quellen stützen. In dieser Hinsicht könnte ein Gleichheitszeichen zwischen die Aufgaben der slowakischen und der ungarischen historischen Forschung gesetzt werden. Nach einer Übersicht über die bis zu jener Zeit verwirklichten Editionen osmanischer Quellen in Ungarn konstatierte er, daß diese Arbeit nicht systematisch und planmäßig gewesen sie und nicht aneinander angeknüpft hätte. Er halte es für notwendig die turkologische Forschung auf die Geschichte des Volkes, auf das Leben des Grenzdorfes und der Grenzstadt, auf das Leben des Bauern, des

---

[28] Diese Aufgaben erfüllte die Osmanistik erst in den letzten Jahren. Die periodische Bibliographie Bibliographie des études balkaniques, Sofia erscheint seit 1966. H.-J. Kornrumpf: *Osmanische Bibliographie mit besonderer Berücksichtigung der Türkei in Europa.* Leiden 1973, umfaßt die Produktion der Jahre 1945—1970. Die neueste und vollständigste Bibliographie ist *Turkologischer Anzeiger*, Wien, seit 1973.

[29] K problematike výberu a vydávania tureckých prameňov (Zur Problematik der Auswahl und Herausgabe türkischer Quellen), Historický časopis, *10*, 1961, Nr. 1, S. 90—100.

Hirten, des städtischen Handwerkers und Kaufmanns zu richten. Er hebt die Wichtigkeit der Erforschung der Arbeit, der Produktion, der Besteuerung dieser Leute, der Ein- und Verkaufsformen, der Märkte, Jahrmärkte und der Maut hervor.

Je nach derer Wichtigkeit räumt er den ersten Platz dem Studium und der Ausgabe von Verzeichnissen der Steuern aus den einzelnen Eyalets (*tahrir defteri*), weiter der *muqāṭaᶜa-defteri,* der *timar defteri* and schließlich der *sicills* und *hüccets* der Kadis ein. Bei der Herausgabe osmanischer Quellen, ob Chroniken oder Schriftstückmaterials, unterstreicht Fekete die Notwendigkeit diese Quellen in der ursprünglichen Sprache und Schrift zu publizieren, und sie erst dann in den Heimatssprachen zugänglich zu machen.

Übersichten über einzelne Arten osmanischer Quellen zur Gesichte der Slowakei samt derer kurzen Charakteristik schrieb V. Kopčan.[30]

Der Autor sammelte bibliographische Angaben über bisdahin herausgegebene Quellen — osmanische Chroniken, Schriftstücke und Defters — und ergänzte sie mit zugänglichen Angaben über nicht publizierte Quellen aus heimischen und ausländischen Sammlungen.

Bis zum Ende der 60er Jahre entstanden einige, verschiedene Fragen der osmanischen Expansion in der Slowakei gewidmete Arbeiten slowakischer Historiker, die`nicht mit türkischem Material arbeiteten. P. Ratkoš befaßte sich mit den Folgen des ersten osmanischen Einfalls in die Slowakei im Jahre 1530.[31] Mit dem türkischen Eindringen in das obere Nitratal und die Westslowakei im Jahre 1663 befaßte sich P. Horváth.[32] J. Beňko befaßte sich mit der Organisation der gegentürkischen Verteidigung in der Mitte des 16. Jahrhunderts im Gebiet der Bergstädte.[33] Der wenig bekannten Frage der Organisation der osmanischen Verwaltung in der Slowakei und den christlichen Hilfstruppen im slowakisch-türkischen Grenzgebiet widmete seine Aufmerksamkeit V. Kopčan.[34]

---

[30] Osmanské naračné pramene k dejinám Slovenska (Osmanische narrative Quellen zur Geschichte der Slowakei). Historický časopis, *13*, 1965, Nr. 1, S. 113—121. Turecké listy a listiny k slovenským dejinám (Türkische Briefe und Urkunden zur slowakischen Geschichte). Historické štúdie, *13*, 1967, S. 105—122. Pramene hospodárskej správy Osmanskej ríše k dejinám Slovenska (Quellen der Wirtschaftsverwaltung des Osmanischen Reiches zur Geschichte der Slowakei). Slovenská archivistika, *2*, 1967, Nr. 1, S. 133—149.

[31] Die Slowakei während der osmanischen Expansion der Jahre 1526—1532. Der erste osmanische Feldzug in die Slowakei vom Jahr 1530. In: Actes du Iᵉʳ Congrès international des études Sud-Est européennes. T. 3. Sofia 1969, S. 737—752. Auch slowakisch in: Historický časopis, *15*, 1967, Nr. 2, S. 219—234.

[32] Turecké vpády na hornú Nitru (Türkische Einfälle in das obere Nitratal). In: Horná Nitra, *4*, 1968, S. 7—23. Turecké vpády na Slovensko roku 1663 (Türkische Einfälle in die Slowakei im Jahre 1663). Vlastivedný časopis, *12*, 1963, Nr. 4, S. 146—150.

[33] Obrana stredoslovenských banských miest v rokoch 1552—1564 (Die Verteidigung der mittelslowakischen Bergstädte in den Jahren 1552—1564). Historie a vojenství, 1969, Nr. 1, S. 1—20.

[34] Príspevok k dejinám osmanskej správy na Slovensku (1541—1686) (Beitrag zur Geschichte der osmanischen Verwaltung in der Slowakei (1541—1686)). Vlastivedný časopis, *17*, 1968, Nr. 3,

Die Verbreitung der Erkenntnisse über die osmanische Expansion in der Slowakei forderte auch deren Zusammenfassung zumindest in populärer Form für einen weiteren Leserkreis. Ein erster Versuch war ein kleines Buch von P. Horváth und V. Kopčan *Turci na Slovensku* (Die Türken in der Slowakei),[35] das vornehmlich Studenten und breiteren Leserschichten zugedacht war. In fünf Kapiteln, deren Kern das zweite „Slovensko v susedstve Turkov" (Die Slowakei in der Nachbarschaft der Türken) und das dritte „Turecká expanzia na Slovensku" (Die türkische Expansion in der Slowakei) darstellen, fassen sie die wichtigsten Vorkommnisse, die osmanische Organisation des eroberten Gebiets und die Folgen der osmanischen Expansion für die Slowakei zusammen. Mit Rücksicht auf die Sendung der Publikation, mieden die Autoren ungelöste Fragen, sowie theoretische Probleme bewußt.

Die Arbeit an der Herausgabe heimatlicher Quellen wurde ebenfalls fortgesetzt, auch wenn nicht in einem solchen Umfang, wie die osmanischen Quellen zugänglich gemacht wurden. Ein kleines Büchlein über Plünderungen türkischer und tatarischer Truppen in der Westslowakei, Mähren und Schlesien im Herbst 1663 und über weitere Ereignisse bis zum Ende des Jahres 1664 entstammt der Feder des Trenčíner Notars M. Vranay.[36] Unter dem Titel *Rabovali Turci...* (Es plünderten die Türken...) veröffentlichte P. Horváth eine Auswahl von Chroniken und Briefen aus dem 16. und 17. Jahrhundert, die die osmanische Expansion in der Slowakei betrafen.[37] Eingereiht sind hier Auszüge aus ungarischen Chroniken von N. Istvánffy, F. Forgách und weiteren lokalen Chroniken, sowie Auszüge aus Evliya Çelebis *Seyahatname* und der Chronik Mehmed Raşid. Unter den Briefen finden wir Drohbriefe an slowakische Städtchen und Dörfer, den Briefwechsel kaiserlicher Befehlshaber, der Städte und Dörfer über die türkische Gefahr. Der Herausgeber veröffentlichte auch einige bisdahin nicht publizierte, vor allem slowakisch geschriebene Briefe.

Für die genauere Kenntnis der osmanischen Expansion in der Slowakei war die Herausgabe der slowakischen Übersetzung türkischer Schriftstücke aus Rimavská Sobota von J. Blaškovič eine bedeutende Editionstat.[38] Das Buch ist in drei Teile geteilt, von denen der erste die Geschichte der Stadt unter der türkischen Herrschaft und die Zahlungsverpflichtungen der Einwohnerschaft bringt. Der zweite Teil

---

S. 116—120. Martalovci na turecko-slovenskom pohraničí v 16. a 17. storočí (Die Martalosen im türkisch-slowakischen Grenzgebiet im 16. und 17. Jahrhundert). Historické štúdie, *15*, 1970, S. 245—252.

[35] Bratislava, SPN 1971. 212 S.

[36] Descriptio Tartaricae depopulationis in anno 1663. Edidit E. Marečková-Štolcová. In: Graecolatina et orientalia I. — Zborník Filozofickej fakulty Univerzity Komenského. Bratislava 1969, S. 125—140.

[37] Bratislava, Tatran 1972. 276 S.

[38] *Rimavská Sobota v čase osmansko-tureckého panstva* (Rimavská Sobota zur Zeit der osmanisch-türkischen Herrschaft). Bratislava, Obzor 1974. 363 S. 31 Tab.

befaßt sich mit der Paläographie und Diplomatik dieser Urkunden, sowie mit derer sprachlichen Charakteristik, und in den dritten Teil sind dann die slowakischen Übersetzungen der Schriftstücke eingereiht. Das Buch wird von Indizes, einem terminologischen Wörterbuch, einem Literaturverzeichnis, den Fotokopien der Urkunden und einem deutschen und ungarischen Resümee vervollständigt.

Seit der 60er Jahre arbeitete J. Blaškovič an Steuerverzeichnissen des Eyalet Nové Zámky, der einzigen osmanischen Provinz, die sich in den Jahren 1663—1685 auf dem Gebiet der heutigen Slowakei befand. Die Ergebnisse seiner Arbeit veröffentlichte er in Teilstudien. Teile aus dem *Defter-i evkâf der eyalet-i Uyvar* (Başvekalet Arşivi, TD Nr. 653) veröffentlichte er in zwei Studien.[39] Aus dem ersten Verzeichnis des Eyalet Nové Zámky aus dem Jahre 1664 (*Defter-i mufassal-ı eyalet-i Uyvar*, BA, TD Nr. 115—698) veröffentlichte J. Blaškovič mit einer Übersetzung Auszüge aus der Nahiye Nitra,[40] das vollständige Verzeichnis der Nahiye Žabokreky mit einer Übersetzung ins Deutsche und einer Fotokopie,[41] sowie einen kürzeren Text und dessen Übersetzung aus der *nahiye* Ňárhíd (im Gebiet der heutigen Stadt Nové Zámky).[42]

Wenn wir die Arbeit an den osmanischen Steuerverzeichnissen erwähnen, muß angeführt werden, daß mehrere, auf das Gebiet der heutigen Slowakei sich beziehende Verzeichnisse, von ungarischen Turkologen veröffentlicht wurden. Bereits im 19. Jahrhundert erschienen Übersetzungen diverser Defters aus Wiener und Budapester Sammlungen, von denen ein nicht unwesentlicher Teil die Sandschaks Esztergom, Nógrád, Szécsény und Fiľakovo betraf, die sich größtenteils auf dem Gebiet der heutigen Slowakei erstreckten.[43] Eine weitere bedeutende Arbeit für die Geschichte der Slowakei war Feketes Ausgabe der Übersetzung des Verzeichnisses des Sandschaks Esztergom aus dem Jahre 1570.[44] Auszüge aus den osmanischen Defters, die die Slowakei betreffen, erschienen auch in Feketes großem Werk *Die Siyāqat-Schrift in der türkischen Finanzverwaltung. I, II.*[45]

Der amerikanische Osmanist Gustav Bayerle gab die Verzeichnisse des

---

[39] Vakfy v novozámockom a nitrianskom okrese (Die Vakfe im Bezirk Nové Zámky und Nitra). Historické štúdie. *18*, 1973, S. 265—275 und Das Sultansdekret (Sünurname) über das Vakf im Bezirk Nové Zámky. Archív orientální, *42*, 1974, S. 300—309, IV.

[40] Turecký daňový súpis Nitrianskej župy z roku 1664 (Das türkische Steuerverzeichnis des Komitats Nitra aus dem Jahre 1664). Agrikultúra, *10,* 1971, S. 29—37.

[41] Ein türkisches Steuerverzeichnis aus dem Bezirk von Žabokreky aus dem Jahre 1664. Archív orientální, *45*, 1977, S. 201—210, IV.

[42] Ziemie lenne (ḫāṣṣ) namiestnika Nowych Zamków w latach 1664—1685. In: Rocznik Orientalistyczny, *38*, 1976, S. 83—91.

[43] Velics, A. — Kammerer, E.: *Magyarországi török kincstári defterek. I (1543—1635), II (1540—1639).* Budapest 1886—1890; Szilády, A.: *A defterekről.* Pest 1872.

[44] *Az esztergomi szandzsák 1570.évi adóösszeírása.* Budapest 1943. 197 S., Karte, Faksimile.

[45] Budapest 1955. 910 S. 104 Tab.

44

Sandschaks Nógrád heraus.[46] Es geht um den zusammenfassenden (*mufassal*) Defter aus dem Jahre 1570 (BA, TD Nr. 507) und den *icmal* aus dem Jahre 1579 (BA, TD Nr. 661).

In diesem Zusammenhang müssen auch die Werke von Gy. Káldy-Nagy erwähnt werden, die aus den osmanischen Steuerverzeichnissen des ganzen osmanischen Ungarns hervorgehen, als eine methodische Anleitung für die Kritik und die Verwertung dieser Verzeichnisse.[47]

Außer der Erforschung des Urkundenmaterials und der Defters wurde die Aufmerksamkeit auch dem Studium der narrativen Quellen gewidmet. H. Turková übersetzte aus Evliya Çelebis *Seyahatname* einen Teil aus dem 6. Band, der die Belagerung und Eroberung von Nové Zámky betrifft.[48]

Mit osmanischen narrativen Quellen zum Feldzug gegen Nové Zámky im Jahre 1663 befaßte sich V. Kopčan.[49] Er verfaßte auch einen übersichtlichen Artikel über die Entstehung, Entwicklung, die Gattungen sowie die spezifischen Züge der osmanischen Geschichtsschreibung und deren Bedeutung für die slowakische Geschichte.[50] Auf Grund von Vergleichen osmanischer Quellen zum Feldzug gegen Nové Zámky bewies er, daß eine der Quellen des osmanischen Geschichtsschreibers Mehmed Ağa Silahdar, sowie auch Mehmed Raşids, das Werk *Cevahir üt-tevarih* von Hasan Ağa war.[51] Auch weitere Studien V. Kopčan gehen aus den osmanischen Chroniken zum Feldzug gegen Nové Zámky hervor.[52] Der Autor gab auch Itinerarien zu diesem Feldzug heraus.[53]

Wenn die zusammenfassenden Arbeiten über die Geschichte der Slowakei nicht miteinberechnet werden, bringen die Studien von Z. Veselá die jüngste Zusammenfassung der Problematik der osmanischen Expansion in der Slowakei.[54] Die Autorin

---

[46] *Ottoman Tributes in Hungary According to Sixteenth Century Tapu Registers of Novigrad.* The Hague—Paris 1973.

[47] Bevölkerungsstatistischer Quellenwert der Ğizye-Defter und Taḥrīr-Defter. In: Acta orientalia ASH, *11*, 1960, f. 1—3, S. 259—269. The Administration of the Sanǰāq-Registration in Hungary. In: Acta orientalia ASH, *21*, 1968, S. 181—223. Macaristan'da 16. Yüzyılda Türk Yönetimi. In: Studia Turco-Hungarica. I. Budapest 1974. 77 S.

[48] Über die Belagerung von Uyvār (Neuhäusel, Nové Zámky) im Jahre 1663 durch die Türken. Archív orientální, *41*, 1973, S. 325—339.

[49] Ottoman Narrative Sources to the Uyvar Expedition 1663. In: Asian and African Studies, *7*, 1971, S. 89—100.

[50] Vznik a vývoj osmanského dejepisectva (Entstehung und Entwicklung der osmanischen Geschichtsschreibung). Historický časopis, *22*, 1974, Nr. 4, S. 575—606.

[51] Eine Quelle der Geschichte Siliḥdārs. In: Asian and African Studies, *9*, 1973, S. 129—139.

[52] Einige Anmerkungen zu Evliya Çelebis Seyahatname. In: Asian and African Studies *12*, 1976, S. 71—84. Bemerkungen zur Benutzung der europäischen Quellen in der osmanischen Geschichtsschreibung. In: Asian and African Studies, *11*, 1975, S. 147—160.

[53] Zwei Itinerarien des osmanischen Feldzuges gegen Neuhäusel (Nové Zámky) im Jahre 1663. In: Asian and African Studies, *14*, 1978, S. 59—88.

[54] Slovensko a osmanská expanze v 16. a 17. století (Die Slowakei und die osmanische Expansion im

sagt selbst, „ich habe vor, diesmal aus unterschiedlichen Positionen, aus den Positionen eines tschechischen Turkologen, unsere heutigen Kenntnisse über die geschichtliche Entwicklung der Slowakei in der osmanischen Zeit zu klassifizieren und einige Anregungen zum weiteren Studium dieser Frage zu geben". Zu den unzweifelbaren Positiva dieser Studie gehört die Tatsache, daß die Autorin außer der politischen und ökonomischen, auch die kulturelle Entwicklung in Betracht zieht und das Problem im Rahmen der osmanischen Geschichte löst. In einer weiteren Studie betrachtet Z. Veselá das Problem der Einstellung verschiedener Schichten der slowakischen Einwohnerschaft zur osmanischen Expansion, sowie auch zu den Türken selbst, und unterstreicht den betont klassenbedingten Aspekt dieser Beziehung.[55]

Die Erforschung osmanischer Quellen, deren Bearbeitung und Studien aus der Geschichte stellen jedoch nicht die Gesamtproduktion der slowakischen Geschichtsschreibung zur Frage der osmanischen Expansion dar. Die Übersicht wäre nicht vollständig, würden wir die Beiträge aus der historischen Archäologie, Numismatik, der Ikonographie der osmanischen Expansion, der Topographie, Toponymie und Onomastik, der Folkloristik, dem Militärwesen, der öffentlichen Meinung, den Migrationen, Vaterlandskunde und den weiteren Problemen nicht zumindest flüchtig erfassen.

Die angeblich von Türken erbaute kleine Festung Sobôtka bei Rimavská Sobota war Gegenstand der archäologischen Forschung zum Ende der 60er Jahre.[56] Sammlungen osmanischer Münzen auf dem Gebiet der Tschechoslowakei wurden nach deren Fundorten von J. Štěpková bearbeitet.[57] Gegenstand der Forschung von K. Jančová-Zavarská waren ikonographische Materialien zu den türkischen Kriegen, sowie zu den Veduten slowakischer Städte.[58] Mit einer ähnlichen Thematik

16. und 17. Jahrhundert). In: Osmanská moc ve střední a jihovýchodní Evropě v 16.—17. století. Praha 1977, S. 8—54.

[55] Ke vztahu slovenského lidu k osmanské expanzi (Zur Beziehung der slowakischen Bevölkerung zur osmanischen Expansion). Československý časopis historický, *23*, 1975, Nr. 5, S. 687—705.

[56] Drenko, Z.: Archeologický výskum tureckého hradu „Sobôtka" (Die archäologische Erforschung der türkischen Burg „Sobôtka"). In: Zborník Slovenského národného múzea 64 — História 10, 1970, S. 139—175. Derselbe: Nové nálezy zo Sobôtky (Neue Funde aus Sobôtka). In: Zborník SNM 65 — História 11, 1971, S. 163—168. Derselbe: Turecký hrad Sobôtka pri Rimavskej Sobote (Die türkische Burg Sobôtka bei Rimavská Sobota). In: Vlastivedné štúdie Gemera, *2*, 1973, S. 79—84.

[57] Coins of the Osmanli Sultans in the Coin-Hoards Found on Czechoslovak Territory. In: Annals of the Náprstek Museum, 2, Prague 1963, S. 141—191. Nálezy osmanských mincí na území ČSSR (Funde osmanischer Münzen auf dem Gebiet der ČSSR). In: Orientalistický sborník. Bratislava 1963, S. 175—179.

[58] Ikonografický materiál z obdobia tureckých vojen (Das ikonographische Material aus der Zeit der türkischen Kriege). Vlastivedný časopis, *13*, 1963, Nr. 4, S. 153—157. *Verný a pravý obraz slovenských miest a hradov, ako ich znázornili rytci a ilustrátori v XVI., XVII. a XVIII. storočí* (Ein wahres und echtes Bild slowakischer Städte und Burgen, wie diese von Stechern und Illustratoren im XVI., XVII. und XVIII. Jahrhundert dargestellt wurden). Bratislava, Tatran 1974.

befaßte sich auch K. Krajčovičová[59] und andere. Die umfangreiche Publizistik über die türkische Gefahr in Böhmen und Deutschland, besonders zu jenen Zeiten, als sich auch diese Länder von türkischen Heer bedroht fühlten, war das Interesse mehrerer Forscher. In einer Beziehung zur Slowakei und Ungarn studierten diese Probleme J. Polišenský mit J. Hrubeš und M. Suchý.[60]

Über die Möglichkeit der Verwertung osmanischer Steuerverzeichnisse, aber auch Evliya Çelebis *Seyahatname* für die Topographie und Toponymie schrieb E. Tejnil.[61] Auf Grund eines umfangreichen Materials aus den osmanischen Verzeichnissen des Eyalet Nové Zámky studierte J. Blaškovič Orts-, Vor- und Familiennamen.[62] Mit der Bearbeitung türkischer Motive in der slowakischen Folklore befaßten sich mehrere slowakische sowie tschechische Folkloristen.[63]

Mit der Geschichte einzelner Gebiete unter der osmanischen Herrschaft und den Bergbauunternehmungen auf dem türkisch-slowakischen Grenzgebiet befaßten sich P. Horváth mit Š. Kazimír, L. Kocsis und V. Kopčan.[64]

[59] Ikonografia k protitureckým bojom na Slovensku v dobových publikáciách 16. a 17. storočia (Die Ikonographie zu den gegentürkischen Kämpfen in der Slowakei in zeitgenössischen Publikationen des 16. und 17. Jahrhunderts. In: Zborník SNM 67 — História 13, S. 163—204. Nové Zámky vo svetle ikonografických prameňov 16. a 17. storočia (Nové Zámky im Licht der ikonographischen Quellen des 16. und 17. Jahrhunderts). In: Zborník SNM 68 — História 14, S. 203—247. Tibenský, J.: Slovensko-turecký svet v ilustráciách A. E. Birkensteina a v Uhorskom vojnovom románe W. E. Happelia (Die slowakisch-türkische Welt in den Illustrationen A. E. Birkensteins und im Ungarischen Kriegsroman von W. E. Happelius). Vlastivedný časopis, *17*, 1968, Nr. 3, S. 105—116.

[60] Polišenský, J.—Hrubeš, J.: Turecké války, uherská povstání a veřejné mínění předbělohorských Čech (Türkische Kriege, ungarische Aufstände und die öffentliche Meinung Böhmens vor der Niederlage am Weißen Berge). Historický časopis, *7*, 1959, Nr. 1, S. 74—103. Suchý, M.: Das türkische Problem in Ungarn im 16. Jahrhundert und die deutsche öffentliche Meinung. In: Gedenkschrift M. Göhring. Wiesbaden 1969, S. 46—59. Derselbe: Das Echo der türkischen Expansion in Ungarn in der ersten Hälfte des 16. Jahrhundert in Deutschland. In: Studia Historica Slovaca, *6*, 1969, S. 63—106. Ratkoš, P.: O protiosmanskej verejnej mienke pred vznikom budínskeho vilajetu (Zdroje a vývinové tendencie) (Über osmanenfeindliche öffentliche Meinung vor dem Entstehen des Ofener Vilayets (Quellen und Entwicklungstendenzen)). In: Osmanská moc v strednej a jihovýchodní Evropě v 16.—17. stol. Praha 1977, S. 287—309.

[61] K problematike tureckej topografie a toponymie na Slovensku (Zur Problematik der türkischen Topographie und Toponymie in der Slowakei). In: Historické štúdie, *14*, 1969, S. 167—178.

[62] Slovenská jména v tureckých daňových soupisech r. 1664 (Slowakische Namen in türkischen Steuerverzeichnissen des Jahres 1664). In: Zpravodaj místopisné komise ČSAV, *19*, 1978, Nr. 1—2, S. 13—25.

[63] Rychnová, D.: Moravské a slovenské lidové balady s tematikou tureckých válek (Mährische und slowakische Volksballaden mit der Thematik der türkischen Kriege). In: Rad Kongresa folklorista Jugoslavije u Varaždinu 1957. Zagreb 1959, S. 251—256. Michálek, J.: Variant povesti o zajatom synovi — janičiarovi (Die Variante der Sage von gefangengenommenen Sohn — dem Janitscharen). In: Slovenský národopis, *11*, 1963, S. 390—397. Kosová, M.: K návrhu interetnického katalógu povestí z čias tureckého nebezpečenstva (Zum Vorschlag eines interetnischen Katalogs der Sagen aus der Zeit der türkischen Gefahr). Slovenský národopis, *14*, 1966, S. 465—467.

[64] Kocsis, L.: Dejiny fiľakovského sandžaku (Die Geschichte des Sandschaks Fiľakovo). In:

Mit der relativ vernachlässigten Problematik der Militärgeschichte, ob es sich um die kaiserliche, gegen die Türken kämpfende Armee, oder die eigentlichen türkischen Heere handelt, befaßten sich einige Artikel.[65]

Den Migrationen der serbischen und kroatischen Einwohnerschaft nach Mitteleuropa in Folge der osmanischen Expansion widmet sich schon seit längerer Zeit K. Kučerová, die nach Teilstudien[66] auch eine Monographie verfaßte.[67]

Über den Einfluß der osmanischen Expansion auf die Fortifikationsarchitektur in der Slowakei schrieb J. Lichner.[68]

Die angeführte Übersicht zeigt, daß in den Erforschung der osmanischen Expansion genug getan wurde. Im Vergleich zur Vergangenheit wurde vor allem in der Zugänglichmachung des türkischen Materials viel erreicht. Vom Gesichtspunkt der Bedürfnisse der slowakischen Geschichte wurden die Fonds der zentralen osmanischen Institutionen in Istanbul noch nicht erforscht, ob es sich um Schriften der Finanzverwaltung oder die *mühimme defteri* handelt. Wie die Studien von Gy. Káldy-Nagy[69] zeigten, bringen die *mühimme defteri* eine Anzahl wertvoller Angaben, und das nicht nur als Ergänzungen zu Steuerverzeichnissen, sondern auch als eine Quelle der Informationen über Entscheidungen des Sultanatsrates in verschiedenen Fragen. Nach einem Verzeichnis dieser Defters, das der jugoslawische

Vlastivedné štúdie Gemera, 2, 1973, S. 53—78. Horváth, P. — Kazimír, Š.: Baníctvo na slovensko-tureckom pohraničí na konci 16. storočia (Der Bergbau im slowakisch-türkischen Grenzgebiet am Ende des 16. Jahrhunderts). Vlastivedný časopis, 23, 1974, Nr. 2, S. 81—84. Kopčan, V.: Hontianska stolica v čase osmanskej expanzie (Das Komitat Hont zur Zeit der osmanischen Expansion). Slovenský národopis, 25, 1977, Nr. 1, S. 145—152.

[65] Picková, V.: Císařské vojsko v Uhrách v 16. století očima současníkú (Die kaiserliche Armee in Ungarn im 16. Jahrhundert mit den Augen der Zeitgenossen gesehen). In: Historie a vojenství, 1965, Nr. 5, S. 789—799. Ratkoš, P.: Memoár habsburského žoldniera Melchiora Haufeho (1526—1543) (Das Memoire des habsburgischen Söldners Melchior Haufe (1526—1543)). In: Sborník FFUK — História 17, 1966, S. 140—158. Kopčan, V.: Vojenský charakter osmanskej expanzie na Slovensku (Der militärische Charakter der osmanischen Expansion in der Slowakei). In: Osmanská moc v strední a jihovýchodní Evropě v 16.—17. století. Praha 1977, S. 235—265.

[66] Migrácia srbského, bosenského a chorvátskeho obyvateľstva z Balkánu do strednej Európy v dôsledku tureckých vojen (Die Migration der serbischen, bosnischen und kroatischen Bevölkerung aus dem Balkan nach Mitteleuropa infolge der türkischen Kriege). In: Studia balkanica bohemoslovaca. Brno 1970, S. 96—103. K problému chorvátskej kolonizácie na Slovensku v 16. storočí (Zum Problem der kroatischen Kolonisation in der Slowakei im 16. Jahrhundert). In: Československo a Juhoslávia. Bratislava 1968, S. 68—76.

[67] Chorváti a Srbi v strednej Európe. (K etnickým, hospodárskym a sociálnym otázkam v 16.—17. storočí) (Die Kroaten und die Serben in Mitteleuropa. (Zu den etnischen, wirtschaftlichen und sozialen Fragen im 16.—17. Jahrhundert)). Bratislava 1976. 327 S.

[68] Lichner, J.: Stavebný charakter mestských pamiatok a opevnení z čias tureckého nebezpečenstva na Slovensku (Der bauliche Charakter der städtischen Denkmäler und der Befestigungen aus der Zeit der türkischen Gefahr in der Slowakei). Vlastivedný časopis, 13, 1964, Nr. 1, S. 1—12.

[69] The Administration of the Sanǰāq-Registration in Hungary und Studia Turco-Hungarica, I, S. 20.

Historiker G. Elezović[70] vor dem zweiten Weltkrieg anfertigte, blieben diese auch jenen Jahren erhalten, als das Osmanische Reich kriegerische Aktionen auf unserem Gebiet durchführte (1593—1596, 1603—1607, 1663—1664, 1678—1681). Es ist unumgänglich die Angaben der narrativen Quellen, bzw. des heimischen Materials durch diese Dokumente zu vervollständigen.

Außer in türkischen Archiven befinden sich reichhaltige Sammlungen osmanischen Materials im Österreichischen Staatsarchiv in Wien, vor allem im Fonds Turcica, aber auch in anderen. Wie eine kürzlich erschienene Herausgabe von Briefen Ofener Statthalter an den Kaiser oder an hohe Würdenträger des Hofes zeigte,[71] berühren viele dieser Dokumente auch das slowakische Gebiet. Ein Teil der Probleme, die in diesen Briefen behandelt werden (z. B. die Vernichtung und Niederbrennung von Dörfern, bewaffnete Konflikte), sind der slowakischen Geschichtsschreibung aus heimischen Archiven bekannt, wir wissen jedoch nicht, wie diese Frage an höchsten Stellen zwischen den Repräsentanten der osmanischen und der habsburgischen Macht gelöst wurden.

Auch das türkische oder von den Türken herausgegebene Material aus ungarischen Archiven, vor allem aus dem Landesarchiv (Magyar Országos Levéltár), ist bislang noch nicht ausreichend genützt worden. In Archiven der Familien, deren Güter sich auf dem Gebiet der Slowakei befanden, wie z. B. der Familie Thurzo, Zichy, Eszterházy, Illésházy usw. befinden sich osmanische Dokumente (z. B. im Fonds von P. Esterházy sind Briefe des Statthalters von Nové Zámky, Küçük Mehmed Pascha).[72]

Was heimische Archive betrifft, haben wir dank der verdienstvollen Arbeit unserer Archivare eine ausreichende Übersicht über türkische Dokumente, wenn auch vereinzelt noch neue auftauchen. Nach der Herausgabe der Sammlung von Rimavská Sobota gibt es in der Slowakei keine größere Kollektion mehr, die eine selbständige Buchausgabe verdienen würde. Sporadisch aufgefundene Dokumente oder kleinere Sammlungen können in selbständigen Studien mit einer historischen und paläographischen Einleitung herausgegeben werden.

Was die Editionen betrifft, am besten ist die Situation in der Herausgabe von Verzeichnissen aus den Sandschaks. Nach Feketes Herausgabe des Steuerverzeichnisses des Sandschaks Esztergom (1943) und Bayerles Edition der Defters des Sandschaks Nógrád (1973) erwarten wir, daß in kurzer Zeit J. Blaškovič die

[70] *Iz Carigradskih turskih arhiva Mühimme defteri.* Beograd 1951 und Heyd, U.: *Ottoman Documents on Palestine 1552—1615. A Study of the Firman according to the Mühimme Defteri.* Oxford 1960.

[71] Bayerle, G.: *Ottoman Diplomacy in Hungary. Letters from the Pashas of Buda 1590—1593.* Bloomington 1972.

[72] Bayerle, G.: Ottoman Records in the Hungarian Archives. In: Archivum Ottomanicum, *4,* 1972, S. 5—22.

Verzeichnisse des Eyalets Nové Zámky zum Druck überreicht. Es wird auch an den Verzeichnissen des Sandschaks Fiľakovo und Szécsény gearbeitet.[73]

Hinsichtlich des beschränkten Umfangs der osmanischen Macht auf dem Gebiet der heutigen Slowakei und die verhältnismäßig kurze Zeitspanne, in der die Türken dieses Gebiet beherrschten, wird es nach Vervollständigung durch heimische Quellen (Urbare, Zehntenverzeichnisse) möglich sein, ein objektives Bild über die Steuerbelastung der Bevölkerung durch osmanische Finanzorgane zu schaffen, und gleichzeitig zur Erkenntnis des Quellenwertes osmanischer Steuerverzeichnisse im Grenzgebiet beizutragen.[74]

Im Falle der osmanischen Schriftstücke in ausländischen Archiven gestatten uns die ungenügenden Kenntnisse über deren Anzahl nicht irgendwelche vorläufige Vorschläge über die Art derer Herausgabe zu machen. Wir würden zuerst deren Bearbeitung in Studien, und erst dann eine Vorbereitung der vollständigen Herausgabe — wie dies schon früher L. Fekete vorgeschlagen hat — befürworten.[75]

Bis vor kurzem gingen unsere Kenntnisse über osmanische narrative Quellen vor allem aus den ungarischen Übersetzungen osmanischer Chroniken vom Ende des 19. und Beginn des 20. Jahrhunderts hervor, die von J. Thúry und I. Karácson vermittelt wurden. Eine verurteilende Kritik des Wertes osmanischer Chroniken aus der Feder des ungarischen Historikers Gy. Szekfü[76] bewirkte, daß dieser Art von Quellen eine kleinere Aufmerksamkeit gewidmet wurde. Erst die jüngste kritische Forschung bewies, daß auch diese Art von Quellen bei einem kritischen Zutritt sehr gut zu verwerten ist. Nach der Übersetzung jener Teile aus Evliya Çelebis *Seyahatname*,[77] die die Slowakei betreffen, wäre es notwendig Übersetzungen aus bedeutenderen Chroniken anzufertigen (Silahdar Tarihi usw.).

Die Herausgabe von Quellen war und ist lediglich eines der Ziele unserer turkologischen und historischen Forschung. Hinsichtlich der erreichten Ergebnisse tritt die Frage einer komplexen Bearbeitung der osmanischen Expansion in der Slowakei, ob schon in Form einer monographischen Arbeit oder als ein Teil der Geschichte der Slowakei immer dringender in den Vordergrund. Als besonders notwendig erscheint es, die Ergebnisse für eine vollständige Bearbeitung der

---

[73] Die Defters beider Sandschaks werden von Prof. G. Bayerle von der Indiana University, Bloomington bearbeitet.

[74] Ein Teil der ungarischen Historiker beurteilt die Verwendung türkischer Steuerverzeichnisse für die Wirtschaftsgeschichte skeptisch, siehe: Mészáros, I.: Történeti statisztikai források a török hódoltság korából. Statisztikai Szemle, *38*, 1960, Nr. 5. S. 501—515. Dagegen Káldy-Nagy, Gy.: siehe Anmerkung 47.

[75] Siehe Anmerkung 29.

[76] Kútfókritikai tanulmány a hódoltság korabeli török történetírókról. In: Török történetírók. III (1566—1659). Budapest 1916, S. 1—63.

[77] *Kniha ciest. Cesty po Slovensku.* Prel. V. Kopčan (Das Buch der Reisen. Reisen durch die Slowakei. Übersetzt von V. Kopčan). Bratislava 1978.

Geschichte der Slowakei zusammenzufassen, ob in einer kürzeren oder umfangreicheren Form, da die kürzlich publizierten Arbeiten dieser Art nicht immer die erreichten Ergebnisse der heimischen und ausländischen Forschung widerspiegeln.

Eine vollständige Bearbeitung der osmanischen Expansion auf unserem Gebiet auf dem heutigen Stand unserer Kenntnisse wird und kann, natürlich, nicht das letzte Wort zu diesem Problem sein. Eine Reihe von Problemen der wirtschaftlichen und politischen Geschichte tritt auf, die in den letzten Jahren von der Osmanistik und durch die Arbeiten der Historiker aus benachbarten Ländern, vor allem der ungarischen, aufgerollt wurden.

Eine der spezialen Fragen, die für unser Gebiet unter der osmanischen Herrschaft typisch erscheint, ist die Frage des *Kondominiums* — also einer gemeinsamen, wenn auch beschränkten Herrschaft beider rivalisierender Mächte — des Osmanischen Reichs und der Habsburger, in den Grenzgebieten. Der typischste Ausdruck dieser Doppelherrschaft war das Steuerzahlen nach beiden Seiten hin. Obzwar die Osmanen im 16. Jahrhundert versuchten diese Doppelherrschaft zu brechen, mußten sie sie später akzeptieren und in Friedensverträgen sogar zugeben. So war im Prinzip das ganze heutige slowakische Gebiet, das die Osmanen beherrschten oder welches sie beanspruchten, ein *Kondominium*, was natürlich für beide Seiten eine Reihe von Problemen mit sich brachte. Deshalb halten wir die Lösung dieser Problematik für einen bedeutsamen Bestandteil der weiteren Arbeit der slowakischen Osmanistik und Geschichtsschreibung.[78]

Eine weitere bedeutende Frage stellt die Erforschung des Aufbaus und der Instandhaltung des Systems von Grenzfestungen gegen die osmanische Expansion dar. Viele Fragen der gegentürkischen Verteidigung sind uns aus älteren Arbeiten, vor allem aus denen von Matunák, bekannt, bislang haben wir uns jedoch wenig mit den konkreten Fragen der finanziellen Erhaltung und der materiallen Versorgung dieser Burgen befaßt. Wir wissen, daß die Verteidigungslinie, d. h. die Garnisonen dieser Grenzburgen in einem bedeutenden Maß aus den Einnahmen der Güter dieser Festungen erhalten wurde. Der Verwaltungsmechanismus und die Verteilung der Einnahmen aus diesen Gütern, die Bereicherung und der Machtanwuchs der Befehlshaber bedeutender Grenzburgen, weitere Formen der Gewährleistung der gegentürkischen Abwehr — außerordentliche Steuer und Auslandshilfe, das alles sind Fragen, deren Lösung noch vor uns steht. Anregend könnten sich hierbei Vergleiche mit den Grenzgebieten des jetzigen Ungarns und Kroatiens auswirken.[79]

Auch die Frage der Gefangenen kann nicht abseits gelassen werden. Das

---

[78] Anregend wirken auf diesem Gebiet die Arbeiten von K. Hegyi, vor kurzem die populäre Monographie *Egy világbirodalom végvidékén*. Budapest 1976.

[79] S z á n t ó, I.: A végvári rendszer kiépítésének és fenntartásának költeségei Magyarországon a XVI. század második felében. In: Acta Historica, 58, Szeged 1977, S. 21—45 und R o t h e n b e r g, G. E.: *The Austrian Military Border in Croatia, 1522—1747*. Urbana 1960.

Kondominium schuf außerordentliche Verhältnisse im Grenzgebiet, aus welchen beiderseits schlecht besoldete oder oft auch ohne Mittel für ihren Lebensunterhalt lebende Soldaten zu profitieren versuchten. Die Beute wurde zum Grundwert und Bedürfnis des Alltagslebens. Alles, inklusive der Menschen, konnte zur Beute gemacht werden. Dal Lösegeld für Gefangene wurde zu einer bedeutenden Einnahmequelle in den Grenzgebieten. Solange sie nicht losgekauft wurden, arbeiteten die Gefangenen für ihre Besitzer. Es kam vor, daß sie auf Gewähr freigelassen wurden, um das Lösegeld schneller einholen zu können. Wir haben Beweise, daß Gefangene kaiserlicherseits von den Türken die Mauteinnahme pachteten, wobei sie dann die Kaufleute ausbeuteten, um schneller zu Lösegeld zu kommen.[80] Das Lösegeld hing von der Stellung des Gefangenen ab, davon ob dieser Soldat oder Bauer war, wobei die Seite, die den Gefangenen festhielt, so viel wie möglich zu erreichen trachtete.[81]

Viele Gefangenen, die man bei großen Kriegszügen oder bei tatarischen Plünderungen (1599, 1663) verschleppt hatte, wurden nicht losgekauft und auf den Balkan oder sogar bis nach Kleinasien verschleppt. Menschenverschleppung gehörte zu den verheerendsten und tragischsten Folgen der osmanischen Expansion.

Fast überhaupt keine Aufmerksamkeit wurde bislang den türkischen Gefangenen auf kaiserlicher Seite gewidmet, obwohl es über diese in den Quellen an Erwähnungen nicht mangelt. Auch diese Frage müßte auf breiterer Vergleichsbasis geprüft werden.[82]

Wir erwähnten lediglich einige der Probleme der osmanischen Expansion in der Slowakei, deren tiefere Kenntnis für das Gesamtbild dringend notwendig wäre. Es gibt, selbstverständlich, noch eine Reihe weiterer Fragen aus der wirtschaftlichen, politischen und kulturellen Geschichte, die die osmanische Expansion vor uns stellt, und die wir auf diesem beschränkten Platz nicht ausführlich behandeln können.

Mit einer tieferen und vielseitigeren Kenntnis der Problematik der osmanischen Expansion in der Slowakei wird unsere Geschichtsschreibung und Turkologie nicht nur zur Erkenntnis der eigenen Geschichte, sondern auch der Geschichte von ganz Mittel- und Südosteuropa beitragen.

---

[80] Blaškovič, J.: Ein Schreiben, S. 65. Sugar, P.: The Ottoman „Professional Prisoner" in the Western Borders of the Empire in the Sixteenth and Seventeenth Centuries. In: Etudes Balkaniques, 7, 1971, Nr. 2, S. 82—91.

[81] Siehe Ungarischer Simplicissimus von D. Speer und Der ungarische Kriegsroman von W. E. Happelius.

[82] Voje, I.: Naseljavanje turskih zarobljenika u slovenačkim zemljama u XVI i XVII v. Jugoslovenski istorijski časopis, 1970, Nr. 4, S. 38—43.

THE STRUGGLE FOR THE RED SEA: MUSSOLINI'S POLICY IN YAMAN, 1934—1943[1]

JOHN BALDRY, Al-Ḥudaydah

After occupying Aden in 1839, Britain progressively concluded agreements with the rulers of Arabia whose territory abutted on the coast of the Peninsula. By 1917 these treaties, by denying the local rulers the right to treat with other powers, had given Britain control of the two sea routes through the Red Sea and Arabian Gulf to its Eastern Empire. By this time Yaman and the odd Ḥijāzī port constituted the sole gaps around the whole Arabian coast where Britain had failed to obtain recognition of its primacy from the local rulers.

Italian intervention in Yaman, 1914—1933

Italy, like Britain, had aspirations in Arabia, due in part to the impoverished state of its colony in Eritrea which needed to trade with the opposite coast. Thus, throughout the First World War both countries attempted to divert Imām Yaḥyā's allegiance from Turkey to their own advantage. When, by the middle of 1915, it had become apparent that Italy was intent on obtaining a footing on the Arabian coast of the Red Sea, Britain responded by occupying the Farasān islands to forestall the Italians.[2] When, the next year, a group of Italian nationalists publicly argued that Yaman should become "a sort of Italian reserve"[3] it was feared in London that the Italian Government might take up the discussion.

---

[1] For earlier aspects of Anglo-Italian rivalry in Yaman see especially my *Anglo-Italian Rivalry in Yemen and ʿAsīr, 1900—1934*. Die Welt des Islams, *XVII*, 1976—1977, pp. 155—193. Other aspects of Italian activities in Yaman are dealt with in my *The Turkish-Italian War in the Yemen, 1911—1912*. Arabian Studies, *III*, 1976, pp. 51—65. For Italian attempts to obtain mineral concessions in Yaman see my *The Powers and Mineral Concessions in the Idrīsī Imāmate of ʿAsīr, 1910—1929*. Arabian Studies, *II*, 1975, pp. 76—107. Anglo-Italian Intervention in Yaman during the Saʿūdi-Yamani War of 1934 is discussed in my *Al-Ḥudaydah and the Powers during the Saʿūdi-Yamani War of 1934* in Arabian Studies, *VI*. The Italian reaction to French pretensions in Yaman is dealt with in my *The French Claim to Shaykh Saʿīd (Yaman) and Its International Repercussions, 1868—1939* (to be published in Arabica in 1980). In connection with the Kamarān Quarantine Station see my *The Ottoman Quarantine Station on Kamarān Island, 1882—1914* in Journal of the History of Medicine, New Delhi, *II*, Nos 1—2, March—June 1978, pp. 3—138. For another examination of Italian interest in the Red Sea, see R a m m, A.: *Great Britain and the Planting of Italian Power in the Red Sea, 1868—1885* in English Historical Review, *LIX*, No. 234, May 1944, pp. 211—236.

[2] L/P&S/10/560.

[3] Hardinge Papers: Rodd (Brit. Amb., Rome) to Hardinge, 9. 9. 1916.

So persistent were the Italians in their attempts to win Imām Yaḥyā's allegiance during the World War, that the India Office stressed in a memorandum the importance of excluding all possible seeds of disturbance from Yaman. It was believed that "Italian ambitions" were "mainly fixed" in Yaman where an Italian presence would "create a ferment... from which we as a limitrophe Power, would be the chief sufferers". Were the Imām, after the War, to acquiesce in Italian domination, there would be a serious likelihood that "part of the price he will ask will be the support (at least tacit) of his claims... in our Protectorate" and Ḥaḍramawt.[4]

At the end of the War both Britain and Italy hoped to acquire political hegemony in Yaman, but there was little possibility that Imām Yaḥyā would conclude any agreement with Britain so long as the Aden Protectorate and Ḥaḍramawt remained under British control. A further obstacle to the establishment of Anglo-Yamani relations lay in continuing British support for the Imām's implacable enemy, Sayyid Muḥammad al-Idrīsī, to whom Britain ceded the Yamani port of al-Ḥudaydah in January 1921 after it had been under British Military Administration for 26 months.[5] It was not until 1922 that France showed any interest in the affairs of South-West Arabia, while the Soviet Union directed its attention to Ḥijāz. The way was thus open to Italy, which by offering economic assistance to Yaman, was able to establish good relations with Imām Yaḥyā immediately after the World War. The Italians also turned their attention to Imām Yaḥyā's northern neighbour, the Idrīsī in ᶜAsīr.

To divert the Idrīsī's loyalty to Britain, the Italians attempted to import Italian silver coins into ᶜAsīr where there was an extreme need for silver currency due to the prohibition of its importation from British territory in 1919.[6]

The Italians then turned their attention to Yaman. At the end of 1921 the Zarānīq shaykh Aḥmad Fatīnī, who had cooperated with the Italians during their war with Turkey ten years earlier, was in receipt of letters addressed to Imām Yaḥyā from the Italian authorities in Eritrea through Linchoni, a doctor formerly in charge of Turkish quarantine at al-Ḥudaydah.[7]

Shortly afterwards, came confirmation that Italy was "actively engaged" in speading anti-British propaganda in Yaman when letters were intercepted, addressed to the Governor of Assab from Maḥmūd Nadīm,[8] the former Turkish Governor-General of Yaman who had remained in the country after the armistice as adviser to Imām Yaḥyā.

[4] IO Nemo, British interests in Arabia, 20. 1. 1917 in L/P&S/18/B247.

[5] See Baldry, J.: *The British Military Administration of al-Ḥudaydah* (to be published in Arabian Studies, *VI*).

[6] Diary of Cpt. M. Fazl ul-Din (Liaison Medical Officer with the Idrīsī) for 28. 12. 1919—12. 1. 1920 in FO371/51444 f. 235.

[7] 1st Aden News Letter, 31. 2. 1921 in FO371/7199 f. 160.

[8] Aden News Letter, 31. 2. 1922 in FO371/7199 f. 172.

The next year — 1923 — the nature of the Italian-Yamani relationship became clearer with the conclusion of semi-official agreements by which an Italian was granted the Customs contract for al-Khūkhah and al-Mukhā'[9] and an Italian shipping line was permitted to make monthly sailings between Massawa and al-Mukhā',[10] al-Ḥudaydah still being under Idrīsī occupation. In 1924 an agreement was concluded with Imām Yaḥyā by which an Italian company would construct a telegraph line between al-Mukhā' and Ṣanᶜā.[11] *Imām* Yaḥyā became so gratified with Italian assistance that in February 1925 he dispatched an envoy to Massawa where an agreement for the purchase of arms was concluded.[12] The same year Italian doctors began to practise in the major towns of Yaman.[13]

When, in March 1925, Imām Yaḥyā seized al-Ḥudaydah from the Idrīsī with the help of Italian arms, he immediately attempted to revive the trade of the town. In this endeavour he was "eagerly seconded" by the Italian Government: Yamani coffee imported at Massawa from al-Ḥudaydah was treated as a product of Italian territory and a duty of only 1% was payable, whereas 8% was levied on Yamani coffee which reached Massawa via Aden.[14] So official had Italo-Yamani relations become by this time that Italian commercial vessels calling at al-Ḥudaydah began to arrive with naval escorts.[15]

Britain hoped that when Imām Yaḥyā occupied al-Ḥudaydah the obstacles to an Anglo-Yamani rapprochement would be removed: however, Britain remained in occupation of the Aden Protectorate, whereas the Italians had met almost all Imām Yaḥyā's requests for arms, telegraphic equipment, medical staff and supplies. The Imām had thus little incentive to reach any accommodation with Britain and instead of normalizing his relations with Britain he concluded an agreement with Mussolini in 1926.[16] A large increase in the flow to Yaman of all kinds of Italian supplies and assistance, including small arms, planes and field guns now followed.[17] These were soon to be used against the tribes of the Protectorate in support of the Imām's claim to those territories: indeed, it has been suggested, undoubtedly correctly, that Mussolini's activities in Yaman at this time were "most certainly undertaken with the

[9] Aden News Letter, 7. 3. 1923 in FO371/8951 f. 204.

[10] L/P&S/611&10th Aden News Letter, 6. 11. 1923 in FO371/8951 f. 264.

[11] L/P&S/10/1109.

[12] L/P&S/10/792.

[13] L/P&S/10/1160.

[14] Res., Aden to CO, 11. 8. 1926 in FO371/10449, f. 37—43.

[15] L/P&S/10/1160.

[16] L/P&S/10/1175.

[17] Craufurd to CO, 11. 7. 1926 in FO371/11445, f. 128—132.

intention of decreasing or containing British influence in the area in the Red Sea where Italy itself had colonial ambitions".[18]

At the end of July 1926 the Imām's request for assistance in the construction of a road between al-Mukhā' and Mawīyah and landing grounds for planes at both places was met by the Italians.[19] Mawīyah was sufficiently close to the Protectorate frontier and also on the road to Laḥaj to cause doubts in British circles as to Imām Yaḥyā's intention towards the Protectorate.

These developments caused considerable concern in London, not only for the security of the Protectorate and the "Imperial route" through the Red Sea, but also for their effect on Anglo-Italian relations. The Cabinet therefore decided that Mussolini should be approached with a view to discussing the situation in South-West Arabia[20] for, as *The Christian Science Monitor* put it, "The situation in the Yemen is by no means a matter of indifference to Britain".[21]

The discussions opened in Rome in October 1926 amid general agreement that it was in both British and Italian interests that no power should establish itself on the eastern shore of the Red Sea and that protection afforded to nationals of the two countries in Yaman should not "assume a political character or complexion". Both parties agreed that they should keep "in close touch" to avoid misunderstandings between them and "misapprehensions" on the part of the Arab rulers as to British and Italian policies. The Italian Government recognized the importance to Britain of the Kamarān and Farasān islands for its communications with India. In return, Britain agreed to delay recognition of the Mecca Agreement between the Idrīsī and Ibn Saᶜūd which would have implied British support for Ibn Saᶜūd's territorial claim to ᶜAsīr against that of Imām Yaḥyā. Britain was made aware of Eritrea's need to trade with Yaman due to the poverty of the Italian colony.[22]

The Rome Understanding reached in 1927 was "somewhat loosely drafted... [and] implied that there was to be what the Italians have described as 'a close parallelism' of policy between Great Britain and Italy in Arabia, and — although this was not stated in the terms — suggested that the territorial *status quo* as it existed in 1927 was to be maintained not only on the Red Sea coast but also in the whole of 'Southern Arabia'".[23] The British Government was satisfied that Italy had recognized its special interest in the area.

However, shortly after the conclusion of the Anglo-Italian Discussions, a Yamani

---

[18] Wenner, H. W.: *Modern Yemen.* Baltimore 1976, 153.

[19] Political Intelligence Summary (PIS) 17, 31. 7. 1926 in FO371/11449 f. 214.

[20] CO to Res., Aden, 10. 12. 1926 in FO371/11445 f. 193.

[21] Christian Science Monitor, 28. 11. 1925, quot. in FO371/10818 f. 133.

[22] L/P&S/10/1175: L/P&S/10/1208: R20/A4C/M.91.

[23] Rendel, G. W.: Anglo-Italian Conversations regarding Arabia: General Summing up to April 9th, 1938 in FO371/21828 f. 173.

delegation headed by Foreign Minister Qāḍī Muḥammad Rāghib and the Imām's son Muḥammad paid an official visit to Mussolini when a supplementary agreement to the 1926 Treaty of Friendship was signed: Yaman was to receive economic and technical aid in addition to military equipment.[24]

It is strange that at this time Italy acknowledged British interests in Arabia, for simultaneously it became part of Fascist dogma that Italy was to embark on the road of conquest to render it "more grand: Fascism was before long said to be imperialist by definition" and Mussolini asserted that Italy was more suited than either Britain or France to be a major colonial power.[25]

Nonetheless, the Rome Discussions were followed by a period of closer cooperation between Britain and Italy in South-West Arabia, although differences arose when Ibn Saʿūd complained of Italian support for the Imām: this resulted in the break-down of the Italian-Saʿūdi negotiations.[26] These differences were not permitted to strain Anglo-Italian relations and, when in 1928, British aircraft bombed Yamani territory, the Italians acted as intermediaries between the British and Imām Yaḥyā[27] while the next year Italian agents in Yaman informed the Imām that he could not expect Italian support for anti-British policies he might pursue.[28]

Italian influence continued to grow in Yaman, especially after Dr. Ansaldi was sent to Ṣanʿā' to supervise the hospital. He had responsibility for "le cure da prestare ai notabili ed alla populazione di Sanaa, e specialmente quelle alla persona stessa dell'Imam ed ai numerosi Principi Reali ed alle rispettive famiglie".[29] Other Italian doctors practised in Taʿiz and al-Ḥudaydah.[30]

These activities, although a blow to British hopes of improving Anglo-Yamani relations, did not affect Britain's relationship with Mussolini, for as I have pointed out elsewhere[31] Mussolini realized that stability in the Red Sea area was essential for the reinforcement of the Italian position in the region, and a period of close cooperation was inaugurated from 1930 until the second half of 1933. Nonetheless, during these three years Italian influence grew in Arabia.

In Ḥijāz, Mussolini's agents were also active. Van der Meulen has described "the few simple" Italians trading in Jiddah who "were only too willing to believe in a faultless leader [Mussolini] who would create a new Roman Empire with the Red

[24] Wenner, H. W.: op. cit., 158: Naval Intelligence, Western Arabia and the Red Sea.

[25] Mack Smith, D.: *Mussolini's Roman Empire*. London 1976, 32, quot. Augustea, 24. 5. 1927, 344—346.

[26] L/P&S/10/1175.

[27] L/P&S/10/1208.

[28] Ibid.

[29] Ansaldi, C.: *Il Yemen nella storia e nella leggenda*. Rome 1933, 5.

[30] Nav. Int., op. cit., 308.

[31] See my *Anglo-Italian Rivalry*, op. cit.

Sea coasts forming a front line of this new imperialism. Proudly they displayed their black shirts in public".[32] Dr. Pisani, one of the Duce's representatives, "through his medical work to all circles of Jedda's society" was able to make an "invaluable" contribution to the extension of Italian influence in Jiddah,[33] but regard for Mussolini was to be short-lived for Ibn Saʿūd fully appreciated that in the event of any dispute between himself and Imām Yaḥyā, Mussolini would give the Imām his fullest support to the detriment of Saʿūdi interests.

The failure of Mussolini's forward policy in Yaman, 1933—1934

In 1933 Mussolini publicly announced his ambition for colonial expansion in Africa and Asia:[34] this coincided with the inauguration of an aggressive Italian policy in the Red Sea. From this time Britain and France acquiesced in Mussolini's gains on the western shore of the Red Sea, whereas in Yaman both powers regarded with apprehension all Italian moves and made concerted efforts to limit the spread of Italian influence.

In the second half of 1933 Mussolini pursued an increasingly more pro-Yamani policy, regardless of the invitable deterioration in relations it would entail with both Britain and Saʿūdi Arabia. Towards the end of the year, when conflict between Saʿūdi Arabia and Yaman appeared invitable over the sovereignty of ʿAsīr, Ibn Saʿūd appealed to the British to request the Italians to urge moderation on Imām Yaḥyā who was being armed from Massawa.[35] Accordingly, representations were made at Rome, but the Italians responded by accusing Ibn Saʿūd of pursuing an aggressive policy against Yaman. In November 1933 abortive Anglo-Italian talks were held in Rome in a bid to avert Yamani-Saʿūdi hostilities: the Italians supported Yamani claims to ʿAsīr, while Britain regarded the disputed territory as part of Saʿūdi Arabia by virtue of the Mecca Agreement concluded between the Idrīsī and Ibn Saʿūd.[36]

Mussolini had succeeded in placing Britain in an invidious position: at the beginning of 1934 whilst Britain was negotiating the terms of a treaty with Imām Yaḥyā in Ṣanʿa', the Italians again pressed Britain to urge restraint on Ibn Saʿūd — yet to have done so at that time would make it appear that Britain "was trying to save the Imām from the attitude which Ibn Saʿūd considers aggressive".[37] In reply, at

---

[32] Meulen, D. van der: *Faces in Shem.* London 1961, 28—29.

[33] Ibid., 29.

[34] Mack Smith, D.: op. cit., 53.

[35] R/20/A4D/14.

[36] FO905/2.

[37] Brit. Min., Jiddah to FO, 21. 1. 1934 in FO905/1.

the beginning of February, Britain informed the Italians that the only means of preserving peace was for Imām Yaḥyā to "recognize unequivocally" Ibn Saʿūd's position in ʿAsīr.[38] When the Italians maintained their view that ʿAsīr should revert to Yamani control, Britain notified Rome that further discussions would serve no purpose due to the conflicting views held by Rome and London as to the sovereignty of ʿAsīr.[39]

It now becomes apparent that Mussolini had no intention of pursuing a policy of pacification in South-West Arabia — as both Britain and Italy had pledged during the Rome Discussions of 1926—27: war suited Italian designs better. Indeed, a peace initiative was already too late, for on 7 April Ibn Saʿūd declared war and his forces rapidly advanced towards al-Ḥudaydah.

The invasion provided Mussolini with just the situation he desired: he accused Britain of failing to abide by the terms of the Rome Understanding by not urging moderation on Ibn Saʿūd and thus felt justified in intervening on behalf of Imām Yaḥyā.[40] The Italian Government informed Britain that it could not "but regard with anxiety the creation of a fresh situation distinct from that which was the basis of the Italian-British agreements embodied in the protocol of the Rome Conversations of 1927".[41] In reply Britain stated that it was examining means of "furthering a peaceful settlement".[42]

Upon the evacuation of Yamani troops from al-Ḥudaydah in face of the advancing Saʿūdi force, a British detachment was landed to secure the safety of its nationals and their property in the town until the arrival of Amīr Fayṣal and the establishment of a Saʿūdi administration which could take adequate measures for the security of European life and property.

The landing of the British detachment afforded the Italians an excuse to take similar action, allegedly in defence of Italian citizens, but in reality, as the Italian Political Officer in al-Ḥudaydah later said, to be in a position to assist Imām Yaḥyā when he took counter-measures against the Saʿūdis. Undoubtedly Mussolini would seek some return in the form of even greater influence in Yaman. However, due to the presence of British and French vessels off al-Ḥudaydah after the embarkation of the British detachment following Amīr Fayṣal's assurances that he could protect foreign life and property, the Italians were unable to intervene on behalf of Imām Yaḥyā, although they too had landed detachments at al-Ḥudaydah.

With the conclusion of peace, the Saʿūdis withdrew from Yaman. The newly

---

[38] FO905/2.

[39] Ibid.

[40] Brit. Amb. Rome, to FO, 3. 5. 1934 in FO905/4.

[41] FO905/4.

[42] FO to Brit. Amb. Rome, 16. 5. 1934 in FO905/4.

installed Yamani administration at al-Ḥudaydah gave guarantees for the safety of foreign nationals and the British, French and Italian warships left Yamani waters.

Appeasement and Mussolini's forward policy elsewhere in the Red Sea, 1934—1938

Mussolini's attempt to gain a privileged position in Yaman had failed, but elsewhere in the Red Sea he made considerable gains as a result of French and British appeasement. In February 1934 the Italian vessel *Ostia* requested permission to land a force on High Peak near Jabal Zuqur Island in order to take "a round of angles of the Arabian Mainland".[43] A month later Italian posts were established on Zuqur and Great Ḥanash Islands to "protect" the transistory fishermen who occasionally spent the night there.[44]

By the Franco-Italian Agreement of the same year, Mussolini obtained possession of a small strip of French Somaliland and the Jazīrat Sawābih, a group of small islands off the French Somali coast and eleven miles from Perim.[45]

Mussolini was indeed keeping his promise made that year to the Quinquennial Fascist Assembly that "Italy's historical objectives have two names: Asia and Africa... collaboration [sic] between Italy and the peoples of Africa, between Italy and the nations of the Near and Middle East".[46]

By mid-1934 Mussolini had decided upon the occupation of Ethiopia and six months later "active preparations" were under way:[47] two attacks — one from Somalia and the other from Eritrea — were planned for the autumn of 1935.[48] It has been suggested that even at that time Mussolini was contemplating for a later date the seizure of the Sūdān, Egypt and "possibly Kenya".[49]

The "early stages of appeasement" were already apparent in Britain in 1935[50] and although Mussolini's aggressive intentions towards Ethiopia were no secret, the British and French delegates who met Mussolini in April that year merely "informally warned" him that his planned occupation of Ethiopia would "arouse strong opposition".[51] In June, Baldwin sent Anthony Eden to Rome "to buy off Mussoli-

[43] HMS Penzance to SNO, Red Sea, 19. 2. 1934 in L/P&S/12/2157.

[44] HMS Penzance to Admiralty, 31. 3. 1934 in L/P&S/12/2086.

[45] Nav. Int., op. cit., 308.

[46] Speech reported by Brit. Amb., Rome to Rendel, 16. 9. 1936 in L/P&S/12/2114.

[47] Mack Smith, D.: op. cit., 60.

[48] Ibid., 69.

[49] Ibid.

[50] Wilson, H.: A Prime Minister on Prime Ministers. London 1977, 167.

[51] Mack Smith, D.: op. cit., 66.

ni"[52] with a plan — unacceptable to Rome as it turned out — by which Ethiopia was to be persuaded to cede certain areas to Italy and receive compensation in British Somaliland.[53] This attempt to avert war failed and the invasion of Ethiopia began on 3 October 1935.

In London there were few audible voices raised against Mussolini's encroachments in the Red Sea. Neville Chamberlain, who succeeded Baldwin as Prime Minister in May 1937, was, in Eden's words, "a man with a Mission to come to terms with the dictators [Mussolini and Hitler]",[54] although Mack Smith has suggested that Chamberlain followed a course of appeasement to avert an Italian alliance with Hitler.[55]

In April 1938 Chamberlain, speaking at Birmingham, referred to the "good prospect of restoring those old friendly relations" with Italy. Indeed, later that month, in an agreement with Mussolini, Chamberlain ratified the conquest of Ethiopia and agreed to cease fortifying the Palestinian coast in return for a reduction of the Italian garrison in Libya. Shortly afterwards, he assured the House of Commons that "we may look forward to a friendship with the new Italy... firmly based, as that by which we were bound to the old".[56]

Appeasement only served to encourage Mussolini. Chamberlain was unaware of his conviction that because Britain had failed to prevent the seizure of Ethiopia Mussolini could, with similar absence of opposition, occupy Egypt.[57] Chamberlain did not "sufficiently appreciate that Mussolini, encouraged by appeasement", believed the West "was in a state of panic and could be pushed even further".[58] The British reaction — or rather its absence — to Italian aggression also led Mussolini to believe that Britain feared Italy more than any other power.[59]

There was some opposition to Chamberlain's policies: Eden was dismissed as Foreign Secretary for opposing his "pathetic approaches to Mussolini",[60] while after the Munich Agreement, Eden warned that "successive surrender brings only successive humiliation and then more humiliating demands".[61] On the other side of the House, Clement Attlee declared that Munich represented "a victory for brute

[52] Wilson, H.: op. cit., 184.

[53] Wilson, H.: op. cit., 184; Mack Smith, D.: op. cit., 67.

[54] A. Eden's Diary for 18. 1. 1938 quot. in Wilson, op. cit., 226.

[55] Mack Smith, D.: op. cit., 127.

[56] Quoted by Wilson, H.: op. cit., 229.

[57] Mack Smith, D.: op. cit., 130, quot. Ciano, 1937—1938, 112.

[58] Mack Smith, D.: op. cit., 137.

[59] Mack Smith, D.: op. cit., quot. Ciano, 227, 230.

[60] Wilson, H.: op. cit., 302.

[61] Quoted by Wilson, H.: op. cit., 232.

force", [62] and warned that friendship with Mussolini's "bankrupt and tottering dictatorship... was no longer worth purchasing".[63] As another put it, "Chamberlain's assertion that a new era had come guaranteeing peace to 'our generation' is considered by all to be an illusion which contact with reality is causing swiftly to fade away".[64] Yet, still undeterred by criticism of his policies towards the Nazi-Fascist regimes, Chamberlain began making friendly overtures to Franco.

Events leading to Anglo-Italian Conversations regarding Arabia, 1938

Mussolini's interventions on the eastern side of the Red Sea and in Yaman in particular met with an entirely different response from Britain. This may perhaps be accounted for by the numerous reports regarding Italian activities submitted by the British Political Clerk in al-Ḥudaydah and by the anxiety expressed by the authorities in Aden, Egypt and India about the vulnerability of the 'Imperial route' to the East through the Red Sea if Mussolini was to obtain a footing on both shores. Certain members of the Committee of Imperial Defence (consisting of representatives of the Armed Forces and the Foreign, Colonial and India Offices) also shared Eden's apprehensions over Mussolini's Middle Eastern pretensions. The Admiralty especially was aware of the possibility of the Red Sea becoming an Italian lake.

For a time after Mussolini's failure in 1934 to secure a paramount position in Yaman, Italian activity again became less overtly aggressive. It was left to Italian medical staff and technicians to spread the "truth" of the great benefits to be derived from Fascism. At the same time the Italian Government expressed its concern, lest either France or Britain obtained a foothold on the Yamani coast, especially as a result of the long-standing French claim to Shaykh Saʿīd.

Imām Yaḥyā, no less than Eden, feared Mussolini's intentions: no sooner had the Ethiopian war begun than the Imām rejected an Italian request to permit casualties to convalesce at Shaykh Saʿīd.[65] The request was interpreted in Ṣanʿā, as part of Mussolini's plan to control Shaykh Saʿūd or even Yaman as a whole. The Imām responded by enquiring as to whether Britain could supply guns for the defence of Shaykh Saʿūd fortress which was then being rebuilt.[66]

---

[62] Quoted by Wilson, H.: op. cit., 231.

[63] Mack Smith, D.: op. cit., 128.

[64] Edward Raczyński (Polish Amb., London) to Min. For. Aff., Warsaw, 16. 12. 1938 in Ministry of Foreign Affairs of USSR, Documents and Materials Relating to the Eve of the Second World War from the Archives of the German Ministry of Foreign Affairs, Moscow, 1948, 302.

[65] Morning Post, 7. 10. 1935.

[66] PIS, 455, 9. 10. 1935 in L/P&S/12/2157.

It was not long before Italian agents in Yaman learnt of the Imām's overtures to Britain and two weeks later their Consul in Aden in an interview with the representative of the Officer Commanding Taʿiz inquired whether British forces were based at Shaykh Saʿūd; if the fortress there was being fortified as a result of British pressure and finally whether Britain had supplied munitions for its defence.[67]

This sudden interest in Shaykh Saʿūd caused concern in London: the India Office proposed that British guns should be supplied if Imām Yaḥyā so requested. If an appeal by the Imām for military assistance were rejected, the Imām would certainly turn to Mussolini: Italian guns at Shaykh Saʿūd, possibly manned by Italians, could pose a threat to Perim and British shipping passing through Bāb al-Mandab.[68] At a meeting of the Committee of Imperial Defence late in November 1935 to discuss the Shaykh Saʿūd situation, the Colonial Office representative stated that he saw no objection to the Imām fortifying Shaykh Saʿīd against a possible occupation by a foreign [i.e. Italian] power. The Foreign Office, more circumspect, was opposed to the presence of any foreign power at Shaykh Saʿīd, but doubted if Mussolini, as a signatory to the 1927 Understanding, would occupy it.[69]

The next month British policy towards an Italian presence on the Yamani littoral — whether "in agreement with the Imām, or by aggression" — was elaborated, although Italian aggression was deemed unlikely, since it would be contrary to the terms of the Rome Understanding. Nonetheless, it was a "vital Imperial interest" that no power should establish itself on the Yamani coast; but the Colonial Office believed that Italy, in view of its possessions on the opposite coast, likewise had no desire to see another European Power established in Yaman. Similarly, Britain would not occupy any part of Yaman outside the Protectorate, since this too would be a breach of the 1927 Understanding: moreover, the Treaty of Sanʿā', concluded between Britain and Yaman in 1934 had left unchanged the frontier established in 1914 between Turkish and British-occupied Yaman.[70]

The Governor of Aden, if questioned by the Imām as to Britain's attitude towards the increasing Italian interest in Yaman, was to inform him that the signatories of the 1927 Understanding had mutually undertaken not to establish themselves on the Arabian coast of the Red Sea. Opportunity was to be taken to advise the Imām that international law required that soldiers after convalescing in a neutral country could neither be returned to their home country, nor to the scene of the war. The Governor was not to offer Imām Yaḥyā arms for the defence of Shaykh Saʿīd, for their use against Italy would adversely affect Anglo-Italian relations. On the other hand, the

---

[67] Aden to CO, 23. 10. 1935 in L/P&S/12/2157.

[68] Minute by IO, 25. 11. 1935 in L/P&S/12/2157.

[69] Minute of Meeting of Standing Official Sub Cttee., Of Cttee. Of Imperial Defence, 26. 11. 1935 in L/P&S/12/2157.

[70] CO to Gov. Aden, Dec. 1935 in L/P&S/12/2157.

Governor was authorized to proffer advice on the best method of fortifying Shaykh Saᶜīd but to do nothing "to give the impression" that Britain accepted responsibility for the defence of Yaman.[71]

The ruthless conquest of Ethiopia had left Yamanis "aghast" and the commander of HMS *Penzance* reported that the Yamani Government had "determined to cultivate the good offices" of Britain as a safeguard against "similar Italian incursions into Yaman".[72] Yamani apprehensions of possible Italian action against Yaman was shared by the British Colonial Office where Ormsby-Gore, after noting "an increasing possibility" of Italian action against Yaman, requested a "rapid supply of information" concerning Italian activities in South-West Arabia.[73]

Britain's Ambassador in Rome also submitted reports which confirmed suspicions in London that Mussolini had hostile intentions against Yaman. In September 1936 he wrote that there could "be no real doubt" that Mussolini, having seized Ethiopia, desired to increase his influence in Yaman and "would be glad enough to establish a footing on the Arabian coast of the Red Sea if a favourable opportunity" occurred, but that in the immediate future he was "more likely to concentrate on preparing the ground".[74] The Ambassador's appreciation of the situation was correct, for in August 1936 the Italian-Yamani Treaty of Friendship of 1926 was extended for a further year.[75] On 4 November 1937 the 1926 Treaty was "brought up to date" by the inclusion of a clause by which Yaman recognized the Italian Empire,[76] that is to say, the seizure of Ethiopia. In commenting on the new treaty the Italian stressed that Italian policy was designed to strengthen the sovereignty and territorial integrity of the Arabian Peninsula.[77]

In the second half of 1936 numerous reports from al-Ḥudaydah concerning Italian activities began to reach London. Many prominent Yamanis, including Rāghib Bey and the governors of both Taᶜiz and al-Ḥudaydah, were said to be in Italian pay,[78] and Italian engineers and doctors spread anti-British propaganda.[79] Dr. Petrie, a Church of Scotland missionary stationed in Ṣanᶜā' from 1937, in describing the Italian medical team, reported that most were captains in the Army Medical Service

---

71 Ibid.

72 Penzance, 1. 7. 1936 in L/P&S/12/2086.

73 Ormsby-Gore to Acting Res., Aden, 2. 7. 1936 in L/P&S/12/2157.

74 Brit. Amb., Rome to Rendel, 16. 9. 1936 in L/P&S/12/2114.

75 Ingrams (Rome) to A. Eden, 29. 8. 1936 in L/P&S/12/2114.

76 Ingrams to Eden, 10. 9. 1937 in L/P&S/12/2114.

77 Ibid.

78 L/P&S/12/2157.

79 Ibid.

sent to Yaman for the dissemination of propaganda: Dr. Lecca in Taᶜiz was "even interested in medicine".[80]

By the end of 1936 London had adopted a very different attitude towards Mussolini's activities in Yaman in contrast with the appeasement the Italian dictator had encountered elsewhere in the Red Sea. On 7 December 1936 the Foreign Office tentatively proposed a revision of the 1927 Understanding so as to provide "a more definite guarantee" of non-intervention in Yaman.[81]

A week later the Committee of Imperial Defence requested the Chief of Staffs Committee to prepare a report on the importance of Yaman "from a strategical point of view": the Committee stressed that in no circumstances should Yaman fall under the control of any European power. Then the likelihood of the elderly Imām dying was discussed and the probability of a subsequent power struggle among his sons, some of whom were provincial governors. With this in view, British agents were "to reach understandings with the *de facto* governors" of al-Ḥudaydah and the provinces adjoining the Aden Protectorate and endeavour "to counter other foreign influence". The meeting ended by accepting a Foreign Office proposal that an initiative should be taken "to re-affirm or review" the Rome Understanding of 1927.[82]

Discussions as to how to counter Mussolini's growing influence in Yaman did not end there. G. W. Rendel suggested that the only way to curtail Italian penetration was to give Mussolini "a clear warning" that Britain would take "drastic measures or retaliatory action".[83] From Cairo, Sir Miles Lampson informed Eden of his conviction that Mussolini would annex Yaman as he had Ethiopia and suggested that two possibilities faced Britain: agreement with Mussolini or a trial of strength.[84]

When, on 19 February 1937, the Chief of Staffs Sub-Committee convened to report "from the strategic point of view on the importance of Yemen as an Imperial interest", it was argued that Yaman derived "its strategic importance from the possibility of its exploitation in relation to our sea and air communications through the Red Sea", and further that in the event of war with Italy, full use should be made of Kamarān island and the Yamani coast for the air defence of shipping. It was thus imperative that Mussolini should acquire no undue influence in Yaman, from whence Italy could launch operations against Aden. The meeting concluded by noting the "strategic interest that neither Yemen nor any part of it should be allowed to fall under the control of Italy".[85]

---

[80] Dr. Petrie, 17. 11. 1936 in L/P&S/12/2157.

[81] FO to CO, 1. 12. 1936 in L/P&S/12/2157.

[82] Meeting Cttee. Imp. Def., Minutes of 14. 12. 1936 in L/P&S/12/2157.

[83] Memo by Rendel, 31. 12. 1936 in L/P&S/12/2157.

[84] Sir M. W. Lampson to Eden, 18. 12. 1936 in L/P&S/12/2157.

[85] Cttee. Imp. Def. Chief of Staffs Sub Cttee., 19. 2. 1937 in L/P&S/12/2157.

The day before the Sub-Committee met, Sir Miles Lampson had suggested to Eden that there would probably be "a gradual penetration" of Yaman by Italian agents. In fact, as has been seen, this had already begun. Sir Miles continued, almost certainly incorrectly, that the Yamani Government was already "subservient to Italian dictates". He urged that a more conciliatory policy be pursued towards the Palestinians so as to remove grounds for Italian anti-British propaganda. Finally, he added his voice to those already pressing for "a [new] effective arrangement" with Mussolini "to protect our interests and avoid a trial of strength with the Italians in the Red Sea".[86]

The debate continued as to how to deal with the threat to British interests presented by Mussolini's growing influence in Yaman. As a first measure Aden and the Protectorate were placed under the direct authority of the Colonial Office in 1937 — an indication of the "awareness of the political situation" in the Red Sea and "a realization that if they were going to keep the area under their 'protection' and jurisdiction, the British would have to take some measures to create a peaceful internal situation".[87] Thus, later in the year Harold Ingrams began his campaign to bring peace to the warring tribes in Ḥaḍramawt. Once peace had been restored, new treaties were concluded between British and the tribal leaders but in Ṣanʿā, these measures were seen as a breach of the 1934 Anglo-Yamani Treaty, and Imām Yaḥyā sent forces to infiltrate those regions where the British had concluded new treaties with the local rulers.[88]

Yet, by mid-1937 there were still few voices raised in favour of a re-negotiation of the 1927 Understanding as is indicated by a memorandum of 2 June, circulated two days later at a meeting of the Committee of Imperial Defence. It was alleged that Rāghib was in Italian pay and that both Imām Yaḥyā and Crown Prince Aḥmad were unpopular, thus raising the likelihood of an uprising — "a fruitful situation for Italian intrigue". The memorandum referred to both the fear mixed with respect with which the Yamanis regarded the Italians after the conquest of Ethiopia; thus, "the danger of their successful penetration in the Yemen has thereby been much increased". But it was still believed that the self-denying ordinance of 1927 would check Italian aggression against Yaman — "the Italians will probably observe it in the hope that Great Britain will do so too". On the other hand, in the event of civil war in Yaman, it was feared that Mussolini might intervene as he had in Spain. The British Government could not therefore remain "indifferent" to the situation in Yaman.

The memorandum rejected the idea of concluding a new agreement with Mussolini, even though the wording of the 1927 Understanding was unsatisfactory and contained provisions "no longer applicable so that the Italians might conceivably

---

[86] Lampson to Eden, 18. 2. 1937 in L/P&S/12/2157.

[87] Wenner, H. W.: op. cit., 161.

[88] Ibid., 163.

invoke the lapse of some of its provisions or the obscurity of others as justifying them in adopting a more forward policy". In conclusion it was argued that it was "clearly impossible with Italy in her present frame of mind, to attach any value whatever to any Italian treaty undertaken as such". Moreover, if the negotiations for a new treaty were to break down, Mussolini might consider himself released from the old undertakings.[89]

At the same meeting Rendel argued that there was evidence to suggest that Italy still held to the 1927 Agreement. If he failed to observe its terms, Mussolini knew Britain would not hesitate to annex Kamarān and Farasān — two convenient landing grounds for the RAF. Rendel suggested that Mussolini was also aware that an Italian renunciation of the 1927 Agreement would provoke Britain into seeking a privileged position in Saʿūdi Arabia: it was therefore in Italy's interest to keep its side of the alliance in the hope of making Britain do likewise.[90]

Throughout June and July 1937 further reports reached London of increasing Italian activity in Yaman and these were eventually to lead the British Government to seek a new treaty with Mussolini over South-West Arabia.

In mid-June the Governor of Aden wrote: "There is no doubt that the Italians are endeavouring to forward their interests in Yemen by every means short of direct and open intervention." The employment of Yamanis in the army in Eritrea, Italian propaganda in the Tihāmah and reports of the presence of Italian warships in the vicinity of Perim were signs of Italian intent to obtain "control of both coasts of the southern Red Sea and to establish themselves in the Yemen".[91] In another communication a few days later the Governor reported that the Italians had turned their attention to the coast near Perim and had communicated with the shore. Elsewhere an Italian submarine had been sighted. Simultaneously Italians lectured Yamani audiences on the weakness of Britain and the strength of Italy.[92]

A barrage of such reports enabled Eden, despite Chamberlain, to inform the House of Commons in July that "It is and always has been a major British interest that no Great Power should establish itself on the eastern shore of the Red Sea. This applies to ourselves no less than to others".[93]

The pursuance of a forward policy by Britain in the Aden Protectorate caused concern in Italy and on 12 July 1937 the Italian Ambassador called on Rendel at the Foreign Office — although Anglo-Italian relations were usually conducted personally by Chamberlain. The Ambassador, while admitting that Italy attached "the greatest importance" to the 1927 Agreement, argued that since then many changes

---

[89] Memo, 2. 6. 1937 circulated to Cttee. Imp. Def., 4. 6. 1937 in L/P&S/12/2157.

[90] Minutes Cttee. Imp. Def,, 4. 6. 1937 in L/P&S/12/2157.

[91] Gov., Aden to C.-in-C., E. Indies, 19. 6. 1937 in L/P&S/12/2157.

[92] Gov., Aden to Ormsby-Gore, 30. 6. 1937 in L/P&S/12/2157.

[93] Quoted in L/P&S/12/2157.

had occurred in the Red Sea, especially the occupation of Ethiopia which had given Italy "a more important" position in the region. The Italian Government was therefore "disturbed by certain recent developments" in the Protectorate which suggested Britain was pursuing a forward policy to which Italy "could not remain unaffected or indifferent".

In reply the Ambassador was firmly told that it was "increasingly difficult [for Britain] to deal with constant unjustified suspicions on the part of the Italian Government in view of the background of hostility and suspicion which was being created by perpetual attacks launched against everything we did by the Italian press". Rendel confirmed Britain's continuing observance of the terms of the 1927 Agreement. However, doubts existed as to "the ultimate intentions of Italy in regard to the Yemen" and Britain desired to see "independent Arab states remain independent and strong. We had no desire to extend our influence beyond those limited spheres in Arabia in which we were legally entitled to extend it and any rumours to the contrary were merely malicious inventions".[94]

The activities of Mussolini's agents now began adversely to affect Anglo-Italian relations: the agents capitalized on British policy in Palestine, while Yamanis returning from Eritrea spread rumours of Italian power in East Africa and the decline of the British Empire. Greater sums of money were distributed to leading officials and "the propaganda falls on soil which the money fertilizes".[95]

Events in 1938 introduced a new dimension into Anglo-Italian relations: Bari Radio began broadcasting in Arabic with the avowed aim of strengthening "the bonds of friendship between Italy" and the Arab World[96] and no opportunity was lost to slander British policy in the Middle East. In an attempt to inflame Arab opinion against Britain, one broadcast spoke of the "great unrest" expected in Palestine as a result of serial bombings of Arab villages[97] — although no such air action had been made by the RAF. So great an effect did this have on Yamani opinion that one of the Imām's sons was quoted as being "particularly gratified by recent Italian statements on Palestine affairs".[98]

Italian public opinion learnt of the success of the Bari broadcasts: the *Corriere de Ticino* claimed that they confirmed Mussolini's "collaboration and intimate union with the Islamic world" and his "interest in the welfare of Islam". The paper added that the BBC's Arabic broadcasts represented "the voice of the Dominator", but

---

[94] Minute by Rendel on his interview with Ital. Amb., 12. 7. 1937 in L/P&S/12/2157.

[95] Report, 11. 4. 1938 by Cpt. B. W. Seager on the present political situation in the Yemen. The above excerpts refer to Aug. 1937: in FO371/21825 f. 211—235.

[96] Summary of Bari Arabic Broadcasts of 1. 1. 1938 in FO371/21834 f. 4.

[97] Bari Broadcast, 16. 2. 1938 in FO371/21834·f. 220.

[98] Bari Broadcast, 21. 3. 1938 in FO371/21834 f. 159.

concluded that "the radio war" was but an aspect "of Italo-British rivalry on the route to India".[99]

Other Italian newspapers manifested an equally overt hostility to Britain. *L'Unione* of 7 February reffered to "English terror in Palestine ... [and] mass arrests" and the confinement of Arab chiefs in "unhealthy territories", amid "cruelty and torture".[100] News sheets seen on board the *Ostia* portrayed John Bull squeezing an Arab by the throat with the caption *"British Courtesy"* below.[101]

Early in 1938 Amīr Ḥusayn, one of the Imām's sons, made an extensive foreign tour: in London before his reception at Buckingham Palace on 11 February, the King was briefed that the prince should return to Yaman with "a favourable impression" of his stay in Britain.[102]

In France similar attempts to impress the Amīr were made: the French Under-Secretary of State for Foreign Affairs invited the Amīr to lunch at the Elysée: he was also received by the French President.[103]

In Rome the Amīr was greeted by banners bearing Qurānic inscriptions. Italy's military strength was stressed when the Amīr visited military establishments where warships were "dressed in his honour".[104] The Amīr's visit to Tokyo appeared "to be a political occasion with a slight anti-British complexion",[105] while in Shanghai the Amīr met the large Italian colony.[106]

In Yaman itself, Italian technicians continued to influence prominent personalities amid ever increasing propaganda.[107] Greater numbers of Yamanis were recruited for service in the Italian army in Ethiopia.[108]

Two elderly inhabitants of al-Ḥudaydah have separately informed me that they recall seeing Italian maps which portrayed a pair of Italian legs astride the Red Sea, with one foot in Ethiopia and the other in Yaman, and it would seem likely that these date from around 1938 at the height of Italian efforts to penetrate Yaman. It would be reasonable to suppose that these maps were seen on Italian ships, as their display in Yaman would have caused grave alarm to the Yamani Government.

---

[99] Article reported by British Legation, Berne, 3. 2. 1938 in FO371/21834.

[100] Reported by W. Knight, British Consul, Tunis, to FO, 7. 2. 1938 in FO371/21834.

[101] Perth to Eden, 11. 2. 1938 in FO371/21834 f. 196.

[102] FO371/21826 f. 23—24.

[103] Sir E. Phipps (Paris) to Halifax, 3. 3. 1938 in FO371/21826 f. 35—36.

[104] FO371/21826 f. 33.

[105] Sir R. Craigie (Tokyo) to FO, 7. 5. 1938 in FO371/21826 f. 58.

[106] H. Phillips (Consul Gen., Shanghai) to FO, 24. 5. 1938 in FO371/21826.

[107] Consul Jakins (Djibouti) on his visit to Yaman in FO371/21839 f. 200.

[108] Jakins: Notes on a journey in the Yemen in February 1938. 18. 3. 1938 in FO371/21825 f. 184—191.

Anglo-Italian conversations regarding Arabia,
March—April 1938

By the beginning of 1938 it had become apparent to the British Government that it was essential to revise the Rome Understanding of 1927 in order to limit Italian influence in Yaman which was not only a threat to the "Imperial route" to India, but also to British interests in the southern Red Sea.

The 1927 Understanding had failed to safeguard Britain's position in Southern, South-Western and South-Eastern Arabia: although reference was twice made in it to "Southern Arabia" there was no mention of Aden or the Protectorate and it gave no indication "of the limits of the areas falling within the British zone. It even seems possible that the negotiators of the Agreement completely overlooked the existence of the Anglo-Turkish Convention of 1914, establishing the boundary between the Turkish and British spheres in Southern and South-Eastern [sic] Arabia".[109]

Partly as a result of "these uncertainties and partly of the extreme tension which developed between Great Britain and Italy during the Abyssinian War, the forward policy which His Majesty's Government were [sic] obliged to adopt in the Aden Protectorate as a result of recent developments in that area led to increasing friction with Italy".[110] "Practically every trouble in Ḥaḍramawt" had "some Fascist flavour about it",[111] but Britain could prepare no defence for fear of offending Imām Yaḥyā.[112] As Philby has pointed out, the Arabs of the Aden hinterland were more familiar with Italian than British rifles.[113]

Suspicion of Italian activities in Yaman "where the internal situation was precarious" and the possibility of Italian intervention and political penetration also made it desirous in the British Government's view for a new agreement to be concluded with Mussolini. It was hoped this would offer "a better guarantee" than that provided under the 1927 Agreement "that Italy would not establish herself in the Yemen, where her presence might have been a cause of serious embarrassment to His Majesty's Government, and at the same time providing that she should formally recognise the British position in the British zones of Southern and South-Eastern [sic] Arabia which she had hitherto refused to do".[114]

The Italians, when approached on the subject of holding new talks, expressed their desire to bring the Rome Understanding up to date: they "were no less nervous of British activities in the Aden Protectorate and of possible British political ambitions

[109] Rendel, G. W.: op. cit., f. 173—174.

[110] Ibid., f. 174.

[111] Stark, F.: *Dust in the Lion's Paw*. London 1961, 21.

[112] Ibid.

[113] Philby, H. St. J.: *Sheba's Daughters*. London, 234.

[114] Rendel, G. W.: op. cit., f. 174.

in Saudi Arabia than His Majesty's Government were of Italian activities and designs in the Yemen".[115] Moreover, the Italians claimed that by the pursuance of a forward policy in Ḥaḍramawt, Britain had extended the boundary of the Aden Protectorate which was contrary to the terms of the 1927 Agreement.[116]

At the talks, Britain's "main concern" was to preclude the possibility of any European power and "particularly Italy", from establishing itself on the Arabian shore of the Red Sea. It was hoped to secure a declaration from the Italians that neither party would do anything to alter the territorial *status quo* in Arabia, nor seek a "privileged position" on the eastern coast of the Red Sea. It was "necessary to avoid the possibility of disputes as to what the territorial *status quo* then was and further to avoid giving scope for Italian interference in the internal management of territories which we consider now to be under our control and protection".[117]

The talks opened in Rome on 15 March 1938 and until 19 March British attention was directed towards obtaining Italian recognition of "British exclusive rights" in territories to the south and east of the frontiers defined in the Anglo-Italian Convention of 1914.

The Italians argued that it was unrealistic that they should be expected "to recognise the exclusive claim of His Majesty's Government over this vast area — of the existence of which they had (so far as could be seen) been genuinely unaware at the time of the conclusion of the Rome Understanding of 1927 — without some kind of *quid pro quo*. In particular, they showed great nervousness at what they described as our apparent intention to convert what had been a loose collection of independent tribal states in purely negative treaty relations with His Majesty's Government — e.g., bound not to cede territory — into what would amount to a highly-organised Crown Colony, which might seriously alter the strategical position in the Middle East".[118]

After Italian objections had been examined in London between 21—26 March, a British Draft Agreement was drawn up which "seemed likely to meet the main Italian *desiderata*, while at the same time giving His Majesty's Government the security and recognition they [sic] required". However, when on 28 March the British Draft was presented to the Italians, they objected that it was terminable at any time at six months' notice, thereby providing no guarantee of stability. Moreover, the Italians did not accept the validity of the Anglo-Turkish Convention of 1914, especially as it had not been recognized by either Saʿūdi Arabia or Yaman.

---

[115] Ibid., f. 175.

[116] FO's First Draft for information of Southern Dept., concerning Arabian aspect of Anglo-Italian Conversations, FO371/21826 f. 113—115.

[117] Memo: Instructions to Brit. Amb. Rome, concerning proposed conversations, FO371/21826, f. 93—96.

[118] Rendel, G. W.: op. cit., f. 175.

The Italians also objected that the economic and commercial rights in the Aden Protectorate conceded to the Italians "were illusory, since they were dependent upon rights granted to other foreign countries while in fact no such rights had been granted at all".[119]

The Italians finally objected that "owing to the differentiation between the provisions of the Draft Agreement regarding the Red Sea coast and those regarding the hinterland, the ostensible object of the Agreement, which was — in the Italian view at any rate — to set up a kind of 'ring fence' round the territory at present occupied by Saudi Arabia and the Yemen, would be largely defeated, since there would be... a gap in that fence in the North and East, where His Majesty's Government were not prepared to give any sort of guarantee against States under their protection or in alliance with them eventually acquiring any part of Saudi territory".[120]

No compromise had been reached by 7 April when it appeared as if the talks would break down. However, the British delegates made a new draft of Article 3 which was approved by the British Government, and accepted by the Italians on 9 April, thereby enabling "complete agreement" to be reached that evening.[121]

The Anglo-Italian Agreement regarding certain areas
in the Middle East, 16 April 1938[122]

By the Agreement the signatories agreed not to undertake any action which would be prejudicial to the independence or integrity of Saʿūdi Arabia and Yaman, nor to seek "a privileged position of a political nature" in the two countries. It was "in their common interest" that no other Power should acquire any political privilege in Saʿūdi Arabia and Yaman.

It was also agreed that neither party would establish its sovereignty or erect fortifications on former Turkish islands in the Red Sea which were not part of Saʿūdi Arabia or Yaman. The Italians accepted the presence of British officials on Kamarān for the sanitary service of pilgrimage to Mecca, while Britain agreed to the stationing

---

[119] Ibid., f. 176.

[120] Ibid., f. 176—177.

[121] Ibid., f. 177.

[122] After the signing of the treaty two 'Confidential Notes' were exchanged between the two parties. The first recognized that the frontiers between Yaman and Saʿūdi Arabia were those established by the Anglo-Turkish Convention of 9 March 1914 and subsequently modified in the Anglo-Yamani Treaty of Friendship and Mutual Co-operation of 11 February 1934. In the second exchange of notes it was agreed that the British Government would use its good offices with the Dutch Government "to secure the acceptance by that Government" of the stationing of an Italian medical officer at Kamarān.

there of an Italian medical officer.[123] Britain also conceded the right of Italy to place Italian officials on Jabal Zuqur and the Ḥanash Islands for the protection of Eritrean fishermen.

The two parties agreed not to intervene in any conflict between Saᶜūdi Arabia and Yaman and that, similarly, no other power should intervene in such a war.

Britain undertook not to "prejudice" the independence of Saᶜūdi Arabia and Yaman, nor to erect fortifications in the Protectorate, except for purely defensive purposes, while Italy would not seek political influence in the Protectorate. Italian subjects were granted freedom to trade, travel, work and reside throughout the Protectorate.[124]

The warning that the signatories were opposed to other powers obtaining a privileged political position in Saᶜūdi Arabia and Yaman did not imply that either power had given any guarantee to protect Saᶜūdi Arabia or Yaman if any power threatened them. Nor were Saᶜūdi Arabia or Yaman advised that they should not grant any other Power such a position. Britain had no objection if the Italian Government was to decide that the activities of a government were such as to threaten the independence of Yaman and that if, in order to protect that independence, Italy took measures in Yaman which might otherwise have appeared to be incompatible with the Agreement.[125]

The Agreement, not unnaturally, met with the disapproval of Ibn Saᶜūd who argued that reference to the "independence and integrity" of Saᶜūdi Arabia and Yaman was "superfluous" as both were independent: it was therefore "derogatory to the dignity" of the two countries and could "only suggest an attitude of protection or a claim to place those countries within an Anglo-Italian sphere of influence". The Agreement constituted "a restriction on the full independence" of Saᶜūdi Arabia and Yaman: they were precluded from conducting their own affairs with other states, "except at the risk of finding themselves opposed" by British and Italian interests as the declaration stated that no power should acquire "a privileged position of a political nature" in the two Arab states.

The Saᶜūdis protested that both Saᶜūdi Arabia and Yaman were debarred from

---

[123] The presence of an Italian medical Officer on Kamarān was scarcely necessary as the number of Italian protected pilgrims passing through the island was only 673 in 1936—1937 and 614 in 1937—1938 (FO371/23186). The Dutch gave their consent to the modification of the Anglo-Dutch Agreement of 1926 concerning Kamarān on 15. 8. 1938 (A. M. Snouck-Hurggronje of Direction Consulaire et Commerciale at the Hague to Sir C. H. Montgomery, Brit. Amb. in FO371/21831 f. 140a). Shortly afterwards an agreement was concluded between Britain, Italy and Holland which accepted the presence of an Italian medical officer on Kamarān. Text in FO371/23186.

[124] Text in FO371/21828 f. 197—203.

[125] FO371/21829.

73

seeking allies in the event of war between them since Article 5 of the Agreement stated that intervention by a third power was contrary to Anglo-Italian interests.[126]

In Britain, however, there was satisfaction that the Italians had recognized the Anglo-Dutch Agreement of 1926 in which the principal British official on Kamarān was described as "Civil Administrator" — a title to which the Italian Government had previously taken exception.[127]

The French Government expressed its wish to adhere to Articles 1—5 of the Agreement, but as Britain and Italy did not concur as to which articles France could accede to, it was impossible for France to sign the Agreement.[128]

Strangely, while a British delegation was negotiating in Rome to lessen Italian influence in Yaman, the British Ambassador in Berlin was informing Hitler that Britain was "earnestly prepared not only to examine the colonial question, but also to make an advance towards its settlement... A solution which, in the opinion of the British Government, would have many advantages would be to work out a plan based on a new regime of colonial administration in some given part of Africa...". In reply, Hitler suggested the best solution to the colonial problem "would be to restore to Germany the property she had lawfully acquired by purchase and treaty".[129]

Italian activity in Yaman,
April 1938—July 1939

Even immediately prior to the opening of the Anglo-Italian talks, agents continued to spread anti-British propaganda[130] and a number of princes and high officials were said to hold pro-Italian sympathies.[131] After the Agreement had been concluded Bari Radio continued to vilify British policy in Palestine, where, it was alleged, British soldiers burnt Qurāns.[132] An anti-British booklet published in Italy in Arabic and widely circulated in Yaman referred to British "atrocities" in Palestine.[133] So effective was this propaganda that whilst visiting members of the

---

[126] FO371/23179 f. 155—161.

[127] FO371/21829.

[128] See particularly FO371/21829 and Baldry, J.: The French Claim to Shaykh Saᶜīd, op. cit.

[129] Minute of a conversation between the Führer and Reichskanzler and His Britannic Majesty's Ambassador in the presence of Reichsminister of Foreign Affairs von Ribbentrop, 3. 3. 1938, in Min. For. Aff. of USSR, op. cit., 50—67.

[130] Jakins: Report on Yemen. 18. 3. 1938 in FO371/21825 f. 200.

[131] Ibid.

[132] CO to FO, 2. 6. 1938 in FO371/21830 f. 189.

[133] Report by Cpt. Seager on his visit to Saif al-Islam Aḥmad in FO371/21830.

Yamani royal family, the Acting Political Secretary from Aden was told by Amīr ʿAlī "how dreadful" it was to learn that the British burnt Qurāns.[134]

In order to counter such propaganda the Colonial Office agreed that two radio transmitters should be purchased for the dissemination of "straight news" by Ṣalaḥ Jaʿfar, the British Political Officer in al-Ḥudaydah, and Dr. Petrie in Ṣanʿāʾ.[135]

The results of this measure were minimal and by the end of the year Italy was said to have more "sway" in Yaman than any other nation. Italian doctors practising in Yaman were, it was alleged, "doctors in name only, as they are quite prepared to admit" and acted as "propaganda agents and spread the fascist doctrine far and wide"[136] and hospitals became "the chief vehicles for Fascist propaganda".[137]

Italian predominance in Yaman was such that Imām Yaḥyā found it politic to purchase all his military requirements from Italy: during the last quarter of 1938 large consignments of cartridges, rifles, machine and anti-aircraft guns from Eritrea were landed in Yaman.[138]

These were not simply for the defence of Shaykh Saʿīd in the event of France implementing its long-standing claim to the Peninsula, but also in support of Imām Yaḥyā's claim to the Aden Protectorate. In October three Italians arrived to train Yamanis in the use of the guns and a fourth to operate the newly-arrived radio equipment.[139]

The arrival of Italian arms created a critical situation in Southern Arabia, endangering not only Anglo-Yamani relations but also those between Britain and Italy, although the *Giornale d'Italia* noted that the supply of Italian arms did not constitute a breach of the Anglo-Italian Agreement as Italy had not acquired "a privileged position" in Yaman.[140]

Yamani forces equipped with Italian arms occupied Shabwa and Ḥusn al-ʿAbr in the Protectorate. This presented Britain with a dilemma, for if the RAF was employed against the Yamani forces, the Italians were likely to protest that such action constituted a breach of Article 1 of the 1938 Agreement which stipulated that no action was to be taken "which might in any way impair the independence or

---

[134] Ibid.

[135] CO to FO, 2. 6. 1938 in FO371/21830 f. 189.

[136] Besse, A.: Impressions on his visit to Yemen. Aden 7. 11. 1938 in FO371/23186.

[137] Stark, F.: *East is West*. London 1945, 26.

[138] PIS 62 of 11. 10. 1938: 64 of 23. 10. 1938: 65 of 18. 11. 1938: all in R20/A4E/Hodeidah Political Records, vol. VII, July 1938—Jan. 1939.

[139] PIS 69 of 15. 12. 1938 in R20/A4E/Hod. Pol. Rec. VII.

[140] Quoted by Perth (Brit. Amb., Rome) to FO, 17. 2. 1939 in FO371/23187.

integrity" of Yaman. By taking up the Yamani cause, Italy would strengthen its position throughout the Arab World at British expense.[141]

However, the expected Italian reaction failed to materialize when the Yamanis were driven from Shabwa later in the month, following RAF bombardments.[142]

The Axis drive to gain support in the Middle East and Red Sea now increased. The Secretary of the Japanese Legation in Cairo spoke of his country's "special feeling towards the Arab Governments and the Moslims", adding that Japan would "act to strengthen the bonds of cooperation with them".[143]

At the same time it was feared that Italy would renounce its agreement of 7 January 1935 with France so as to gain possession of Domairah Island at the southern end of the Red Sea. The British Government accordingly requested France not to cede the island in any new treaty it might conclude with Mussolini.[144]

Early in 1939 Italy directed its attention to Kamarān where Dr. Moise took up his post as medical officer. He was a naval captain and accompanied by Italian naval ratings as servants.[145] He had no sooner taken up his appointment than two Italian destroyers, the RTC *Nullo* and the RTC *Battisti* called: their crews spread rumours that they would regularly visit the island. More threatening, from the British point of view, was the story put out that Britain had occupied the island for 25 years, which was its allotted span, and therefore Italy would take over the administration of Kamarān in 1940 with Moise replacing Captain Thompson as Civil Administrator.[146]

Soon after Moise's arrival on Kamarān, his activities caused anxiety to Thompson: Moise was "rather troublesome" and appeared to have political as well as medical functions. Moreover, he was to reside on Kamarān throughout the year for the treatment of the population, whereas his Dutch and British counterparts practised there for the $4\frac{1}{2}$ months of the pilgrimage season.[147]

Imām Yaḥyā's apprehension of Mussolini's intentions,
January—July 1939

The Italian occupation of Ethiopia in 1935 led Imām Yaḥyā to suspect that Mussolini harboured similar designs against Yaman and during the next four years his concern steadily grew. However, he feared to oppose Italian activities in Yaman lest he offend Mussolini and provoke him to take military action against Yaman. To

---

[141] Minute on Cttee. Imp. Def. Paper 14908, "Air Action against Yemen", 7. 12. 1938 in FO371/21838 f. 80—82.

[142] PIS 79 of 15. 2. 1938 in R20/A4E/Hod. Pol., Rec. VII.

[143] FO371/21838 f. 112.

[144] L/P&S/12/2157.

[145] FO371/23186.

[146] FO371/23189 f. 236.

[147] CO to FO, 31. 7. 1939 in FO371/23185 f. 301—302.

avert such an eventuality, Imām Yaḥyā accepted almost all Italian offers of economic, military and technical assistance.

The Imām's fears were somewhat allayed as Mussolini never failed to avail himself of every opportunity to represent Italy as the ally and friend of the Arab World, while Britain and France were condemned as potential threats to the independence of not only Yaman but the Arab World as a whole.

In the early months of 1939 Mussolini devoted considerable attention to the Middle East. The mass emigration of Italians into Libya was designed to break "Arab preponderance in the Mediterranean",[148] although this intention was strenuously denied. A few days later, on 8 January 1939, Mussolini, after discussions with his Foreign Minister, Ciano, decided that Italian policy should seek to acquire a joint administration of Djibouti with France and that there should be "a strong [Italian] participation in the administration of the Suez Canal".[149] A month later Mussolini informed the Grand Council that Italy "should prepare to march to the Ocean" and assert its authority at Gibraltar and Suez.[150] At the same time the Egyptian Ambassador to Berlin was to be informed of Italian approval for any weakening of "ties between Egypt and London".[151]

It was these declarations of intent and the annexation of Albania in March 1939 that made it increasingly apparent to Imām Yaḥyā that acceptance of every offer of Italian assistance and acquiescence to every Italian demand was no way to safeguard Yamani independence.

Thus, in May 1939 Imām Yaḥyā took his first cautious steps towards lessening his dependence on Italy and dispatched Qāḍī Ḥusayn Ḥilalī to Aden to open negotiations for the purchase of arms for the defence of Shaykh Saʿīd against possible attack by either France or Italy.[152]

The Qāḍī informed the British of Imām Yaḥyā's "alarm" at both recent reports that certain powers had designs on Shaykh Saʿīd and of the aggressive policy pursued by Mussolini, especially after the seizure of Albania. The envoy continued that the Imām was concerned at the possibility "of a general war in the event of which he was convinced that an attempt would be made by all belligerents to obtain possession of important strategic points of which Sheikh Said was an example". The Imām therefore wished to put Shaykh Saʿīd into a state of defence against air and sea attacks, and, for this purpose he required anti-aircraft guns and gas masks. He requested British help and advice in the matter as "the two Governments had

---

[148] Ciano's Diary (Ed. M. Muggeridge). London 1947, entry for 4. 1. 1939, p. 4—5.

[149] Ibid., entry for 8. 1. 1939, p. 8.

[150] Mack Smith, D.: op. cit., 139.

[151] Telegram Gov., Aden to Sec. State Cols., 12. 5. 1939 in FO371/23188 f. 25—27.

[152] Ibid.

a common interest" in the defence of Shaykh Saʿīd.[153] The Imām would accept advisers of any nationality recommended by the British Government.[154] The Governor of Aden, in communicating the nature of the discussions to London, added that it was "desirable on political grounds" to meet the wishes of the Imām.[155]

Within three days of the receipt in London of the Imām's request for British arms, the Committee of Imperial Defence met: the Colonial Office delegate argued that the guarantee of "active assistance" to Yaman would be "inconsistent" with the provisions of Article 5 of the Anglo-Italian Agreement and that reference to that agreement should allay the Imām's fears regarding Italian pretensions in Yaman. He continued that British assistance to Imām Yāḥyā should be limited to the supply of small guns and equipment.[156]

The Foreign Office concurred with this view, for there was the danger that if Shaykh Saʿīd was heavily fortified and subsequently fell to the Italians, Italy's position would be strengthened at the mouth of the Red Sea. Financial assistance to the Imām was undesirable as it would create resentment in Saʿūdi Arabia where ʿAbd al-ʿAzīz had unsuccessfully requested British financial help.[157]

The Foreign Office also felt that the provision of military equipment would be seen by the Italians as affording Britain a privileged position in Yaman, contrary to the terms of the 1938 Agreement. But the matter was complicated by doubt as to whether Mussolini intended "to respect the neutrality of the Yaman in the event of hostilities". The Italian attitude "would doubtless depend on the question" whether or not Mussolini believed he was "more likely to obtain substantial additional advantages" than he already derived from the occupation of Eritrea.[158]

In a communication to the Colonial Office, the Foreign Office observed that the Italians would continue to observe the Anglo-Italian Agreement "for so long as, but for no longer than, they think that to do so will serve their interests better than to face an open struggle for power in Arabia... It is also undoubtedly the case that the Italian Government continue to court the favour of Yemeni officials and to intrigue in the Yemen generally. But even so, there is no very obvious reason why Italy should wish to embark on an open struggle for power at this time, unless she is willing to extend the area of the contest to the Mediterranean and even to the whole world".[159]

---

[153] Ibid.

[154] Gov., Aden to CO, in FO371/23188 f. 30—32 (14. 6. 1939).

[155] Gov., Aden to CO, in FO371/23188.

[156] Cttee. Imp. Def.: Standing Official Sub Cttee., for Questions concerning the Middle East — the Yemen fortification of Sheikh Said, in CO Memo of 16. 5. 1939 in FO371/23188 f. 38—39.

[157] Memo by Baggallay, 17. 5. 1939 in FO371/23188 f. 30—32.

[158] Ibid.

[159] FO to CO, 7. 3. 1939 in FO371/23187 f. 176.

The wish to avoid embittering Anglo-Italian relations appears to have been the over-riding consideration that led Britain to decide against accepting "a formal commitment to secure the Yemen against aggression". Moreover, the fortification of the Yamani coast by Imām Yaḥyā would be a breach of the Anglo-Italian Agreement, since it would endanger Yamani neutrality. Assistance to Imām Yaḥyā by either of the signatories of the 1938 Agreement would cause the other party to regard such action as hostile to it and thence destroy any confidence in the Agreement and increase the possibility of conflict in the Red Sea and of drawing Yaman into the conflict. For these reasons the possibility of British assistance in fortifying Shaykh Saʿīd was rejected. The Imām was to be advised to defend his coast by machine guns and wire entanglements, thus avoiding the necessity for foreign assistance.[160]

In mid-June Qāḍī Ḥusayn Ḥilalī returned to Aden with a new request for arms, despite the notification the Imām had received of the British refusal to sell arms to Yaman. Nonetheless, the Imām was "still anxious" to obtain four or five anti-aircraft guns for the defence of Shaykh Saʿīd and 10,000 gas masks for the garrison. The Imām appreciated that the employment of British instructors in the use of such guns could arouse "international jealousy"; he was, therefore, willing to accept any advisers — such as Iraqis, Egyptians or Turks — recommended by the British Government.[161]

Several factors soon led the British Government to reconsider the question of arms supplies to Yaman. Firstly, they could be supplied through a third party. Secondly, German and Italian companies had been asked for quotations for anti-aircraft guns.[162] Thirdly, Italian influence in Yaman was increasing: the Ṣanʿā' paper al-Imān attacked the British presence in Shabwa and it was believed that the Italians were responsible for the article.[163] Fourthly, the head of the Italian medical mission had offered to supply anti-aircraft guns "of the best quality...at reduced prices" for the defence of Shaykh Saʿīd, Dhubāb and al-Mukhā' against possible French aggression and even a temporary Italian occupation of Shaykh Saʿīd "until the danger had passed" was proposed.[164] Finally, late in May considerable Italian military equipment, supplied the previous year, was moved to Shaykh Saʿīd.[165]

---

[160] CO to Gov., Aden, 31. 5. 1939 in FO371/23188 f. 57—59.

[161] Gov., Aden to CO, 14. 6. 1939 in FO371/23188 f. 84.

[162] Gov., Aden to FO, 15. 5. 1939 in FO371/23188 f. 42—44.

[163] Political Clerk, al-Ḥudaydah to Pol. Sec., Aden, 10. 2. 1939 in R20/A4E/Hodeidah: Copies of Letters from Political Clerk, Hodeidah to Political Secretary, Aden, 1939.

[164] Gov., Aden to CO, 23. 5. 1939: reported by CO to FO on 31. 5. 1939 in FO371/23188 f. 60. Also Intelligence Report 40 of 13. 6. 1939 in R20/A4E/Hod. Pol. Rec., op. cit.

[165] Int. Rep. of 23. 5. 1939 in R20/A4E/Hod. Pol. Rec., op. cit.

The Governor of Aden suggested that Britain could supply anti-aircraft guns of a kind for which no other power would be able to supply ammunition.[166]

In view of this new information the Committee of Imperial Defence concurred that "on political grounds" it was "desirable" as far as possible to meet the Imām's wishes to purchase anti-aircraft guns and respirators from Britain. However, as it was impossible to give early delivery due to the re-armament programme, the Colonial Office was requested to ascertain which countries could supply the respirators. In the meantime, the Imām was to be informed "that Turkey would probably provide the most efficient personnel".[167]

However, by the end of June the Imām had still not been informed of the British decision and the Crown Prince asked a British official then visiting al-Mukhā' for an early decision.[168]

Meanwhile, the Italians had convinced the Imām that France was intent on occupying Shaykh Saʿīd. Thus, in face of British procrastination in reaching a decision on the question of arms, Imām Yaḥyā requested Italy to take responsibility for the defence of Shaykh Saʿīd from possible French aggression.

The arrival of Italian armaments in Yaman,
August 1939

Whilst the Yamanis were awaiting the arrival of guns from Eritrea, two mountain guns reached al-Ḥudaydah from Ṣanʿā' on 14 August: the Governor of the former, Sayyid ʿAbdallāh al-Wazīr, was instructed to forward them to al-Mukhā'. Days earlier the garrisons at Shaykh Saʿīd, al-Mukhā' and Dhubāb were again strengthened.[169] However, on the 11th, four 8-ton Italian guns and a large quantity of shells were landed at al-Mukhā'. Four Italian officers also disembarked[170] and were to remain for six months to train the Yamanis in the use of the guns.[171] Shortly after their arrival the Italian military instructors surveyed al-Ḥudaydah pier and the harbour at Rā's al-Kathīb.[172]

When at this time a French Mission visited Yaman, the Yamani Foreign Minister

---

[166] Gov., Aden to FO, 15. 5. 1939 in FO371/23188 f. 42—43.

[167] Minutes, 68th Meeting Sub Cttee. Questions concerning Mid. East, 19. 6. 1939 in FO371/23188.

[168] Record of an interview between the Yemeni Crown Prince and Cpt. Seager at Mocha on Friday June 30th, 1939 in FO371/23186.

[169] R20/A4E/Hod. Pol. Rec., op. cit., 45, 4. 8. 1939.

[170] Ibid., 56, 16. 8. 1939. Also in FO371/23189 f. 145.

[171] Pol. Rec., op. cit., 42, 20. 8. 1939 & 51, 29. 8. 1939.

[172] Ibid., 67, 6. 9. 1939.

explained that his Government was convinced that if Mussolini joined Hitler, Yaman would be occupied by Italy and in an attempt to avert the possibility of an Italian occupation, Imām Yaḥyā refrained from giving offence to Mussolini.[173] The French Mission suggested that Britain should cede ᶜAbr and Shabwa to Yaman as a means to prevent the Imām from joining Italy.[174]

British measures to counter Italian propaganda in Yaman,
September 1939—March 1940

With the arrival of Italian military equipment for the defence of Shaykh Saᶜīd in August 1939 against a possible French attack, Italian influence predominated in Yaman: in London it was feared that if Mussolini joined Hitler, Yaman might be used as a spring-board for an invasion of Aden and British East Africa. Thus, in September 1939 the Chief of Air Staff proposed strengthening Aden by a squadron of aircraft,[175] but the Foreign Office requested "a final opportunity" of expressing its views and to have sufficient time to inform Mussolini before such action was taken.[176] In reply, the Chief of Air Staff stated that it was not his intention to maintain a squadron at Aden for "an idenfinite period before the possible entry of Italy into the war, as this might lead to a concentration of further Italian units in East Africa". But, "on the other hand, we ought to have the squadron there at the outbreak of war with Italy".[177]

In the meantime, Italian agents in Yaman became increasingly active: it was even reported that a secret agreement had been concluded by which Italy would come to the support of Crown Prince Aḥmad in the event of a power struggle for the succession if the elderly Imām were to die.[178] The Imām however, feared total reliance and dependence on Italy and in January 1940 once again approached Britain for arms for the defence of Shaykh Saᶜīd[179] from Italy. Aden recommended that his request be met as a means of inducing him to resume negotiations on the question of ᶜAbr and Shabwa,[180] but the arms situation was so critical in Britain that

---

173 Ibid., 51.

174 Ibid., 63, 20. 8. 1939.

175 Air Chief Marshal Sir Cyril Newall to Sir A. Cadogan, Sep. 1939 in FO371/23179 f. 257.

176 Cadogan to Newall, 11. 9. 1939 in FO371/23179 f. 258.

177 Newall to Cadogan, 16. 9. 1939 in FO371/23179 f. 271—272.

178 Sir R. Bullard to FO, 28. 10. 1939 in FO371/23186 f. 175.

179 Gov., Aden to CO, 15. 2. 1940 in FO371/24545 f. 321.

180 Gov., Aden to CO, 5. 1. 1940 in FO371/24544 f. 55—59.

81

none could be spared for the Imām:[181] this refusal by Britain caused the Imām considerable "hurt".[182]

More positive British measures to win Imām Yaḥyā's allegiance were taken at the beginning of 1940, although there remained numerous obstacles to the establishment of satisfactory Anglo-Yamani relations, especially British policy in Palestine and the forward policy in the Aden Protectorate which was seen in Ṣanᶜā' as a breach of the 1934 Agreement between the two countries.[183] The forward policy in the Protectorate was abandoned not only to placate the Imām, but also because "any untoward incident was considerably magnified by Italian broadcasts and rebounded to the discredit of Great Britain".[184]

In February 1940 Miss (now Dame) Freya Stark arrived in the Yamani capital — "a fascist reserve"[185] with the object of countering Italian influence and of convincing the Yamanis of an "eventual [Allied] victory".[186] To achieve this she took a projector and films which she projected in the chief houses of Ṣanᶜā'.[187] Her presence caused considerable concern to the Italians who unsuccessfully attempted to persuade two ministers to approach the Imām with a view to having her deported.[188]

The Imām's son Qāsim expressed his surprise when he learnt that Italy did not rule the Mediterranean,[189] while the Prime Minister, after seeing the films, said that they should be projected to the royal family.[190]

After the projections, Radio Berlin announced that all the British ships shown in the films had been sunk,[191] but Berlin broadcasts soon became "less credited".[192] Moreover, such was the effect of the films depicting British victories by land, air and sea that the Imām ordered the closure of a shop which sold Fascist literature and distributed Italian flags.[193]

---

[181] Lake, Note on an audience with H. M. the Imam of Yemen, 31. 1. 1940 in FO371/24544 f. 321.

[182] Gov., Aden to CO, 15. 2. 1940 in FO371/24545.

[183] Gov., Aden to CO, 15. 2. 1940 in FO371/24545 f. 321.

[184] Wenner, H. W.: op. cit., 164.

[185] Stark, F.: Dust, op. cit., Letter to Sir Kinahan Cornwallis, 9.

[186] Stark, F.: Dust, op. cit., 2.

[187] Stark, F.: East, op. cit., 32—33.

[188] Ibid., 30.

[189] Stark, F.: Letters iv: Bridge of the Levant, 1940—1943. Salisbury, 1977; letter to Stewart Perowne, 12. 2. 1940, p. 13.

[190] Ibid., letter to Perowne, 13. 2. 1940.

[191] Ibid., letter to Perowne, 21. 2. 1940, p. 22.

[192] Ibid.

[193] Ibid., letter to Lord Halifax, 29. 1. 1940. Stark, F.: Dust, op. cit., 31.

In her letters from Ṣanᶜā', Miss Stark described the Italian propagandists in Yaman as "riff-raff": there were three "innocent young men but the rest [were] just the worst, commonest and low products of the regime".[194] The Italians, although disliked, owed their success to "sheer bribery" and the "entrée they have got in the palaces" and their influence over the two princes ᶜAlī and Aḥmad, who by February 1940 had, however, turned against the Italians.

Miss Stark used three arguments to lessen Yamani allegiance to the Italians: without British friendship, she argued, Yaman "would long ago have [been] swallowed" by Mussolini; that neither of the two Axis dictators came from "good families" [sic] and finally that Italian behaviour towards Abyssinia and Albania before they had been occupied, was similar to that of the Italians towards Yaman.[195] Miss Stark found that the population of Ṣanᶜā' was predominantly pro-German: the present writer has likewise been informed that during the early months of the war German military might was greatly admired in al-Ḥudaydah.[196] There was only one German — and engineer — in Yaman at this time,[197] but it was through him that German pictures and literature were distributed.[198]

Miss Stark left Yaman after a few weeks when most of the population had been convinced that the Allies were winning the war, although "every notable" was still "in Italian pay".[199]

With Miss Stark's departure from Yaman there remained only the British Political Clerk in al-Ḥudaydah and Dr. Petrie in Ṣanᶜā' to counter Italian propaganda: their resources were minimal when compared with those at the disposal of the Italians. Moreover, Mussolini continued to supply the Imām with military equipment: on 5 March 1940 four Italian guns were landed at al-Mukhā'[200] although Crown Prince Aḥmad permitted only two Italian officers to disembark instead of the 15 officers and 50 men the Italians had proposed putting ashore.[201]

---

[194] Stark, F.: Letters, op. cit., to Perowne, 16. 2. 1940, p. 16.

[195] Ibid., letter to Perowne, 28. 2. 1940, p. 28—29.

[196] I have found a collection of correspondence dating from just before the beginning of the Second World War between Hitler and German officials and Imām Yaḥyā's envoy to Berlin which I hope to publish shortly.

[197] Stark, F.: Letters, op. cit., Letter to Col. Clayton, 28. 2. 1940 and also information gathered in al-Ḥudaydah by the present writer.

[198] Stark, F.: Letters, op. cit., Letter to Col. Clayton, op. cit.

[199] Ibid., Letter to Lord Llyod, 18. 5. 1940, p. 57—58.

[200] Stark, F.: *Dust*, op. cit., 36.

[201] Ibid.

Mussolini joins Hitler, 10 June 1940

By March 1940 Mussolini had become "more definitely pro-German" and openly spoke of entering the war on the side of Germany and planned an offensive from Ethiopia against Djibouti and Kenya.[202] Two months later, it was evident to the Allies that Mussolini had every intention of participating in the war: Miss Stark feared "a fifth column descent" on the Yamani Tihāmah,[203] while in London it was believed that "small scale" Italian landings on the Red Sea coast might occur. The Admiralty was accordingly instructed to be prepared "to intercept any kind of Italian landings" on the Red Sea coast.[204]

At the end of May when Ciano, the Italian Foreign Minister, met Poncet and proposed a deal with France over Tunisia or Algeria,[205] the nature of Italian pretensions in the Middle East became clearer and the Allies took further precautions against possible Italian hostilities in the Red Sea. In Saʿūdi Arabia, Ibn Saʿūd was informed that British dispositions had been made to forestall any attempt by the Italians to land a small mobile force and precautions taken to secure the command of the Red Sea.[206]

When on 10 June 1940 Mussolini declared war, the Italian position in the Red Sea and Indian Ocean appeared very strong. Allied shipping in the Red Sea could be attacked from Massawa and Assab: the Cape route was threatened from Mogadiscio, while from Italian East Africa strikes could be made against Uganda, Kenya, Khartūm, the Nile and Aden.[207] In Egypt, Italy "had bought up a large part of the press and used it unscrupulously to foster her plans".[208] The position of Sūdān was even more precarious, being bordered by the Italian possessions of Libya and Ethiopia.

For the Allies the defence of the Mediterranean and the Red Sea was of great importance and one of the prime tasks of the British Navy was to guard the Mediterranean, "a vital passage to and from the Suez Canal and the East",[209] and if the Navy had not controlled the eastern basin of that sea, Malta, Suez and

---

[202] Ciano's Diary, op. cit., 225, entry for 23. 3. 1940.

[203] Stark, F.: Letters, op. cit., Letter to Lord Lloyd, 18. 5. 1940, p. 57—58.

[204] Baggallay to Maj. Spraggett, May 1940 in FO371/24590 f. 163—164.

[205] Ciano's Diary, op. cit., 225, entry for 27. 5. 1940.

[206] FO to Stonehewer-Bird (Jiddah), June 1940 in FO371/24590 f. 162.

[207] Rowan-Robinson, H.: *Wavell in the Middle East*, n.d., 20—21.

[208] Ibid., 25.

[209] HMSO, *East of Malta. West of Suez.* London 1943, 7.

Alexandria might have fallen and the Axis would have reached the Indian Ocean from the West.[210] Similarly, it was the responsibility of the RAF to hold the line of communications between Gibraltar and the Indian Ocean.[211]

The failure of Mussolini's Yaman policy, 10 June 1940—26 February 1943

Mussolini's plans were soon thwarted: in Aden the British defence forces put up "such a good show" after the first air raids, that Italian planes "were content to drop their bombs in the sea".[212] Before the end of June an Italian submarine was captured beyond Aden harbour.[213] Indeed, such were the early successes of British sea and air forces against Italian naval and air force attacks in the Red Sea that by July the Italians had renounced all plans for an eastward invasion of Aden from Eritrea[214] and a convoy of British ships was able to sail unmolested from Aden to Egypt,[215] most Italian vessels in the eastern Mediterranean and Red Sea having been rounded up by patrol vessels.[216] Within a year of the Italian declaration of war, sixteen Italian submarines had been either captured or destroyed there.[217]

Aden and the Red Sea were thus relatively immune from the Italians, but initial Allied victories were offset by the establishment of a Vichy régime in Djibouti following the fall of France on 26 June 1940 and the loss of Somaliland two months later. These Axis successes gave an immeasurable boost to Italian propagandists in Yaman and Mussolini's morale was such that on 7 July 1940 he dispatched Ciano to Berlin to put forward Italy's claims for Nice, Crosica, Malta, Tunisia, Sūdān and Aden.[218] Mussolini's aspirations to dominate the Red Sea pre-supposed an Italian occupation of "Aden, Perim, and Socotra, as well as the nearby British and French colonies on the African coast... [and] some areas in the Sudan would have to be

[210] Ibid., 6.

[211] HMSO, *RAF Middle East: the official story of Air Operations in the Middle East from February 1942 to January 1943*. London, n.d., 11.

[212] Ingrams, H.: *Arabia and the Isles*. London 1952, 323.

[213] Stark, F.: *Dust*, op. cit., 48.

[214] Stark, F.: *East*, op. cit.

[215] Stark, F.: *Dust*, op. cit., 51.

[216] *East of Malta*, op. cit., 12.

[217] Ibid., 25.

[218] Mack Smith, D.: op. cit., 225, quoting Documents on German Foreign Policy 1918—1945, D/10/45, 245; Simoni, L.: *Berlino ambasciata d'Italia, 1939—1943*. Rome 1946, 141—142.

taken from Egypt in order to provide a link between Libya through Ethiopia to Somalia, thus opening a land route to the Indian Ocean".[219]

Although during the next few months the Allies suffered several setbacks, Imām Yaḥyā maintained a strict neutrality, but he must have welcomed the Axis victories and hoped for the elimination of Britain from South Yaman.

In September 1940 Marshal Graziani launched "a ponderous offensive" from Libya into Egypt[220] with the object of capturing the Suez Canal. Had the invasion succeeded, Britain would have lost control of the eastern Mediterranean and probably the whole of the Red Sea, thereby enabling German troops to be "freely transported" to Africa.[221] However, during December 1940 and January 1941, Italian forces in Egypt had taken several "knocks" at the hands of Wavell[222] and Mussolini was obliged to accept German assistance to extricate Italian troops from their difficulties: Rommel received the command of Axis forces in North Africa with orders to recapture Tubruk and then "investigate ways of invading" Egypt from the west. The Wehrmacht, after seizing the Caucasus, would then invade Egypt from the East.[223] It has been pointed out that with the German assumption of affairs in North Africa, Mussolini "ceased to be a war leader in any meaningful sense".[224]

In January 1941, Eritrea was selected by the Allies as the first target in East Africa and within three days of opening hostilities British forces had advanced 40 miles inside Eritrea. Allied advances were also made inside Somalia the same month and by mid-February Kismayu — "the best natural harbour" — fell and at the end of the month the whole of the Juba river in Somalia as well as Mogadiscio were in Allied hands. In Ethiopia, Asmara fell to the Allies on 1 April followed by Addis Ababa four days later and Massawa on the 7th.

The Allied victories in North and East Africa at the beginning of 1941 were welcomed in Yaman,[225] and given full press coverage in Ṣanᶜā':[226] the Italian doctor in Taᶜiz was so abashed that he remained in his house.[227] The capture of Mogadiscio

[219] Mack Smith, D.: op. cit., 226 quoting Quartara, 467—468: Politica Sociale, Sep. 1942, 218: Vademecum Africano, 1943, 2/75—76: Orientamenti, 37: Le Vie del Mondo (Ed. L. Arpenti& G. Saitta), Bologna, Oct. 1940: Senato commissioni, 30. 5. 1942, 1576 (Aloisi).

[220] Irving, D.: The Trail of the Fox: the Life of Field Marshal Erwin Rommel. London 1977, 58.

[221] Rowan-Robinson, H.: op. cit., 25.

[222] Irving, D.: op. cit., 58; Rowan-Robinson, H.: op. cit., 68—78. Wavell seized Sīdī Barrani on 12 Dec.: on the 16th Sullum fell and British forces entered Libya. In Jan. 1941 Wavell occupied Bardia, Tubruk and Darna and during the first week of February advanced as far as and occupied Benghazi.

[223] Irving, D.: op. cit., 102.

[224] Mack Smith, D.: op. cit., 234.

[225] R20/A4E/Hod. Pol. Rec. — vol. for 1. 1. 1941—28. 9. 1941; report for 25. 2. 1941.

[226] Al-Imān No. 174, Feb. 1941, quoted in R20/A4E/Hod. Pol. Rec., op. cit.

[227] Hod. Pol. Rec., op. cit., 25. 1. 1941.

by British forces received a warm welcome in al-Ḥudaydah.[228] Even greater was the reception given to British subjects in Yaman after Italy lost Asmara.[229] The Yamani Government shared the popular enthusiasm and confiscated Italian propaganda leaflets dropped over Zabīd and Ibn ʿAbbās.[230]

However, the arrival in North Africa of Rommel and his soon-to-be-famous Afrika Korps appears to have given new spirit to Italian propagandists in Yaman. In May 1941 rumours were widespread that Britain was planning to occupy Shaykh Saʿīd and the Tihāmah. These were taken so seriously that the population of al-Ḥudaydah evacuated the town for the interior.[231] Days later, Italian doctors spread rumours that British troops were deliberately destroying mosques in Palestine.[232]

When Harold Ingrams visited Ṣanʿā', the Italians publicly alleged that the object of his visit was to negotiate the lease of Shaykh Saʿīd and airfields elsewhere in Yaman:[233] they went on to declare that Germany would shortly be mistress of the Red Sea[234] — a public admission that Mussolini's role in the war in the Red Sea was minimal.

For the remainder of 1941 Italian propagandists in Yaman were chiefly engaged in convincing both Government and people that Britain was contemplating an occupation of Yaman. In this they were so effective that in July Government circles in Ṣanʿā' believed that British forces would land at Shaykh Saʿīd and Dhubāb under cover of darkness:[235] Imām Yaḥyā summoned all the shaykhs of the Tihāmah to Ṣanʿā' where they had to "declare their allegiance" and "to act as a united body" in the event of British aggression against the Yamani coast.[236] Amid growing rumours of British intentions to occupy Shaykh Saʿīd, Crown Prince Aḥmad went to the vicinity[237] to arrange for its defence. Reinforcements were dispatched and in February 1942 Aḥmad ordered the merchants of al-Mukhā' to open their businesses at Shaykh Saʿīd to serve the needs of the large garrison.[238]

---

[228] Ibid., 27. 1. 1941.

[229] Ibid., 2. 4. 1941.

[230] Ibid., 3. 3. 1941.

[231] Bayt al-Faqīh and al-Marāwaʿh: Hod. Pol. Rec., 2. 5. 1941.

[232] Hod. Pol. Rec., 7. 5. 1941.

[233] Ibid., 15. 5. 1941.

[234] Ibid., 22. 5. 1941.

[235] Ibid., 5. 7. 1941.

[236] Ibid., 25. 8. 1941.

[237] Ibid., 15. 9. 1941 & R20/A4E/Intelligence Summaries, Hodeidah, Oct. 1941—Dec. 1942, No. 1, 26. 10. 1941.

[238] R20/A4E/Int. Summ. Hod., op. cit., 15, 2. 2. 1942.

Japanese propaganda was also disseminated. As early as August 1941 Sayyid Ḥusayn al-Qibsī was actively spreading propaganda on behalf of Tokyo.[239] The Japanese proposal in April 1942 that the Axis should issue a tripartite declaration in favour of the independence of India and Arabia, although rejected by Hitler, met with Mussolini's approval[240] and following Japanese successes in Burma in May 1942, Italians in Yaman spread pro-Japanese propaganda.[241] However, the British occupation of Madagascar lessened the impact of the Axis propagandists.[242] Yet, propaganda booklets from Aden in Arabic distributed in Yaman and entitled "Adolf and his Ass Benito" were confiscated by the Yamani authorities in August.[243] This action coincided with Rommel's advance across the Libyan frontier to within 70 miles of Alexandria and it would seem that Imām Yaḥyā was then anticipating an Axis victory. However, with the defeat of Rommel in Libya in November 1942, American landings in Algeria and Morocco, and the presence of American tanks at the gates of Tunis, it became evident that the Axis powers were on the way to losing the war in the Middle East.[244] Now "ordinary Italians...displayed an instinctive revulsion against the gang of people who had landed the country in such a sorry plight",[245] and the Italians in Yaman refused to act as agents of Fascist propaganda: "Italy from every point of view — from the naval point of view, from the military point of view — was a defeated power."[246]

With Rommel's total defeat in North Africa in 1943 Imām Yaḥyā too realized that it was only a matter of time before the Allies were assured of complete victory and on 26 February 1943 ordered the arrest and imprisonment of all Italian and German citizens in Yaman. Diplomatic relations with both countries were severed, thus bringing an end to Mussolini's dream of establishing an Italian lake in the Red Sea. The Imām was correct: following the Allied invasion of Sicily in July 1943, the King prepared his coup d'état and exiled Mussolini after which "Fascism collapsed overnight; not a single Fascist attempted to defend the regime...it simply fell down like a house of cards, which was all it really was".[247]

---

[239] R20/A4E/Hod. Pol. Secret Reports, 21. 8. 1941.

[240] Ciano's Diary, op. cit., 457.

[241] R20/A4E/Int. Summ. Hod., 29, 10. 5. 1942.

[242] Ibid.

[243] Ibid., 42, 9. 8. 1942.

[244] On 21. 11. 1942 the Allies occupied Benghazi and on 23. 1. 1943 Tripoli fell.

[245] Mack Smith, D.: op. cit., 246.

[246] Taylor, A. J. P.: *The War Lords*. London 1977, 33.

[247] Ibid., 35.

Had Mussolini joined Hitler at the beginning of the Second World War, it is very probable, as the Yamani Foreign Minister himself believed, that Italy would have immediately attempted to occupy Yaman, the capital of which, as has been seen above, was as early as the beginning of 1940 "a fascist reserve". However, by the time Mussolini finally decided to join Hitler, the fascist threat to the independence of Yaman was easily thwarted due to the international alliance against Fascism and Nazism. The successes of Allied military operations were so adverse to Fascist Italy, not only in Europe but also in Africa and Asia, that the independence of Yaman was assured.

In the immediate vicinity of Yaman the possibility of an occupation was finally removed by the early successes of the RAF from its base in Aden and British army operations in East Africa. Thus, Yaman was saved from the fate which had befallen the Ethiopians and Albanians.

Perhaps the only partial successes of Mussolini's Yaman policy were in temporarily embittering relations between Imām Yaḥyā and the French by exaggerating the nature of French claims to Shaykh Saʿīd and secondly by supplying armament and military advisers to Yaman with which the Imām was able to embarrass the British by infiltrating the Aden Protectorate, thus dividing what should have been a united front opposed to fascism.

Yet, paradoxically, when Imām Yaḥyā broke with the Axis powers he had temporarily to lay in abeyance his campaign for the British evacuation of South Yaman and the subsequent unification of the two Yamans.

THE QUESTION OF JAPANESE REPARATIONS AFTER WORLD WAR II AND ITS DEVELOPMENT UP TO THE YEAR 1949

KAROL KUŤKA, Bratislava

The aim of the present study is to outline the overall course of development in solving the question of Japanese reparations during the period of occupation of Japan, pointing on the one hand, to the way this issue was treated within the competence of the Far Eastern Commission and to the agreements arrived at, and on the other, to the manner in which the United States of America misused the solving of this question for their own strategic goals in Asia.

The Question of War Reparations During World War II

The obligation to pay reparations as a way of compensation for material war losses caused by an aggressor derives from international law, the legal basis being given by international treaties on the right of military conflicts,[1] multilateral and bilateral agreements and peace treaties. Such a legal base was also set up by the United Nations' Declaration aimed against economic plundering, spoliation of occupied territories by the enemy in which the signatories warned that after the war they would assert their claims. The Declaration was signed by the governments of 17 countries on 5th January 1943, in Moscow, London and Washington.[2]

The failure of the reparation policy following World War I and its overall sequelae prompted the allies already during the hostilities of World War II seriously to ponder over problems relating to reparations and their form, quantity and guarantees. The first concrete plan concerning German post-war reparations was submitted by the Soviet Union at the *Crimean Conference* (4th—11th February 1945). In contrast to the mode of financial indemnification imposed on Germany after World War I — which was one of the causes of its fiasco — the Soviet Union proposed that reparations be made in the form of payments in kind and that they be simultaneously

---

[1] E.g. Article 3, of the *IVth The Hague Convention* signed 18th Dec. 1907, enjoining on the belligerent violating the principles of law and customs, the obligation of compensation. *Encyklopedia prawa międzynarodowego i stosunków międzynarodowych*. Warsaw 1976, p. 231.

[2] The Declaration was signed by the governments of Belgium, Czechoslovakia, China, France, Greece, The Netherlands, India, Luxemburg, Norway, New Zealand, Poland, Austria, South Africa, Great Britain, U.S.A., U.S.S.R., Yugoslavia.

accompanied by a demilitarization of the economy. The closing communiqué, Art. III *Reparations Imposed on Germany* speaks of its obligation to compensate the Allies for damages caused to their countries. The protocol signed on this occasion determined also the forms of payments:

(a) in the form of a single take-over of part of the national property located on the territory of Germany or outside it;

(b) in the form of annual supplies of goods from current production during a period the length of which would be stipulated;

(c) in the form of utilizing German manpower.[3]

The Allies simultaneously agreed that an *Allied Reparations Commission* would be established in Moscow whose task it would be to work out a detailed reparations plan.[4]

The essential principles of the reparations policy towards Germany were, in view of their universal character, also applied to Japan. The most important document dealing with the future of Japan was the *Potsdam Proclamation* drawn up by representatives of the United States, Great Britain and China on 26th July 1945, summoning Japan, still fighting, to surrender unconditionally.[5] The Potsdam Proclamation formulated conditions of capitulation and traced out the direction which Japan would have to follow in future. The political platform adopted in this Proclamation corresponded to that accepted towards Germany, this policy being the result of a strong anti-fascist front and primarily of the growing democratic forces in the world.

Article 11 of the Potsdam Proclamation says: "Japan will be permitted to maintain such industries as will sustain her economy and permit the exaction of just reparation in kind, but not those which would enable her to re-arm for war. To this end, access to, as distinguished from control of, raw materials shall be permitted..."[6]

Occupation of Japan and Participation of the Allies

Japan's militarist attempt in the first half of the 20th century to dominate Asia, become its leader politically and economically and thus to oust from this territory the old colonial powers ended in its defeat, its acceptance of the Potsdam Proclamation and its signing of unconditional surrender on 2nd September 1945.

---

[3] *Teheran — Yalta — Potsdam. Collection of Documents.* Bratislava 1972, p. 185.

[4] Kowalski, W. T.: *Wielka koalicja 1941—1945.* Vol. 3. Warsaw 1977, pp. 101—104.

[5] The Soviet Union signed the Potsdam Proclamation simultaneously with its entry into war against Japan.

[6] *Potsdam Proclamation Defining Terms for Japanese Surrender*, July 26, 1945.

After Japan's capitulation, government circles in the United States were faced with the problem of the Allies' participation in the ensuing occupation of Japan, as well as the question of a concrete formulation and implementation of their policy towards this country. The *State War-Navy Coordinating Committee* (SWNCC) prepared proposals, towards the end of April, for the President regarding this problem, in which it stood that:

(a) "In view of political and psychological aspects, Allies' participation in the occupation is desirable."

(b) "The United States must play a decisive role in formulating policy towards Japan."[7]

The proposals by SWNCC were based on the premise that Japan would not be divided into occupation zones and any eventual military units of other countries would be under the Commander of Allied Forces who would be an American. Allied participation in realizing occupational policy towards Japan was to have been ensured solely through the *Far Eastern Advisory Commission* (FEAC) with headquarters in Washington. The Allies determined the setting up of such a commission by constituting a controlling organ with headquarters in Japan. At the conference of foreign ministers of Great Britain, the United States and the Soviet Union in Moscow, 16th to 26th December 1945, an agreement was reached on the competence of two allied organs: 1. *Far Eastern Commission* (FEC) with headquarters in Washington,[8] 2. *Allied Council for Japan* (ACJ) with its seat in Tokyo.[9] In reality, however, the United States of America, pursuing their own designs, did not lose their dominant position in the occupation of Japan and in the formulation of post-war policy towards it. True, the FEC did acquire the right to formulate the political line and general principles deriving from the Capitulation Act, as well as the right to resolve issues submitted by individual members in relation to directives, or orders of the *Supreme Commander of Allied Powers (SCAP)*,[10] but its recommendations required unanimity of decision on the part of the Great Powers and could be

[7] Góralski, W.: *Stany Zjednoczone — Japonia, 1945—1972. (Sojusz-Współpraca-Sprzeczności).* Warsaw 1976, pp. 49—51.

[8] The FEC comprised 11 member States, viz. U.S.A., Australia, China, the Philippines, France, Holland, India, Canada, New Zealand, Great Britain, the U.S.S.R. The commission started work on 26th February 1946. In 1949 it was enlarged by cooption of Burma and Pakistan.

[9] The ACJ was made up of representatives of U.S.A., U.S.S.R., China, Great Britain. It started its activity on 4th April 1946.

[10] *Supreme Commander for the Allied Powers,* also *General Headquarters* (GHQ), the principal occupation organ in Japan. This was headed up to 11th April 1951 by General Douglas MacArthur, who exercised considerable influence on U.S. policy towards Japan. The abbreviation SCAP will be used in this study in both the above meanings — and even for General D. MacArthur personally, and in the sense of "occupation organ".

forwarded to SCAP uniquely through the intermediary of the United States government. In case no decision could be reached by FEC, the United States had the right to issue *interim directives*[11] to SCAP with the clause that such directives would not be related to reparations.[12]

Demilitarization of the Economy and Reparations

As in the case of Germany, the question of demilitarization of Japan's economy was closely connected with reparations. The guiding principles of the policy of demilitarization and of reparations of the United States towards Japan were embodied in a document entitled: *U.S. Initial Post-Surrender Policy for Japan,* which was approved by the President on 6th September 1945 and was forwarded as an order to "SCAP". The document carried on in the spirit of political decisions arrived at by the Allies at conferences in *Cairo* and *Yalta* and concretized the conditions embodied in the Potsdam Proclamation.

According to this document, the programme of demilitarization presumed the destruction of the existing economic base of Japan's military strength and prevention of its renewal in future; a ban on the production of all items destined for the equipment, maintenance or use of any military force or institution whatever; a ban on all special equipment for the production or repair of war material including naval craft and airplanes; dismantling of those industrial branches liable to create a capacity for renewed rearming. The decision how to dispose of the means of production that come under this list — either by way of exporting them abroad in the form of reparations, by demolition or utilization for other purposes — would be taken following the appropriate stock-taking.[13]

The document spoke of two forms of reparations:

(a) through the transfer — as may be determined by the appropriate Allied authorities — of Japanese property located outside of the territories to be retained by Japan,[14]

---

[11] *Politika SShA v stranakh Dalnego Vostoka* (U.S. Policy in Countries of the Far East). Moscow 1964, p. 23.

[12] *Department of State Bulletin* (DSB), *The Official Weekly Record of the United States Foreign Policy* (GPO), Washington, *XVI*, 1946, No. 406, p. 674.

[13] B r e n n, Bruce M.: *United States Reparations Policy Toward Japan, September 1945 to May 1949.* Studies in Japanese History and Politics. Edited by Richard K. Beardsley. The University of Michigan Press 1967, Center for Japanese Studies, Occasional Papers No. 10, p. 105.

[14] The problem of Japanese property abroad, as also questions concerning restitution and indemnification for private persons constitute a separate issue and are not included in this study.

(b) through the transfer of such goods or existing capital equipment and facilities as are not necessary for a peaceful Japanese economy or the supplying of the occupying forces.[15]

The fact that in the initial stage of the occupation of Japan the United States pursued a policy close to that agreed on by the Allied powers towards Germany was an outcome of four factors, viz. :

(a) the authority of the Great Coalition in which the Soviet Union played the leading role,

(b) a change in the international position of the Soviet Union due to its growing authority in international affairs,

(c) the wide anti-fascist resistance and the growth of democratic forces in the world,

(d) a reflection of the situation within the governing circles of the USA themselves.[16]

Questions of reparations were embodied in a far more precise and detailed manner in a document approved after lengthy discussions by FEC on 19th June 1947, under the heading: *The FEC Basic Post-Surrender Policy for Japan.* This document became the basic politico-legal guide for the Allies when dealing with reparations.

The document states: "For acts of aggression committed by Japan and for the purpose of equitable reparation of the damage caused by her to the Allied Powers and in the interests of destruction of the Japanese war potential in those industries which could lead to Japan's rearmament for waging war, reparations shall be exacted from Japan through the transfer of such existing Japanese capital equipment and facilities or such Japanese goods as exist or may in future be produced and which under policies set forth by the Far Eastern Commission or pursuant to the Terms of Reference of the Far Eastern Commission should be made available for this purpose. The reparations shall be in such a form as would not endanger the fulfillment of the programme of demilitarization of Japan and which would not prejudice the defraying of the cost of occupation and the maintenance of a minimum civilian standard of living. The shares of particular countries in the total sum of the

---

[15] *United States Initial Post-Surrender Policy for Japan;* Brenn, B. M., op. cit., pp. 106—107.

[16] There were two basic approaches in U.S. government circles to the solution of Asian policy, represented by the so-called *China Crowd* and *Japan Crowd.* Until the defeat of Japan, the decisive role in Asian policy was played by the pro-Japanese group, supported by monopolies which were closely connected with their Japanese counterparts. This "*Crowd*" defended the view of a moderate treatment to be meted out to Japan after the war (the so-called "*soft peace*") which meant preserving the State system, the monopolies "Zaibatsu" and the conservative forces. Towards the end of the war, the principal aim of U.S. policy in the Far East — defeat of Japan — becomes shifted to a solution of the situation in China in a manner that would be convenient to them. At this time, the pro-China Crowd standing for a tough attitude towards Japan (the so-called "*hard peace*") begins to gain the positions of the pro-Japanese Crowd in government circles and thus has a decisive word in forming U.S. Far Eastern policy.

reparations from Japan shall be determined on a broad political basis, taking into account the scope of material and human destruction and damage suffered by each claimant country as a result of the preparation and execution of Japanese aggression, and taking also into due account each country's contribution to the cause of the defeat of Japan, including the extent and duration of its resistance to Japanese aggression."[17]

As implied in these documents, Japanese reparations were intended to meet two principal aims:

(1) They were to serve as a means to achieve military and industrial demilitarization of Japan, so that it would represent no further menace to the Allies;

(2) To compensate the Allies, up to a certain degree, for the expenses and damage caused by Japanese aggression.

Pauley's Report on Japanese Reparations

The first concrete proposal concerning reparations was elaborated by Edwin W. Pauley — personal representative of the President of the United States in matters of reparations — who headed a group of American experts investigating the economic situation of Japan and the possibilities relating to the size and mode of payment of reparations. Pauley's survey resulted in two reports: 1. the so-called *Interim Report* submitted to the President on 18th December 1945, and 2. the final report of Pauley's Commission, completed in April of 1946 under the heading *Report on Japanese Reparations to the President of United States.*

Pauley in his reports took into account the preceding agreements and political documents and, as in the case of Germany, put the question of Japanese reparations in close relation with liquidation of its military potential and demilitarization of its economy. His supporting assumption here was that reparations ought to serve as a means of raising the standard of industrialization of the various Asian countries whose economy had suffered in that Japan took away raw materials and brought in ready-made goods and thus these countries could not develop their own economies. In Pauley's view, such a reparation policy would contribute not only to a stabilization of economy in underdeveloped Asian countries, but in its further impact also to political stability[18] in this region.[19]

---

[17] *The FEC Basic Post-Surrender Policy for Japan.* Text of Document. DSB, *XVII*, 1948, No. 422, pp. 221—222.

[18] A characteristic phenomenon in the Far East and countries of Southeast Asia following World War II was the powerful growth of a national liberation movement and revolutionary process which took up momentum during the Japanese occupation of this region. The principal aim of the colonial powers after the defeat of Japanese militarism was to liquidate this movement and this process in these countries and to reinstate their colonial rule.

[19] *Recommendations by Ambassador Pauley on Japanese Reparations.* DSB, *XV*, 1946, No. 386, pp. 957—959.

Pauley's report comprised a large number of concrete political economic and organizational measures which, after having been scrutinized at the SWNCC and amended, were approved of by the U.S. Government.

As regards reduction of military potential, Pauley proposed total disruption and transfer of the armament industry which ultimately meant restriction of production in the other industrial branches supporting war aims.[20] He considered as basic to Japan's war industry: machine-tools, army and naval arsenals, aircraft industry, ball bearings and antifriction ball bearings, ship-building yards, plants for processing steel, iron, magnesium, aluminium, thermal power stations, manufactories for producing sulphuric acid, calcinated soda, sodium hydroxide and chlorine. He recommended a transfer of the capacity, which was evidently excessive for the needs of peaceful economy, in the form of reparations. These industrial units producing *in excess* earmarked for transfer were designated by the term *interim removals* for they did not cover the final and total height of industrial reparations that should be exacted of Japan. Interim removal was to affect only capital investments, i.e. machine equipment and factories.[21] Pauley further suggested an increased production in the domain of light industry, consumption goods, building and construction, food industry, mining and other branches in order to fill in the gap left by the removal of the armament industry.[22]

In addition to a removal of all the armament capacities, Pauley also recommended the transfer

(a) in the field of iron and steel, removal of approximately 5,000,000 metric tons of blast furnace capacity,

(b) nearly 3,000,000 tons of electric furnace capacity,

(c) over 6,000,000 tons of open hearth capacity,

(d) 6,000,000 tons of rolling mill capacity,

(e) Japan's machine tool inventory was proposed to be reduced to 175,000 machine tools by the transfer of 600,000 in reparations. A maximum annual capacity of 10,000 new machine tools was to be permitted,

(f) three-fourths of the ship-building facilities. It was proposed that Japan's shipping be limited to an overall gross tonnage of 1,500,000 including wooden ships, with no vessel to exceed 5,000 gross tons, or 12 knots.[23]

The problems concerning classification of production units from the aspect of their share in arms production proved fairly complicated in the first months of occupation.

---

[20] DSB, *XV*, 1946, No. 386, p. 957.

[21] *The Far Eastern Commission. A Study in International Cooperation: 1945 to 1952.* Washington (GPO), 1953, pp. 124—125.

[22] DSB, *XV*, 1946, No. 386, p. 957.

[23] Cohen, Jerome B.: *Japan's Economy in War and Reconstruction.* Minneapolis, University of Minnesota 1949, p. 420.

After protracted considerations and partial decisions, the Far Eastern Commission approved the final document entitled *Reduction of Japanese War Potential,* dated 14th August 1947. This document defined in precise terms which industrial plants and equipment fell into the sphere of *Primary War Facilities*..., i.e. plants and establishments primarily engaged in the development, manufacture, assembly, testing, repair, maintenance, or storage of combat equipment and products and civil aircraft, and establishments building merchant vessel above a size to be determined by FEC,[24] and into the sphere of *Secondary War Facilities*..., i.e. plants and establishments primarily engaged in manufacturing, repairing, or maintaining major fabricated component parts, subassemblies, accessories or equipment especially designed for use in the products of primary war facilities.[25] In addition, the document also delimited for the future the capacity of Japanese *War Supporting Industry* and categorically forbade Japan to produce in the sphere of Primary War Facilities. The connection between reparations and destruction of military war potential was intimated in the introduction: "...industrial machinery and equipment in primary war industries and such other industrial facilities in secondary war industries and war-supporting industries as may be in excess of the peaceful needs of the Japanese economy, should be made available for claim as reparations."[26]

According to Pauley's proposal, subsequent reparation policy towards Japan, as in the case of Germany, ought to have been directed by an *Inter-Allied Reparations Commission,* made up of representatives of member States of the Far Eastern Commission, which would work according to directives of this commission (FEC). To implement FEC's decisions, he suggested setting up in Japan an executive organ that would work as a separate section of SCAP.[27] The United States of America, on the other hand, repeatedly suggested during 1946 the setting up of a semi-autonomous organ, independent of FEC's political decisions, a stratagem that would give the United States an opportunity to deal with the issue of reparations according to their own designs. The Commission refused this project and thus remained an authoritative Allied organ in formulating the reparations policy.

Subsequent Reparations Policy of the United States
and the Far Eastern Commission

Pauley's report was submitted to SWNCC which, after careful reflection, set down an *Interim Reparations Removals Program* favouring Japan in some points against

---

[24] *Reduction of Japanese Industrial War Potential.* DSB, *XVII,* 1947, No. 428, p. 513.

[25] Ibid., p. 514.

[26] Ibid., p. 513.

[27] Brenn, B. M.: op. cit., p. 78.

Pauley's original suggestions. The SWNCC programme was further forwarded to FEC which, after lengthy deliberations between 13th May to 6th December 1946, approved a total of 8 directives of the Interim Reparations Removals.[28] This programme set down the following points for SCAP, in the spirit of the subsequently approved final document called *Reduction of Japanese War Potential:*

(a) which industrial branches are to be earmarked for reparations,

(b) the size of production to be left in place.

In accordance with this programme Japan was left, among other things, the right annually to produce:

(1) 3,000,000 tons of steel,

(2) 2,000,000 tons of pig-iron,

(3) 3,500,000 tons of sulphuric acid,

(4) 25,000 pieces of machine tools.[29]

At the same time, FEC made the recommendation to SCAP when selecting establishments for dismantling, to take into consideration primarily factories belonging to the industrial concern Zaibatsu.

In addition to documents already referred to, FEC passed numerous weighty directives, including the decision guaranteeing Japan maintenance of a certain productive capacity within the framework of its peaceful needs. On 23rd January 1947, on the basis of Pauley's report, the Commission drew up the document *Determination of Peaceful Needs of Japan* which states that: "... the peaceful needs of the Japanese people should be defined as being substantially the standard of living prevailing in Japan during the period of 1930—1934. Data about the standard of living 1930—1934 should for the present purposes be used to make an estimate of Japan's peaceful needs in 1950..."[30]

All the Commission's directives and documents dealing with the reparations policy (FEC unanimously voted for 14) were of a partial and an interim nature and during its entire period of activity the Commission never drew up a final document that would have unambiguously and definitely resolved the question of reparations. The FEC could not agree on the solution of two basic problem circuits, viz:

(a) determination of the total height of industrial reparations for transfer,

(b) assignment of the percentage share to individual countries claiming reparations.[31]

From the beginning of 1946, SCAP taking support in Pauley's report recommending immediate payments of reparations, began taking an inventory of plants of

---

[28] *The Far Eastern Commission* ..., p. 125.

[29] Góralski, W.: *Stany* ..., p. 90.

[30] DSB, *XVI*, 1947, No. 409, p. 806.

[31] *The Far Eastern Commission* ..., p. 129.

a military character that were intended for reparations. By October, the list contained some 1,100 plants that did not conform with a peaceful development of Japanese economy.[32] Yet, this stocktaking failed to bring the liquidation of Japan's war potential to a definite end. American military circles were not interested in dismantling but rather in exploiting Japanese war factories on the spot. SCAP often revised the lists of plants destined for reparations, curtailed them, arguing that those struck off the list did not meet the reparations requirements, or that they had been damaged during the war, or that the original data on them had not been exact. Thus, from a total of 164 plants excluded from the lists, 153 belonged to the group of aircraft industries which, according to the document *Reduction of Japanese Industrial War Potential,* belonged to the sphere of Primary War Industry.[33] Such an attitude on the part of the occupation forces is clear evidence of an effort at limiting demilitarization of Japan, at preserving its military industrial potential as their reserve.[34]

As FEC failed to agree on the percentage division of the requisitioned assets, its decisions proved *a priori* a dead letter. The total value of the inventoried property proved far too low to satisfy the claims put in by individual countries that had fought against Japan and had suffered considerable damage. In this complex situation, when FEC had decided which industrial branches were destined for reparations and SCAP, in the spirit of these directives, had made an inventory of such plants, and as no agreement could be reached by FEC, the United States issued a unilateral directive to SCAP — in April of 1947 — under the title *Advance Transfers of Japanese Reparations.*[35] This was in effect an order to dismantle the establishments destined for reparations amounting to 30 per cent of the total — 15 per cent being allotted to China, and 5 per cent to each of the following: The Philippines, Holland (for the Netherland Indies) and Great Britain (for Burma, Malaya and its colonies in the Far East).[36] The remaining 70 per cent of plants destined for reparations were to have been divided among the various claimants after a final decision would have been reached by FEC.

As evident from Table 1, the claims of the various countries were practically double of the total value determined within the *Interim Reparations Removals* project. Their implementation of this as well as of other economic directives issued by FEC was slowed down, till these were finally revoked by SCAP

---

[32] Shinobu, Seizaburō: *Sengo Nihom Seijishi.* Vol. II, p. 510. Tokyo, Keisō Shobō, 1972.

[33] *Reduction of Japanese Industrial War Potential.* DSB, *XVII,* 1947, No. 428, pp. 513—516.

[34] For more details see: *Ocherki noveishei istorii Yaponii.* Moscow 1957, pp. 295—297.

[35] In February 1947, the U.S.A. submitted this directive for approval to FEC who rejected it and thus the U.S. procedure went counter to previous agreements of the Allies.

[36] *Transfer of Japanese Industrial Facilities to Devastated Countries.* Statement by Frank R. McCoy. DSB, *XVI,* 1947, No. 406, p. 674.

Table 1. The situation at FEC as regards the share in reparations[37]

Member Countries FEC	Claims to reparations in %	USA suggestions for reparations in %
China	40	29
U.S.A.	29	29
Australia	28	8
Great Britain	25	10
The Philippines	15	8
India	12.5	4
France	12	2
Holland	12	4
USSR	12	3
New Zealand	2	1.5
Canada	1.5	1.5
Total	189 %	100 %

in May of 1949 in view of the changing situation in Asia and a growing distaste on the part of a section of American economic circles towards the entire reparations programme and demilitarization of Japanese industry. During the whole period of two years (April 1947 to May 1949), the industrial facilities and equipment transferred from Japan[38] amounted to some 40,000,000 dollars, of which China received one half, the other half being divided among the Philippines (8,000,000 dollars), Great Britain (7,000,000 dollars) and Holland (5,000,000 dollars).[39]

The aim of American occupation policy in Japan was to eliminate Japan as a competitor of the U.S.A. in the Far East, to create for themselves a monopoly on economic, political and military control and thus to deprive Japan of national independence. Gradually, with the manifest failure of American policy in China, this strategy of American policy was supplemented with a further, not less important design — to make of Japan a point of support for U.S. policy in the Far East. American monopolies endeavoured to prevent the realization of any deeper reforms that might hinder the achievement of these aims.[40]

From the year 1947, American occupation organs openly pursued a policy of reconstruction and modernization of various types of military installations, such as

---

[37] *The Far Eastern Commission* ..., p. 144.

[38] On 13th February 1949, FEC passed a resolution on transfer of reparations goods to claimant countries, which stated that Japan would bear all expenses connected with dismantling, packing and transporting to a determined inland or sea port on Japanese territory (DSB, *XVI*, 1947, p. 433).

[39] *The Far Eastern Commission* ..., p. 141.

[40] *Mezhdunarodnye otnosheniya na Dalnem Vostoke 1940—1949*. Moscow 1956, p. 668.

harbours and airports. American government circles endeavoured to weaken their competitor — Japan — only to a measure just indispensable to keep it under American control, but they were not interested in bringing true democracy into the country.[41]

The fact that the United States were forced to carry out certain democratic reforms in Japan had some objective reasons. It was in the first place the unflinching fight of the Soviet Union in international organizations for a complete demilitarization and democratization of Japan. But the occupation policy of the United States also came in under strong pressure of the working class and democratic movement inside Japan, that had been suppressed during the military-fascist régime.[42] Still, American occupation authorities did all they could to confine the reforms to a necessary minimum and simultaneously impart to them a character that would be in harmony with the aims of American expansionism and would preserve in Japan the foundations of a reactionary socio-economic system.[43]

Change in United States' Attitude Towards the Economic Problems and Reparations of Japan

The evolution of the international situation in 1947—1948, the strained relations between the United States and the Soviet Union and the declaration of the *cold war* by Anglo-American imperialism against the Soviet Union and countries of the socialist commonwealth of nations exerted a decisive influence on U.S. policy towards Japan. This became manifest in a marked deviation from pursuing a political line based on the Potsdam Declaration and in the spirit of the so-called *hard peace*, as also in efforts to prevent expressions of the growing democratic forces in Japan.

Tendencies to weaken the democratic process appeared in SCAP's policy as far back as the year 1946 and in 1947 they already had a conspicuous character. This was evident, for instance, in their support of the first government headed by Yoshida, banning a general strike in February 1947. This process of a changing U.S. attitude was even more tangible in the economic sphere, particularly as regards liquidation of Zaibatsu and resolving the question of Japanese reparations.

Japanese economy was in a deep crisis with its concomitant symptoms of a rising inflation,[44] unemployment, lack of foodstuffs, booming black market, low standard

---

[41] Ibid.

[42] *Vneshnyaya politika Yaponii posle vtoroi mirovoi voiny.* Moscow 1965, pp. 30—31.

[43] Ibid., p. 42.

[44] At the time of Japan's capitulation, a total of 28.6 milliard yen was in circulation; in February 1946, it was 60 milliard and in January 1947, 100 milliard yen (*Rekishigaku Kenkyūkai Hen, Sengo Nihonshi,* Vol. I, pp. 146—147. Tokyo, Aoki Shoten 1974).

of production brought about, on the one hand, by a slow retooling of military plants for peaceful production, and on the other, by business undertakers' stalling tactics, waiting to see how the situation would develop. This applied especially to reparations in the form of removals of plants. Although the maximum limit of productive capacity in the various industrial branches (ten earmarked branches according to Pauley's report) were guaranteed, nothing definite had been decided as to which industrial facilities and equipment would be moved out and which were to remain in Japan; this uncertainly discouraged businessmen from starting production;[45] however, the principal reason for sabotaging the economy on the part of Japanese monopolies lay in their efforts to attain a lowering or even total cancelling of reparations.[46]

None of the Japanese post-war governments succeeded in efficiently coping with economic crises which brought about dissatisfaction among the population and activated the working-class movement. An interesting phenomenon in the Japanese working-class movement of this period was the frequent effort on the part of employees of various production units standing idle to take these over into their own hands and initiate operations which the owners delayed due to the uncertain situation in the reparations policy. By the end of May 1946, there were 108 such cases of take-overs[47] (*seisan kanri*) and in May 1946 alone, a total of 38,847 workers took part in 56 such cases.[48]

Such an intrapolitical development of the situation in Japan forced U.S. government circles, already in conditions of the "containment" policy, to deal with this economic phenomenon which might prove a danger for further political evolution in Japan.

A pretext for a shift from a policy of weakening Japan's economic power to one of renewal of its economy so that it would become self-sufficient, was an effort at easing the burden of American tax-payers for aid granted in the form of various credits and loans, principally through the "GARIOA" fund (*Government and Relief in Occupied Areas*). By the end of the year 1949, the sum of these credits and loans amounted to 2.5 milliard dollars, but it should be observed that Japanese expenses

---

[45] E.g. in the production sphere of steel ingots, plants and establishments capable of producing over 3,500,000 tons annually were made available for reparations; selected plants producing 2,000,000 tons might be retained; the future of plants producing 1,500,000 tons annually was uncertain. (*The Far Eastern Commission ...*, p. 127).

[46] For details see Pevzner, Ya. A.: *Monopolisticheskii kapital Yaponii (Dzaibatsu) v gody vtoroi mirovoi voiny i posle voiny.* Moscow 1950, p. 356. See also: *Ocherki noveishei istorii Yaponii*, p. 291.

[47] Shinobu, S.: op. cit., Vol. II, p. 348.

[48] Ibid., p. 350.

connected with the occupation for the same period amounted to 3.181 milliard dollars, hence, exceeded by some 700 milliard dollars the aid provided.[49]

The change of United States' attitude towards Japan became strikingly manifest also as regards destruction of its war industry, lowering its industrial potential and the closely related question of reparations. This entire process was of course affected by the changes on the international arena and particularly by the situation in China. Early in 1947, signs of a gradual dissatisfaction became apparent in United States' government circles, in particular in the War Department, with the conclusions and suggestions made by Pauley's Commission, as they did not fit in with their new plans intending to renew Japanese economy.

The representative of the United States at the FEC session, Major-General Frank R. McCoy in his statement of 21st January 1948 on U.S. policy towards Japan, justified his country's new political course towards Japan by declaring that the principal aims of occupation as they had been set up in the Potsdam Declaration had been fulfilled and that in the present situation the principal aim of occupation was the recovery of Japanese economy so that it would be self-sufficient.[50]

The Far Eastern Commission took up a negative stand towards this new attitude on the part of the United States. The Soviet representative in the Commission criticized McCoy's declaration on the grounds that the United States were setting up the new political line towards Japan independently and without consulting the FEC or obtaining its agreement, which runs counter to the Commission's authority. At the FEC session of 8th April 1948, the Soviet representative Panyushkin declared: "... the Far Eastern Commission which is called to formulate the policies, principles and standards in conformity with the fulfillment by Japan of its obligations under the Terms of Surrender may be accomplished, remains in ignorance on such an important political question as the planning of reconstruction of Japanese industry... in the American press there are again and again appearing articles which refer to the fact that the U.S. Government is working out its policy in regard to reconstruction of the Japanese industry and is planning the allotment of certain credits for this purpose in evasion of the Far Eastern Commission... the Soviet delegation considers it necessary to state, in order to make clear that without the policy decision of the Far Eastern Commission on the question of the reconstruction of Japanese industry no other unilateral decision and actions could be considered legal."[51]

The official declaration on the change in United States' policy towards Japan had been preceded by a detailed survey of the state of Japanese economy and her ability

---

[49] Pevzner, Ya. A.: op. cit., pp. 378—380.

[50] *Major General Frank R. McCoy's Statement of the United States Policy for Japan, at the Meeting of the FEC,* January 21, 1948 (Brenn, B. M., Appendix I, pp. 109—110).

[51] *The Far Eastern Commission ...,* p. 155.

to pay the reparations. In February 1947, U.S. War Department sent a commission to Japan, headed by Clifford S. Strike, to study Japan's possibilities of paying reparations. Strike in his concluding report proposed a reinvestigation of the whole problem and suggested that removals of industrial facilities and equipment destined for reparations should be limited only to the armament industry, i.e. the Primary War Facilities. These conclusions were approved by the War Department, but caused U.S. Government circles to split into *Pauley's* and *Strike's factions*: the former supported Pauley's conclusions and suggestions, with the use of more reliable statistical data. Strike's faction, also known as *War Department Faction*, backed Strike's report on the inevitability of revising the reparations policy.

Edwin W. Pauley in his report drew attention to the fact that the statistical data which he had used must be verified as, "... at the time the Commission was making its survey, the reliability of statistics relating to Japan was questionable. During the year 1946, SCAP unceasingly evaluated Japan's economic capacities."[52]

In April 1947, following protracted discussions within the U.S. Government between the various Departments (State, War, Navy) and representatives of Pauley's and Strike's factions, the parties agreed on United States' attitude towards the final and total reparations removals from Japan. The final proposals were approved in SWNCC document No. 236/43. This document, called *Reparations Removals of Industrial Facilities and Merchant Shipping from Japan*, was forwarded to the Far Eastern Commission.

Document No. 236/43 meant a further step in the United States' attitude as regards lowering the amount of reparations that were to have been exacted from Japan. Through their new policy, the United States repudiated the preceding standpoint which held that the final shares of reparations from Japan ought to be stricter than those embodied in *Interim Reparations Removals*.[53] In general, this document was based on Pauley's report and confirmed its conclusions, drawing support in the more reliable statistical data prepared by SCAP.

In June of that same year, the U.S. War Department again sent Clifford S. Strike at the head of a twelve-member delegation of experts from Overseas Consultants, Inc., to study in more detail the economic situation of Japan and to elaborate new proposals for implementing the reparations programme in the spirit of the altered U.S. attitude. After nearly six months of survey by the Overseas Consultants, Inc., Strike completed his report in March 1948 under the heading *Report of Industrial Reparations Survey of Japan to the United States of America*.[54]

---

[52] Brenn, B. M.: op. cit., p. 81.

[53] *The Far Eastern Commission* ..., pp. 153—154.

[54] Brenn, B. M.: op. cit., p. 84.

Strike's report comprised two sections:

Section A listed those facilities that should be removed in conformity with SWNCC document No. 235/43.

Section B gave the opinion of Overseas Consultants, Inc., as to productive facilities which should be retained in Japan to permit it to achieve a self-supporting economy, irrespective of previous decisions by the U.S. Government or the Far Eastern Commission. The report recommended that reparations from Japan should be limited to Primary War Facilities and a limited proportion of the productive capacity of the following industries: nitric acid, synthetic rubber, ship-building, aluminium and magnesium fabricating, and magnesium reduction.[55]

The pretext for carrying out a general survey of Japanese economy was a perspective selection of production units most suitable for removal within the industrial standards set down in SWNCC document No. 235/34. The latter estimated the total value of reparations in the form of industrial equipment removal at 990,033 thousand Yens (at the 1939 rate of exchange), and the value of primary war facilities amounted to 1,475,887 thousand yen.[56]

Strike in his report, whose principal motive was a renewal of Japanese economy, recommended that the dismantling and removal of equipment in war-supporting industry be reduced to the lowest limit, and as regards Primary War Facilities, to abide by SWNCC document No. 236/43. The reduction of the reparations sum proposed by Strike represented 800 million yen, equivalent to one-third of the original amount.[57] Strike's programme reckoned in this connection with the fact that of the 1,100 plants singled out on the basis of previous decisions during 1946 for reparations removal, as many as 845 would be left in Japan[58] and simultaneously he suggested an increase of industrial production so that by 1950/51 Japan would achieve the standard it had in 1935.[59]

Strike's report is an expression of the altered attitude of the United States and although it purports to take support in SWNCC document No. 236/43, it differs essentially from Pauley's report.

The conclusions from which Clifford S. Strike made his deductions in his report may be summarized into three points:

(a) Reconstruction of Japanese economy so that it might become a sufficiently strong partner and ally of United States' policy in Asia.

(b) Utilization of Japanese reparations as part of United States general policy

---

[55] *The Far Eastern Commission* ..., op. cit., p. 156.

[56] Cohen, Jerome B.: op. cit., pp. 423—425.

[57] For more details see Table 3, p. 111 of the present study.

[58] Pevzner, Ya. A.: op. cit., p. 399.

[59] Shinobu, S.: op. cit., Vol. III, pp. 772—773.

towards countries of Far Eastern and Southeast Asia.The Overseas Consultants, Inc. report states: "...We realize that other Far Eastern countries are in need of industrial equipment, and the ultimate decision with respect to reparations should be based upon a balancing of needs to obtain optimum benefits for the region as a whole... It is our opinion that this can be achieved most surely by leaving Japan free to reconstruct and use as quickly as possible the bulk of her industrial capacity...".[60]

(c) An industrially strong Japan "...would be less dangerous to the peace and prosperity of the Far East than a continuance of the present state of instability and economic maladjustment in this vast populous region..."[61]

These conclusions derived from the situation prevailing in the Far East. Originally, all the FEC countries held the view that should Japan rearm, it would become the greatest threat in the region of the Pacific and the Far East. On this premise was also based the reparations policy (removal of excess equipment). Later, in the spirit of the *cold war,* the United States became aware that their greatest danger in this region would not be Japan, but the national liberation movements and revolutionary processes that began to sweep through countries of the Far East and Southeast Asia. In view of this "danger" it was in the interests of the United States of America to aid Japan in the reconstruction and development of its industry and not to remove its installations.

Strike's report clearly documents the nature of the change in U.S. policy towards Japan in the domain of economy and reparations.

Within U.S. Government circles this change is an expression of an altered attitude on the part of the so-called pro-Chinese group holding the view of *hard peace* towards Japan, to a more benevolent procedure expressed by the term *soft peace.* This change was primarily determined by two factors:

(a) The general strategy of American imperialism which had its concrete form in Truman's and Keenan's doctrines. (Stability of Japanese economy, in the views of American imperialism, was inconceivable without a lowering of the number of facilities earmarked for reparations and was indispensable for creating suitable conditions for conservative forces in order that they might eliminate the rising progressive and leftist forces, and for resuming cooperation between Japanese and American monopolies, interrupted during the war.)

(c) The outcome of the changes that had taken place on the international arena. (The changing situation in China and the spread of the national liberation movement in South and Southeast Asia forced American imperialism to look for another potential ally in this region.) Such a suitable ally was Japan which the U.S.

---

[60] *Overseas Consultants, Inc., Report on Industrial Reparations Survey of Japan to the United States of America.* New York 1948 (Brenn, B. M.: op. cit., pp. 89—90).

[61] Ibid., p. 90.

Government circles decided to transform, in lieu of China, into a military-strategic base for aggression against the Soviet Union and the national liberation movement in the countries of Asia and the Pacific Ocean.[62]

The New Political Situation and Its Reflection on United States' Policy Towards Japan Within the Framework of Reconstruction of Japanese Economy and Reparations

The development in the international situation in 1948, the formation of a world socialist system, the growth of the national liberation movement and revolutionary process in Asia and in Japan itself, the disintegration of the Allied Coalition and "*the cold war*" of Anglo-American imperialism had a fundamental influence on United States' policy towards Japan; they took up an entirely contrary attitude in their occupation policy which became manifest in SCAP's deviation from previous Allied agreements, setting on an opposite course, the principal aims of which were:

(a) reconstruction of Japan's economic and war potential, remilitarization, rehabilitation, reinforcement of and support to monopolies and rightist-bourgeois forces;

(b) suppression of democratic rights and liberties, weakening and total elimination of all leftist movements.

In this novel situation, in the spring of 1948, the Department of the Army sent to Japan and Korea a commission made up of representatives of the highest government circles headed by the Under-Secretary of the Army William H. Draper,[63] and of representatives of the top monopolist circles headed by the chairman of the Chemical Bank and Trust Company, Percy Johnston.[64]

The task of this commission, whose official name was *United States Committee to Inquire into Economic Problems of Japan and Korea*, often referred to as Johnston's or Draper's Committee, was to carry out a depth analysis of the economic situation in these two countries and simultaneously to propose measures for overcoming economic difficulties as early as possible.

The Committee in its final *Report on the Economic Position and Prospects of*

---

[62] *Ocherki noveishei istorii Yaponii*, pp. 314—315.

[63] William H. Draper headed the economic division of American occupation organs in Germany in 1945—1947. His most significant decision in this function was to put an end to the policy of decartelization of German monopolies and thus open the way to their revival.

[64] Further representatives of American monopolies were: Paul G. Hoffman, President of the "Studebacker Corporation", Robert H. Streuer, representative of "Streuer and Co.", Robert F. Lorce, chairman of "National Foreign Council" (Shinobu, S.: op. cit., Vol. III, p. 774).

Japan and Korea and the Measures Required to Improve Them, published towards the end of April 1948, recommended a number of measures concerned with fundamental changes in United States policy towards Japan, primarily in the field of deconcentration of industry, foreign trade and reparations.

In the economic field, the Committee suggested:

(a) to limit to a minimum deconcentration of large monopolist concerns (this ensues from the fact that Draper — as in the case of Germany — combined reconstruction of Japanese economy with restitution of Japanese monopolist capital);[65]

(b) to increase foreign trade (to help Japan to accumulate adequate dollar exchange to be able to acquire means for purchasing enough raw materials whose lack causes low production and low export);

(c) to reconstruct Japanese merchant shipping.

In the question of reparations, the Committee expressed anxiety over removal of plant equipment which would paralyse for a long time Japan's economy; hence, it recommended the following measures:

(1) "Japan will hand over its assets to the countries that have legal jurisdiction over the territory where these assets were deposited at the end of the war."

(2) "Japan will release from its territory for reparations equipment from the Primary War Facilities except the following:

(a) those that SCAP considers necessary for occupation purposes, or for the smooth run of Japanese economy;

(b) those that the Far Eastern Commission set aside for interim removal. In addition, it recommended

(c) to release the stipulated number of definite plants and equipment

(d) to give priority to these proposals over preceding directives and to order member countries of the Far Eastern Commission to submit percentage shares from the total reparations sum that they claim, and to stipulate a date by which they must do this;

(e) to release for reparations only those industrial facilities and equipment specified in this report, and SCAP alone will have the right to alter them."[66]

According to Johnston's report, the primary aim of the occupation of Japan at that time was to create a self-supporting Japanese economy. In this connection he advised acceptance of the United States' government programme, approved also by the Department of State, according to which Japan and Korea were to receive during the course of twelve months the sum of 220 million dollars as aid in the reconstruction of their economies.

---

[65] Shinobu, S.: op. cit., Vol. III, p. 774.

[66] Overseas Consultants, Inc. (Brenn, M. B., op. cit., pp. 96—97).

In contrast to all the preceding reports, that by Johnston lowered reparation removals in all the industrial facilities excepting those producing aluminium and magnesium. However, he recommended the largest cut in reparations in the ship-building industry and the sphere of Primary War Facilities (by more than 60 % of the total value in each case).[67]

Percy Johnston's recommendations as regards reparations went along the line taken up by Strike but gave even greater support to monopolist capital and to efforts to make of Japan an economically strong ally of the U.S.A. in the Far East. His scheme revealed evident attempts on the part of the military-monopolist circles in the U.S.A. to combine reconstruction of Japanese economy with that of its military-industrial complex. A member of Johnston's Committee, Paul G. Hoffman (later an administrator of Marshall's plan) worked out a schedule according to which pig-iron smelting would attain, by 1955, a total of 6 million tons, steel manufacture 11 million tons and rolled iron 16 million tons.[68]

Table 2. Comparison of Hoffman's Plan with Real Pre- and Post-War Production of Metallurgic Items in mil. tons[69]

	1938	Hoffman's plan for 1955	1955	1956
Pig-iron	2,563	6,000	5,217	5,987
Steel	6,472	11,000	9,408	11,106
Rolled iron	5,128	16,000	7,351	17,220*

* Production from the year 1960

The overall evolution of change in U.S. policy in the domain of reparations from Pauley's report (SWNCC No. 236/43) up to the last one is clearly documented in Table 3.

Suspension of Reparations Removals

The Draper-Johnston Committee was the last mission to deal with the question of Japanese reparations. Subsequent commissions that visited Japan during the years 1948—1949 were openly concerned with a "stabilization of its economy" and deepening the cooperation between U.S. and Japanese monopolies. Japan was coming to be the principal ally and support of U.S. policy against the national liberation movement and the revolutionary process in Asia. Simultaneously with the

[67] The total lowering of reparations proposed by Johnston is shown in Table 3 on p. 111

[68] Pevzner, Ya. A.: op. cit., p. 400.

[69] *Aziya i Afrika 1950—1960 g. Statisticheskii sbornik*. Moscow, Izd. Nauka 1964, p. 402.

Table 3. Value of Japanese Reparations Proposed by Pauley, OCI and Johnston's Report*
Value of 1939 Yen

Industries	Pauley	OCI	Johnston
Machine tool manufacturing	145,695,000		
Precision bearing	24,537,000		
Electric power	7,851,000		
Iron and steel	390,314,000		
Soda ash	22,632,000		
Nitric acid	9,648,000	9,648,000	8,000,000
Sulphuric acid	25,201,000		
Synthetic rubber	10,236,000	10,236,000	10,000,000
Ship-building	163,121,000	118,138,000	50,000,000
Light metals	166,821,000	21,688,000**	21,688,000
		12,599,000***	12,599,000
Subtotal	966,156,000	172,269,000	102,247,000
Primary War Facilities	1,475,887,000	1,475,887,000	560,000,000
Total	2,442,043,000	1,648,156,000	662,247,000

* According to Brenn, B. M., pp. 94—97.
* Aluminium and magnesium fabricating.
*** Magnesium reduction.

111

progress of the people's revolution in China and the fall of Kuomintang, a change occurred also within the government circles of the United States of America. The pro-Chinese group which under the pressure of the international political development had retreated from its standpoint of a *hard dealing* with Japan, lost its position in the governing circles in favour of a pro-Japanese group. This change became manifest in the occupation policy by a continuance of the *opposite course.*

A concrete expression of this process in the economic domain was the publication of a *Programme of Economic Stabilization* in Japan, approved by the United States Government in December 1948 and immediately dispatched to SCAP in the form of an *interim directive* without any preceding notice being given to the Far Eastern Commission. It comprised a whole series of economic measures, similar by their character to the *Marshall Plan*, the principal aim of which was a remilitarization of the Japanese economy. The so-called programme of economic stabilization of the Japanese economy represented the foundation of a close alliance and cooperation qualitatively different from the one that had prevailed between U.S. and Japanese monopolies before World War II, and simultaneously it opened the way for a large-scale penetration of American capital into the Japanese economy.[70]

Soviet representatives in the Far Eastern Commission and in the Allied Council for Japan often expressed sharp criticism of the occupation policy aimed directly against an implementation of FEC decisions and designed to subjugate the Japanese economy, to enforce proposals whose aim was to accelerate reconstruction of the Japanese national economy and ensure its independence.[71]

At the FEC session of 23rd September 1948, the Soviet representative Panyushkin put forward a weighty proposal dealing with an industrial development of Japan and advanced the following motions for approval:

(1) Not to restrict the reconstruction and development of Japanese peaceful industry, the aim of which is to satisfy the needs of the Japanese population, nor the development of export which is in harmony with the needs of Japanese peaceful economy.

(2) To proscribe a reconstruction and development of Japanese war industry and to set up a control for some years to see to it that these decisions are implemented; this control should be carried out by countries that are most interested in preventing a new Japanese aggression.[72]

The programme of the so-called economic stabilization meant an essential revision of the entire economic policy of American occupying organs which they had practised during the period 1945—1948.

---

[70] For more details see Pevzner, Ya. A.: op. cit., pp. 423—447.

[71] Ibid., p. 443.

[72] *The Far Eastern Commission,* op. cit., p. 162.

A successful pursuance of this new policy required an urgent solution of the question of further reparations removals. In this connection, General McArthur informed the U.S. Government that "...he could not carry out the provisions of the interim directive on the Economic Stabilization, doubtless especially in regard to increasing Japanese manufactured products and Japanese export, and at the same time continue to remove from Japan as reparations industrial facilities in accordance with the Advance Transfer Program."[73]

Under these circumstances, the U.S. Government, taking support in preceding reports, prepared by Strike's and Johnston's commissions, and in SCAP's attitude, decided not to undertake any further steps in the question of reparations; rather the opposite — to abandon its previous decisions.

This new attitude of the U.S. Government towards the question of reparations and industrial standard, was announced to the Far Eastern Commission by the U.S. representative General McCoy, on 12th May 1949. In his statement he declared that the form of reparations through removals of industrial facilities is an obstacle to achieving a stable and self-supporting Japanese economy and that its reconstruction requires to put into effect all the means at its disposal.[74] In conclusion, General McCoy declared: "... the United States Government is impelled to rescind its interim directive of April 4th 1947, bringing to an end the Advance Transfer Program called for by that directive. It is impelled also to withdraw its proposal of November 6, 1947, on Japanese reparations shares ... the U.S. Government takes this occasion to announce that it has no intention of taking further unilateral action under its interim directive powers to make possible additional reparations removals from Japan ...".[75]

The programme of Japan's economic stabilization according to the plans of the United States and its decision to stop all payments of reparations was received with disapproval by member States of the Far Eastern Commission and their representatives sharply criticized this decision, as it contravened previous agreements among the Allies. The Philippines representative in FEC, Carlos Romulo warned: "... the programme of stabilization of Japanese economy and the efforts on the part of the United States to make of Japan a factory of Asia may lead in the future to a full revival of Japanese militarism."[76]

General McCoy's declaration practically meant an end to efforts at solving the

---

[73] Ibid., pp. 157—158.

[74] *Statement by the United States Representative on FEC Concerning Japanese Reparations and Level of Industry* (B r e n n, B. M.: Appendix I, p. 111).

[75] Ibid., p. 111.

[76] S h i n o b u, S.: op. cit., Vol. III, p. 962.

113

question of reparations on the floor of the Far Eastern Commission in view of the right of veto by the United States of America.

●

In conclusion, it may be stated that the development of the question of reparations imposed on Japan was essentially determined by United States' home and foreign policy — the principal occupying power — and its foundations were given principally by the designs of a general strategy of American imperialism.

The share of the Allies in the occupation of Japan was minimal right from the beginning and the activity of the Far Eastern Commission was complicated by the fact that when it actually did initiate its activity (February 1946), the main principles of the occupation policy had already been formulated, and also by the other fact that the Commission's competence was determined by the attitude of the United States who paralyzed implementation of decisions approved, often after lengthy discussions, on the FEC forum.

As a result of U.S. policy oriented towards an elimination of its war-time allies from participating in the occupation of Japan and in international cooperation, the Commission (FEC) never held the place which it rightly ought to have occupied in working out an occupation policy towards Japan. A positive aspect of the existence of FEC and ACJ was that the Soviet programme for democratization and demilitarization of Japan, founded on the Potsdam Proclamation, received wide-ranging publicity and came to the notice of the Japanese democratic public at large. Pronouncements by Soviet representatives in Allied commissions uncovered the aggressive, reactionary policy pursued by American imperialism and outlined concrete programmes for putting into effect the principles of the Potsdam Proclamation.[77]

The attitude of the United States of America towards the question of reparations that had been right from the beginning associated with a demilitarization of the Japanese economy and liquidation of its military-industrial complex, is characteristic of the overall occupation policy and reveals its imperialist character. The entire process may be divided into two stages documenting a change in U.S. policy, conditioned by the development of international relations and the situation in Asia.

During the first stage of the occupation of Japan, questions relating to reparations were dealt with in a spirit of agreement among the Allies, but the United States endeavoured in all manner of ways to exploit this solution in their favour regardless of whether this suited the other Allied powers or countries that had suffered most through Japanese aggression, or not. Reparations were to have been an inseparable part of the strategic aim which the United States had set themselves towards Japan in

---

[77] *Ocherki noveishei istorii Yaponii*, pp. 269—270.

114

the final stage of the war and at the start of the occupation; viz., a weakening of Japanese militarism, creation of guarantees against Japan's relapse into a totalitarian régime of the military-fascist type which would again be capable of becoming a potential adversary of the United States, weakening and elimination of Japanese capital from the Asian continent and thus creating conditions and possibilities for exercising a long-term influence in Japan itself. On the other hand, a solution of the reparations issue served the designs of U.S. foreign policy in the Far East and Southeast Asia, oriented as it was to support colonial powers in their efforts to regain their positions and in their struggle against the national liberation movement and the revolutionary process in Asia, and to support a local rightist bourgeoisie ever willing to cooperate with American imperialism.

It was also in this spirit of a *hard peace* towards Japan that Pauley's report on Japanese reparations had been drawn up; it was strongly influenced by the wide-ranging antifascist resistance during World War II and after it, as well as by the grown of democratic forces in the world.

The second stage of U.S. occupation policy and the solution of the reparations question was determined by the post-war upsurge of the national liberation movement in the Far East and Southeast Asia, and by the declaration of the *cold war* by Anglo-American imperialism. The development of the international situation had a substantial influence on the attitude and occupation policy of the United States of America towards Japan. The principal aim of the strategy of American imperialism was no longer a weakening of Japan, but its rapid reconstruction in the politico-economic domain, protection of its military-economic potential so that it would become a support of U.S. policy in the Far East — a policy more and more oriented against the national liberation movement in Asia and against the Soviet Union. At the same time, the United States was concerned about setting up favourable conditions for keeping conservative governments in power, for counteracting the growing influence of progressive forces, and also for creating economic stimuli that would encourage the Japanese bourgeoisie to cooperate with American monopolies.[78]

In the solution of the reparations question, the new aims of the United States — diametrally opposite to the Potsdam Proclamation — became concretely manifest, on the one hand, in their gradual lowering of the sum stipulated for reparations as proposed by American experts, their lowering of the number of plants and industrial facilities earmarked for reparations, and their ultimate cancelling of all reparations and removing this issue from the programme of FEC; on the other hand, this aim was evident in the revival of Japanese monopolies and their cooperation with American capital, which received its concrete shape in the so-called programme of stabilization of Japanese economy.

[78] Cf. Góralski, W.: op. cit., pp. 93—94.

The fact that of the total sum destined for reparations on the basis of Pauley's report only about 6.5 per cent were actually paid, constitutes a blatant testimony to the manner in which one of the principal aims of the occupation of Japan — viz. demilitarization of its economy — had been accomplished. Japanese military-industrial potential not only failed to be destroyed, it even came under the special, *individual* protection of the United States of America. This fact became strikingly evident at the moment of the outbreak of war on the Korean Peninsula. As a matter of fact, as the Japanese military-industrial potential had not been destroyed, the war became a means of enrichment to the reinstated Japanese monopolies.[79]

A second important result of U.S. reparations policy was that reparations, in their subsequent development, helped Japanese capital to penetrate into Southeast Asia and contributed to binding economies of Southeast Asian countries to Japan.[80]

---

[79] Special U.S. orders for equipping their army from the year 1950 to 1953 reached the sum of 2,374 milliard dollars (*Sengo Nihonshi*, Vol. II, p. 72).

[80] See also *Mezhdunarodnye otnosheniya na Dalnem Vostoke v poslevoennye gody 1945—1957*, Vol. I, pp. 106—108.

SOME COMMENTS ON THE NATURE OF SIGN

VIKTOR KRUPA, Bratislava

Linguistic signs are classified into iconic and conventional. Neither of them are in a causal relation to their referents. There are various degrees of iconicism. The problem of unilaterality or bilaterality of sign is regarded as a pseudoproblem. Language as a means of reflecting reality is discrete, being continuous as an object of investigation. Sign, as the cognitive process in general, is based upon the principle *pars pro toto*.

As a consequence of advances in the field of humanitarian research, language is investigated as a partial instance of the sign system in semiotics.

Although sign is a central notion of this discipline, many questions concerning it remain open. Traditionally, three basic types of signs are distinguished, i.e., indexical, iconic, and conventional signs (e.g., Reichenbach, 1947). Indexical signs occur in nature — in this sense smoke would be a sign of fire, wet streets a sign of rain — but also in the world of human beings — e.g., laughter is a sign of gaiety, cry is a sign of pain, etc. Iconic signs signalize the object they represent both by means of their form and content (which are parallel). Finally, conventional signs are notable for their lack of reflexivity upon the formal level.

Reichenbach's subdivision harmonizes with Peirce's definition of sign as something that replaces something in a certain relation or quality. At the same time, it explains some features of the sign process. Thus, indexical signs occur in an immediate context of the object or event to which they refer. This object or event may be said to cause them. If a given object does not occur, neither does the appropriate indexical sign.

However, the dichotomous classification of signs into (a) signs connected with their denotates by means of causal relations and (b) signs which are not connected with their denotates by means of causal relations, (cf. Gorskii, 1963, pp. 14—15), seems to be preferable here.

Indexical signs have virtually no content, being only symptoms of something and, to be precise, they do not represent any objects. This is what distinguishes them from iconic and conventional signs both of which are signs in the true sense of the word. Iconic signs are a lower type of true signs which represent their objects upon the level of both content and form, being in a sense their "abbreviations". Neither iconic nor conventional signs are automatically evoked by some stimuli and are not determined

117

or caused by their objects (i.e. by objects they stand for). They reflect only some of the properties of these objects and the selection of these properties depends upon the human subject, its attitude and interests. The subject plays no part as far as an indexical sign is concerned. If a fire burns, smoke appears in the natural order and the subject may only be an observer and interpreter here. Likewise, the painful outcry is an involuntary, automatic reaction to an unpleasant stimulus. As mentioned above, an iconic sign has both form and content. It is, like the conventional sign, a way of reflecting reality, of cognizing it and enabling communication about it. "Iconicism" of a sign has various degrees of intensity. Signs may be more or less iconic, which becomes manifest when we compare, e.g., a colour photograph with a black and white one, with a painting, with an interjection or with, e.g., reduplication as a marker of plural in some languages. This sequence is arranged so as to stress the gradual emancipation of form. A good example of the gradual conventionalization of a system of iconic signs is found in Chinese writing which was originally pictographic.

Conventional signs reflect reality as iconic signs do, but this holds only as far as their content is concerned; their form is relatively independent of content. The sign form or signal (Král, 1974) has a structure of its own, but the latter does not correlate with the structure of content in an unambiguous way. A total mutual diversity of sign forms would be inefficient and too exacting for memory — this is why the particular sign forms do not differ mutually as wholes but only partially, which means that they are structured. Content, information carried by the signal is likewise articulated, structured. Contents of various signals may overlap to a greater or smaller extent. This reflects the existence of similarities, regularities and connections both in reality and in the way people perceive them. The sign content reflects reality in accordance with the needs of the subject. It is motivated externally (from the viewpoint of the sign system). The sign form conforms to the demand of consistency of language as a system. However, the gap between the obvious external motivation of the content and the internal function of the form is not so deep if viewed in a historical perspective. It is observed that an incessant shift from the level of content to that of form takes place in language. The structure of sign forms arises so that particular, motivated elements lose their original reflexive adequacy, transparence and motivation and the sign form in question is reduced to a formal distinctive element. Analogous phenomena occur elsewhere as noticed, e.g., by K. Lorenz: "This simplification of originally independent subsystems in the course of their integration into a superior whole is a phenomenon which may be observed at any phase of evolution" (Lorenz, 1973, p. 52). An abundance of examples is furnished by derivational processes when particular derivate morphemes, originally independent elements of a reflexive nature, lose their productivity and become petrified, cf. the sequence of phonemes -tēr in Greek kinship terms patēr—father, mētēr—mother, thygatēr — daughter, -na in Maori kinship terms as tuakana elder sibling, teina younger sibling, tupuna ancestor, grandfather, -su in Japanese names of some flying

118

animals, e.g., *uguisu* nightingale, *hototogisu* cuckoo, *karasu* crow, *kirigirisu* cricket, or *t-* in Slovak pronouns as *ten* that, *tu* here, *tam* there, *teda* thus, *teraz* now, *taký* such.

The question of the content of sign leads to the problem of unilaterality vs. bilaterality of sign which, in a sense, may be regarded as a pseudoproblem (cf. Kráľ, 1974, p. 139) since each occurrence of a sign is at the same time an occurrence of its content.

Sign does not refer to reality directly. It represents reality for human beings who cannot, naturally enough, communicate without perceivable carriers of information. The complexity and essential continuity of reality as well as the impossibility of a direct transfer of reflections means that we cannot communicate about it directly, upon the level of a mechanical reflection, but only via the cognitive process which discretizes the continuum by means of the communicative instrument. Sign is unilateral in the sense that reality to which it refers in the act of communication is not its part. However, it is bilateral in the sense that it has both form and content. Content is not communicable without sign and sign without content is no sign at all. If we tried to separate content from form, we should have to postulate the existence of ideal content entities which, however, do not exist independently of either communicating subjects or sign forms. That is why we do not accept the view according to which there exists "a universal system of ideal linguistic referents and common to all natural languages" (Vardul, 1977, p. 32). Such a system may be regarded merely as a useful theoretical construct.

Zvegintsev stresses that the semantic content of sign is created by discreteness (Zvegintsev, 1973, pp. 217—218). To be more precise, the semantic content and discreteness of sign are interdependent. We can communicate about continuous reality only if we break it up into a set of components, if we discretize it. This mosaic projection remains essentially discrete despite all subtlety and possible overlaps. Meanings are discrete projections of continuous phenomena and are bound to discrete carriers. Continuum may be discretized in manifold ways and the number of discrete approximations is theoretically unlimited, although one way of discretization may be more frequent or probable than another one. This implies that a continuum cannot be discretized by means of a limited inventory of forms; the latter remains open in all languages. Language as a means of reflecting reality is discrete. On the other hand, language as an object of investigation, as a part of reality, is continuous. To be sure, our picture of language is discrete. The continuity of language as an object of investigation is manifest not only upon the acoustic level but also, e.g., in grammar. Thus there is a gradual transition between what is termed a fully-fledged word and an affix, but our metalanguage discretizes this continuous scale.

Sign, as the cognitive process in general, is characteristically based upon the principle *pars pro toto*; sign is in a way metaphorical because it helps us to cognize the whole and communicate about it by means of its part. Since the whole as such is unfathomable in its entirety, cognition inevitably leans upon a mere part of its features and upon their basis proceeds to conclusions about the whole. Thus, the cognizing subject presumes a certain homogeneity of the object. This, however, is never complete and that is why the process of cognition remains open. The principle *pars pro toto* operates also in mythology. Thus, the meaning of a sign reflects only a part of the features of the object that is represented by that sign. This selection of reflected features is not casual. The features included in it are essential (also from the subject's standpoint); this holds to a much greater extent for vocabulary than for grammar. As far as grammatical categories are concerned, the features selected serve largely distinctive, i.e., formal purposes.

Since there is, on the one hand, unlimited reality, while on the other, the faculties of the cognizing subject are limited, language is a device that enables us to map what is infinite with the aid of finite means. In accordance with this, the simplest signs consist, after all, of elementary distinctive elements of linear nature, of phonemes. The simplest signs combine according to some rules into more complex formations so that language enables communicating about new objects and events via combining available linguistic means. This possibility warrants an efficient advance of cognition from more familiar to less familiar and utilizes a partial similarity of various phenomena. An analogous procedure is exploited when the meaning of unfamiliar, new signs is explained, or of signs representing objects that are not directly observable. This is a premise upon which Carnap bases his method of semantic postulates (Carnap, 1956). His method is formally equivalent to the componential analysis that describes meaning as a set of semantic components.

However, when applying these two methods of semantic analysis one should not be misled by the idea that semantics is based upon a set of fundamental semantic atoms from which any meaning can be derived combinatorially. The set of semantic components is obtained inductively, as a consequence of comparing more or less similar linear meaningful units. These components do not correspond directly with reality but are of a formal nature, being abstract theoretical entities brought forth as results of the cognitive process.

An ability to denote something is inseparable from signs and there is no point in isolating meaning from sign as is done by those who adhere to the unilateral theory (cf. about this Kráľ, 1974, pp. 109—120). The ability to denote something establishes a link between sign and reality. Meaning as a reflection represents a selection of features characteristic for a certain aspect of reality. At the same time, it is a compromise between reality and human subject; the selection of features is carried out by the subject.

Meaning as defined above is not accessible to direct observation. It is no thing, its nature is relational. It is a relation holding between subject and reality in the society of subjects. It exists neither outside their consciousness nor outside the system of all signs. Meaning is a fuzzy relation and as such it is open so that various signs may overlap semantically. This is an advantageous property since it makes semantic change and development possible. Due to this property, any sign may start to denote a new class of objects if the need arises.

Since meaning is not amenable to direct observation, it cannot be measured. Attempts at a quantification of meaning known from psychology (e.g., Noble, 1952; Osgood — Suci — Tannenbaum, 1957) measure, in fact, the results of the impact of meaning upon human behaviour, although they are concerned with the so-called psychological meaning (Noble, 1952, p. 421). In his paper Noble interprets meaning as a relation between stimuli and reactions to them. The number of these reactions is regarded as an index of semantic richness. The psychological attitude to meaning is instructive for linguists because it stresses the primary goal of cummunication which consists in the exchange of information about things external to our consciousness, in the need to coordinate activity of the members of a community. True, this approach ought to be complemented by the semantic analysis of meaning as a reflexive category (cf. Panfilov, 1977, p. 81) correlating reality with the cognizing subject.

REFERENCES

Carnap, R. (1956): *Meaning and Necessity.* 2nd Ed. Chicago, University of Chicago Press.
Gorskii, D. P. (1963): *Logika.* Moscow, Uchpedgiz.
Král, Á. (1974): *Signál — znak — slovo.* Jazykoved. Čas., *25*, pp. 99—116.
Král, Á. (1974): *Model rečového mechanizmu.* Bratislava, Veda.
Lorenz, K. (1973): *Die Rückseite des Spiegels.* München — Zürich, R. Piper and Co.
Noble, C. E. (1952): *An Analysis of Meaning.* Psychol. Rev., *59*, pp. 421—430.
Osgood, C. E. — Suci, G. — Tannenbaum, P. (1957): *The Logic of Semantic Differentiation. The Measurement of Meaning.* Urbana, The University of Illinois Press, pp. 1—20, 25—30.
Panfilov, V. Z. (1977): *Filosofskie problemy yazykoznaniya.* Moscow, Nauka.
Peirce, C. S. (1960): *Collected Papers.* Cambridge, Mass.
Reichenbach, H. (1947): *Elements of Symbolic Logic.* New York, Macmillan.
Vardul, I. F. (1977): *Osnovy opisatelnoi lingvistiki.* Moscow, Nauka.
Zvegintsev, V. A. (1973): *Yazyk i lingvisticheskaya teoriya.* Moscow, Izdatelstvo MGU.

NOUN CLASSES IN FIJIAN
AND THEIR SEMANTICS

VIKTOR KRUPA, Bratislava

This is an analysis of the content of the category of possession in Fijian. There are four classes which seem to be a later elaboration of a simpler binary opposition as known from, e.g., the Polynesian languages.

The categorization of nouns into several classes, the number of which varies from language to language, is known throughout Oceania. While Polynesian is notable for its dichotomy of alienable versus inalienable nouns, many Melanesian languages and among them Fijian have developed more complex patterns. The categorization of nouns has developed after the decay of the Proto-Austronesian unity and before this happened, possession had been marked by means of possessive pronominal suffixes which could combine with all nouns. The same situation also prevails in present-day Indonesian languages.

In Melanesian languages mentioned above, possessive suffixes have been pre-served only to some extent, namely, as markers of the inalienable possession. They are compatible with nouns referring to objects that are organic parts of a higher whole such as, e.g., body parts or family members. In other instances, possession is marked by means of possessive pronouns that are usually prepositive. Unlike these languages, Polynesian has completely eliminated possessive pronominal suffixes so that all types of possession are expressed by two series of possessive pronouns, i.e., alienable (marker -a-) and inalienable (marker -o-).

Four noun classes or genders have been traditionally distinguished in Fijian (Milner, 1956, pp. 64—72; Cammack, 1962, pp. 57—63). They are termed (1) neutral, (2) edible, (3) drinkable, (4) familiar.*

Class (1) is usually defined in a negative way as including all nouns that are not members of the other three classes. It is marked by *no-* ～ *ne-*, cf. *na noqu vale* my house, *na nona gauna* his time, *na nona caa* his bad deeds, *na nona itukutuku* his story (i.e., a story by him). This class includes more items than any other class.

Class (2) includes nouns referring to articles of solid food considered from the

---

* In another Melanesian language, Kaliai-Kove, there are three classes, neutral, edible, and intimate (Counts, 1969, pp. 99—100).

point of view of consumption, i.e., as distinguished from planting, selling, etc., and nouns referring to qualities, properties or attributes of someone or something (Milner, op. cit.). This class is marked by *ke-* ~ *kei-*, e.g., *na kedatou kakana* our food, *na kena dalo* his taro.

Class (3) includes nouns that refer to items of drink or containers of drinkable fluids. Its markers are *me-* ~ *mei-*, e.g., *na medatou wai* our water, *na memudrau sucu* your milk, *na medratou yaqona* their kava. Besides, it incorporates also such nouns as *dio* oyster, *suka* sugar, *maqo* mango which would not be classified as drinkable in our culture. However, the Fijians use these words with the verb *gunuva* to drink.

Finally, class (4) includes nouns that refer to component parts of a whole such as, e.g., the parts of human body, of plants or members of the family. This class has no special marker. Instead, its membership is indicated by possessive suffixes which directly combine with the respective nouns, cf., *na yacaqu* my name, *na batina* his teeth, *na matana* his eye.

At a first glance the Fijian system of noun classes seems to be significantly different from the Polynesian pattern. However, a more detailed analysis shows that they are merely an elaboration of a simpler and basically identical opposition. The deviant way of marking the class (4) opposes it to the other three classes; the former represents integral, inalienable possession and the latter three may be regarded as a result of the decay of a hypothetical class *(4̄). This class would include nouns referring to objects in a nonintegral, alienable possession. This class may be considered as unmarked and its relation to (4) as privative, in Polynesian. It is worth mentioning that this elaboration of the system has taken place via the differentiation within the unmarked member of the opposition; probably because the unmarked member of the opposition displays a greater semantic heterogeneity than its marked member. Thus in Fijian two classes have split away from the hypothetical class *(4̄), i.e., edible (2) and drinkable (3) nouns. Now there is the question of interrelations among these three classes, namely (1), (2), and (3). Class (2) opposes immediately class (1). This is because the *k*-markers are used if an otherwise neutral noun is to be presented as inalienable or specific to somebody or to something. As a consequence of this, we obtain pairs such as *na nona itukutuku* his story (told by him) and *na kena itukutuku* his story (about him). Class (2) markers may transform neutral nouns into ad hoc inalienable nouns; perhaps it is a rationalization of the observation that what is eaten becomes, in fact, an organic part of the consumer. Class (2) is regarded as marked and class (1) as its unmarked counterpart. These two classes together again represent an unmarked pendant to class (3) which includes a restricted number of nouns classified as drinkable. This is in accordance with, e.g., Kaliai-Kove where there are only three classes, i.e., familiar (termed intimate by Counts, 1969, pp. 99—100), neutral and edible; the class of drinkable nouns has not split away and established itself as a separate category.

If the owner is expressed by a noun in Fijian, the particular classes are indicated by means of particles *nei* (class 1), *kei* (class 2), *mei* (class 3), and *i* (class 4), e.g., *na vale nei Jone* John's house, *na uvi kei Sala* Sala's yam, *na bia mei Senitieli* Senitieli's beer, *na taci i Bale* Bale's brother.

Classes in Fijian are a typical illustration of how the classification of nouns takes place in any language. This category, no doubt, has a semantic background. It consists of a selection of features that are reflexive in origin. This selection has no chance character. Since it is carried out by human beings, it cannot be regarded as a mechanical reflection of the objective reality. Rather it should be regarded as the result of an interaction between reality and subject (the latter is part of the objective reality itself). This interaction includes, first, the impact of the external reality upon the subject and, second, the utilitarian, pragmatic attitude of the subject to the external reality. The former aspect may be equated with the ability to distinguish objects which create an organic whole from more or less chance aggregates. This distinction exists independently for the subject's attitude. The latter aspect, however, manifests the interests of the subject who regards some objects as edible, other objects as inedible and yet another group as drinkable. Thus, the selection of particular semantic features reflects both objective and subjective factors; their balance may vary from language to language. From the cognitive point of view the categorization of nouns in Fijian is tentative only, which is the case of all grammatical categories. The criteria used when classifying the particular nouns are unable to break down the whole set of nouns in a satisfactory and unambiguous way into mutually exclusive classes. In some instances the criteria work better while in other instances they tend to be not very adequate, which leads to an increasing formalization. The category itself undergoes a conventionalization and becomes a component of a higher whole, of the language system. As such it loses part of its essence and becomes subordinate to the demands of the language structure. As Lorenz says, structure is materialized knowledge but cognition requires that an old structure must be replaced by a new one (Lorenz, 1973, p. 261) which is a *conditio sine qua non* of the adaptive evolution of each system.

REFERENCES

Cammack, Floyd Mc Kee: *Bauan Grammar.* An Unpublished Thesis. Cornell University 1962.
Counts, David R.: *A Grammar of Kaliai-Kove.* Honolulu, University of Hawaii Press 1969.
Lorenz, Konrad: *Die Rückseite des Spiegels.* München — Zürich, R. Piper and Co. 1973.
Milner, G. B.: *Fijian Grammar.* Suva, Government Press 1956.

ON THE CATEGORY
OF DEFINITENESS IN BENGALI

ANNA RÁCOVÁ, Bratislava

This is an attempt to show how the universal logico-semantic deep category of definiteness becomes manifest in the surface structure of the Bengali language.

The present study is based on the premise that every language possesses a mode how formally to express the fact that a name designates either some definite, concrete, known item, or only an object in general, as the representative of a certain class of objects. It is therefore assumed that the opposition "definiteness — indefiniteness" which exists as a universal logico-semantic deep category, will become manifest also in the surface structure of a language.

A large number of languages exists in which this opposition is grammaticalized, i.e. is expressed with the aid of an article; but even here the rules governing the use of articles need not be uniform. Thus, for instance, the general rule in French or German is that an article (definite or indefinite) stands in front of an appelative, while in English a substantive is normally without an article and a knowledge of when and why to use an article, and which, is absolutely indispensable; at the same time, clearness of concept by itself is insufficient for definiteness. A more detailed definition of the term is usually required (Mathesius, 1961).[1]

It is only natural that attention is traditionally devoted to the grammatical category of definiteness in languages with grammatical articles. Nevertheless, here too, a re-evaluation of existing theories on articles takes place, and this in connection with the need to investigate contextual, syntactic and semantic conditions, a search being simultaneously made for mutual affinities between an article and other words that may have the function of a determinator (Buzássyová, 1971).[2]

Grammatical descriptions of languages that have no grammatical article pay but sporadic attention to the question in what manner one expresses, in the surface structure, whether a concrete or nonconcrete object, not mentioned as yet, is involved. This applies in the fullest measure also to Bengali.

The aim of this study is then to systematize existing notions on expressing the

---

[1] Mathesius, V.: *Obsahový rozbor současné angličtiny na základě obecně lingvistickém*. Praha, Nakladatelství Československé akademie věd 1961.

[2] Buzássyová, K.: *Príspevok ku kontrastívnemu skúmaniu kategórie určenosti (maďarčina — slovenčina)*. In: Jazykovedný časopis, *XXIII*, 1, Bratislava, Vydavateľstvo Slovenskej akadémie vied 1972, pp. 13—25.

opposition definiteness — indefiniteness in Bengali, to verify them on a given set of texts and to supplement them with findings from these texts.[3] We are aware that this involves a very complex issue, one that has received scant attention thus far in Bengali, hence, no claims are made at completeness.

In Bengali, the most current, the most frequently occurring indicators of definiteness are the particles *-ṭā, -ṭi, -khānā, -khāni, -gāchā, -gāchi*, which, alongside others, have two principal functions: (1) they set apart the given object or person from a group of similar objects or persons: *rāmsundar kampita hāste noṭbādhā cādarṭi kådhe tuliyā ābār corer mata sakaler dṛṣṭi eṛāiyā bāṛi phiriyā gelen* (Th II/36) — With trembling hands Ramsundar threw his chadar, in which he had tied his money, across his shoulder and returned home, avoiding the looks of everyone, like a thief; (2) they point to the object or person already referred to or known: *anatibilambe duṭi gāl phulāiyā kalikāy phū dite dite rataner prabeś. hāt haite kalikāṭā laiyā poṣṭmāṣṭār phaṣ kariyā jijñāsā karen* (Th II/18) — Ratan entered without delay, blowing into a pipe with all her strength. The postmaster took away the pipe ... and asked her.

In works by Soviet linguists, these particles are called determinative-indicative affixes. In our view, the designation "determinative-indicative" is suitable for it justly indicates how the particles function in a text. The same, however, cannot be said of the designation "affixes", for the given particles do not refer to the domain of word formation. As has been rightly observed by Zograf (1976),[4] morphologically they do come closer to agglutinative affixes, but semantically they fail to achieve the same level of abstraction as do "true" affixes. They combine within them several meanings. Alongside definiteness, they may point to the size and shape of an object, and also to the relation of the speaker towards what is indicated.

The particles *-khānā, -khāni* are added to substantives designating a broad, flat object: ... *kṣārkāpaṛkhānā niyā ghāte giyāche* (M 227) — She took her clothes and washing powder and went to the ghat.

The particles *-gāchā, -gāchi* are affixed to substantives designating a long, slender object: *daṛigāchā dhara* (Page, 1934)[5] — Catch hold of the rope.

More neutral are the particles *-ṭā, -ṭi*, which are added to substantives designating objects of any shape whatever, but also a person, an animal or an abstract noun: *yekhāne sakale āsiyā basibār kathā, seikhāne baiṭā pheliyā rākhilen* (Th I/21) — She

[3] We have analysed the following texts: Ṭhākur, R.: *Galpaguccha, dvitīya bhāg, dvitīya saṃskaraṇ.* Kalikātā, Iṇḍiyān Pābliśiṃ Hāus, 224 pp. Ṭhākur, R.: *Galpaguccha, caturtha bhāg, tṛtīya saṃskaraṇ.* Kalikātā, Iṇḍiyān Pābliśiṃ Hāus 1920, 159 pp. Majumdār, D. M.: *Ṭhākurmār jhuli.* Kalikātā 1974, 274 pp. The numbers in brackets denote volumes and pages.

[4] Zograf, G. A.: *Morfologicheskii stroi novych indoariiskikh yazykov.* Moscow, Nauka 1976.

[5] Page, W. S.: *An Introduction to Colloquial Bengali.* Cambridge 1934.

tossed the book to where all were to sit. *jaygopāl kichutei bujhite pārita nā ei krisakāy brihaṭmastak gambhīrmukha śyāmabarna* **cheleṭār** *madhye eman ki āche ye-janya tāhār prati etaṭā sneher apabyay karā haiteche* (Th I/6) — Jaygopal could not understand what was in that dark-skinned boy with that big head and serious face that she should so much love towards him. *ye maner ākśep mukh phuṭiyā balibār jo nāi, tāhāri* **ākroṣṭā** *sab ceye beśi hay* (Th IV/4) — The greatest is that anger which man cannot express.

Variants of particles with -*i* may be used when a minor object or person is to be designated: **grāmṭi** *ati sāmānya* (Th II/16) — That was an insignificant village. *ei ghatanāy śiśu* **bhrātāṭir** *prati śaśikalār bhāri rāg haila* (Th IV/3) — Therefore, Śaśikalā became very cross with her little brother.

Occasionally it is used with persons of the female sex: *pratham* **kanyāṭi** *yakhan pitār bakṣer kāch paryyanta bāṛiyā uṭhila, takhan tārāprasanner niścintabhāb ghuciyā gela* (Th IV/19) — When the eldest daughter had grown up to her father's chest, T. ceased to be carefree.

Variants with -*i* may, however, indicate also a familiar or pejorative relation on the part of the speaker: **poṣṭmāṣṭārer chātrīti** *anekṣan dvārer kāche apekṣā kariya basiyāchila* (Th II/20) — The postmaster's pupil sat long at the door and waited. *ei dupur rātre beś* **kājṭi** *bāhir kariyācha!* (Th II/57) — Fine work you've found now at midnight!

It appears that such cases, too, involve some sort of definiteness, a closer designation of the speaker's relation to the object or the person referred to. In contrast to such languages as, for instance, English or Hungarian (here the article does not serve to express the grammatical category of gender), in which the definiteness category is achieved in communication, in Bengali it is achieved already in nomination. Hence, Bengali, by using the above particles, may determine an object or person both in nomination and in communication.

If a single object is to be specified more closely, particles -*ṭā*, -*ṭi*, -*khānā*, -*khāni*, -*gāchā*, -*gāchi* are added directly to the substantive: *poṣṭmāṣṭār balilen, "*śarīrṭā *bhāla bodh hacche nā"* (Th II/21) — The postmaster said: "I don't feel well" (literally, the body does not feel well).

When a group of equivalent objects is enumerated, particles are added to the numeral (in such cases they resemble a numerative): *tārāprasanner* **cāriṭi** *santān, cār kanyā* (Th IV/19) — T. has four children, four daughters.

The above particles may be joined to a substantive also when it is preceded by a demonstrative pronoun or a personal pronoun in the genitive case (expressing possessiveness), or even by both simultaneously: *anek gurutar ghatanār ceye* **sei kathāṭāi** *tāhār mane beśi uday haita* (Th II/18) — That item became fixed in her memory more strongly that very important events. **āmār sei kaṅkālṭā** *kothāy geche, tāi khūjite āsiyāchi* (Th II/56) — I have come to find out what has become of the skeleton of mine.

That means that although by their function, Bengali particles *-ṭā, -ṭi, -khānā, -khāni, -gāchā, -gāchi* resemble very much the definite article, especially the most neutral of them *-ṭā*, the rule of noncompatibility with a demonstrative pronoun and a personal pronoun in the genitive case does not apply to them (in contrast to e.g., English, or German, but in harmony with, say, Hungarian).

Particles (similarly as the article in English) are not used to express definiteness with general substantives which function in a text as proper nouns, e.g., father, mother within the context of family, daughter-in-law, bride, groom in wedding ceremonials, etc.: *śvaśurbāṛi yāibār samay nirupāmāke buke laiyā **bāp** ār cokher jal rākhite pārilen nā* (Th II/29) — When she was leaving for her father-in-law's house, her father pressed Nirupama to his breast and could not keep back his tears. ***bar** sahasā tāhār pitṛdebatār abādhya haiyā uṭhila* (Th II/28) — The groom suddenly opposed his father.

The above particles allow expression of the fact that there is question of an indefinite, unknown object, an animal or a person and this in connection with the numeral *"ek"* (one) one isolated, undefined object, animal or person from a class of similar objects, animals or persons, or with indefinite numerals if a larger indefinite quantity of undefined objects, animals or persons is indicated: *sahare **ekṭā** nutan byāmo āsiyāche* (Th II/32) — There is a new epidemic in the town. *noṭ **ko'khāni** rumāle jaṛāiyā cādare bādhiyā rāmsundar behāiyer nikat giyā basilen* (Th II/32) — R. wrapped a few bank notes in his handkerchief, tied them in the chadar and set out for his father-in-law's.

When undefined persons or animals are meant, this can be expressed in Bengali also with the aid of the locative case terminating with the suffix *-te (-e, -y)*, which acts in the text as the subject of the sentence in the plural: ***loke** āmār kāche lukāite ceṣṭā karita* (Th II/58) — People endeavoured to get out of my way. *gharer mejete hār gor, ajagarer kholās! **ajagare** sukhuke khāiyā giyāche* (M 235) — There are bones, a snake's skin on the floor. Pythons devoured Sukha. ***chelete chelete** nānā upalakṣe jhagrā bibad haiyā thāke* (Th IV/7) — Boys will always quarrel and fight for various trifles.

A further means to express definiteness in Bengali is with the suffix of the objective case *-ke*. It is added only to a concretized, known object, while a nonconcretized object is expressed by the direct case: *yakhan mānuṣ chilām ebaṃ choṭa chilām, takhan ek **byaktike** yamer mata bhay karitām* (Th II/57) — When I was human and small, I was afraid of one man as of the devil. *yakhan chele haibe, ei śikale nāṛā dio, āmi āsiyā **chele** dekhiba!* (M 80) — When a child is born, pull on this cord, I shall come to have a look at it.

The above rule, however, has but a limited validity. It applies fully only to animate substantives; generally *-ke* occurs also with inanimate substantives only exceptionally: *śyyātale tāhār svāmi ye aṃśe śayan karita sei aṃśer upar bāhu prasāraṇ kariyā pariyā śūnya* **bāliske** *cumban karila*(Th IV/1)—She stretched out her hand towards that part of bed where her husband used to sleep and kissed the empty cushion.

In contrast to particles -*ṭā*, -*ṭi*, -*khānā*, -*khāni*, -*gāchā*, -*gachi*, the suffix of the objective case -*ke* may be added also to proper names and to general nouns which function in a text as proper nouns: *yāibār samay* **ratanke** *ḍākiyā balilen* (Th II/24) — On getting ready to leave, he called Ratan and said. **bāpke** *alpa alpa mane āche* (Th II/18) — She remembered her father slightly.

With the suffix of the objective case -*ke*, the law of incompatibility fails to apply not only with the demonstrative pronoun and the genitive case of personal pronouns, but also with particles; this goes to show that definiteness is expressed with the suffix -*ke* secondarily only, and that -*ke* constitutes primarily a gramatical aid for expressing direct object and animateness, but also the fact that the category of definiteness in Bengali is not grammaticalized to the same extent as in typical "articled" languages.

In Bengali there exists an evident connection between expressing definiteness and possessiveness: an object may be more closely determined by designating its possessor and this by means of the genitive case of substantives or personal pronouns: *yāite yāite pathe ek gāi dukhuke ḍāke* — ... **āmār** *goyālṭā kāṛiyā diyā yābe? dukhu* ... **gāier** *goyāl kāṛila* (M 227) — As Dukhu was walking along, the cow called her: Wouldn't you clean up my byre? D. cleaned the cow's byre. **tāhār** *nāti* **tāhār** *dui hātu sabale jaṛāiyā dhariyā mukh tuliyā kahila* (Th II/35) — The nephew embraced his knees with all his strength, lifted his face up to him and said.

As has already been stated in connection with particles and the suffix of the objective case -*ke*, expressing definiteness by means of the genitive case of personal pronouns and that of substantives does not exclude the employment of other indicators of definiteness, as may be noted in the preceding examples.

Occasionally, the genitive case of a personal pronoun may lose its primary function in a text, i.e. designation of the owner of an object, and retains only that of the indicator of definiteness: **āmāder** *poṣṭmāṣṭār kalikātār chele* (Th II/16) — (Our) postmaster came from Calcutta.

Similarly, an object may be more closely determined with the aid of determinative pronouns: *nā bābā, e ṭākā diye tumi āmāke apamān koro nā* (Th II/36 — No father, don't offend me by giving him this money.

On the other hand, indefinite pronouns designate closely unspecified objects: **kon** ... *dāsī Nirur śvāśurike ei khabar dila* (Th II/36) — Some ... servant told it to Niru's mother-in-law.

131

In Bengali, a certain object or person may be more clearly specified or set apart from a class of similar objects or persons also syntactically, and this by means of subordinate sentence in a relative clause:

Here, three eventualities may arise:

(1) The substantive to be more clearly specified is named in the subordinate sentence where it is introduced by a relative, but also in the main clause (introduced by a correlative): *ye **din** sandhyār samay nirur śvās upasthita haila, **sei din** pratham ḍākṭār dekhila* (Th II/37) — The doctor saw Niru for the first time only that evening when she gasped for breath (literally, which evening Niru ..., that evening ...).

(2) The specified substantive is named only in the subordinate sentence, with only the correlative standing in the main sentence: *eman samay gharer koṇe ye teler **sej** jvalitechila, **seṭā** prāy miniṭ pā̃cek dhariyā khābi khāite khāite ekebāre nibiyā gela* (Th II/25) — The oil lamp burning in a corner of the room, flickered for some five minutes and finally went out completely (liter., ... which oil lamp burned ... that one five minutes flickered ...).

(3) An independent correlative stands in the subordinate sentence and a relative in the main sentence: *tāhār abhiprāy katadur saphal haiyāche **yāhārā** āmādigke jānen **tāhāder** nikat prakāś karā bāhulya* (Th II/55) — It is superfluous to explain to those who know us, how far his efforts have been successful (liter., who know us, to those it is superfluous ...).

The following observations may be made by way of conclusion:

(1) Although Bengali lacks the grammatical category of definiteness, the logico-semantic opposition is reflected also in the surface structure of the language. It may be expressed with the aid of several linguistic means, viz. grammatical means (morphological suffixes -*ke*, -*e*, genitive of nouns and personal pronouns expressing an owner of closely determined object; syntactically by a subordinate sentence in a relative clause); lexical means (determinative pronouns, indefinite pronouns, indefinite numerals, the numeral one) and by such means as stand on the margin between lexical and grammatical ones (particles). Hence, there is always question of an implicit expression of the category of definiteness.

(2) The use of one indicator of definiteness does not rule out a simultaneous employment of another one. From this it clearly follows that the definiteness category is not grammaticalized; therefore, several competing means are available to express it. Their choice is governed by complex rules, bound to an expression of other properties (possessiveness, speaker's relation, features of the object, e.g. its appearance).

(3) These properties go to show that the category of definiteness in Bengali is realized not only in communication, but very often already during nomination.

WORD-FORMATIONAL ASSIMILATION
OF LOANWORDS IN ARABIC

LADISLAV DROZDÍK, Bratislava

The study is concerned with a number of the most outstanding word-formational aspects of lexical borrowing in Modern Written Arabic. An attempt is made at establishing a significant relation between the ability of the borrowed units to be subsequently resegmented in accordance with relevant linguistic structures of Arabic, and their capacity for being integrated into the Arabic lexicon.

1. The steadily growing needs to expand and modernize the Arabic lexicon, largely stimulated by new political, cultural, scientific and technological developments all over the Arab world, have brought considerable amounts of foreign lexical elements into Arabic. The bulk of the 19th and 20th century borrowings, recently occurring in Arabic, are drawn from modern European languages. Nevertheless, the root-and-pattern morphemic system of Arabic, quite dissimilar to anything known in Indo-European, is one of the most serious obstacles for any easy and problemless word-formational assimilation of borrowings and their integration into the Arabic lexicon. It accounts, at the same time, for a surprisingly vacillating attitude of Arab innovators and all concerned language users towards this word-formational procedure, ranging from an elated enthusiasm up to a total rejection with many variously shaded in-between stages.[1]

The root, as the core of the Arabic (Semitic) root-and-pattern system, is, dissimilar to Indo-European, an exclusively consonantal formation and, when approached statistically, it may most frequently be identified with tri-consonantal, much less currently with quadri-consonantal, and quite rarely with bi-consonantal phonemic sequences which are intercalated with the stem-formative vocalic constituents of the pattern morpheme.[2]

---

[1] For some of these attitudes towards $ta^c r\bar{\imath}b$, see e.g. Stetkevych, J.: *The Modern Arabic Literary Language. Lexical and Stylistic Developments.* Chicago—London, The University of Chicago Press 1970 (Chapter 3: The Assimilation of Foreign Words (*Al-Ta^c rīb*)), pp. 56—65. Cf. also Sa'id, Majed F.: *Lexical Innovation Through Borrowing in Modern Standard Arabic* (Sa'id, in what follows; for the linguistic data quoted in the text of the present study, abbreviated to (S)). Princeton University 1967, p. III. Cf. also our paper *Lexical Innovation Through Borrowing as Presented by the Arab Scholars* (in: *Asian and African Studies*, XV, 1979, pp. 21—29.

[2] In terms of classification proposed by W. M. Erwin, a *simple pattern* consists of one or more vowels distributed among the consonants of a root, while a *pattern complex* is a combination of a simple pattern and one or more affixes. See Erwin, W. M.: *A Short Reference Grammar of Iraqi Arabic.* Washington, D.C., Georgetown University Press 1963, p. 52 (the first definition is slightly abbreviated).

2. The discrepancy between the predominantly tri-consonantal root in Arabic and the typically more-than-tri-consonantal root (or what might be from the point of view of a common native speaker of Arabic indentified with a root) in the donor languages of a non-Semitic genetic background generates, together with other features of structural dissimilarity, several problems. First of all, it prevents both linguistic participants in the process of lexical borrowing, the recipient and the donor languages, from their meeting each other at the statistically culminant points of the relative frequency of occurrence of their morphemic constituents undergoing the morphemic transfer from the donor to the recipient language. From this point of view, two distinct classes of borrowing[3] may be distinguished:

(1) borrowings which did not undergo resegmentation along the morphemic boundaries of the Arabic root-and-pattern system and are treated as one-morpheme units:

e.g.:

tilivisyōn (W, 96), *talavizyōn* (S, 49), *tilivisyōn/tilifizyōn* (B, 115), *tilīfizyōn* (Sch, 393: *Fernsehen*; no Romanized transcription available in the source quoted, possibly *tilīvizyōn*) "television";[4]

trānzistōr (D, 1287; Kh, 631; no Romanized transcription is given in any of these sources; in a more conservative representation possibly *trānzistūr*, like in the preceding example, *tilīfizyūn*), *trānzistar* (S, 57), *tirānzistōr* (Sch, 1211) "transistor";

tilifūn, talīfūn (W, 96), *talifōn, talifūn* (S, 53; the latter variant is labelled as an example of a conservative rendition in which certain phonemic substitutions replace direct phonemic transfers), *tilifūn* (Kh, 610; no Romanization provided, possibly *tilifōn*), *tilīfūn* (Sch, 1188; possibly *tilīfōn*), *tilifūn, tilīfūn* (Bar, 104; possibly *tilifōn, tilīfōn*), etc. "telephone";[5]

fītamīn (W, 734), *vītāmīn* (S, 35), *fitamīn, faytamīn* (B, 115; both variants are said to reflect the French and English origin respectively), etc. "vitamin";[6]

mikrōfōn (W, 935), *maykrofōn* (S, 67), *mikrōfōn, maykrūfōn* (B, 115), etc. "microphone", etc.;

(2) borrowings that did undergo a resegmentation in accordance with the root-and-pattern system of Arabic, e.g.:

(2.1) tri-consonantals:

film "film" (W, 727), analysed into a root *f-l-m* and a pattern *CiCC*, plural formed by pattern modification *CiCC — 'aCCāC: film — 'aflām*;

---

[3] For the definition of lexical borrowing, as conceived in the present paper, see § 4 in what follows.

[4] Various loan translations which may sometimes co-occur with this and other loanforms, quoted throughout the present study, are disregarded.

[5] Co-occurring with the native creation *hātif*.

[6] Co-occurring with a recent loanblend *hayamīn* the first constituent of which is related to *hayāh* "life".

bank "bank" (W, 77), analysed into a root *b-n-k* and a pattern *CaCC*, plural obtained by pattern modification *CaCC — CuCūC: bank — bunūk;*

warša "workshop" (W, 1061), analysed into *w-r-š* and *CaCCa*, pluralized by pattern modification *CaCCa — CiCaC: warša — wiraš,* or by an extra-root affixation: *waršāt; warša — wuraš* (S, 72); etc.

(2.2) quadri-consonantals:

qunṣul "consul" (W, 729), analysed into *q-n-ṣ-l* and *CuCCuC*, pluralized by pattern modification *CuCCuC — CaCāCiC: qunṣul — qanāṣil,* by analogy with e.g. *bulbul — balābil* "nightingale";

duktūr "doctor" (W, 288), analysed into *d-k-t-r* and *CuCCūC*, pluralized by pattern modification *CuCCūC — CaCāCiCa: duktūr — dakātira,* by analogy with four-consonantal singulars having a long vowel between the third and the fourth root-constituting consonant, as in *tilmīḏ — talāmīḏ/talāmiḏa* "student; disciple" or *'ustāḏ — 'asātiḏa* "master; teacher; professor", etc.

3. Another limitative factor, preventing a massive introduction of tri-consonantally resegmented borrowings, is exactly the peak frequency of occurrence of the tri-consonantal root in Arabic which may tend to interfere with the mass of the indigenous tri-consonantals and thus produce an undue homonymy,[7] as in:

numra, nimra (W, 1000) "number, numero; figure", analysed into a tri-consonantal root *n-m-r* and a pattern *CuCCa, CiCCa,* pluralized by pattern modification *CuCCa, CiCCa — CuCaC, CiCaC* resp.: *numra — numar, nimra — nimar;* the root is homonymously related to another root *n-m-r* in e.g. *namir* "leopard; tiger";

biyān, biyāna, biyānō "piano" (W, 84), *biyān* (S, 86), analysed into a root *b-y-n* and a pattern *CiCāC* or its variant *CiCāCa* (the last variant, *biyānō,* since it does not coincide with any native word-formational pattern, cannot be analysed in these terms and has to be treated as a mono-morphemic unit), pluralized by means of affixation (viz., the suffix *-āt*); the root enters a homonymous relationship with another root *b-y-n* conveying the general idea of 'clearness, obviousness and evidence', as in *bayān* "clearness, obviousness; explanation etc.", *bayyin* "clear, evident, obvious";

munāwara (Fr. *manœuvre;* Engl. *manoeuvre, maneuver*) "maneuver; trick", plur. in *-āt: munāwarāt* "military maneuvers" (W, 1010), coinciding with an actual Arabic word which may be analysed into a root *n-w-r* and a pattern *muCāCaCa;* root homonymy between the latter and another root *n-w-r* implying the general concept of "light, gleam, fire", as in *nūr* pl. *'anwār* "light", *nār (*nawar)* "fire", *nawwara* "to light, illuminate", etc.

A certain preference is therefore given to quadri-consonantals which, in tune with their restricted representation in the Arabic lexicon, do not incur the danger of

---

[7] See Sa'id, pp. 91—92.

producing this type of unwanted multiple meaning relationship in any significant degree, e.g.: *qunṣūl, duktūr* (as quoted above), etc.

4. As evident from the examples quoted so far, as well as from the aim of the present paper to study word-formational aspects of lexical borrowing which may be found relevant to the process of assimilation of foreign lexical elements and their integration into the Arabic lexicon, only a relatively small part of what is possibly associated with the general procedural frame of lexical borrowing is taken into account. On the strength of this restriction, only such borrowings will subsequently be examined which display full morphemic transfer from the donor into the recipient language, as is also the case of all examples so far quoted. Technically, in descriptions covering the whole spectrum of phenomena related to lexical borrowing, such borrowings are usually referred to as loanforms,[8] as against e.g. loanblends which combine morphemic substitution with morphemic transfer,[9] as in *faḥmāt* "carbonate" (M, 143), analysable into the Arabic lexeme *faḥm* "coal" (here standing for "carbon") and the foreign suffix *-āt*, or *ḥadīdīk* "ferric" (Kh, 218), consisting of the Arabic *ḥadīd* "iron" and the suffix *-īk*, corresponding to the French *-ique* or the English *-ic*. Since loanblends may never achieve a complete word-formational assimilation, they will be excluded from the scope of the present inquiry, together with the whole vast domain of loan translation, loanshift and other phenomena possibly associated with linguistic interference.

From a phonological point of view, no attempt will be made at classifying borrowings in accordance with whether they predominantly display features of phonemic transfer, as in *film* (English) — *film* (Arabic), or rather show various eye-striking combinations of both transfer and substitution elements, as in *talifōn, talavizyōn*, etc.

5. The identification of the immediate source language may appear, in most cases, to be extremely difficult, especially in the internationally circulating terms like *malyūn, malyōn* "million", *kīlōmitr* "kilometer", *tilifūn, talīfūn, talifōn* etc. "telephone", etc. Neither is it possible to rely, in this respect, on the seemingly self-evident phonological features, as is, for instance, the occurrence of diphthongs in terms like *haydrujīn* (S, 67), alternating with *hidrōžēn* (W, 1042) "hydrogen", or *saykolōjī, sīkolōžī* (W, 448), where the phonological picture of the diphthong-free variants seems to point to the French, while that of the diphthonguized alternants, to the English origin of the borrowing. At the same time, however, the same feature may reflect various aspects of linguistic prestige or, quite simply, an individual

---

[8] The definition is that of M. F. Sa'id (p. 38), based on that given by E. H a u g e n, in *The Norwegian Language in America: A Study in Billingual Behavior*. 2 vols. Philadelphia, University of Pennsylvania Press 1953. Some terminological innovations should be attributed to M. F. Sa'id (e.g. Sa'id's 'transfer' for the Haugen's 'importation').

[9] For the definition of loanblends, see S a ' i d, p. 38.

proficiency in one language or another, within various patterns of bi- or multilingual-ism, as statable with the early 19th and 20th century innovators and lexicon-makers, as well as with the recent language users.[10]

In some single instances, the relation between the donor and the recipient language may present a rather complicated picture, especially when observed through a sufficiently long period of language contact and cross-cultural interference. The mediaeval term *dār aṣ-ṣināʿa* "workshop, esp. for manufacturing weapons", for instance, by way of the Italian *darsena* (Dozy I, 145), came back to Arabic as *tarsāna* (co-occurring with a loanblend *tarsxāna*) "arsenal; shipyard, dockyard" (W, 93).[11] So we have:

(1) *tarsāna* — an Europeanized modern term for 'arsenal', and

(2) *dār aṣ-ṣināʿa* — a mediaeval model word for the latter, syntactic construction of a head-modifier type, "workshop (esp. for manufacturing weapons)"; as a modern term, synonymously related to *tarsāna* (W, 299).

Since it is impossible to discover the first recorded attestation of lexical borrowings in every particular case, owing to the lack of appropriate documentary material, a rather impressionistic and indiscriminative attitude towards the European source languages is mostly adopted.[12]

6. The degree of word-formational adaptation of foreign lexical units to the existing word pattern of Arabic is reflected at all linguistic levels.[13] Most immediately, however, it is mirrored in the set of their derivational and inflectional manifestations. Since the present study is quite specifically concerned with word-formational phenomena, inflectional manifestations of the ongoing process of assimilation will to a considerable extent be disregarded and no systematic presentation of the latter will be provided. Nevertheless, the inflectional phenomena may provide some very useful issues for a systematic examination of word-formational processes under consideration. Since the word-formational assimilation cannot be achieved without a simultaneous inflectional assimilation of the borrowed units, the latter will be used, in the frame of the present study, as a sort of testing criterion in relation to the former. Vacillations in the loanform gender assignments, alternatively stimulated by gender classification in the source language (if the latter happens to be a gender language) or by various analogical pressures emanating from the recipient

---

[10] Cf. Belkin, V. M.: *Arabskaya leksikologiya* (Arabic Lexicology) (— Belkin, in what follows; for the examples quoted in the text, abbreviated to (B)). Moscow, Izdatelstvo Moskovskogo Universiteta 1975, p. 115.

[11] From the Italian *darsena*, after the elision of /d/, mistakenly identified with the Italian preposition, it passed into the European languages as 'arsenal'.

[12] For a similar attitude, cf. also Saʾid, p. 33 ff.

[13] For the significant relationship between the degree of word-formational assimilation (Saʾid's 'pattern congruity' or 'morphemic congruity') and that of phonemic substitution, see Saʾid, p. 87.

language, as well as particular ways of gender- and number marking, are the inflectional phenomena most immediately associated with the process of word-formational assimilation.

7. From the word-formational point of view, the most conclusive criterion for establishing the degree of word pattern assimilation is the capability of borrowings for resegmentation along the structural boundaries of the Arabic root-and-pattern system.

7.1 Nonresegmentable borrowings, treated as mono-morphemic units (of course, when inflectional markers involving affixation are disregarded), may mostly be identified with lexical units considerably exceeding, by the number of their consonants, that of the typical Arabic root (see §3 in what precedes), as in the following internationally circulating terms: *transistor* (*trānzistar*; S, 57), *galvanometer* (*galvānūmitr*; S, 67), *television* (*tilivisyōn*; W, 96), etc. Besides, they frequently coincide with shorter units that however display word patterns too dissimilar to the native stock, as in the French *mademoiselle* (*madmwāzel*; S, 61) "mademoiselle", *colonel* (*kolonēl*; S, 61) "colonel", *maréchal* (*mārišāl*; S, 61) "marshal", or in the Italian *consulato* (*qunṣulātū*; W, 792) "consulate", *maestro* (*māyistrō*; W, 889) "maestro, conductor", and the like.

7.1.1 The capability of nonresegmentable borrowings for producing derivatives is very limited. Being treated as one-morpheme units, pattern modifications cannot be used either as derivational or inflectional markers. Accordingly, the affix-based derivation and inflection is the only possible one. The set of derivational affixes which can operate independently of pattern modifications is rather limited. The most frequently occurring affixes are represented by the following suffixes:

(1) the relative adjective (*nisba*) suffix -*ī*, as well as its inflected forms, e.g. *tilifizyūnī* "television — (adj.)", as in *mursil tilifizyūnī* "television transmitter" (Kh, 611), *baṭṭ tilifizyūnī* "television broadcasting" (Kh, 611), or *tilifūnī (-iyya)* "telephone — (adj.), telephonic", as in *mukaṭṭif tilifūnī* "telephone condenser" (Kh, 610), *mukālama tilifūniyya* "telephone call" (Kh, 610), etc.

(1.1) In a number of instances, the *nisba* suffix -*ī*, as one element of the *zero/-ī* opposition, may signal the derivational relationship between the collective (CN) and unit nouns (UN), as in *(al-) 'amrīkān* (CN) "the Americans", as opposed to one single individual out of this ethnic whole, *'amrīkānī* (UN) "(an) American" (W, 28), by analogy with the native CN—UN pairs of the latter type, like *'ins* (CN) "man (as a generic term), mankind, human race" vs. *'insī* (UN) "human; human being" (W, 30) or *jund* (CN) "soldiers; army" vs. *jundī* (UN) "soldier, private" (W, 613), etc.

It should be noted, however, that a quite independent inflectional relationship does co-occur with the derivational CN — UN system:

'amrīkānī (singular) "American" — *'amrīkāniyyūn* (plural) "(the) Americans" (W, 28)[14] etc.;

(2) the *nisba*-abstract suffix *-iyya,* used to produce abstract nouns from the *nisba* adjectives, as in:

'ūtūmātīkiyya "automatism; automatic device", derived from *'ūtūmātīkī* "automatic" (Bar., 49; since no Romanized transcription is available, both examples have been rewritten from Arabic), by analogy with the native coinages like *māddiyya* "materialism" (from *māddī* "material; materialistic"), *ḏātiyya* "subjectivism" (from *ḏātī* "subjective; subjectivist"), etc. Or else, the suffix *-iyya* may simply be applied as a regular and quite nonspecific substantivizer, as in *qunṣul* "consul" — *qunṣulī* "consular" — *qunṣuliyya* "consulate" (W, 792), etc.;

(3) the suffix *-a,* a derivational-and-inflectional marker associated with the *zero/-a* opposition as its constitutive element. As a derivational marker, it signals the membership of a noun in the derivational class of unit nouns, as against that of collectives, singalled by the *zero*-marker. As an inflectional marker, it signals the feminine gender class membership, as against the *zero*-marked masculines. Some examples:

sardīn (CN) — *sardīna* (UN) "sardine(s)" (B, 114: *sardīnah*);

'asbirīn (S, 47: *'aspirīn*) (CN) "aspirin" — *'asbirīna* (UN) "a single pill of aspirin" (B, 114: *'asbirīnah*), etc.

These and similar examples are modelled on the native CN—CN pairs, like:

waraq (CN) "foliage, leafage, leaves" — *waraqa* (UN) "leaf" (W, 1062), or:

naml (CN) "ant(s)" — *namla* (UN) "(an) ant" (W, 1001), etc.[15]

7.1.2 A number of hasty borrowings belonging to this class had a truly ephemeral existence and have long since been supplanted by native creations, like *mūtūr* (S, 79: *mōṭōr*) *'āryāksyūn* (K, 21), from the French *moteur à réaction,* "jet engine", now *muḥarrik naffāṯ* (the native coinage *naffāṯ* substitutes for the French-based borrowing since 1944 (K, 21)).

On the other hand, a number of clearly unassimilable borrowings of this class tend to persist, especially when used in the nontechnical language, e.g. *mītrdūtīl* (B, 111), from the French *maître d'hôtel,* "steward, hotel manager"; *rūb dīšambr* (B, 111), from the French *robe de chambre,* "morning gown", etc.

7.1.3 A number of borrowings, belonging to this class, despite their world-wide spread and well-established place in Modern Written Arabic, do not seem to produce any derivatives, as may be seen in the Russian origin term *bulšafīk* (Russian *bolshevik*), treated as a collective noun, "Bolsheviks, Bolshevists". The corresponding unit noun, which in this type of the CN — UN relationship is signalled by the

---

[14] Sa'id, alternatively, qualifies both pairs as members of a singular — plural relationship (p. 76).

[15] The phenomenon may be detected in colloquial variants of Arabic, too. In Takrūna Arabic (a rural variety of Tunisian Arabic), for instance, we have the following CN — UN pair: *kebbār* (CN) "capers; caper shrubs" — *kebbāra* (UN) "one single unit of the latter" (T 7, 3362). From the Greek *kapparis,* probably by way of Italian.

nisba suffix *-ī*, is related to another derivational basis, viz. *balšaf-* (of *balšaf-a* "Bolshevizing; Bolshevism"), producing in this way *balšafī* (UN) "Bolshevist; Bolshevist, Bolshevik", hence also *balšafiyya*, synonymously related to *balšafa*, "Bolshevizing; Bolshevism" (Bar., 83).

The latter type of loan derivatives, as illustrated by the series of examples just quoted, is based on the process of resegmentation and root abstraction and, accordingly, belongs to another class of borrowings which is treated in §7.2 in what follows.

It should be noted that the abstracted quadri-consonantal root **b-l-š-f*, obtained by the process of elision of /k/ of the underlying loanform *bulšafīk*, permits the use of the inflectionally relevant pattern modification to mark the plural, e.g. *balšafī* (sing.) — *balāšifa* (plur., co-occurring with the suffix-marked plural *balšafiyyūn*) (Bar., 83).

7.1.4 Similar distinction between unsegmented and segmented formations is of a relatively frequent occurrence in the inflectional domain of number marking where it usually displays the following pattern:

singular: one-morpheme thematic segment,
plural: two-morpheme thematic segment.

The following examples have to account for this structural discrepancy:

faylasūf (singular) "philosopher", at this stage non-resegmentable, as against:

falāsifa (plural), resegmentable into a quadri-consonantal root **f-l-s-f*, obtained by a shortening of the number of consonants of the underlying loanform, and a plural pattern *CaCāCiCa*, by analogy with the (mostly foreign-origin) quadri-consonantals, like *'ustāḏ*, plur. *'asātiḏa* "master; teacher; professor" or *tilmīḏ*, plur. *talāmiḏa* (co-occurring with another plural pattern, viz *talāmīḏ*) "pupil, student; disciple", etc.

Similarly:

kardīnāl, plur. *karādila* "cardinal" (W, 808);

tarjumān, plur. *tarājīm*, *tarājima* "translator, interpreter" (W, 93), etc.

7.2 Resegmentable borrowings, by their structural properties, sharply contrast with the class of borrowings just examined. Owing to their capability for morphemic resegmentation, they present the highest possible degree of word-formational assimilation of foreign-origin lexical elements to the word-formational patterns of Arabic, as well as their adaptation to the native scheme of their inflectional behaviour.

The class of what we call resegmentable borrowings may be subdivided into two distinct subclasses:

7.2.1 Borrowings in the proper sense of the term, technically identifiable with loanforms (see §4), are resegmentable on the strength of an accidental, complete or nearly complete overlap of their word-formational patterns, as occurring both in the donor and the recipient language, for derivational and/or inflectional purposes. With

140

the present type of loanforms, the procedure of resegmentation may be presented as consisting of:

(i) root abstraction, and

(ii) pattern identification (with one of the set of native word-formational and/or inflectional patterns); e.g.:

film, plur. *'aflām* "film" (obviously, a from-English-to-Arabic oriented borrowing), resegmentable in terms of

(i) root abstraction: **f-l-m*, and

(ii) pattern identification with the native *CiCC*, possibly pluralized by means of a pattern modification, viz. *CiCC — 'aCCāC,* as in *fꜥl*, plur. *'afꜥāl* "deed, act, action"; *milḥ*, plur. *'amlāḥ, milāḥ* "salt", ro *milk*, plur. *'amlāk* "possession", etc. (For more evidence see §2(2) in what precedes.)

Since the processes of derivation and inflection are substantially identical with those associated with the far more productive class of loan derivatives, they will be shortly described with the latter type of borrowings in what follows.

7.2.2 Borrowings, displaying a combination of borrowed roots with native word-formational and/or inflectional patterns, are by most recent authors identified with the class of loan derivatives (cf. S, 109). With loan derivatives, the process of resegmentation has its starting point in the foreign term or one of its regularly numerous Arabic reflexes which are based on morphemic transfer with inclusion, however, of various combinations of phonological elements due to transfer and/or substitution, as in the French term *télévision* or one of its numerous morphonological reflexes in Arabic, e.g. *tilivisyōn, tilifizyōn* (B, 115). At this stage, similar terms behave as one-morpheme units. As a preliminary procedure, prior to the very process of resegmentation, a phonological and morphological adaptation should take place. For purposes of the present inquiry, the most important preliminary procedure is the consonant sequence shortening whenever the unit to be resegmented exceeds, by the number of its consonants, that of the most favoured (from the point of view of loan derivation) quadri-consonantal root in Arabic: **t-l-f-z*, in relation to the example quoted above.[16]

The genuine process of resegmentation, as associated with loan derivatives, may be presented as involving the following procedures:

(i) root abstraction (borrowed element): **t-l-f-z*, for the example quoted, and

(ii) pattern assignment (native element), by analogy with patterns belonging to the native stock as well as with the derivational and/or inflectional values they display, e.g.:

*t-l-f-z combined with the pattern *CaCCaCa: talfaza* "television" (W, 96), possibly producing even external derivatives, e.g. the relative adjective *talfazī*

---

[16] Here, the extent of phonological variation is drastically reduced by maximizing the substitution phenomena (here the elimination of the variant with voiced labio-dental spirant /v/).

"television (adj.)", as in *'iḏā͑a talfaziyya* "television broadcast, telecast" (ibid.), contrasting with what we call non-resegmented derivative *tilifizyūnī* (cf. 7.1.1 (1) above), or

*t-l-f-z combined with the pattern *CaCCaCa* (generating perfective verbs from quadri-consonantal roots): *talfaza* "to televise, transmit by television" (W, 96), or

*t-l-f-z combined with the verbal noun pattern of quadri-consonantals *CiCCāC*: *tilfāz* "television set" (W, 96; Kh, 610), here apparently reinterpreted in terms of *nomina instrumenti* by the impact of a remote analogy with the instrumental pattern *miCCāC* (cf. also S, 96), as in *miftāḥ* "key", derivationally related to *fataḥa* "to open", etc.

7.2.2.1 Loan derivatives drawn from tri-consonantal roots:

(1) *CaCCaCa*, producing perfective verbs of a denominative background (here); the apparent quadri-consonantal type of the root is due to the gemination of the middle root-constituting consonant, e.g.:

nammara (seemingly from the Fr. *numéro*) "to mark with numbers, to number" (W, 1000; M, 158; K, 103; S, 93: *nammaṛ*);

maṭṭar (Fr. *métro*; locally used by the Algerians living in Paris; M, 158; K, 104) "to travel by subway";

tarran (Fr. *train*; locally used by the Algerians in Paris; M, 158; K, 104) "to travel by train";

ġawwaza (from *ġāz* "gas"), re-etymologized in terms of a nonexisting root *ġ-w-z*, "to gasify" (S, 92; K, 104; Kh, 247);

kawwaka (from *kūk* "coke") "to coke" (K, 104; Kh, 103), etc.

(2) *taCaCCaCa*, a reflexive variant of the latter, e.g.:

taġawwaza "to gasify (intr.)" (Kh, 247), etc.

(3) *taCCīC*, a verbal noun pattern related to the verbal pattern *CaCCaCa*, e.g.:

tanmīr "numbering, numeration, count" (W, 1000; S, 93);

taġwīz "gasification" (Kh, 247; S, 92);

takwīk "coking" (Kh, 103; K, 104), as in *waḥdat at-takwīk* "coker", lit. "coking unit" (Kh, 103); etc.

(4) *taCaCCuC*, a verbal noun pattern related to the verbal pattern *taCaCCaCa*, e.g.:

taġawwuz "gasification" (as a spontaneous process, as against *taġwīz*, implying a man-stimulated process) (Kh, 247); etc.

(5) *CaCCāCa*, a nominal pattern mostly denoting instrumentality, e.g.:

nammāra "numberer, numbering machine, date stamp" (W, 1000), by analogy with the native derivatives molded on this pattern, like *sayyāra* "car", *ġassāla* "washing machine", *ṭayyāra* "airplain, aircraft", etc.

Etc.

7.2.2.2 Loan derivatives drawn from quadri-consonantal roots:

(1) *CaCCaCa*, generating perfective quadri-consonantal verbs, as in:

talfana "to telephone" (W, 96; S, 90; etc.);

fabraka "to fabricate, manufacture" (M, 158);

maġnaṭa "to magnetize" (W, 916; M, 158);

farnasa "to make French, Frenchify" (W, 710; M, 158; S, 93);

ṭalyana "to Italianize" (S, 93);

'amraka "to Americanize" (S, 93);

bastara "to pasteurize" (Kh, 432);

balmara "to polymerize" (Kh, 456; K, 101);

baltana "to platinize" (Kh, 451; K, 101);

karbana "to carbonize" (Kh, 81; K, 101);

'aksada "to oxidize, cause to rust" (W, 21; Kh, 425);

kalwara "to chlorinate" (Kh, 92; K, 101);

saynada "to cyanide" (K, 101);

galfana (Egyptian reading) "to galvanize" (W, 131; Kh, 245: *ġalvana*), etc.

(2) *CaCCaCa* (*CaCCaCatun*, in a contextual presentation); a verbal noun pattern related to the preceding one, e.g.:

'amraka "Americanization" (S, 93);

bastara "pasteurization" (Kh, 432);

karbana "carbonization"; *waḥdat karbana* "carbonizing plant" (Kh, 81);

'aksada "oxidation, oxidization" (Kh, 425); etc.

(3) *taCaCCaCa*, a reflexive verbal pattern related to *CaCCaCa*, e.g.:

ta'amraka "to become Americanized, adopt the American way of life" (W, 27; S, 96: "to act like an American");

ta'aksada "to oxidize, rust, become rusty" (W, 21; Kh, 425), etc.

(4) *taCaCCuC*, a verbal noun pattern related to *taCaCCaCa*, e.g.:

ta'amruk "Americanization" (W, 27; S, 96: "the act of getting Americanized");

ta'aksud "oxidation, oxidization (intr.)", cf. *mānīᶜ at-ta'aksud* "oxidation inhibitor (Chem.)" (Kh, 425), etc.

(5) *CiCCāC*, e.g.: *tilfāz* (see § 7.2.2 in what precedes);

(6) *muCaCCid,* an active participle pattern derivationally related to the verbal pattern *CaCCaCa*, e.g.:

mu'aksid "oxidant" (Kh, 424); "oxidizer" (Kh, 425); cf. *ᶜāmil mu'aksid* "oxidizing agent" (Kh, 425), etc.

(7) *muCaCCaC*, a corresponding passive participle pattern, e.g.:

mubastar "pasteurized" (S, 95);

mukarban "carbonized" as in: *fūlāḏ mukarban* "carbonized steel" (Kh, 81);

mu'aksaj (from *'uksijīn* "oxygen") "oxygenated" (Kh, 425), etc.

(8) *mutaCaCCiC*, a participial pattern related to *taCaCCaCa*, e.g.:

muta'aksid "oxidized", in e.g. *xām muta'aksid* "oxidized ore" (Kh, 425), etc.
Etc.

8. In accordance with the classificatory criteria adopted and the documentary

143

evidence adduced, the two available models of derivation (and, of course, inflection, even if the latter is not represented to the full in the present study) may be presented as interlinked with the main classes of modern borrowings into Arabic as follows:

8.1 Simple model of derivation, coinciding with an extra-root (affix-marked) procedure, as in *tilifizyūn* + *ī* = *tilifizyūnī* "television (adj.)", or *'asbirīn* + *a* = *'asbirīna* "a single pill of aspirin", etc., is related to the class of what we call nonresegmentable borrowings, technically identifiable with loangforms.

8.2 Complex model of derivation (and, of course, inflection), infolving both intra-root (pattern-marked) and extra-root (affix-marked) procedures, as in *talfazī* "television (adj.)":

(i) internal procedure:

*t-l-f-z plus *CaCCaCa* = *talfaza* "television", and

(ii) external procedure:

talfaz(a) + *ī* = *talfazī* "television (adj.)", should be related to the class of borrowings we call resegmentables. The latter consists of a limited number of loanforms which accidentally coincide with some of the native word-patterns or at least closely follow them, as in *film* "film", *qunṣul* "consul", and with the relatively massive subclass of loan derivatives, the number of which is rapidly increasing from day to day.

ABBREVIATIONS

B — Belkin, V. M.: *Arabskaya leksikologiya* (Arabic Lexicology). Moscow, Izdatelstvo Moskovskogo Universiteta 1975.

Bar. — Baranov, Kh. K.: *Arabsko-russkii slovar* (Arabic-Russian Dictionary). 5th ed. Moscow, Izdatelstvo 'Russkii yazyk' 1976.

D — Doniach, N. S.: *The Oxford English-Arabic Dictionary of Current Usage.* Oxford, Calrendon Press 1972.

Dozy — Dozy, R.: *Supplément aux dictionaires arabes.* I—II. 2nd ed. Leide—Paris, E. J. Brill-Maisonneuve Frères 1927.

K — Krahl, G.: *Die technischen und wissenschaftlichen Termini im modernen Arabisch — eine Untersuchung zur arabischen Wortbildung.* Inauguraldissertation, Leipzig 1967 (mimeographed).

Kh — Al-Khatib, Ahmed Sh.: *A New Dictionary of Scientific and Technical Terms. English-Arabic.* Beirut, Librairie du Liban 1971.

M — Monteil, V.: *L'arabe moderne.* Paris, Librairie C. Klincksieck 1960.

S — Sa'id, Majed F.: *Lexical Innovation Through Borrowing in Modern Standard Arabic.* Princeton University 1967.

Sch. — Schregle, G.: *Deutsch-Arabisches Wörterbuch* (German-Arabic Dictionary). Wiesbaden, Otto Harrassowitz 1963—1974.

T — Marçais, W. — Guïga, A.: *Textes arabes de Takroūna,* II. *Glossaire.* Fasc. I—VIII. Paris, Librairie orientaliste Paul Geuthner 1958—1961. The extremely involved allophonic transcription is here considerably simplified.

W — Wehr, H.: *A Dictionary of Modern Written Arabic.* Edited by J. M. Cowan. Wiesbaden, Otto Harrassowitz 1971. The English equivalents are given either in full or in somewhat reduced quotations. The transcription is slightly modified in accordance with the system of writing adopted in the present paper.

MODERN ASIAN LITERATURES: TOWARDS A POTENTIAL COMPARATIVE APPROACH TO THEIR STUDY

MARIÁN GÁLIK, Bratislava

This article is devoted to a potential project to study modern Asian literatures within an international framework using the systemo-structural approach.

Comparative study of Asian literatures has its own history. Oriental literatures constituted in part the starting point and the base on which foremost Soviet comparatists, for example, V. M. Zhirmunsky or N. I. Konrad, set up their theoretical works.[1] Until now, however, little if any attention has been devoted to operative theory directly applicable in practice that would help to overcome that "marking of time" so characteristic at present of international cooperation of orientalists-comparatists. It would contribute to an achievement of "minimum of agreement on methodology" of which Professor D. W. Fokkema wrote in his letter of 2nd December, 1976 addressed to the participants of the Eighth Congress of the International Comparative Literature Association (Association Internationale de Littérature Comparée) interested in Asian and African literatures.[2] Precisely this "minimum of agreement", along with a bold direction, a setting up of problems and an organizational work might become one of the guarantees of crossing the Rubicon.

Before that, however, two problems should be pointed out. The first refers to the realizers of this activity, its organizational forms, and the other to the methodics of study (methodics is mentioned here because Comparative Literature has no methodology of its own, it shares the latter in common with the general theory of

[1] Zhirmunsky, V. M.: *Epicheskoe tvorchestvo slavyanskikh narodov i problemy sravnitelnogo izucheniya eposa* (The Epic Creation of the Slavic Nations and the Problems of a Comparative Study of the Epos). Moscow 1958; *K voprosu o literaturnykh otnosheniyakh Vostoka i Zapada* (On the Questions of Literary Relations Between East and West). Vestnik Leningradskogo universiteta, 4, 1947, pp. 100—119; *Literaturnye otnosheniya Vostoka i Zapada v svete sravnitelnogo literaturovedeniya* (Literary Relations Between East and West in the Light of Comparative Literature). Leningradskii gosudarstvennyi universitet. Trudy yubileinoi nauchnoi sessii, sektsiya filologicheskikh nauk, 1946, pp. 152—178. Konrad, N. I.: *Problemy sovremennogo sravnitelnogo literaturovedeniya* (Problems of Contemporary Literary Studies). In: *Zapad i Vostok* (West and East). Moscow 1966, pp. 348—364; *O literaturnom posrednike* (On the Literary Intermediary), ibid., pp. 348—364; *Problemy realizma i literatury Vostoka* (The Problems of Realism and Oriental Literatures), ibid., pp. 304—331.

[2] Cf. also Neohelicon, *5*, 1977, No. 1, pp. 283—284.

literature, it only has certain research procedures, its own "methodics"). The first problem will here be dealt briefly, the second one in more detail.

1

During the past quarter of this century we have been the witnesses and often also the participants of various international projects. In the contemporary world international scientific projects (ISP) as efficient means of dealing with the most diverse issues of a scientific, technological and cultural character, have come to be accepted as a matter of course. If modern Asian literatures (MAL) are thought of as a possible ISP, then sets of certain factors restricting our work have to be done away with. These exist, firstly, in the domain of information exchange (weak or no contacts at all among scholars working in this area, inadequate bibliographic knowledge, insufficient equipment with books and source references); secondly, in the domain of coordination (the latter has not as yet been initiated as regards modern Asian literatures, and is in the embryonic stage in the field of chronologically nondifferentiated Asian literatures).

These factors have to be removed if a truly effective project is to be set up and later also agreed upon. This may be partially achieved in the form of symposia, conferences and, if no other possibility exists, then also through a rational utilization of various international and national congresses and meetings. Numerous items of information may be mediated through other channels, for instance, in bulletins, international directories, etc., further through an effective exchange of offprints, reviews and review articles. Much can be done through a purposeful initiative, a survey of possibilities, abilities and good will of various centres. Coordinating limitations will not be removed without effective interventions of an operative nature. A prerequisite of success of every ISP is the existence of an international committee, further of a guiding centre, one that would be capable quantitatively (number of researchers) and qualitatively (methodical drive, knowledge, overall equipment) to carry the burden of the project and win the confidence of those involved.

Optimum results of each ISP depend on the possibility of removing the above limiting factors. Much depends, of course, also on the ISP itself, the form of its organization, its systemo-structural arrangement, its variability. It is assumed that ISP/MAL ought to have a clearly defined object of investigation, aim (or aims) of investigation, methodics, elements, relationships between them, and its operative code. The elements at the "man-man" level should be efficient teams, eventually individuals; at the "object-object" level the various Asian and other literatures or other comparative phenomena as parts of MAL. Individual tasks ought to be dealt with at centres ensuring their optimum solution. The work ought to be directed by an international committee responsible for setting up the tasks, their control, the required corrections in the style of work; of course, everything in agreement with the teams or individuals participating in the project.

Since only optimum results of every ISP or such as come close to this ideal are decisive, it would be desirable, if this international effort is to have its *raison d'être,* that certain fundamental principles be satisfied: Firstly, a minimum representation of various countries or of such that investigate modern literatures of individual Asian countries (i.e. all important Asian literatures should be followed at the time of their modernization, and later as qualitatively new literatures; further representatives of various countries should be engaged in this study); secondly, a minimum information exchange ought to be ensured (among various ISP/MAL elements, then between the main centre and the international committee); thirdly, there should be at least a minimum "agreement on methodics" of the study; there should be a minimum technico-economic base required for the acquisition of necessary materials, books, journals, possibilities of publishing; and finally, care should be taken to ensure an efficient "feedback". This last should be in the hands of the coordinating centre in cooperation with the international committee and should reside in an operative briefing on the state of the project, in the required corrections of the style of work (methodical model) and in scientific "service" which should be provided to the various elements participating in the project.[3]

2

Every methodics assumes an object of investigation, its optimum range corresponding to the aim and possibilities. In the case of MAL, the above principle of minimum representation would be satisfied if a larger number of Asian literatures were studied during the period of their modernization, the rise and the development of new Asian literatures during the second half of the last and the first half of the present century. Literatures that would come into consideration are the following: Chinese, Japanese, Indian (particularly Bengalese and Hindu), Iranian, Turkish, eventually some others.

"The origin of literary comparative study is related to an endeavour to know the literary process within a wider interliterary context and the appropriate development of literary history. This has led to a 'crossing of boundaries' of any national literature and to an investigation of relationships and affinities ..., and in the final consequence, to an investigation of world literature."[4]

---

[3] Povzner, A. D.: *Mezhdunarodnyi nauchnyi proekt kak sistema* (International Scientific Project as System). In: *Sistemnye issledovaniya* (Systems Research). Moscow 1977, pp. 91—103.

[4] Ďurišin, D.: *Teória literárnej komparatistiky* (Theory of Comparative Literature). Bratislava 1975, p. 56. Cf. also his argumentation in the book *Sources and Systematics of Comparative Literature.* Bratislava 1974, pp. 113—122 or in the book *Vergleichende Literaturforschung.* Berlin, Akademie-Verlag 1972, pp. 23—46.

This "crossing", however, should not be an end in itself, and in the methodics we intend to propose here, it should not constitute the only mode of the study. The ultimate aim of every literary research is a knowledge of the genesis and essence of the literary phenomena, the inner laws of literature, and the most diverse relationships between the literary context and all the other contexts into which a literary work enters, could provide an aid to this knowledge. It is hardly correct to lay emphasis on the idea that the object of Comparative Literature is beyond the confines of one particular country,[5] hence, investigation is directed solely to interliterary relationships and affinities (i.e. those existing between various national literatures) leaving aside a study of intraliterary (national literary) relationships and affinities. As in the case of a comparative study of literature in general, so also with MAL, the object of investigation will be various genetic-contact relationships (of interliterary and intraliterary origin) and various typological affinities. In either case, the dialectical tension existing between the inter- and intra- may be to the advantage of literary research. A thorough knowledge of the inner relationships and affinities presumes a knowledge of the external impact, and the other way round; external relationships and affinities make possible a thorough comprehension of the inner response.

The aim of investigation of MAL will be a reconstruction of the modernization process of old Asian literatures, the rise and development of modern Asian literatures, a deeper insight into the specificity of the literary process or laws of these literatures, and finally, a determination of their place in the development of world literature. The first part of this aim is the more pressing and the more actual. Asian literatures are among the least known in the world. The subsequent parts of the aim designed to follow up the specificity of the contributions by modern Asian literatures (in their relation among themselves and to other, for instance, European literatures) to the literary process and to world literature, can be responsibly dealt with only in connection with the first part of the above aim.

Modern Asian literatures as an inseparable part-and-parcel of world literature — and with regard to it — have gone through the so-called "accelerated development". The reasons for this are to be looked for in the typical genetic-contact relations, the typological affinities of various kinds connected to or existing in parallel with the ideologically more effective and socially more operative literature of the West; or in such parts of modern Asian literatures that had passed earlier through the modernizing processes or the first stages of the rise and development; further in the emphasis on the socio-political and other functions of literature. This development should be looked upon also as the outcome of a sudden intensive Western impact in various spheres of social consciousness, socio-political conditions

---

[5] E.g. Remak, H. H. H.: *Comparative Literature. Its Definition and Function.* In: Stallknecht, N. P. — Frenz, H. (Eds): *Comparative Literature. Method and Perspective.* Carbondale 1971, p. 1.

prevailing at various periods, ideological climate, economic possibilities, etc. This process should be studied in regard to the different power of the indigenous literary traditions, norms and functions.[6]

An optimum study of the material context spoken of in the preceding passage will provide the necessary basis for a study of the literary context with the aid of methodics of national and comparative studies. The former will not be taken up here. The methodics of Comparative Literature will have to be applied first to the study of the so-called external contacts: bio-bibliographical data on literary relations, various reports, references, various studies of foreign literatures, reviews, notes, and sometimes also translations of literary works if they possess an "informational function" only and organically do not fit "into the contemporary endeavours of the receiving literature". Note will here have to be taken of what is occasionally spoken of as *mirage* (image), further of the "transmitters" of the most diverse kinds. This group of phenomena is usually spoken of as reception or *Wirkung*.[7]

In addition, the internal contacts will have to be investigated, that is, those that may have affected the structure of the receiving literature in the most various aspects. This is often termed "influence studies".[8] Influence may be defined as an objectification of very many kinds of the successful stimuli applicable to the recipient systemo-structural entities and enabling their new originality in literature under impact. The various forms of these internal contacts may be divided into integrating (reminiscence, borrowing, similarity, paraphrase, allusion) or differentiating (parody, travesty).

The intense interest in translation, its theory and utilization in historical practice ought to be manifest also in the work of MAL, for these literatures could hardly have been possible without the mediating function of translation (or frequently of translation-adaptation).

Typological affinities are an important part of modern comparative studies and partially intervene into what we have termed: material context. By this we have in mind principally socio-typological analogies, similarities, but also divergencies, due to the enormous Euro-American impact in the economic and political domain which prevailed during many decades of a colonial or semicolonial domination, further to cultural (philosophical, ideological, religionist) impact finding a broad and deep response in the literary realm: i.e. in the relation towards traditional cultures, in an accelerated development and accelerated periodization, in genological "re-hierarchization", in the advent of journalism, literary periodicals, professional writers, in

---

[6] Cf. *Contributions to the Study of the Rise and Development of Modern Literatures in Asia*. Vols 1—3. Prague, Academia 1965—1970.

[7] Weisstein, U.: *Comparative Literature and Literary Theory. Survey and Introduction*. Blomington—London, Indiana University Press 1973, pp. 48—65.

[8] Ibid., pp. 29—47.

efforts to link up with the European and American literary development, in literary "evolutionism", and later, under the impact of the Great October Socialist Revolution, the Soviet literature and literary criticism, often with proletarian literature, and under the influence of Western literature, with modernist tendencies.

Literary-typological or structual-typological affinities are part of the literary context. Insofar as MAL is concerned, developmental trends in our century come principally into consideration and they comprise the most diverse questions from the domain of poetics, genology and stylistics, periodization, relations to literary traditions and to the most varied aesthetic issues.

A study of external contacts in MAL should primarily contribute towards a deeper understanding of the internal relationships, and a study of socio-typological analogies towards a better comprehension of literary-typological analogies. This would provide the preconditions for an internal, systemo-structural investigation which is methodologically the most adequate.

MAL (as a form of ISP) may have solely the character of a working hypothesis, a variable model, constantly subject to adjustments and corrections, as may be required by the "feedback" referred to above.

●

Much was done in the domain of Comparative literature in Soviet Oriental studies until the year 1975.[9] This work is being further pursued.[10] Something similar may be said of the efforts by American Orientalists. The Indiana Conferences on Oriental-Western Literary Relations have been held regularly since 1954. American Orientalists present papers at the triennal meetings of the American Comparative Literature Association (ACLA). The section known as Literature East-West is an intrinsic part of these conferences. Sinologists are unusually active here. Of the fifteen papers with orientalist themes presented at the Sixth Triennal Meeting of the ACLA in April 1977, eight dealt with relations between Chinese literature and literatures of other nations.[11] At the Eighth AILC/ICLA Congress in Budapest in 1976, one of the three main subjects was concerned with problems of relations between new literatures of the twentieth century and Western literatures. This involved primarily literatures of

---

[9] Cf. Gálik, M.: *Comparative Literature in Soviet Oriental Studies.* Neohelicon, *3,* 1975, Nos. 3—4, pp. 285—301.

[10] The following books are at least partly of comparative character: Belova, K. A. (Ed.): *Literatury zarubezhnoi Azii v sovremennuyu epokhu* (Contemporary Foreign Asian Literatures). Moscow 1975; *Sovetskaya literatura i literatury zarubezhnoi Azii* (Soviet Literature and Foreign Asian Literatures). Moscow 1977, and *Literatura Vostoka v noveishee vremya* (Contemporary Oriental Literatures). Moscow 1977.

[11] Cf. the programme of the meeting.

Asia and Africa. During the past few years, Research Conferences on Comparative East Asian Literatures began to be organized; the first such conference was held in 1973 at Bloomington.

Several comparative journals are published at the present time devoted predominantly to problems of East-West literary relations, or to these same problems among Asian countries. Several issues of journals were taken up principally by contributions of this kind, and of course, proceedings from special conferences have also appeared.[12] A valuable work, currently available is *An Annotated Bibliography of English, American and Comparative Literature for Chinese Scholars*, Taipei 1975, which also carries items relating to other Asian, mainly Japanese, literatures. Much space is devoted to Oriental literatures and their relation to these of the Western world also in Etiemble's book, now in its third edition, *Essais de littérature (vraiment) générale*, Paris 1975.

All in all, however, it could not be said, at least not for the time being, that the conditions would be ripe for a wider, purposeful cooperation in this field either on a national or an international scale. But step by step, they will be created. These reflections might perhaps be of help to those who may opt for a similar undertaking.

---

[12] Weisstein, U.: op. cit., pp. 278 and 281.

SUGGESTIONS REGARDING PERIODIZATION OF LITERATURE IN THE PEOPLE'S REPUBLIC OF CHINA

ANNA DOLEŽALOVÁ, Bratislava

The specific conditions of literary development in the People's Republic of China require that suitable criteria be set up for its periodization. As the most adequate, we may consider the criteria of China's cultural policy directly related to the country's political development and on this basis, three principal stages of literary development in the PRC may be set up.

Attempts at setting up periodic landmarks in the development of Chinese literature after the year 1949 make it manifest that none of the conventional criteria deriving from the inner laws of literary development can be effectively applied here, as extraliterary factors, campaigns with an extraliterary background, repeatedly intervened into this developmental process in the PRC. During the greater part of this period, literary production was directively controlled and its function confined to that of a direct tool for propagating predetermined ideas, concepts and political aims. The role of literature as an analyser of social tendencies and an emotional educator of an all-round, harmonic personality, came to be negated.

In a situation when literary production is governed by demands that either partially or totally ignore the fundamental and irreplaceable characteristics of literature and lay emphasis solely on the imposed politico-propaganda function, these circumstances must naturally be taken into account when searching for criteria of periodic landmarks. An analysis of the problems relating to periodization shows that in the case of literature of the PRC, the most adequate criteria are those of the cultural policy which, in turn, consistently follows and expressively illustrates the peripeteia in the political development of the PRC.

More complex works on Chinese literature after the year 1949 are but modestly represented in sinologic literature. Such are, for instance, books by Soviet authors — L. Z. Eidlin *O kitaiskoi literature nashikh dnei* (On Contemporary Chinese Literature), Moscow 1955, dealing with prose and drama up to the year 1955 and the book by I. M. Nadeev "*Kulturnaya revolyutsiya*" *i sudba kitaiskoi literatury* ("Cultural Revolution" and the Fate of Chinese Literature), Moscow 1969, comprising the period up to the "Cultural Revolution"; the concluding part of *A History of Modern Chinese Fiction 1917—1957* by C. T. Hsia (New Haven 1961), the work processed in the PRC *Chung-kuo hsien-tai wen-hsüeh shi* [1] History of Contemporary Chinese Literature — by a group of students and lecturers of the Peking University (Peking 1959) giving an overview of literary development in that

153

country up to the year 1958. These works are not concerned with questions of periodization. Joe C. Huang in his book *Heroes and Villains in Communist China* (London 1973) dealing with the novel in the PRC from before the "Cultural Revolution", divides novel writings solely according to the thematic aspect. A collection of biographies of 180 writers of the PRC, *Chung-kuo tang-tai tso-chia hsiao-chuang* [2] Concise Biographies of Contemporary Chinese Writers edited in Paris in 1976 by Lin Man-shu [3], Ch'en Hai [4] and Hai Feng [5], divides the writers into four generation groups: the first two groups comprise authors who began to publish at the time of the May Fourth Movement and in the thirties, the third group includes those who entered literature during the anti-Japanese war and the fourth those whose first works appeared after the foundation of the PRC.

At present, two fairly complex histories of literature of the PRC are available, in the introductions of which the authors also give some thought to questions of periodization. The Japanese sinologist Minoru Takeuchi in his book *Gendai Chūgoku no bungaku* (Contemporary Chinese Literature), Tokyo 1972, processed the history of literature of the years 1949—1970 and divides this period into four stages: I. the years 1949—1955 (the First and Second All-China Congress of Literary and Art Workers, Criticism of Hu Feng [6], the enforcement of Mao Tse-tung's line in literature); II. the years 1956—1959 (Hundred Flowers Campaign, Anti-Rightist Campaign, the People's Communes Movement, nomination of Liu Shao-ch'i President of the PRC); III. the years 1960—1964 ("liberalization and deliberalization" — consolidation of Liu Shao-ch'i's policy, the prevailing new policy towards literature, the demand of a description of the "middle-men", Wen-i shih-t'iao [7], Ten Points on Literature and Art, Mao Tse-tung's criticism of these tendencies); IV. the years 1965—1970 (proscribed writers and works based on the policy of preceding periods, the Cultural Revolution that ended in 1969; a new period, the fifth, begins with the year 1970). When comparing the first three periods, the author deems each to mean an advance over the preceding one.

The second extensive history of contemporary Chinese literature appeared in Paris in 1978 in Chinese under the title *Chung-kuo tang-tai wen-hsüeh shih kao* [8] *Histoire de la littérature en République populaire de Chine (1949—1965)*. The authors Lin Man-shu, Ch'en Hai and Hai Feng judge the problem as they themselves write in the preface, "from the standpoint of a struggle of realism and anti-realism, a struggle of revisionism and dogmatism" and subsequently delimitate and characterize three periods: I. the years 1949—1954, the application of Mao Tse-tung's views on literature and art and the first act of Hu Feng's disagreement with dogmatic literary and artistic theories; II. the years 1956—1957, the first wave of resistance against dogmatic literary and artistic theories; III. the years 1958—1965, the second wave of resistance against dogmatic literary and artistic theories (the authors give a fairly detailed account of the principal events of each of these periods). In practice this means that both these histories of literature of the

PRC apply cultural-political, political and ideological aspects in their periodization.

Questions of the cultural policy of the PRC, including its concrete application in the domain of literary thinking, are dealt with in a variety of monographs. Among the more complex are those by R. Mac Farquhar (the order is here given chronologically according to the year of publication) *The Hundred Flowers Campaign and the Chinese Intellectuals* (New York 1960), D. Fokkema *Literary Doctrine in China and Soviet Influence* (Hague 1965) for the period 1956—1960, M. Goldman *Literary Dissent in Communist China* (Cambridge, Mass. 1967) comprising the period up to the sixties, I. Bakešová *Kulturní politika komunistické strany Číny v letech 1942—1966* (Cultural Policy of the Communist Party of China in the years 1942—1966) (Prague 1968), L. S. Kyusadjan *Ideologicheskie kampanii v KNR* (Ideological Campaigns in the PRC) (Moscow 1970) for the period up to 1966, C. Johnson *Communist Policies Toward the Intellectual Class* (Hong Kong, first reprinting 1973) devoted to the period up to 1955, K. Dietsch *Der Weg der sozialistischen Literatur in China nach 1949* (Munich 1973) processing the years 1949—1966, and M. Markova *Maoizm i intelligentsiya. Problemy i sobytiya 1956—1973 gg.* (Maoism and the Intelligentsia. Problems and Events 1956—1973) (Moscow 1975). Problems relating to cultural policy are also comprised in the books referred to above devoted to the history of literature in the PRC and are analysed in a number of part studies. Recently, a book has appeared in Moscow entitled *Sudby kultury KNR 1949—1974 gg.* (Fate of Culture in PRC 1949—1974), the second part of which includes an extensive chapter devoted to the history of literature, while the first part dealing with issues of cultural policy is divided into three chapters: I. the years 1949—1956 (For a Socialist Way of Cultural Development), II. the years 1956—1965 (From 'Hundred Flowers' to 'Cultural Revolution'), III. the years 1965—1974 ('Cultural Revolution' and Its Consequences). With the exception of the authors of this collection, published in 1978, none of the others, cited above, had aimed to delimitate and specify the various periods of development. They assign the issues into a chronological sequence; at the same time, they mutually differ not only by their objectivity and scientism, but also by the interest and attention they devote to the various problems — which ultimately derives from their different methodological premises and approaches. In the collection on culture in the PRC during the period 1949—1969, now being prepared in Czechoslovakia, the year 1958 is taken as the periodic dividing line.

From an analysis of the development of cultural policy in the domain of literature, which is in logical harmony with the development of political and ideologic history of the PRC, an optimum division appears to me to be that into three periods. Naturally, a more detailed processing permits these to be further subdivided and may briefly be specified and characterized as follows:

I. The years 1949—1957. A period ushered in by the First All-China Congress of Literary and Art Workers. Up to approximately the year 1956, it is characterized in particular by efforts to create a Chinese socialist literature, taking contact principally with the Yen-an traditions and models of Soviet literature. In 1953, socialist realism was declared to be the fundamental creative method. The first campaigns relating to the film *Wu Hsün chuan* [9], The Story of Wu Hsün and the novel *Hung lou meng* [10] Dream of the Red Chamber, did embody indeed elements of the subsequently "improved" methods of campaignings, yet one could also note in them an effort at elucidating a new approach to a revaluation of national history and China's literary heritage. An evident turn in the nature and impact of the campaigns was signalized by the stupendous repressive campaign against Hu Feng. This was followed, without any great respite, by the adventurous policy of the Hundred Flowers Campaign. The original interpretation of the term *pai-hua* [11] as "*all* flowers",[1] came to be limited within a year by Mao Tse-tung's "six political criteria" (anchored in his work *Kuan-yü cheng-ch'üeh ch'u-li jen-min nei-pu mao-tun ti wen-t'i* [13] On the Correct Handling of Contradictions among the People), allowing diverse interpretations in practice. This first period was concluded by the Anti-Rightist Campaign. Several literary works of lasting value were created during this period and a number of literary discussions took place with the purpose of elucidating fundamental issues involved in literary creation.

II. The years 1958—1965. The creative method of socialist realism is replaced by the "method of combination of revolutionary realism and revolutionary romanticism" which is made to pass for Mao Tse-tung's original contribution to Marxist literary theory. Accent was laid on revolutionary romanticism which in practice, led to a moulding of idealized reality and an idealized man. Emphasis on features specifically Chinese began to be blatantly apparent also in the domain of literature, where the "Great Leap Forward" policy was likewise pursued, and great store was laid on amateur production. As a result of a weakening of Mao Tse-tung's prestige, brought about by the failure of the "Great Leap Forward" policy, works began to appear criticizing his policy, using some allegory. Renewed efforts were made to enrich literary production with theses about portraying middle-men, about the veracity of literature, etc., as well as with an extension of the compromising Ten Points on Literature and Art. As of 1962, Mao Tse-tung takes the offensive again. New ideals and models are vaunted.

This period was concluded by the "first shot of the 'cultural revolution'", Yao Wen-yüan's [14] attack on Wu Han's [15] play *Hai Jui pa kuan* [16] Hai Jui's

---

[1] To designate the campaigns, I use the expression Hundred Flowers which is generally current in English, though the term "pai-hua" was not always interpreted as "Hundred Flowers". See, e.g. the publication Lu Ting-i [12]: *Pust rastsvetayut vse tsvety, pust sopernichayut vse uchenye* (Let *All* Flowers Bloom, Let *All* Scholars Contend), published in Peking 1956, in Russian. The same speech by Lu Ting-i was published in English in Peking 1957 with a title Let Flowers of Many Kinds Blossom, Diverse Schools of Thought Contend!

Dismissal from Office. Besides several complex and conflicting discussions, this period has also left a few important literary works.

III. The period since the year 1966. It was initiated by the "Cultural Revolution", which in fact meant liquidation of literary creation and silencing of the great majority of literary authors. The "Summary of the Forum on the Work in Literature and Art in the Armed Forces with which Comrade Lin Piao Entrusted Comrade Chiang Ch'ing" became a programme document and artistic consumption became limited to so-called model plays. After the year 1972, a partial resumption of literary production took place, adhering strictly to political requirements. A pragmatic and utilitarian relation to literature and art became clearly evident, and this aspect was also the criterion for judging foreign works and the entire previous Chinese literature. Literary works and postulates from these years essentially have but an extraliterary value as documents of the period of their origin.

After Mao Tse-tung's death and the removal of the "Gang of Four", the most vulgarizing theses on literature and art were condemned, new approaches proclaimed in the interpretation of literary creation, and a number of writers and works became rehabilitated. The blame for all the erroneous theses and manipulations, from which the new leadership in cultural policy decided to distance itself, is ascribed to the "Gang of Four", particularly to Chiang Ch'ing and is alleged to be a consequence of their disobedience or distortion of Mao Tse-tung's line of conduct, Chou En-lai's directives, etc. The aim of these as yet insufficiently crystallized measures is a more effective enforcement of cultural-political designs of the new leadership of the PRC. Literary circles remain diffident and the novel situation has not as yet become reflected in literary production, as admitted by contemporary Chinese sources.[2]

A characteristic trait is the appraisal of the cultural policy of the PRC in China today. According to it, during the entire existence of the PRC, Mao Tse-tung's correct line generally prevailed also in the cultural policy despite the "harmful interventions of traitors". The press makes more global comments as regards the first two of the above periods, especially within the framework of its criticism of "the theory on the dictatorship of the black line in literature and art", by which Chiang Ch'ing and her adherents had condemned a seventeen-year-old development since the foundation of the PRC up to the "Cultural Revolution". The period of the fifties and early sixties is assessed as one of reinforcement of socialist revolution and a matching of strength between socialism and capitalism which was particularly virulent and complex in the domain of ideology, including culture. The years 1949—1955 are being described as a period of successful struggles in culture (here

---

[2] See, e.g. proceedings of the Committee Session of All-China Federation of Literary and Art Workers (Kuang-ming jih-pao [17] Bright Daily, 17th June 1978), an article by Tan Ch'i [18] in Jen-min jih-pao [19] People's Daily, 25th June 1978 and other sources.

are meant the campaigns since the criticism of the film The Story of Wu Hsün, up to the campaign against Hu Feng). The "Anti-Rightist Campaign" of the year 1957 is assessed as a decisive victory of the proletariat over the bourgeoisie, the Hundred Flowers Campaign and the "creative method of combination of revolutionary realism and revolutionary romanticism" are further made to pass for Mao Tse-tung's important contribution to a Marxist-Leninist theory of literature and art. The years 1961—1962 are presented as a period in which some "poisonous weeds" grew up in all the domains of literature and art. In the view of these Chinese authors, this was made possible by Liu Shao-ch'i's "revisionist line" that, according to them exploited temporary economic difficulties and, as they demagogically assert, profited by the "pressure" made on China "by Soviet revisionists" and caused a rightist step backwards. These "dangers", however, as is now often emphasized in the PRC, were pointed out in time by Mao Tse-tung at the Tenth Plenary Session of the Central Committee of the Chinese Communist Party in 1962, and in the directives of 1963 and 1964. That is how the contemporary Chinese press concludes its assessment of the cultural policy of the PRC before the "Cultural Revolution".[3] "Cultural Revolution" itself in the domain of literature, and the period of the seventies, from the end of 1976 receive, in fact, a negative evaluation in the PRC in connection with the criticism of the cultural policy of the "Gang of Four".

The development of literature in the PRC or its cultural policy in the domain of literature, bears evident marks of the social evolution in its whole complexity, and this in creative practice, theoretical postulates and ideological leadership. Concrete elements of the cultural-political development in the PRC as of an important part of its ideological evolution, reflect and often anticipate all the characteristic traits of the developmental process of the PRC's policy. It is only within the frame of reference of these aspects that I consider it possible to evaluate questions of periodization of the PRC's cultural policy in the domain of literature.

---

[3] In the whole of this passage I draw on an article by a group of the Department of Culture of the Principal Political Administration of the People's Liberation Army, published in Jen-min jih-pao, 6th February 1978.

1) 中国現代文学史　　2) 中國當代作家小傳

3) 林曼叔　　4) 程海　　5) 海楓　　6) 胡風

7) 文艺十条　　8) 中國當代文学史稿

9) 武訓傳　　10) 紅樓夢　　11) 百花　　12) 陸定一

13) 關於正確處理人民内部矛盾的問題

14) 姚文元　　15) 吳晗　　16) 海瑞罷官

17) 光明日报　　18) 丹赤　　19) 人民日报

THE PROBLEM OF MAN'S RELATION
TO SOCIETY IN THE WORKS
OF ERDAL ÖZ

XÉNIA CELNAROVÁ, Bratislava

The work of the contemporary Turkish writer, Erdal Öz (born 1935), rather small in extent, reflects the efforts of the Turkish petty bourgeois intellectuals to find their bearings in the complex social situation prevailing in their country during the past three decades. While in the writings from the fifties—sixties, Erdal Öz leaves the hopelessly lonely hero to stand aloof from all political events, in those from the early seventies he draws him into the maelstrom of social reality.

In 1975 Erdal Öz won the Orhan Kemal Literary Award[1] for his second novel *Yaralısın* (1974, You Are Wounded). In an interview given on the occasion of the presentation of this award, Erdal Öz admitted than in his very first short stories published in literary journals as far back as 1952, he endeavoured to imitate Orhan Kemal,[2] one of the foremost Turkish realists. However, the budding author's inclination to the so-called social realism as Turkish literary criticism chose to term his critical-realistic work touching on the most burning social issues of the day, proved to be but a transient phenomenon.

Erdal Öz entered literature at a time when open and, up to a measure, justified objections began to be heard from critics, his contemporaries, against *littérature engagée* written by representatives of the New Poetry and social realists, in which a trend towards schematism began to be apparent. Labelling such works as 'commissarial, descriptive and primitive', young poets and prosaists beginning to write in the fifties, advocated an introverted, introspective, apolitical type of literature, unrelated to the needs of society. Evasion of real problems, escape into a world of dreams, abstractness, absurdity, pessimism, experiments in the domain of language and form, these are the characteristic traits of the so-called new literature, also designated by the term *"bunalım"* (dejection). Fethi Naci, the literary critic, draws attention to these unhealthy tendencies in the development of Turkish literature right at the beginning when they were as yet in an incipient stage, with a note of anxiety. He understood right away that the origin of this "state of dejection

---

[1] The Orhan Kemal Prize, founded by his family in 1972, is awarded every year for a novel. A decisive criterion for awarding the prize is a social commitment of the work and a realistic processing.

[2] *Orhan Kemal ödülünü kazanan Erdal Öz* (Erdal Öz, Laureate of the Orhan Kemal Prize). In: Milliyet Sanat Dergisi (Istanbul), 1975, No. 134, p. 3.

and depression" in literature has to be looked for in the social situation prevailing in Turkey.[3]

The government of the Democratic party which came to power in 1950 did not bring the promised welfare and democraty to the Turkish people, but on the contrary, economic chaos and political terror. In the stuffy atmosphere of Menderes's régime ruthlessly persecuting the progressive intelligentsia, a part of it succumbs to pessimism, despondency, despair. Under these circumstances, intellectual circles in Turkey manifested an extraordinary interest in the works of F. Kafka, J. P. Sartre, A. Camus and in authors of the French *noveau roman* which contributed in no small measure to the fact that at that time, works oriented to plots estranged from society, buffeted by feelings of terror and impotence in the face of reality, made such a vehement claim to be heard. The Soviet turkologist S. N. Uturgauri in her analysis of the topic of estrangement in the works of two typical representatives of the "*bunalım*" literature, viz. Necati Tosuner and Leyla Erbil, adopting the Marxist standpoint, pointed out that the young Turkish writers had reduced the entire complex of life problems into that of loneliness.[4]

A turning away from objective reality and an orientation to the subject, his inner world had already marked Erdal Öz's stories written in the period 1954—1958, included in the collection *Yorgunlar* (1960, Tired). Motifs of pessimism and loneliness are already sounded in them, although as yet not with such an intensity as in his first novel *Odalarda* (1960, In the Rooms).

The subject whose innermost feelings and moods the author strives to express, is represented in all the eight stories in the collection by the figure of the narrator in the first person. Of Erdal Öz's stories, those produce the most convincing and rounded impression in which the author penetrates into the psyche of the child hero. The stories *Çocuk* (1954, The Child), *Mumçiçekleri* (1957, Wax Flowers) and *Babamdı* (1958, He Was My Father) bear in a considerable measure the positive influence of Orhan Kemal who was truly a master at moulding child characters, their world of fancy. In this respect, the story *Çocuk* in particular comes very close by its form to those of Orhan Kemal. Of the mental confusion that accompanies the first childhood love of the protagonist in the story, to his friend's elder sister, we learn as if "by the way", in an off-hand manner, from the narrator's short monologue reflections, interrupted by lapidary spoken dialogues, through a recall or reproduction of sensory percepts. The narrator's detailed recording of these sensory percepts throughout the visit in his friend's house is neither accidental nor an end in itself.

---

[3] Fethi Naci: *İnsan tükenmez* (Man is Eternal). Istanbul, Yenilik Basımevi 1956, pp. 6, 73.

[4] Uturgauri, S. N.: *O freidistskoi i ekzistentsialistskoi tendentsiyakh v turetskoi proze 60-kh godov* (On Freudian and Existentialist Tendencies in Turkish Prose of the 60s). In: *Ideologicheskaya borba i sovremennye literatury zarubezhnogo Vostoka* (Ideologic Struggle and Contemporary Literatures of non-Soviet East). Moscow, Nauka 1977, p. 57.

A sharpened perception of all the sounds, changes in the nuances of voice, transitions from light to darkness and the other way round, all this speaks of itself of the boy's tension in the presence of his secret love. Sensory perceptions, as an important component in producing the overall atmosphere, also figure in the author's other stories in which the hero-narrator finds himself in a situation of stress.

A creative approach to Orhan Kemal's work as the model is evidenced by the story *Mumçiçekleri*. In it, Erdal Öz took over the episode of a flight before the enemy from Orhan Kemal's autobiographic prose *Baba evi* (1949, Paternal House) which he reshaped into a symbol of man's flight from an inimical world and a search for a new one in which he would find peace, from efforts doomed beforehand to failure. The fictive conversation of the boy with the moon reflects a child's way of looking at the most fundamental relations and things making up his child world. On the other hand, in the story *Babamın elinde bıçak* (1956, Knife in My Father's Hand), it is the split consciousness of an individual persecuted by an instinct of fear that is reflected in the hero-narrator's surrealistic vision.

A total departure from realism to the surrealistic method is evident in the story *Kuklacı* (1957, Puppet-Player). The passenger-narrator's forebodings and hallucinations enframed with a detailed description of the progress of the train across the night-veiled countryside, finally lead to his identifying himself with a demigod. The crushing, oppressive sense of loneliness and nothingness that overpower the hero when he becomes conscious of this presumed exceptionality, here appear purely as a consequence of his morbid imaginativeness.

One of the characteristic procedures in modern Turkish literature was to deduce the mental states of personages solely from the action of ubiquitous elemental forces in the spirit of S. Freud's subjective psychoanalytical theory. However, in the story *Sular ne güzelse* (However Pretty Be the Waters), written in the same year as *Kuklacı*, Erdal Öz already relates his hero's depressive states with concrete social affinities prevailing within a bourgeois society. His view on the impasse of the bourgeois society condemning man to loneliness, he enclosed in the hero-narrator's inner monologue:

> ... We, the middle strata of the society, are respected, poor bourgeois ... We are constantly waiting for luck which never comes true. We do not realize that the thing called happiness is our own stupidity ... In no other period was the human individual left so lonely and helpless. We are lonely ... Look, I am a man exactly as required by our times. Look, I have destroyed all my feelings ... I am a great nothing that has killed our epoch. And not even great, perhaps only a little nothing.[5]

This typical apprehension of a human being by contemporary existentialist philosophy as "emptiness amidst reality" condemns adherents of existentialism to

---

[5] Öz, E.: *Yorgunlar* (Tired). Istanbul, A Dergi Yayınları 1969, pp. 60, 62.

accept loneliness as a state natural to a man's existence in the split, bad and misunderstood world. Such an existential isolation of the individual from society was brought "ad absurdum" by Albert Camus in his personage Antoine Roquentin, the hero in the novel *The Stranger*. Having arrived at the conviction that human existence is mere nothingness and all human strivings are therefore vain, absurd, Camus's hero reduced his existence to the ensuring of essential needs of life and hedonistic experiences, totally ignoring the social and moral codes of the society to which he belonged.

An internal contact of authors of Turkish new literature with Albert Camus's work became also apparent in Erdal Öz's first novel. Certain analogies in the motives and situations in the novel *Odalarda* point to Öz's relation to the novel *The Stranger*. However, in contrast to Camus portraying estrangement between an individual and society as a process definitively completed, when life in isolation appears to his hero as the most adequate form of human life and consequently the hero does not feel his loneliness as something tragic, Erdal Öz looks upon this phenomenon as something unnatural to human essence, causing it to die, something man instinctively abhors. The young Turkish prosaist moulded his hero's estrangement as a dynamic prosaist in its most agonizing stage for man. The principal figure in the novel *Odalarda* is continuously tossed and swayed between a glorification of his loneliness and its desperate, though vain refusal.

The presentation of the novel *Odalarda* is reminiscent of that of *The Stranger* not only by a similarity in plot — death of the hero's mother and the scene of her funeral — but also by an absence of any emotion in the hero over the loss of a being so close to everyone as is one's mother. However, while the emotional coldness will accompany Antoine Roquentin throughout the entire plot as a leitmotiv right up to the scaffold, the impassivity in the hero of Öz's novel is only apparent. That which takes place in the hero immediately after his mother's death is in reality only a numbness, supineness deriving from the psychic shock, which he will experience as soon as he becomes conscious of his frightful dereliction. Öz's hero suffers even from a pathological oversensitivity which prevents him from reflecting logically. In the case of Camu's Roquentin, on the other hand, his deadening of intellect is connected to his practically animal relation towards life. Conformably to the different conception of the principal figures in the two novels, which simultaneously fulfil the function of personal narrator, the narrative style in *The Stranger* also differs from that in Erdal Öz's novel.

Antoine Roquentin's narration represents an even, unexcited recording of events as they took place from the moment he was handed the wire informing him of his mother's death, up to the time when only a few hours separated him from his execution. All these events are given as if the narrator looked at them from above without any personal involvement. Hence, the narrative unwinds calmly, even monotonously. It is a stylized confession of a man at peace with himself, with his way of life, despite the face that his senseless existence is about to end in an even more senseless death. The only passage in the plot where the diction in the narrative changes is in the finale of the novel. At the moment when society, represented here by the priest, urges Roquentin to accept, at least on the border between life and death, its moral code, in a moment of discomfiture and excited monologue he flings his life truth to the priest's face. But is it truly only the priest and society whom he wishes to convince of his truth? Did he not himself, too, a stranger in a peopled world, on the threshold of real nothingness, feel the tragedy of his loneliness?

The nameless hero in the novel *Odalarda*, constantly experiencing the intensive oppressive feeling of loneliness, views everything about him through the prism of this sensation. Hence, his narrative is frequently coloured with a tragic undertone, his statements about events and facts of his own life, due to some association of a sudden emotion, break abruptly and pass into excited inner monologues in which the narrator reveals his innermost feelings, trying to come to understand his own self. The localization of the hero on one of the lower rungs of the societal ladder in the novel *Odalarda* also acquires a different sense from that in *The Stranger*, in view of Öz's different conception of his estranged hero. With Camus, the hero's insignificant social standing does not appear as the cause of his estrangement, but as its result. Roquentin, ignoring all the aims after which society about him strives, does not feel the need to alter his status of a minor clerk which ensures him a modest standard of life, refuses an offer of a more advantageous position. In Erdal Öz's conception, it is precisely the position of an outsider in society expressing appreciation and confidence solely to the successful and the powerful one, a torturing consciousness of this position, that drives the hero into isolation, that forces him to doubt his own human dignity. While in his *Stranger*, Camus made no attempt at uncovering the social causes of man's estrangement, of his moral and emotional destruction, Erdal Öz in his novel outlined the affinities among feelings of anxiety, loneliness, hopelessness, desperation, inferiority complex in an individual on the one hand, and a lack of social security in a chaotic world, on the other.

The material deficiency in which Öz's hero lives is firmly anchored in the plot of *Odalarda* as a constantly and intensively recurring motif. The hero's childhood, too, is marked by poverty and this motif is indirectly projected into the title of the novel. He is painfully conscious of the misery of the rooms in which he grew up and in which he hid from the outside world, when he confronts them with the simple, modestly furnished room of his future wife.

> ... That which was most striking in the room was its whiteness: white-washed walls, white flax curtains, the white bed cover. I should have seen such pretty, clean-kept rooms in childhood. But somehow, we never had such rooms as this. I grew up in rooms that were poor, without furnishings. And it is still so even now. I lie down on a miserable rugged mattress spread on the ground in a desolate, unfurnished, dusty room. And I am alone. As always.[6]

The grinding, painful social situation of Öz's hero — a little official — comes most conspicuously to the foreground in the second chapter of the novel, in a scene reminiscent of the meeting between the copyist Makar Devushkin and the general in Dostoevsky's first novel *Poor Folk*. Like Dostoevsky's hero, Öz's clerk becomes most conscious of his social and human degradation at the moment when he comes face to face with a highly-situated person, although the latter behaves in both cases condescendingly even magnanimously. The role of the missing button which defeated all Devushkin's efforts a preserving at least some remnant of human dignity, is taken over in Öz's novel by the motif of a dirty handkerchief.

Dostoevsky was the first in world literature to portray a minor clerk as a definite social type not from the author's position, for already Gogol had summarized the objective traits making up a characterizing portrait of such a petty official, transposing it into the hero's field of vision and thereby making him the object of his own self-torturing self-awareness.[7] In the consistent self-analysis of the tormenting feelings by Öz's minor clerk, conscious of his insignificance and hopeless position, we may note parallels pointing to Öz's relation towards F. M. Dostoevsky's works *Poor Folk* and *Notes from the Underground*.[8] His ambition (the hero pretends a nonexisting recognition of his work in order that at least in this manner he would rise in other people's eyes), his yearning for contact with people, his submissiveness to the will of others and his acceptance of other people's views, his devotedness and magnanimity in relation to his wife bring him closer, on the one hand, to Makar Devushkin, on the other hand, through his morbid oversensitivity making him approach everything with mistrust and suspicion, be constantly preoccupied with it, analyse everything into the minutest details, through his impulsive expressions which he immediately bitterly regrets, his ludicrous rebellions of whose helplessness he is himself aware, through his cynical looks at women, Öz's hero comes closer to the character study of "the man from the Underground".

Makar Devushkin's emotional relation to Varenka Dobroselova, just as the absurd escape into the "Underground", cannot represent, for Dostoevsky's heroes, an escape from the vicious circle in which they found themselves through the fault of the existing social order. The question how and what to live for remains unresolved both in *Poor Folk* and in *Notes from the Underground*. And neither does Erdal Öz find an answer to it in his novel, the hero of which finds himself at its conclusion in a situation analogous to that at the start. In addition, the impasse of his position at the

---

[6] Öz, E.: *Odalarda* (In the Rooms). Istanbul. Varlık Yayınları 1960, p. 49.

[7] Bachtin, M.: *Dostojevskij umělec* (Dostoevsky the Artist). Prague, Československý spisovatel 1977, pp. 66—67.

[8] Dostoevsky is after Tolstoy the most translated Russian classic in Turkey. The first work to have been translated into Turkish was precisely the novel *Poor Folk* (1846), published in instalments in the journal Yeni Mecmua already in 1924.

end is made worse by the fact that not even his love to another being is able to protect him from loneliness.

Erdal Öz as a member of a generation of Turkish writers whose *Weltanschauung* began to be formed under the influence of existentialist philosophy could not arrive at any other conclusion. Man, failing to find his social self-realization, tries to escape nothingness to reach love that will unite him to a being equally reserved and lonely as he is himself. Starting from a spirit of individualism, the existentialists understand relations among people as those between two persons, between "me and the other one", considering relations among human groups, between an individual and a group, between one isolated individual and another as the member of a group, to be abstract and derived.[9] But what else can a man, clinging to his loneliness to which he is condemned by existentialism, bring to another lonely person if not a twofold loneliness? Öz's hero, too, came to realize this, and at the moment when he finally succeeded in getting closer to his wife also emotionally. At the moment when he succeeds in achieving that in what he had ceased to hope, he understands that for him there is no escape from loneliness.

Diametrically opposite to this impasse in the hero's fate from the novel *Odalarda* stands the conception given by Orhan Kemal to his picture of a minor official. His scribe from the autobiographical prose *Avare Yıllar* (1950, Roving Years) carries on an intensive, bitter struggle to overcome his sense of inferiority complex, made even more complicated by his love, which only multiplies his suffering. However, the author gives real hope to his hero of finding his lost self-confidence. This perspective solution resides in the hero's clinging to the working class, represented by the characters of the foreman İzzet and the hero's sweetheart — a working girl.

After his initial attempts at prose writing, Erdal Öz stopped writing for fully twelve years.[10] They were years of searching for his place in life, in literature, a search in the ideological and the formal domain, years of considerable changes in the life of the author's country. These searchings and changes found a reflection in the collection of short stories *Kanayan* (1973, Bleeding) and in the novel *Yaralısın* (1974, You Are Wounded).

After the overthrow of Menderes's régime through a military coup on 27th May 1960, an easing of the political, economic and social life was felt in Turkey and it livened up also the literary domain. Social realists whose works, in contrast to the intellectual writings of representatives of *bunalım* literature, enjoyed popularity among the reading public, now began, free from the threat of persecution and censorship, an all-round analysis of actual problems in their country. But some

---

[9] Kossak, J.: *Existencialismus ve filozofii a literatuře* (Existentialism in Philosophy and Literature). Prague, Svoboda 1978, pp. 40—41.

[10] Erdal Öz justifies his silence saying he could not carry on along the line he had chosen as a beginning author, designed to study an individual's inner confusions. *Orhan Kemal ödülünü kazanan Erdal Öz*, p. 3.

representatives of the new literature also began to turn to reality, to the life on society, from their own introspective sphere. Those among them succeeded best who had not belonged to its radical wing, who had always made their introspective heroes to be involved to some extent in a concrete social environment.

The economic problems which Turkey had to face in the sixties aroused greater and greater doubts in the young progressive intelligentsia and the student world about the correctness of the capitalist system in the country. Many of them found the correct approach to Marxist-Leninist ideas and endeavoured to make contact with the growing and activating working class. However, part of the young remained disoriented, associating in small, mutually isolated extreme leftist organizations. Their terrorist activities had no small share in the unrest in the country which finally led to the unfortunate March Memorandum and to the state of emergency on 28th April 1971. The wave of political terror that began in the following months brought untold sufferings to thousands of progressively-minded people, tortured in prison cells by a mediaeval regime. This bitter experience of the Turkish people found its reflection in numerous poetic and prose works, designated by Turkish critique as literature of 12th March. An attempt at a more complex view of this literature was made by the young literary critic Murat Belge, but his approach is marked by a certain one-sidedness and superficiality.[11]

A foremost place among writers who in their works turn to this unhappy period in contemporary Turkish history belongs precisely to Erdal Öz. During his detention on remand and the interrogations to which he was subjected as owner of a bookshop with leftist literature, he had the opportunity to come to know at first hand not only the procedures followed by enemies of progress, but also those against whom such procedures were adopted. The cruel post-March reality found its reflection in four short stories of Öz's collection *Kanayan* and in the novel *Yaralısın.*

In contrast to his collection *Yorgunlar* with direct first-person narration, the narrator simultaneously being the hero in each story, Öz in the six stories of the collection *Kanayan* had recourse to various narrative attitudes.

Direct narration in the first person is met with only in the title story, the narrators here being alternately the father and mother, while the hero is their son. Recounting the last months of their son's life before he joined the guerillas, the parents, independently of each other, endeavour to understand his decision, to elucidate their mutual relations. Their son's interior world, however, remains an enigma to them.

A narrator in the third person, confining himself to a description of the personages' external expressions, their way of acting, their gestures, to a reproduction of their dialogues, appears in the two stories: *Masa* (1970, The Table) which is a critical view of a false apprehension of humaneness, and *Ernesto* (1970).

---

[11] Belge, M.: *12 Mart Romanlarına Genel Bir Bakış* (An Overall View of the 12th March Novels). Birikim, 1976, No. 12, pp. 8—16.

The charge of criticism contained in the story *Ernesto* is directed against the nihilistic approach by Orhan Duru to the immortal person of the Latin-American revolutionary Ernesto Che Guevara, and against his warped interpretation of an artist's freedom and independence. In this story, Erdal Öz successfully made use of a nontraditional compositional procedure. In the first part of the story, the true drama of Guevara's death is made to unroll in a lyricized form and contrasts sharply with the fictive episode of the origin of Duru's story in the second section where irony, passing even into sarcasm, replaced lyricism. In this story, although it is in fact an experiment in the domain of satire, Erdal Öz made proof of an extraordinary discernment in the matter of choice of means of form and a sense of proportion in their application. The story may rightly be considered to be the peak of the author's production so far.

A character's innermost feelings and thoughts became the basis of a plot in the stories *Kurt* (1971, Wolf), *Güvercin* (1972, Pigeon) and *Sığırcıklar* (1972, Starlings), connected by the inhuman sufferings of victims of political terror. However, in contrast to the stories in the collection *Yorgunlar* and the novel *Odalarda*, the emotional and psychic world of the characters is here revealed from the standpoint of the author narrator.

In the central figure of the story *Kurt*, i.e. in the workman İsa, there still remained a great deal of the tragically lonely hero from the novel *Odalarda*, despite the fact that İsa arrives at the prison as one of a large collective of workers fighting for their rights. İsa's episode is enframed by his meeting with his father and his wife in the prison visitors' box after two months of separation. During the entire meeting İsa remains immersed in his own thoughts and memories and his mind is far away not only from his visitors, but also from his comrades of whose solidarity his father is talking to him. The only news from the outside world that makes some impression on him is that his dog, by the name of Wolf, had perished. The suffering he had undergone made of İsa a broken man, passively resigned to his fate instead of mustering and activating his strength to resist violence and his determination to carry on the struggle.

An analogous interpretation of the image of victims of political terror in the land also applies to the stories *Güvercin* and *Sığırcıklar*. Their heroes, having passed through the hell of tortures — or in their expectation, apathetically adapt themselves to the life in the prison cell without reflecting why, by what right they had been deprived of their freedom, so that hatred would be roused in them against their torturers. They remain alone, reserved, without any sense of "togetherness" towards their comrades in the other cells.

The story *Sığırcıklar* develops two episodic ideals in parallel, although seemingly incongruent. Nevertheless, there is a deep-running affinity between the episode of the young man into whom the author projected the fates of thousands of illegally imprisoned and tortured young people and that of the starlings and black kites,

169

symbolizing the growth of fascist tendencies in the land. The author's design was to bring out the fact that fascism had come to be a concrete, palpable danger for the entire nation. He certainly could not be accused of intentionally intimidating the masses, still less of rendering a service to the governing classes, as does Mehmet Ant in his critical essay analysing the collection of stories *Kanayan,* although, it should be noted, he rightly criticized Öz's concept of fascism as a robust, indestructible phenomenon, as a danger that sprang up nobody knows whence.[12] Nor can one agree with Erdal Öz's image of the people symbolized by the starlings. The writer transmits the passivity of his heroes to the entire nation when he presents the starlings in the tops of plane-trees as a terrified flock, submitting silently, without a fight, to the attack of black kites.

A new deeper sense is imparted to the image of victims of political terror in the novel *Yaralısın,* called by the foremost Turkish novelist Yaşar Kemal, an epos of defiant man.[13]

While Öz's novel was very favourably received by the representatives of social realism, as attested by the enthusiastic response from many of them, and the award of the Orhan Kemal literary prize, the young Turkish critics took up a negative stand towards it.

Erdal Öz did not have too happy a hand with the choice of his narrative procedure. The use of the atypical second person singular in narration obscures issues — who is actually being spoken of, whether the second person is being addressed, or whether this person is not himself, or whether this involves a shifting from one person to the other, an oscillation between me and you, that is, an oscillation between a dialogue and a monologue.[14] A suspicion has been raised also, whether Öz in his choice of the narrator attitude, had not been influenced by Michael Butor's novel *Transformation.* The writer resolutely refutes this insinuation and justifies his use of this form by his own personal experience in prison, where, as he states, fellow-prisoners usually spoke of their experiences in the second person. In the writer's view, such a mode of narration takes the events related out of the personal frame and in a sense makes them objective.[15] This effort at objectivization in the author's design was also noted by the critic Murat Belge, who, in his analysis of the novel *Yaralısın* wrote: "It is evident that the reason for using you is an effort at conveying the idea that every one of us may find himself in such a situation."[16]

---

[12] A n t, M.: *Yılgınlık edebiyatına bir örnek: Kanayan* (Example of the Literature of Intimidation: Kanayan). Yeni Adımlar, 1974, No. 21, p. 67.

[13] See foreword by Yaşar Kemal to the first edition of the novel *Yaralısın.* Öz, E.: *Yaralısın* (You Are Wounded). Istanbul, Cem Yayınevi 1974, p. 8.

[14] K r a u s o v á, N.: *Rozprávač v románe* (Narrator in the Novel). Slovenská literatúra, 1965, No. 2, p. 147.

[15] *Orhan Kemal ödülünü kazanan Erdal Öz,* p. 3.

[16] B e l g e, M.: *12 Mart Romanlarına Genel Bir Bakış,* p. 14.

Erdal Öz admits that the creators of the *nouveau roman* are concerned, in their search for new, nontraditional moulding processes, with objectivization; however, he decidedly distances himself from this movement, which he considers unhealthy. Yet, certain formal procedures in the novel *Yaralısın* betray that Öz's contact with the *nouveau roman* had a certain influence on the development of his own creative method.

The concrete hero was dislodged from the plot in the novel *Yaralısın* by a personal pronoun in the same manner as is the case in several works by representatives of the *nouveau roman*. In contrast to these, however, Öz's grammatical figure addressed by the pronoun you, did not lose its historical and social determination.

A characteristic feature of the creative method in the *nouveau roman* is a detailed description of things and phenomena, and to this is related also the use of attributes in their purely descriptive function, and of similes deprived of any poetic tone. In the novel *Yaralısın*, Erdal Öz manifests a tendency towards such a formal approach, lingering on details of the various stages of tortures and the physiological functions of a tortured body. Compared to the writer's earlier works, abounding in images and picturesque expressions, the aesthetic function of the artistic style in the novel *Yaralısın* is much weakened by such a procedure. But on the other hand, this aesthetic imbalance is partially compensated by the positive development in the author's lexicality and particularly his syntax where ramified, complicated subordinate clauses, overloaded with nonfunctional inversions have been replaced by simple sentences adhering to the stabilized word order. In the novel *Yaralısın* the author could apply in a greater measure than in works strictly oriented to the character's inner world, spoken dialogue which to him, in contrast to the dialogue in the *nouveau roman*, does not cease to be the bearer of dramatic tension.

While in his first novel Erdal Öz is guided by the traditional scheme of plot development commonly valid for fabulated structure, the novel *Yaralısın* is based on an intentional disruption of the time course and causality of the various episodes in one of his two lines of events. This procedure, typical for the *nouveau roman*, has its logical justification in the plot of Öz's work.

Two lines of events of the story run on two different temporal planes, that is, on the plane of actual narration and on that of reminiscences, episodes of the two planes alternating regularly. The first line, running on the level of actual narration, observing the causal and the spatio-temporal chronology and follows the principal character during the course of a little over twenty four hours. This line of events may be denoted as a story of knowledge. It has incorporated within it the fates of prisoners with whom the principal figure became familiar after his arrival to the common cell and who are the mediators on his way to knowledge.

This first line of events essentially enframes the second one, made up of the principal figure's reminiscences. This line, let us call it a story of defiance and indestructibility of human dignity, the reader has to reconstruct from recollections recorded in the sequence in which they are recalled by the fictive memory of the principal figure. The reminiscences are an evoking of events from the two months that passed since a young graduate, hiding under the pronoun you was arrested until he was put into a common cell.

The principal figure in the novel *Yaralısın* returns in his reminiscences to his interrogation and tortures. Here, however, in contrast to the stories *Kurt* and *Güvercin*, what is of importance is not the act of torture as such, but rather the way the victim will behave face to face to inhuman torments, what attitude he will take towards his tormentors. In the stories referred to, there is not the least indication whether their heroes resisted their tormentors by refusing to speak, but the way they behaved during their ordeal implies that they broke down.

The young man in the novel *Yaralısın* realizes that his tormentors are out to degrade man by humiliating tortures, to kill in him human dignity and pride, but he also knows that only when he resists, when he does not permit them to achieve their end, will he come out clean from this unequal contest.

> If you do not die, if they do not kill you, even if they maim you and a day will come when you will leave that place, if some day you come away from there, you do not wish to walk the earth, under the sun, among men as a scoundrel hiding your face.[17]

The principal character does not hide his fear of torture, however, he knows he must not succumb, that it is better to die than to talk. If man is to remain a man, he must become a hero.

The Czech journalist and writer Julius Fučík, a fighter against fascism, in his *Reports from Under the Gallows* speaks of the great moral strength that prisoners in Nazi prisons draw from a consciousness of fellowship and mutual solidarity.[18]

The young man in Öz's novel, with his fear, sufferings and determination to resist, is alone, surrounded by his tormentors and their obedient lackeys. Yet it is not the loneliness of an estranged individual, but an enforced isolation from people at liberty with whom he had been linked by common interests, and also from those who, like him, equally suffer in prison. However, even the strictest precautions cannot prevent the young man from feeling in his most difficult moments, that he is not alone. He finds a moral support in the expressions of protest by his fellow prisoners as the

---

[17] Öz, E.: *Yaralısın*, p. 95.

[18] A translation of Fučík's *Reports from Under the Gallows* appeared in Turkish for the first time in 1974 and during three years went through three editions. It found an extraordinary response among the young progressive intelligentsia. Erdal Öz had completed his novel *Yaralısın* in 1973. The analogies between the real episode of the revolutionary-communist and the fictive episode of an apolitical member of the intelligentsia derive from a similar social situation, which conditioned the origin of both the works, although the possibility of Erdal Öz's having read Fučík's *Reports* in one of the world languages even before it appeared in the first Turkish edition, cannot be excluded.

172

guards drag him so ill-treated, in front of their cells, as well as in meeting a guard who, in the midst of the horrible machinery, remained human.

> Look at those types! Look at those figurines! After all, it's nothing but a riff-raff. It is but a piece of the political army of Nazism. Pillars of the régime. Supports of its society ...[19]

In these words Julius Fučík characterizes German prison guards in his reports from the threshold of death. In the novel *Yaralısın*, the appurtenance of the investigators and guards to the régime, which is an enemy of progress, is expressed figuratively:

> ... These people live in a never-ending night. Everywhere in this building electric lights are on for twenty-four hours on end. As if interminable night reigned everywhere. Day, daylight, brightness do not exist here. Perhaps they do not like that. Everywhere, always night. Infinite night.[20]

This picture comprises also the answers to the question which the principal character in the novel poses to himself during the interrogation:

> "... All right, but what do these people want from you? They have not asked yet about anything. They only beat you... Who has made those people so angry?"[21]

The principal character of the novel belongs to the intelligentsia. In Turkish the word "*aydın*" has a double meaning: "bright" and "intelligent". The reactionary régime inclining towards fascism, and its helpers who feel how precarious their position is see the intelligentsia as the bearer of progress, a potential danger, a threat, hence, they hurry to break it before it grasps where its true place is.

The principal character finds a direct answer to his questions on his arrival at the common cell, when he became more familiar with its involuntary inmates. From their mouth he hears the bitter truth about the abyss separating the intelligentsia and the people. The simple-minded man understood that the existing tragic situation would not occur if the intelligentsia would not meet the common people only behind prison gates. At the same time, he expresses his conviction that in future, the intelligentsia will find its way to the people. This unification of the intelligentsia with the people is symbolically expressed in the concluding part of the novel. The principal character willingly accepts the name Nuri as a sign that he identifies himself with the simple men in his cell, that he wishes to be one of them.

Necati Mert in his criticism giving an oversimplified view on the issues dealt with in the novel *Yaralısın*, designates Erdal Öz to be a representative of escapist literature, ignoring in his work social struggle and class reality.[22]

---

[19] Fučík, J.: *Reportáž psaná na oprátce* (Reports from Under the Gallows). Prague, Odeon 1970, p. 115.

[20] Öz, E.: *Yaralısın*, p. 198.

[21] Ibid., p. 99.

[22] Mert, N.: "*İşkence" ve kaçış edebiyatı* (Literature of "Torture" and Escapism). Yansıma, 1975, No. 38, p. 42.

This opinion of the Turkish critic cannot be accepted. Erdal Öz in his novel *Yaralısın* takes in hand a pressing and a very actual problem, namely, that of a political passivity on the part of a section of the Turkish intelligentsia. The principal character, even though coming from the impecunious social strata (this ensues from an association evoked by reminiscences to his mother — p. 209), before his imprisonment stood outside the political events, a fact that the author indicates in a dialogue with a fellow prisoner:

"What was your offence?"

What was your offence? What will you say now?

Should you perhaps say 'I don't know'?

"They say you are a 'political'."

"Well then," Nuri saves you from the indecisiveness into which you have fallen. "I am political".

So you are political. That is good. If anybody asks you, you will be able to say without hesitation why you are here.[23]

The principal character of the novel represents that type of Turkish young man with university training to whom reading of Marxist literature is more a fashionable matter than one of any political conviction and Marxist *Weltanschauung* or world outlook. True, he distances himself from the existing régime, does not agree with it, but the idea of a collective fight against it is still strange, foreign to him.

Necati Mert in the passage referred to above speaks of two worlds in the novel *Yaralısın*, one of torture, the other without torture.[24] Nevertheless, the novel clearly speaks of three worlds: of the world of interrogators and guards from which the young man distances himself, the world proper to the young man and from which he has been torn away and to which he longs to go back, and "Nuri's" world which is at first strange to him, yet one in which he will finally take his place voluntarily. And it is precisely this idea of an inevitable union of the intelligentsia with the people in a struggle for common aims, for a brighter future of their country, which embodies the perspectives of Öz's work. Hence, the problems in the novel *Yaralısın* cannot be spoken of as issues of existentialism, as does Murat Belge in his study on the 12th March novels, already referred to.[25]

In conclusion, let us compare Erdal Öz's solution with the impasse in which an educated petty bourgeois is left by a representative of an earlier generation of Turkish writers, Vedat Türkali (born 1919) in his novel *Bir gün tek başına* (1975, One Day of Loneliness), likewise awarded the Orhan Kemal prize. The hero of the novel, a middle-aged owner of a bookshop, in his youth an active participant of the

---

[23] Öz, E.: *Yaralısın*, p. 19.

[24] Mert, N.: *"İşkence" ve kaçış edebiyatı*, p. 43.

[25] Belge, M.: *12 Mart Romanlarına Genel Bir Bakış*, pp. 14—16.

Student Movement, although drawn by his woman friend into the vortex of revolutionary events in the last months before the overthrow of Menderes's régime, remains only a passive, frightened observer of what is going on around him and ends in suicide.

REWIEW ARTICLES

NEW SOVIET WORKS ON THE YOUNG TURKS' MOVEMENT AND REVOLUTION

NAĎA ZIMOVÁ, Prague

The more historians became interested in socio-economic phenomena, structures and processes, the more they discovered that they needed new analytical tools. It was possible to study political ideas, institutions and international relations without the explicit use of such disciplines as political science, psychology, etc. But it turned out to be extremely difficult to study the question of economic growth or the relations between social classes without making use of the theories and methods developed by economists and sociologists. Marxist-Leninist history is conceived of as a historical social science owing to its socio-economic foundations. Thus, due to their common rooting in the theories of historical and dialectic materialism, history, political economy and sociology are regarded as closely-related sciences.

Our purpose in this short review article is to analyse two recent Soviet publications in this line of research: Yu. A. Petrosyan's and V. I. Shpilkova's studies on the Young Turks' movement and revolution.[1] Much has been written on Turkey in the stage of its decline, on the Ottoman Empire as spoils to be divided among the European powers, as well as on the efforts to save the Empire by means of internal reforms. Starting at the beginning of the 19th century and continuing into modern times, reform movements sprang up in Ottoman Turkey. The new concept of reform, which was usually identified with the constitutional movement of the Young Ottomans, began to shape in the sixties of the 19th century. In 1876, the reformers seemed to have finally reached their goal — i.e. the first Ottoman Constitution. Shortly after, however, the autocratic system of Abdülhamid II, put a stop to the possibility of any further development or improvement of the Empire. Nevertheless, despite the failure of the Young Ottoman movement, the results achieved were by no means abolished.

The suppression of this reform movement only aggravated the process of continuing chaos, degeneracy and disintegration of the Empire, which in turn gave vital impetus to the movement of the Young Turks. The latter, for their part, were

---

[1] Petrosyan, Yu. A.: *Mladoturetskoe dvizhenie (vtoraya polovina XIX—nachalo XX vv.)* ((The Young Turks' Movement) (second half of the 19th and the beginning of the 20th centuries)). Moscow, Nauka 1971, 327 pp.; and Shpilkova, V. I.: *Mladoturetskaya revolyutsiya 1908—1909 gg.* (The Young Turks' Revolution of 1908—1909). Moscow, Nauka 1977, 292 pp.

later to play a predominant role in the revolution of 1908. Their movement spread rapidly and, led by the political society called İttihad ve Terakki Cemiyeti (the Committee of Union and Progress), it successfully carried out the revolution of 1908 and restored the Constitution of 1876. Subsequently, however, this movement too, began gradually to degenerate. Nevertheless, it continued to guide the destinies of the Ottoman Empire until its own final disintegration in the wake of the Empire's defeat in World War I.

The number of articles and books concerning various aspects of the Young Turks' revolution which have appeared during the last twenty-five years has not only provided a basis for a more balanced appraisal of this movement, but it has also increased the need for a comprehensive study of that important period. Yu. A. Petrosyan and V. I. Shpilkova have clearly sought to write such studies and, to a considerable extent, they have succeeded in their aim. Both authors share a common concern, as reflected by the emphasis they place on the social and economic background of the political events of that period. But while Shpilkova examines in detail the outbreak and course of the revolution in the years 1908—1909, Petrosyan concentrates his attention on its origins. He analyses the socio-economic and ideological basis of the Young Turks' movement within the broader framework of the constitutional movement of the Ottoman Empire.

Petrosyan's study is a strictly professional one; it has filled a gap in the intellectual history of the Turkish constitutional movement. The author is eminently qualified to undertake this task, as he has already produced several important works on the development of Ottoman-Turkish ideological trends.[2] The first four chapters of the volume under review are devoted to the Young Ottoman movement which constitutes, he suggests, a prelude to the events of 1908. According to the author, the Young Ottomans' activities, seen as a protest against the prevailing absolutism, precipitated the Young Turks' movement. Thus, both movements must be considered as two different stages of one single process of socio-economic and political development, in which the old mode of production was in the process of decaying and a new one was emerging. Similarly, B. Lewis considers the Turkish revolution as a process within which "The basic change in Turkey — from an Islamic Empire to a national Turkish state, from a mediaeval theocracy to a constitutional republic, from a bureaucratic feudalism to a modern capitalist economy — was accomplished over a long period, by successive waves of reformers and radicals".[3]

Petrosyan concentrates his attention on the economic and social factors which constituted the dynamics of the Turkish political system, as well as on its ideological development. He presents a critical description of the Young Turks' organizations

---

[2] Cf. Petrosyan, Yu. A.: *"Novye osmany" i borba za konstitutsiyu 1876 g. v Turtsii* (The Young Ottomans and the Struggle for the Constitution of 1876 in Turkey). Moscow 1958.

[3] Lewis, B.: *The Emergence of Modern Turkey*. London 1961, p. 474.

and their activity at about the turn of the century and shows that the Committee of Union and Progress was by no means a monolithic structure. This fact resulted in the formation of a number of groups within it, each of which comprised the protagonists of a different theory. The author concentrated in this connection, on Ahmed Riza and his supporters (who were influential in the early days of the constitutional régime) and on Prince Sabaheddin, an ideologue of the liberals and a leader of the anti-Unionist groups. We may justly and responsibly say that this contribution by Yu. A. Petrosyan is a thorough and exhaustive study. It is strictly scientifically based and its incontestable value lies in the wide range of information it presents, gleaned from source materials investigated in depth.

In recent years, V. I. Shpilkova has published a number of articles on various aspects of the Young Turks' movement and revolution[4] and now, in this work, she has attempted to integrate her findings into a compact study. The present work is based on an extensive study of Russian and Bulgarian archival materials, as well as on a wide range of published books and articles. Shpilkova describes at length the social and economic conditions that affected the historical development of Turkey before the revolution of 1908 and assigns them their due place in the general Ottoman context. She devotes special attention to the period 1905—1907 and emphasizes the effects of the Russian revolution of 1905, as well as the growing unrest of all the subject peoples and oppressed groups of that time.

A major positive aspect of the book lies in the manner in which the theoretical research is combined with a practical analysis of the revolutionary-democratic movement. A large part of it is devoted to the overall process of the workers' movement, since it was this movement that was to play a significant role in the country's future development. Summarizing her ideas, the author considers that the most immediate result of the Young Turks' revolution was the fact that it put an end to the absolutism of Abdülhamid II, and set Turkey on the road toward becoming a modern state.

The movement of the Committee of Union and Progress and the participation of the Young Turks in the Turkish national awakening in the Ottoman Empire have usually been attributed to the despotic government and repressive policies of Abdülhamid II. These new Soviet works on the Young Turks' movement are particularly welcomed because they stress the hitherto underestimated socio-economic background of these events. Moreover, the Young Turks' movement should be analysed within the broader context of the growing Turkish national consciousness. The emergence of this consciousness, resulting from the corresponding socio-economic basis, is thus a more extensive topic which deserves to be dealt with in greater detail in future.

---

[4] Cf., for example, Sphilkova, V. I.: *Pervyi proekt politicheskoi programmy mladoturok* (The First Project of the Young Turk Political Programme). Narody Azii i Afriki, *4*, 1973, pp. 61—68.

In a brief review article such as this, it is impossible to give these works the detailed analysis they would deserve. Thus, one must leave almost unmentioned some of the authors' freshest, most interesting insights into such subjects as the significance of the army, the question of military-civilian relationships, those of the constitutional reforms and the motive forces of progressive development.

Both authors rightly point out, however, that although seen retrospectively the Young Turks' revolution proved a failure as far as its further development was concerned, it nevertheless constituted a crucial aspect of Turkey's revolutionary history. It was, actually the first Turkish bourgeois revolution[5] which represented, in fact, the first attempt to express protest and put up a resistance to foreign powers' economic and political expansionism in the region comprised by the Empire. Both studies under review constitute a new approach to this field. They analyse the Young Turks' revolutionary movement and its ideology as a conflict of old versus new social forces within the broader socio-economic context.

---

[5] Miller, A. F.: *Burzhuaznaya revolyutsiya 1908 g. v Turtsii* (The Bourgeois Revolution of 1908 in Turkey). Sovetskoe vostokovedenie, 6, 1955, p. 29.

BOOK REVIEWS

Farmer, Edward L.—Hambley, Gavin R. G.—Kopf, David—Marshall, Byron K. — Taylor, Romeyn: *Comparative History of Civilizations in Asia*. Reading, Addison-Wesley Publishing Company 1977. 797 pp.

The idea of comparing the history of civilizations received a new impetus in connection with the growing interest on the part of scholars in an interdisciplinary approach to the investigation of history and contemporary problems of the human society. Attempts had been made even earlier in historical sciences and outside them to compare civilizations, but in most cases these were confined to individual cultural-historical, ethnographic or psychological elements. Others again were marked by a tendency on the one hand, to underscore the priorities, the creative character and universal validity of values set up within one particular civilization and on the other, to prove the dependence or the inferiority of another cultural unit. Such a mode of investigation of course led neither to an improved knowledge of the contemporary significance of diverse civilizations, nor to an understanding of the historical processes that moulded them.

A group of five American historians has now published an original comparative history of the civilizations of Asia spanning a period from prehistory up to modern times. These authors see the Asiatic continent within the framework of five great cultural zones, three of which — viz. the Western, Southern and Eastern Asia — represent the focus of their attention, for they are the cradle of three great, essentially independent civilizations. The use of purely geographical terms to delimitate civilization units presents a double advantage. First, it permits the authors to leave out the traditional designations of Near and Far East that embody a politically tainted Eurocentric view of the world, rejected by Asian nations. On the other hand, it enables them better to emphasize the fact that one may not indiscriminately identify, say South-Asian with Indian civilization, or East-Asian with Chinese, for their development was considerably and often creatively influenced not only by the biggest, but also by several other nations of these regions. This mode of approach and the contents of the work make it clear that the authors endeavoured to achieve a balanced view of the historical destinies and the place of

185

Asian nations in the history of mankind. At the same time, however, they stress that this presupposes a study of several civilizations at once, without becoming satisfied with that overall, indiscriminate apprehension of Asian civilization that is applied to European one.

The first volume comprises an enormous time interval reaching from the very birth of civilization in Asia up to the Eurasian integration under Mongol dominance. The second volume deals with the period from the origins of modern empires up to the emergence of nationalism and the new forces of change in modern Asia. The authors have elaborated and applied an original method. Each chapter is divided into two parts: the first follows up processes strictly on a common plane, while the second one shows them in concrete patterns on the soil of the various empires and regions. In addition, each chapter has a summary introduction and a valuable section of concluding remarks in which ideas or questions elicited by a comparison of concordant or divergent elements are presented as stimuli for reflection. The authors express the view that certain broad parallels allow comparative generalizations which, although instructive on the abstract plane, need not be necessarily valid for every unit within a common civilization. The book has not the aim to explain Asian history in casual terms. Its purposeful methodical arrangement will prove particularly useful to the reader interested in a solid introduction to the study of Asian history. A comprehensive bibliography is attached for his benefit. In addition, the authors lead the reader to reflections on the origin and effect of several fundamental factors in the history of Asia, such as, for instance, the discovery of agriculture, class stratification and relations, the origin of universal empires and religions, crises and social disintegration, impact of European imperialism and the coming of modern political forces. Although the authors are for the most part experts on the contemporary epoch, they have nevertheless succeeded in capturing of at least touching on the most significant problems from the entire spectrum of Asian civilizations across a span of twelve millennia and in pointing out the more outstanding stages in their historical development. A priority of the book is its uniform manner of processing — a felicitous outcome of a long-term collective effort. The reasons for which the connecting Chapter Nine and the Introduction from the first volume are reproduced in the second one, do not sound quite convincing. At the same time the authors state that because of lack of space, they dropped their original design to extend their comparison of Asian civilizations to the whole of Eurasia. However, they did fulfil their principal aim — to show the history of Asian nations by the method of a selective comparison of great civilizations, which is more fecund in stimulating historical concepts than a study of anyone single Asian culture.

Ivan Doležal

Gillard, David: *The Struggle for Asia 1828—1914*. London, Methuen and Co., Ltd. 1977. 214 pp.

Dr. Gillard's book makes the struggle for Asia in the 19th and early 20th century appear essentially as rivalry between Great Britain and Tzarist Russia. A spate of books and studies have been devoted to the contention between these two powers, but as the author remarks in his introduction, none of them processes this issue within the framework of the all-Asian continent and with equal impartiality for British and Russian policy. He sees his task in an endeavour to fill this gap.

On the basis of extensive research of British, American and partly also pre-revolutionary Russian and the new Soviet literature on the subject, he presents a detailed analysis in 8 chapters of the growing role of Russia and Britain on the Eurasian continent, the mutual distrust of these two States and their diplomatic and armed struggles on the soil and 'before the gates' of Asia. Although the author does make brief references to the situation then prevailing in China, his principal interest clearly lies in Western Asia, in regions where Britain's and Russia's interests most often touched or crossed. Short-term clashes between these two powers and their temporary agreements certainly had a significant impact on Asian development, but further countries, too, shared in no small measure in the struggle for Asia during the period under study, e.g. the United States of America, France, Germany, Japan. The author, however, devotes far less attention to their role.

Another factor narrowing down the scope of the subject is the author's tendency to interpret the Anglo-Russian hostility as a specific power rivalry in which the two parties endeavoured to ensure their position repeating, mirror-like, each other's offensive or defensive gestures which, through a correct or a wrong interpretation by leading politicians, then led either to agreement or to conflict. In this spirit the author compares not only the political attitudes and aims of the two countries, but also such political personalities as were the British minister Salisbury and the Russian Witte.

The work rests on a solid knowledge of the wide international-political context and derives from concrete situations on the Asiatic scene. Nonetheless, the author's explanation gives the impression that the events took place according to some abstract model of relations which, in virtue of inherent contingencies, might recur anywhere when two powers with equal fears for their security, interests and future grow side by side. Against a background of such a premise, the author compares, in the concluding part of his book, the period of the Great Game, a term applied to this epoch of Anglo-Russian rivalry, with the "Cold War" period following World War II. His design, although comprising certain realistic elements, shows also sensibly weak points primarily in its separation from economic, and in the more recent period also from ideological factors which, as determining motives, have a far more penetrating effect than the rules of diplomatic or political fencing.

D. Gillard undertook to process a concrete historical theme and on its background, in contrast to many preceding authors, he posed himself weighty questions of a general character relating to the mechanism of relationships between contending powers, a mechanism that eventually acts also against the will of statesmen and may bring about conflict situations. His answers, however, move within the narrow scope of evaluating diplomatic abilities, their perspicacity and the psychology of leading political personalities.

An extensive selection of commented literature is appended.

Ivan Doležal

Keyes, Charles F.: *The Golden Peninsula.* New York, MacMillan Publishing Co., Inc. 1977. 370 pp.

A research of the cultural traditions of Southeast Asia belongs among the more demanding tasks, for since the remotest ages up to the present times, this region has been the scene where alongside home sources, also numerous and powerful influences from abroad were at play, primarily from nearby Asian countries, but in modern times also from Europe and the United States of America. The image of this crossroads of nations and cultures was made even more complex by subsequent migratory streams of a motley ethnic appurtenance, by the effects of Asian religious and philosophical systems, the impact of Indian and Chinese culture, the conquest-seeking interventions on the part of Chinese, European and American expansionism, the subjugation of Southeast Asia by the world capitalist economy and the coming of revolutionary ideas that have inspired movements for national liberation and national independence.

Against this background, the American anthropologist Charles F. Keyes has endeavoured to show how local cultural traditions originated and how they affected the processes through which the populations came to be permanently adapted to the prevailing conditions and the changing historical circumstances. He focused his research on a few characteristic regions in which various types of cultural traditions were crystallized. He studied the ways of life, customs and ways of thinking of people living in primitive mountain settlements, in villages of fertile lowlands and in both historical and modern towns of Indo-Chinese States, as well as of Burma and Thailand. The author has designedly left out the region of the Malay Peninsula, for although a part of the continental Southeast Asia, he considers it, in accordance with the view of the other experts, to be closer in its cultural affinities to the Indonesian Archipelago which was mostly influenced by Islam. The problem circuits examined reach from clan traditions, through Buddhist practices, up to such modern phenomena as is nationalism of the minority nation of the Karens on the Thai-Burma borders,

Communism in Vietnam, certain changes in ideology and way of life of nations affected by the sequelae of Western colonialism.

The work draws support from a wide range of more recent results of anthropology and several related scientific disciplines, principally history, orientalist studies and social sciences. It refers to the author's earlier attempt to classify the heterogeneity of the sociocultural systems and to similar attempts by earlier European authors connected with the beginnings of colonialization which Keyes designates here as examples of "applied" orientation in the interests of contesting colonial empires. He considers as extreme the theories of these historians of Southeast Asia according to which Indian and Chinese cultures were merely transplanted to this region. The author's principal care was to elucidate the sociocultural systems within the defined area of continental Southeast Asia and to analyse the changes that are making themselves felt more and more distinctly and insistently also at the present time.

In five chapters the author deals with primitive clan cultures, the Theravada Buddhist civilization, its role in the life of farmers, the oft-discussed problem of tradition and revolution in Vietnam and the significance of modern towns in the life and political attitudes of the population of this part of the world. The author has not given an analysis in his work of all the problems and aspects involved in the making of and the changes taking place in the culture of local nations, but has concentrated on only some of them, those which he considers as characteristic for the entire region. He has succeeded to show not only the different patterns of cultural adaptation in Southeast Asian societies, but also certain sources of tension and of the ongoing socioeconomic processes.

Ivan Doležal

Lean, Geoffrey: *Rich World, Poor World.* London, George Allen and Unwin 1978. 352 pp.

The journalist and historian G. Lean, active in the domain of scientific journalism, has collected in his book a wealth of data on some of the more important issues of our times. He has specially focused his attention on the deepening abyss between the rich and the poor world. He feels convinced that the poor world may become rich and that we already have the ability and the means to ensure a positive life for all.

But for this optimistic perspective to become reality, the author considers radical changes in imagination and attitude to be a prerequisite condition. As one example of a change of attitude he mentions the prognostic report of a scientific institution according to which, by the year 1985, over 35 million American citizens will be willing to adopt a less-consumptive way of life and to maintain a "voluntary simplicity" (p. 332). His argument, however, is not too convincing, for he leaves aside the question as to what will be the attitude of the remaining roughly 200 million Americans and in what manner of ways could or should the means derived from the theoretical presumed voluntary simplicity of the small minority be utilized. The author lays emphasis on moral and spiritual factors if a new world, that is technically possible, is to be built. A tangible difference is evident in the work between a factual and abundantly documented description of inadequate supply of foodstuffs and sources of energy, of population increase in both poor and wealthy countries, of deep social tensions provoked by urbanization and an unjust division of wealth, as well as the increasing use of nuclear energy, on the one hand, and his shorter passages in which this author expresses his conviction that the existing contradictions may be resolved by individual efforts at overcoming greed and envy.

G. Lean does not include references to books and journal sources in his text, but — as he mentions in the appendices — he made use of more than 2,000 of them, of which he lists only about 200 of the most important ones in his Select Bibliography. Yet, despite this stupendous amount of sources studied by the author, some of his evaluations remain on the surface of events. In his view, e.g., "Mahatma Gandhi ranks with Mao Tse-tung as a pioneer of the new philosophy of the rural development" (p. 105). True, both politicians devoted attention to the countryside, only, while Gandhi was an advocate of equality between the town dwellers and villagers, Mao Tse-tung professed the theory of an encirclement of the town by the village. Gandhi was a prominent preacher of non-violence, while Mao Tse-tung, commander and theoretician of a long-term war, is the author of the statement that "power grows out of a gun-barrel". A comparison of such inherently contrasting personalities appears forcible, even if only a partial aspect is involved.

The author points to the depth and urgency of the existing problems, but his attempts at formulating solutions remain misty. Most often he satisfies himself with such undefined terms as "new philosophy", "new economic order", or the need for a "new world order". In this connection he cites the Financial Times and subscribes to their opinion that "moral considerations rather than economic ones ought to be our guide" (p. 321). The author's zealous, but in view of mankind's past experiences hardly effective or practical appeal on individuals' morality is most clearly expressed in the concluding 17th chapter "Changing Philosophy". It is however, characteristic for the ideological base of the whole book, which otherwise has the form of a factual work, built up on a large quantity of data on economic and social tensions prevailing in contemporary society.

Ivan Doležal

Todaro, Michael P.: *Economic Development in the Third World*. London and New York, Longman 1977. 445 pp.

The gradual deterioration in relations between underdeveloped and advanced countries in the seventies and the concomitant difficulties and symptoms of crisis in the capitalist economy helped to focus attention on the unfavourable situation prevailing in former colonial and dependent countries. Efforts were also made to give a theoretical expression to new economic problems and tendencies of the steadily growing number of developing countries, but very few systematic and broadly conceived works have appeared on all the facets and ways of their economic development.

Michael P. Todaro has devoted to these issues a comprehensive, teaching-oriented book, abundantly provided with summary data, tables and figures. Reader orientation in the complex problems is facilitated by a graphic and purposeful division of the topic, succinctly formulated conclusions in all the 17 chapters, a clear readable style, and by stimuli through which the author leads the reader to reflections, and discussions on the principal concepts and ideas.

One of the priorities of this work is its concentrated attention on the concrete situation prevailing in underdeveloped countries, their relations and in a lesser measure their attitude to capitalist and socialist states. The author points out the mutual dependence of all the spheres of world economy, considers as indispensable a coordinated approach towards a solution of problems facing the developing countries and underlines that they may be considered solely within the context of a socio-political system, a fact often ignored by narrowly-oriented economic and technical theoreticians.

The work is divided into four parts. Part One presents a systematic explication of the principles and concepts of development, Part Two comprises a review of the fundamental problems as well as of the internal policy directed to economic development, while Part Three is concerned with conditions and relations of its foreign policy. Into Part Four the author has included present-day possibilities and prospects, pointing at the same time to some of the difficulties and serious weaknesses in development planning. This section also contains the principal conclusions tending towards the idea of a global mutual interdependence.

Todaro's work, arranged methodically and purposefully, elucidates the fundamental concepts, the initial state, a concise historical background, problems, processes and theories of growth of underdeveloped countries. He deals with the best known theoretical concepts without any polemic evaluation and indicates indirectly only which of them he considers to be obsolete or unsuitable for the sphere of the "Third World".

The book is supplemented with a 24-page glossary of the most frequent terms and abbreviations.

Ivan Doležal

Panfilov, V. Z.: *Filosofskie problemy yazykoznaniya* (Philosophical Problems of Linguistics). Moscow, Nauka 1977. 288 pp.

V. Z. Panfilov is notable for his work in the field of philosophical aspects of language study. These have been the object of much research; nevertheless, the linguists ought to tackle this problem repeatedly, especially in the crucial or, as Panfilov puts it, critical periods of the development of their discipline.

The range of the so-called philosophy of language is considerable. It includes problem of language ontology, as well as problems of general principles of language study, i.e., gnoseological problems (see p. 4).

Structuralism assumes that language is a set or network of relations and thus the language units are to be interpreted as intersections of these relations, which implies that language is immanent in its development and that it is a sign system. These assumptions are not acceptable in their totality. Language is indeed a system but it does not exist in a vacuum since it functions in an environment that likewise displays a systemic nature. Closed systems are merely theoretical constructs and language as a partially open system is subject to external influences. At the same time, language is a vehicle, a medium of communication, and as the aim of communication lies outside communication itself, language necessarily undergoes changes that render it more suitable to fulfil its functions. Thus, there is no doubt that language is not immanent and that its autonomy is only relative and subordinate to the requirement of its adequacy. V. Z. Panfilov has developed such a conception of language which is in accordance with what had been said before. His book consists of five chapters.

In Chapter 1 (pp. 16—44), Panfilov examines the interrelations of language and thought. He rejects the so-called theory of linguistic relativity which, however, does not amount to denying the existence of a certain influence exerted by language upon thought and cognition. This is due to the fact that language is the vehicle of a specifically human thought and, besides, the results of the previous cognitive phases are fixed in its vocabulary and grammatical categories (p. 29). They reflect subjectivity and selectivity, features which are inseparable from the process of cognition.

Chapter 2 (pp. 45—98) discusses the role of natural languages in reflecting reality and the problem of linguistic sign. Panfilov defines the latter as a unilateral unit. The reviewer prefers regarding sign as a two-layered unit. Sign is unilateral if we maintain that it stands for or points to something in the external reality and the aim of communication lies in solving nonverbal tasks. But this definition of the linguistic sign would not be exhaustive because, e.g., smoke points to fire and may be regarded as its sign. However, while in the latter instance the relation is causal, the relation between the linguistic sign and the particular section of reality is based upon convention. And it is this lack of causality that makes the linguistic sign a two-layered unit. The material (acoustic or written) shape of the sign represents the meaning and the meaning represents the proper section of reality or denotate. Contrary to Panfilov, this does not mean that the ideal aspect (= meaning) is denied the reflexive nature (p. 55). Meaning reflects some relevant features of the denotate and in this sense it may be characterized as iconic in relation to reality. This structure of the linguistic sign corresponds to two important demands to be fulfilled by language, i.e. those of adequacy and coherence. Meaning in its relation to the denotate is subject to the dictate of adequacy, while the material shape of the linguistic sign in relation to meaning lies in the domain of coherence.

Panfilov in his sophisticated analysis is well aware of the fact that the relative autonomy of language is linked with the presence of both meaning and valency (in the Saussurean sense). This is parallel to our distinction of adequacy and coherence. Both play different roles upon various language levels (see pp. 80—81). Panfilov regards language as a system organized hierarchically, so that the meaning of units of a higher level is no mechanical sum of the meanings of its component units (p. 85).

Chapter 3 (pp. 99—129) deals with language universals the existence of which is conditioned by various factors including the expressive and communicative functions of language (p. 100). Many interesting ideas are pronounced by the author; the relative autonomy of language is conceived as a consequence of the fact that language represents a system which is sufficiently complex in its organization; although the external factors (thought and society) determine the behaviour of language elements, this influence may be said to be modified by intrasystemic factors (p. 104). Put in a different way, the tendency to adequacy is realized in language in an interaction with the tendency to coherence. A good deal of attention is paid to sentence universals as conditioned by the structure of thought (pp. 106—129). Here, syntactic and logico-grammatical levels are distinguished by Panfilov. The reviewer wonders to what extent these may be compared with surface and deep structures. One ought to appreciate Panfilov's ideas on the interrelations holding between the typology of word, on the one hand, and the sentence organization, on the other. Word is regarded as the basic object of typology (pp. 128—129), to which most Czechoslovak and other linguists would readily subscribe.

A concrete example of the application of Panfilov's approach to language is given in Chapters 4 and 5 (pp. 130—157 and pp. 158—285) where the categories of quality and quantity are analysed, again in their relation to thought. The author uses data from various languages. His conclusions are persuasive and plausible. He discovers parallels between the development of thought and that of these categories. However, the reviewer would like to have a more explicit statement on the cyclical character of the development of grammatical categories.

Panfilov's book may be recommended to all linguists as an essential contribution to the study of language in relation to thought and society.

Viktor Krupa

Vardul, I. F.: *Osnovy opisatelnoi lingvistiki. Sintaksis i suprasintaksis* (Foundations of Descriptive Linguistics. Syntax and Suprasyntax). Moscow, Nauka 1977. 352 pp.

Language as an object of investigation requires that a distinction be made between linguistics proper and external linguistic disciplines. The former considers language in isolation from its connections with other phenomena; that is why it ought to utilize purely linguistic notions. The internal organization of an object under examination cannot be discovered if we do not abstract from what is external to language. At the same time, however, no object can be understood in its entirety if we do not complement its isolated examination with an investigation of its interaction with its environment.

Vardul has devoted his book to linguistics in the proper sense, i.e., to what he terms descriptical linguistics. He rejects both descriptive synchronous and taxonomical as unsuitable terms. The aim of descriptical linguistics consists in distinguishing everything that can be distinguished in any language and in identifying everything that can be identified.

According to the author, descriptical linguistics is hampered in its further advance by two factors. First, by surviving remnants of psychologism and, second, by a neglect of the deductive approach.

The volume under review consists of 21 chapters which discuss problems of language description. The author's aim is to construct a formally consistent theory of descriptical linguistics, starting from the most basic notions, e.g., sign, speech, discourse and language, system and its structure. Semantics is distinguished from presemantics. Finally, the syntactic level is discussed at considerable length. Vardul pays a good deal of attention to the analysis of sentence; he introduces and defines such terms as glosseme, lexeme, vocabula, part of speech, syntaxeme, part of sentence, sentence and period, phrase and phraseme, etc. His approach is in many respects original and interesting, although sometimes his effort to be consistent leads to unacceptable conclusions. Thus, the reviewer would not accept the thesis that there exists a universal system of ideal language referents (p. 32). Further, it is

194

thought that signs may also reflect reality (cf. p. 104). Structure is defined by Vardul as a summary property of an object (p. 148). This may be true but it could be added that properties of an object can become manifest only in the latter's relations to other objects, in their interaction.

Vardul's model of descriptical linguistics is notable for its internal consistence and absence of contradictory statements. Its application to particular languages may give many fruitful results and, besides, it may lead to certain modifications of the proposed approach.

Viktor Krupa

Pidgin and Creole Linguistics. Edited by Albert Valdman. Bloomington and London, Indiana University Press 1977. xvi + 399 pp.

This is a collection of fourteen papers divided into five sections. All of them, except for Keith Whinnom's paper *Lingua Franca: Historical Problems,* appear here in printed form for the first time (Whinnom's paper was originally delivered at a specialized European colloquium).

Section I — **The Field of Pidgin and Creole Studies,** is represented by two papers, i.e. *The Development of Pidgin and Creole Studies* (pp. 3—20) by David DeCamp and *On the Beginnings of Pidgin and Creole Studies: Schuchardt and Hesseling* (pp. 21—45) by Guus Meijer and Pieter Muysken. The authors of both papers deal with pidgin and creole languages diachronically. DeCamp gives a survey of pidgin and creole studies, but he lays stresses mainly on the activities after 1959 when the First International Conference devoted to the Creole Language Studies was held in Jamaica. Meijer and Muysken describe works and views of the most prominent of the early creolists, the German Schuchardt and the Dutchman Hesseling. However, they also discuss the nineteenth-century views and works of the Portuguese Coelho and the Frenchman Adam.

Section II — **Pidgins, Creoles, and Problems of Language Acquisition and Language Universals** contains three papers, namely, *Pidginization and Creolization: Language Acquisition and Language Universals* (pp. 49—69) by Derek Bickerton, *Pidginization, Creolization, and Language Change* (pp. 70—98) by Elizabeth Closs Traugott, and *Simplified Registers, Broken Language, and Pidginization* (pp. 99—125) by Charles A. Ferguson and Charles E. DeBose. In this section, the authors occupy themselves with the processes of pidginization and creolization. In particular, Bickerton interprets pidginization and creolization as special types of second- and first-language learning, Traugott investigates the implications of pidginization and creolization for three theories of linguistic change, i.e. the genetic, the acquisitional and the dynamic wave theory, and Ferguson and DeBose discusses pidginization as the interaction of foreigner talk and broken language; all three varieties (foreigner talk, broken language and pidgin) are a transformation of normal language input.

Section III — **The Life-Cycle: Pidginization, Creolization, and Decreolization** brings four papers: *Processes of Pidginization in African Languages* (pp. 129—154) by Gabriel Manessy, *Creolization: Elaboration in the Development of Creole French Dialects* (pp. 155—189) by Albert Valdman, *The Question of Prior Creolization in Black English* (pp. 190—221) by John R. Rickford, and *Processes of Pidginization and Creolization* (pp. 222—255) by Robert Le Page. Here, the three stages of the life cycle of pidgins are dealt with. Manessy demonstrates these questions on the material of African languages; his approach is predominantly descriptive. Valdman focuses on Creole French dialects and analyses the relationships between syntactic and phonological features in their development. Rickford investigates the creole origin of American Black English and the influence that had moulded its features on the levels of phonology, morphology, syntax and lexicon. Finally, Le Page summarizes his insights concerning processes of pidginization and creolization; his emphasis rests on the sociolinguistic as well as the psychological aspects of the problem.

Section IV — **Problems of Genesis and Development: The Historical and Social Matrix** contains three papers: *Toward the Reconstruction of the Social Matrix of Creole Language* (pp. 259—276) by Robert Chaudenson, *Recovering Pidgin Genesis: Approaches and Problems* (pp. 277—294) by Ian F. Hancock, and *Lingua Franca: Historical Problems* (pp. 295—310) by Keith Whinnom. This section concentrates upon the question of the origin of pidgin and creole languages. Chaudenson shows how anthropological, historical and sociological facts allow to identify those languages that have played a role in the process of formation of creole languages. His conclusions are based on data from the history of the settlement of Bourbon Island in the Indian Ocean. Hancock's suggestions that Lingua Franca (Sabir) originated much earlier than is recognized and that Yiddish is an offspring of Lingua Franca, are rather inconclusive. Whinnom's evidence, as far as this problem is concerned, is more convincing.

Section V — **Creoles and Pidgins and National Development** contains two papers: *Creole Languages and Primary Education* (pp. 313—332) by Dennis R. Craig, and *Pidgins, Creoles, Lingue Franche, and National Development* (pp. 333—357) by Stephen A. Wurm. Craig discusses educational problems in creole-speaking areas in Jamaica and Haiti, while Wurm inquires into problems connected with Melanesian Pidgin English (Tok Pisin) and Hiri Motu (formerly Police Motu).

The volume is supplemented with a Summary Bibliography (pp. 358—361), an excellent list of pidgin and creole languages compiled by Ian F. Hancock (pp. 362—391) with maps, and an Index (pp. 392—399).

All in all, the reviewed collective volume presents valuable papers in the field of the evolution of pidgin and creole languages. Some of the problems involved are discussed here in a more serious and detailed way than before, e.g. the long neglected or unsatisfactorily treated problem of the origin of pidgins and creoles, and some other problems of relevance to sociolinguistics, bilingualism and language contact, but possibly instructive also to general and theoretical linguistics.

Jozef Genzor

Literatura Vostoka v noveishee vremya (1917—1945) (Modern Literature of Asia). Moscow, Izdatelstvo Moskovskogo universiteta 1977. 559 pp.

This is the work of a numerous team of scholars attached to workplaces of the Moscow and Leningrad: Institute of Asian and African Countries at the Moscow State University, Eastern Department of the Leningrad State University, Oriental Institute of the Academy of Sciences USSR and the Institute of World Literature, Academy of Sciences USSR, and was editorially prepared by a group of four Soviet literary scholars-orientalists: I. S. Braginsky, V. I. Semanov, E. V. Paevskaya and N. B. Nikitina.

Literatura Vostoka is the last but one of a five-volume series of studies *Istoriya literatur zarubezhnogo Vostoka* (A History of Literatures of Foreign Orient) which began to appear in 1962 and whose publication will end in the first half of the eighties. This volume begins with the times of the October revolution which "made an enormous impression in the East and resulted in an essential change in the historical fates of colonial and dependent countries" (p. 3) and ends with the year 1945, with the defeat of the fascist and militarist régimes in Germany and Japan. This defeat in which the USSR played a very weighty role, "opened up new possibilities for the development of progressive literatures of Eastern countries" (p. 9).

With the exception of the literature of Egypt which geographically belongs to Africa, all the others dealt with in this book are Asian literatures. As might be expected, being the work of 20 different authors, the book is not uniform in style, although for the most part, it combines the form of a historical treatise, with shorter or longer biographical sketches devoted to the most prominent authors of the various countries. For the sake of clarity the historical treatment is presented so as to bring out the genological wealth of the individual literatures. The book is pedagogically oriented and is destined to undergraduates of Soviet institutions of higher learning.

Besides Egyptian literature already noted, the book analyses, from Asiatic Arab literatures, also that of Lebanon, Syria and Iraq; from Indian literatures, we find Hindi, Urdu, Bengalese and Tamil and in a few further languages. In addition, there

197

are national literatures, viz. Turkish, Iranian, Afghan, Indonesian, Japanese, Chinese, Korean and Vietnamese.

The historical treatment adheres to the chronological course of events. It may be noted that the twenties and thirties were characterized in all the Asian countries by an extensive organizational activity in the literary field. Unions, leagues, societies and other associations were being founded which later intervened in a significant manner into the artistic and political life of the various countries. During that period, a revolutionary and proletarian literature came into being in numerous countries, particularly in the Far East, which became most developed and bore fruit especially in Japan and China. The possibilities of this development had not been conditioned solely by the socio-cultural tenor of the various countries, but also by the great impact of Soviet and European revolutionary and proletarian literature. Asian countries came into contact with the works of M. Gorky, V. Mayakovsky, H. Barbusse, with the literary-critical and theoretical studies of V. I. Lenin, G. V. Plekhanov, A. V. Lunacharsky and others.

Besides proletarian and revolutionary literature, more or less typical for these countries were various genres of modernism, symbolism, impressionism, but literary freudism and surrealism, too, were fashionable and greatly in vogue.

Above all, the more important among literatures of these countries, e.g. Japanese and Chinese, were the arena in which literary trends that in their original homelands, European countries, had appeared in a chronological sequence, here existed in parallel, side by side. The most vigorous works, both socially and artistically, were those that may be characterized as works of critical realism. Here belong, e.g. the short stories by Lu Hsün, the most eminent Chinese writer of modern times, or the stories and novels by Premchand, the most outstanding representative of modern Hindi literature.

Various Asian literatures, particularly from the twenties, contain numerous works with striking romantic tendencies, occasionally linked with modern European literary trends, e.g. expressionism. An interesting passage is, for instance, that about Chinese literature, where mention is made of romanticism of an expressionist orientation into which the author E. A. Tsybina includes poets and writers of the Creation Society (Ch'uang-tsao she): Kuo Mo-jo, Ch'eng Fang-wu, Yü Ta-fu, Chang Tzu-p'ing and others living at that time in Japan.

Asian literatures of the 1920s and 1930s even more than those from the second half of the 19th or the first two decades of the 20th century, joined the trend of world literature. This is evidenced by the genetic-contact relations between Asian and European or American literatures, or those between Asian literatures themselves, as well as typological affinities of different kinds. As regards the former, i.e. genetic-contact relations, a foremost place in modern Asian literatures in the period 1917—1945, belonged to classical Russian literature of the 19th century and to

198

Soviet literature. Readers may repeatedly convince themselves of the enormous impact of V. I. Lenin or M. Gorky on Asian literatures.

The end of the 1930s and the first half of the 1940s in Asia were greatly marked by war events. In several countries, particularly in China, India and Iran, antifascist and antimilitarist literatures came into being, while in other parts, e.g. in Southeast Asia which came under Japanese domination, literature was strictly censored. In Turkey and in Japan, progressive literature was practically silenced.

A perusal of this book reinforces the reader's conviction that the writing of similar literary history, particularly if this refers to modern times and deals with more than one national literature, may not neglect or lose sight of the international and comparative aspect of investigation. The authors of this work were fully conscious of the importance of the social function of these literatures, their mission in the struggle for national and social liberation, against the oppression of colonialism and imperialism, home reactionary forces, their role as a means of struggle for the emancipation of women and socio-political progress. This also applies to the communicative function of literature, its far more extensive application, its ideological action and the origin of concerned mass literature. Asian literatures of this period achieved their artistic and aesthetic apogee in the twenties and thirties. A gradual substitution of old aesthetic standards of the preceding period by new ones found a relatively fertile soil during the years 1917—1935 for the creation of new literary works of the most diverse genres. The works by Sadek Hedayat, Lu Hsün, Nazim Hikmet, Akutagawa Ryunosuke have achieved world fame and have been translated into many languages.

The book under review deserves to be read by students in the domain of Asian literatures and fulfills a pioneering mission in its efforts at studying national literatures both by the methods of comparative as well as national study of literature.

Marián Gálik

O yazykakh, folklore i literature Okeanii (On Languages, Folklore and Literature of Oceania). Edited by A. S. Petrikovskaya. Moscow, Nauka 1978. 192 pp.

This collection comprises papers concerned with some linguistic and cultural problems of present-day Oceania by Soviet scholars.

Oceania is the last part of the world to get rid of the colonial heritage. This complicated process of decolonization is accompanied by various changes in the spheres of language and culture. The new independent countries need their respective national languages as well as culture to back their national identity. Most attention is paid to New Guinea which is probably more important than any other country in Oceania. Altogether there are three papers discussing the linguistic problems while the other three deal with folk music and literature of some peoples of Oceania.

A. A. Leontiev (in his paper Social, Linguistic and Psychological Factors of the Language situation in Papua-New Guinea, pp. 5—15) analyses the role of Pidgin English in the political and cultural life of Papua-New Guinea. Various intertribal languages are judged as to their prospects, and Pidgin English is regarded as the language with the most promising future in the whole country.

M. A. Zhurinskaya's contribution (Nominal Possessive Constructions in Melanesian Languages, pp. 16—38) describes the so-called category of possession typical not only for Melanesian, but also for other Oceanic languages. She is right when rejecting a complete identification of thought forms with language forms (p. 24) and believes that this category deserves further investigation.

A characteristic of the present-day speech of the Easter Island is drawn by I. K. Fiodorova (Some Features of the Development of the Rapanui Language, pp. 39—81). Her paper is based upon available folklore texts which are classified by Fiodorova into contemporary stories by the Easter Islanders, Bible translations, texts reflecting the features of the language of the 19th century, exoteric versions of Easter Island myths, and texts similar to those supplied by Ure Vaeiko as informant. The Easter Island language is characterized as agglutinative analytical (p. 40). While both characteristics are true for the Easter Island language, the former attribute loses its weight to a considerable degree if a language is analytical. Fiodorova pays a good deal of attention to variation of vowels and consonants (pp. 41—42) and also discusses some phonotactic regularities. Derivative processes are also described at some length and reduplication is stressed as one of the most important devices employed in derivation. Neither are syntactic problems neglected by Fiodorova (pp. 53—79). Fiodorova's study is one of the few works dealing with the Easter Island language. It cannot be ignored by those who are engaged in the decipherment of the kohau rongorongo.

During his field trip, B. N. Putilov (Problems of Research in the Folk Songs of Oceania, pp. 82—99) has recorded some 350 songs in various parts of Melanesia, i.e., in New Guinea, Nauru, New Hebrides, New Caledonia, Fiji, and, besides, in the Tuvalu and Gilbert groups. Putilov publishes extensively upon the Oceanic folk music in the past and his present paper is an attempt at some generalizations and conclusions (loss of ancient traditions, acceptance and adoption of western models, role of folklore in the modern society).

The same author has contributed another paper (Connections of the Musical Folklore of New Guinea Papuans with Their Mythology, pp. 100—130), devoted to the alleged mythological origin of Papuan musical instruments, songs and ceremonies. A knowledge of these links is a necessary prerequisite for a correct interpretation of Papuan music.

200

The last paper by A. S. Petrikovskaya (The Rise of National Literatures in Oceania, pp. 131—190) deals with a key problem of Oceanic culture — with the beginnings of literature in Oceania. Again, considerable attention is paid to New Guinea. Because of the lack of local public, Oceanic authors prefer writing in standard English. In addition to New Guinea, the author discusses literary problems of Samoa, Fiji, Tonga, and New Zealand (Maori).

All contributions are supplied with useful bibliographical lists.

The present volume is another piece of evidence that a new centre for Oceanic studies has arisen in addition to those of London, Paris, Honolulu, Auckland, and Sydney.

Viktor Krupa

Croghan, Richard V.: *The Development of Philippine Literature in English (Since 1900)*. Quezon City, Philippines, Alemar-Phoenix Publishing House, Inc. 1975. vii + 511 pp.

This book presents the latest revised and considerably enlarged edition of a manual compiled on the basis of several text-books, but especially of one in mimeographed form from the year 1972, which the author — a literary scholar and a translator from Tagalog — used when teaching Philippine literature at the University of the Philippines. As a matter of fact, it is a voluminous anthology of the Philippine literature written in English, perhaps, the most representative one available so far.[1] This anthology covers the whole period of the development of Philippine fiction in English during the last three quarters of this century. It is accompanied by brief excursions into its history, and provides bibliographic references and several useful appendices.

The author's aim was to illustrate the development of the Anglophone Philippine literature in its dynamics, as well as to reflect the improvement of various genres — poetry, fiction and essays. "The main criteria for selecting material to go into the book," he writes, "were that the work must be written by a Filipino, it must be interesting and it should reflect some literary qualities for that particular period in Philippine literature" (p. vii). While repeatedly emphasizing a close connection between the literary process and the historical development of the country,

---

[1] See, for example, Yabes, L. Y.: *Philippine Literature in English, 1898—1957, a bibliographical survey*. Quezon City, 1958, 92 pp.; Florentino, A. S. (Comp. and ed.): *Midcentury Guide to Philippine Literature in English*. Manila, 1963, 194 pp.; Roseburg, A. G. (Ed. and comp.): *Pathways to Philippine Literature in English, anthology with biographical and critical introductions*. Quezon City, Alemar-Phoenix P. H. 1966, 294 pp.

R. Croghan divides the history of the Philippine literature written in English into three periods: early, middle and contemporary. However, his periodization is not documented in a convincing manner. Samples of literary writings from every period are furnished with brief critical introductions where the most important literary works are discussed and evaluated.

I. The main features characterizing the early period, 1900—1930 (pp. 3—64) are the introduction of the American system of education, the rise of the Anglophone press (Manila Times, Philippines Free Press and others), the rise and gradual development of poetry and prose written by Filipinos in English. This development had a remarkably dynamic course: in 1900, English was declared the official language of education in all public schools of the country; in 1907, the first poem written by a Filipino (Justo Juliano) in English was published; in 1908, the first short story appeared as a poem in the Philippines Free Press; in 1921, Zoilo M. Galang published the first novel written in English, *A Child of Sorrow* and the first collection of essays *Life and Success*. The twenties of this century are especially remarkable, for then the Philippines Herald, the Philippine Magazine, several university journals, first collections of stories and anthologies began to be published. These favoured the consolidation of the Philippine short-story production. From 1925 on, the Free Press awarded an annual prize for the best story; in the same year the Association of the Philippine Writers was founded and in 1927, the PEN Club of the University of the Philippines (hitherto a directive organ) publishing mainly works by short-story writers, was established. The most notable of the early stories are *Dead Stars* (1925) by Paz Marquez-Benitez, *The Small Key* (1927) by Paz Latorena, *Harvest* (1930) by Loreto Paras-Sulit, *The Fence* and *Footnote to Youth* by J. G. Villa, *Zita* (1930) by Arturo B. Rotor; they are included in the present anthology; essays by Fr. Benitez, J. Bocobo, M. Kalaw are also included. Poetry is represented by the best poems of that time — *The Spouse* by Luis G. Dato, *The Rural Maid* by F. M. Maramag, *Rain* and *Loneliness* by M. de Gracia Concepcion, sonnets by J. Villa.

II. The middle period, 1930—1960 (pp. 67—246) bear witness both quantitatively and qualitatively to the considerable advances of the Philippine literature in English, and the consolidation of all its genres in the literary life of the country, in spite of the adverse circumstances of their development during the years of Japanese occupation (1942—1945). During this period several organizations were formed, i.e. the Philippine Book Guild (1936), the League of Philippine Writers (1939) and the Association of Philippine Writers (1955), the first Conference of national writers took place at Baguio in 1958; numerous students' literary journals written in English at universities and colleges, as well as a special journal devoted to poetry (Signatures, 1955) were launched; many collections and anthologies of poetry and prose in English were issued. In 1940, at the first Literary contest of the Autonomous Philippines, prizes were awarded to the essay by Salvador P. Lopez *Literature and Society,* to Manuel E. Arguilla's story *How My Brother Leon Brought Home a Wife,* to the poem by R. Zulueta da Costa *Like the Molave* and to Juan C. Laya's novel *His Native Soil* — the best works in English included in anthologies. In 1949, the journal Philippines Free Press instituted an annual prize for the best short story; in 1950, the Palanca Memorial Award for achievements in the field of literature was established. In accordance with the Constitution of the Philippines of 1935, English and Spanish (from 1946 on also Tagalog or the National Language) were declared official languages.

In addition to the works mentioned above the anthology contains the best short stories of the period: *Night in the Hills* (1931) by P. Marquez-Benitez, *Morning in Nagrebcan* and *Rice* by M. Arguilla, *Three Generations* and *May Day Eve* by N. Joaquin, short stories from the collection *The Wound and the Scar* (1937) by A. B. Rotor, stories by E. Alfon, D. Fresnosa, D. Paulo Dizon, H. Ocampo, N. V. M. Gonzalez and some others.

III. The contemporary period, 1960—1975 (pp. 249—484) brings us practically to present-day literature of the Philippines. This era has experienced quite a few political upheavals and internal changes that have brought about the rise of a "New Society" in the country in 1972. A new constitution was declared in 1973; according to it both English and Tagalog or Pilipino are the official languages of the country. All genres of Philippine literature are cultivated. In 1960, a State prize, i.e. the Republic Cultural Heritage Award was founded; in 1966 the title of "Poet-Laureate" and in 1973 the honorary title of "National Artist" were introduced (one of the first was awarded to José Garcia Villa). In 1975, the Fourth symposium of Afro-Asian writers was held in Manila.

Short-story has come to be a predominant genre of the Philippine literature in English, romantic subjects of the previous period are giving way to "subjects of rebellion and violence", mainly towards the end of the 60s– beginning of the 70s (p. 249). In the present anthology, this trend is represented by selected works from collection of leading contemporary authors, such as *Distance to Andromeda* by Gregorio Brillantes, *The Butcher, the Baker, the Candlestick Maker* (1962) by Gilda Cordero-Fernando, *Stories* (1968), *Author's Selection* (1971) and *Adventures in Forgotten Country* (1975) by Kerima Polotan-Tuvera, *Loneliness Is a Volcano* (1966), *Nocturne for Piano and Heartstrings* (1967) and *The Three Faces of the Hero* (1969) by José A. Quirino, *Children of the City* (1974) by the talented young story writer Amadis Ma. Guerrero and some others. The essay genre of this time has been perfectioned by K. Polotan-Tuvera, F. Tutay, historiographic articles by O. de la Costa, publicist and literary essays by Miguel A. Bernad, Nick Joaquin (samples of their creation have been given a place in the anthology), and also by M. Soliven, J. V. Cruz, J. Sison, T. Agoncillo, C. Quirino and some others. It should also be noted that the best novels were published at this time; first of all *The Bamboo Dancers* (1959, 1960) by N. V. M. Gonzalez, *The Hand of the Enemy* (1961) by K. Polotan-Tuvera and *The Woman Who Had Two Navels* (1961) by N. Joaquin,

The Pretenders (1961) by Fr. Sionil José, *The Volcano* (1965) by B. N. Santos, *Like a Big Brave Man* (1961, 1963) by C. Carunungan, *But for the Lovers*... (1970) by W. D. Nolledo, and some others.

In the contemporary Philippine poetry the compiler makes references to poems of the 60s written in the macaronic Anglo-Tagalog language (R. Tinio, J. Lansang, E. Torres, S. F. Bautista), satirical poems by F. Daus, A. Cuenca and A. Hufana, poetic miniatures by N. V. M. Gonzalez, selected works by R. Demetillo (collections *Dedal*, 1961, *Masks and Signatures,* 1968 and others), G. Burce Bunao (collection *Trembling and Fear*, 1968), Mauro R. Avena (collection *Rain*, 1970, *Evening Verses*, 1971), Tita Lacambra-Ayala and some others. Specimens of almost all of them are represented in the anthology.

The Appendices bring a list of winners of the Philippines Free Press short story contests (1949—1971, pp. 487—489), a list of laureates of the Carlos Palanca Memorial Awards for literature in English (1950—1976, pp. 490—496), a list of winners of short-story prizes of the Graphic Magazine and Focus Philippines (pp. 497—498), the Glossary of Non-English Words and Expressions (pp. 499—509) — which is very useful — comprises about 400 Tagalog, Ilocano, Visayan, Javanese, Malayan, Chinese, Spanish, Latin and other words and combinations of words, place names encountered in the Philippine literature in English. An Author and Title Index (pp. 509—511) is also appended.

As a whole, R. V. Croghan's book *The Development of Philippine Literature in English (Since 1900)* is obviously of great interest as a systematic aid. It is a detailed and thoroughly documented work, well illustrated with carefully selected specimens and will be useful not only to Philippinists, but also to those interested in a comparative study of literature of the countries of Asia and Africa, to specialists in general literary criticism, and to all those interested in literature written in English.

Vladimir Makarenko — Jozef Genzor

Graaf de, H. J.—Kennedy, J.—Scott, W. H.: *Geschichte*. Handbuch der Orientalistik, Dritte Abteilung, Erster Band, Zweite Lieferung. Leiden/Köln, E. J. Brill 1977. VII + 247 S., 1 Karte.

In diesem Handbuch wird die Geschichte dreier Staaten Südostasiens — Indonesien, Philippinen, Malaysia — deren geschichtliche Entwicklung viele gemeinsame Züge aufweist, in drei in sich abgeschlossenen Beiträgen behandelt. Es sind Staaten, die erst nach dem zweiten Weltkrieg durch harte und wechselvolle Kämpfe ihre formelle politische Unabhängigkeit erlangten und heute im Rahmen der ASEAN zusammenarbeiten. Ihr Geschichtsbild wurde von einer mehr als dreihundert Jahre währenden Kolonialherrschaft geprägt. Auch wenn sich die Kolonialherren durch Machtkämpfe ablösten, blieb doch der Charakter ihrer nationalen Unterdrückungsmethoden gleich. Diese Entwicklung wird Anfang des 16. Jh. ausgelöst durch die Entdeckungsfahrten der Portugiesen (bzw. Spanier) auf der Suche nach neuen Reichtümern, findet ihren Anfang in den ausländischen Handelsniederlassungen (Vereinigte Ostindische Kompanie und English East India Company) im 17. Jh. und führt direkt zur offenen kolonialen Unterdrückung, d.h. politischen Unterwerfung und völligen ökonomischen Ausbeutung.

Dieser Problematik räumen die Autoren den größten Raum in ihren Studien ein. H. J. de Graaf betrachtet im ersten Artikel die *Geschichte Indonesiens in der Zeit der Verbreitung des Islam und während der europäischen Vorherrschaft* (S. 1—118). J. Kennedy beschäftigt sich mit der *Geschichte Malayas seit 1400 u.Z.* (S. 119—195) und W. H. Scott gibt einen kurzen Überblick über die *Geschichte der Philippinen* (S. 196—229). Leider ist die Geschichtsdarstellung nicht immer objektiv, sondern wird vom Blickwinkel der bürgerlichen Geschichtsschreibung aus betrachtet. So entbehrt der Satz von de Graaf (S. 89) nicht einer gewissen Ironie, wenn er schreibt, daß „große Teile Indonesiens die Autorität des Gouvernements nicht anerkannt hatten, obgleich sie zur niederländischen Einflußsphäre gehörten" und, daß „die Indonesier sich 1945 von einer 350-jährigen Kolonialherrschaft befreit hätten, also wenigstens eine starke Übertreibung" sei. Dagegen sprechen eindeutige Fakten, die selbst aus seiner eigenen Arbeit zu entnehmen sind. Am Schluß dieser Abhandlung, in *Die Liquidation der kolonialen Verwaltung* (S. 113—118), geht der Autor auf das letzte traurige Kapitel der Kolonialgeschichte, auf die Versuche der Aufrechterhaltung der niederländischen Kolonialmacht mit allen Mitteln, entgegen den UNO-Beschlüssen, ein.

Malaya (bzw. Malaysia), Gegenstand des zweiten Beitrages, stand schon seit dem frühen 15. Jh. unter dem Königreich Malacca im Mittelpunkt ausgedehnter Handels- und Kulturbeziehungen zwischen asiatischen und arabischen Staaten. Seit Beginn des 16. Jh. mischten sich die Portugiesen in diese Beziehungen ein und versuchten auf Malaya Fuß zu fassen bis sie hundert Jahre später von den Niederländern abgelöst wurden. 1824 fällt Malaya unter britische Oberherrschaft. Der Problematik der britischen Kolonialherrschaft, die bis in die 60-iger Jahre u. Jh. andauerte, widmet der Autor sein größtes Augenmerk. Er geht dabei auch auf die Rolle des benachbarten siamesischen Staates ein, weist auf die maßgebenden ökonomischen und politischen Einflüsse der in der zweiten Hälfte des 19. Jh. eingewanderten Chinesen hin und zeichnet die innen- und außenpolitischen Konflikte Malaysias nach Erringung der Unabhängigkeit auf. Ihren zeitlichen Abschluß findet die Arbeit mit dem Beitritt Malaysias in die ASEAN und den Wahlen 1969. Eine Bibliographie (S. 193—195) ist eingefügt.

Der Autor des letzten Beitrages befaßt sich nach kurzer Erwähnung der vorspanischen philippinischen Geschichte (S. 196—200) mit der spanischen Kolonialherr-

205

schaft bis zur Proklamation der Unabhängigkeit 1898. Drei Jahre später übernehmen die Amerikaner die Rolle der Kolonisatoren, die auch nach der Ausrufung der unabhängigen Republik der Philippinen 1946 ihre militärischen Stützpunkte aufrechterhalten.

Der Verfasser benutzt innerhalb der einzelnen Kapitel die Regierungsperioden der Generalgouverneure als chronologischen Leitfaden. In den Kapiteln werden bestimmte Probleme besonders hervorgehoben: die Durchsetzung des spanischen Lebensstils und die Bildungsprivilegien der Spanier, Resultate der Kolonisation, das Erwachen des Nationalbewußtseins und die philippinische Revolution, die japanische Okkupation und der Weg der Republik nach 1946. Ein Verzeichnis (S. 224) weist auf die verwendete Literatur hin.

Im Anhang befinden sich ein Sachregister (S. 230—238), ein Geographisches Register (S. 239—242) sowie ein Personen-Register (S. 243—247).

Durch die Zusammenstellung aller drei Beiträge in einem Handbuch wird ein interessanter Geschichtsvergleich geliefert, der vielleicht noch durch eine Zeittafel im Anhang hätte ergänzt werden können.

Cornelia Trunkvalter

Casparis de, J. G.: *Indonesian Palaeography. A History of Writing in Indonesia from the Beginning to C. A. D. 1500.* Handbuch der Orientalistik, Dritte Abteilung, Vierter Band, Erste Lieferung. Leiden — Köln, E. J. Brill 1975. 96 pp., 10 plates.

There is hardly any book on the ancient history of Indonesia that would not mention inscriptions. In addition, scientific papers frequently appear that deal with particular inscriptions. However, the study under review presents for the first time since F. K. Holle's work from the year 1882 a comprehensive summary of inscriptions materials in their overall complexity. It covers a time span of over one thousand years, beginning with the earliest known inscriptions in the Early Pallava script from the mid-eighth century (p. 12 ff.) and following up the development through Kawi of Old Javanese scripts from the years 750 to 1250 (p. 28 ff.) and Javanese and regional scripts of the Majapahit period (from the year 1250 to 1450), up to the Indonesian scripts from the mid-fifteenth century (p. 63 ff). Two brief sections mention also Tamil and Arabic scripts. The history of Indonesian writing is divided into five distinct periods, involving 200 to 300 years each, with a continuous development being clearly manifest. Such an image is created by a thorough processing of the peculiarities and differences of symbols, signs and possibilities of their variations in the manner of writing. At the same time, there is a noticeable tendency to simplification from earlier towards more recent periods.

In his investigations, the author does not dwell solely on ancient scripts and the development of their written forms, but sees their development in relation to political, economic and cultural history of the particular regions in which they were in use. He also points to certain relations in the type of writing (Sanskrit, Nāgarī) in other parts of Asia (Northern and Southern India, Sri Lanka, Cambodia).

An evaluation of inscriptions may contribute to an elucidation of the history of Indonesia, nevertheless, such inscriptions must be dealt with critically, as several subjective influences might bring about a distorted image of its history. A correct solution of inscriptions and their dating require a well-grounded palaeographic knowledge — and this, the present author certainly possesses. As an epigraphist in the archaeological service in Indonesia, Casparis had opportunity enough to acquire practical experience on the spot, and thus, the author not only describes the techniques and modes of resolving scripts, but also endeavours to present an objective view in connection with inscriptions.

Practically all the materials come from Central and East Java and Bali and only a modicum from Western Java and Sumatra. This of course permitted a continuous development of scripts to be given only from East and Central Java. The existing knowledge of ancient scripts is based on inscriptions in stone and metal – coopper, for text on organic materials, understandably enough, failed to survive.

At the end of his study, the author arrives at two interesting conclusions: (1) No direct relation exists between political history and the history of scripts. Regional territories within large empires (Śrivijaya and Majapahit) retained a *local genius* in their own script. (2) Alongside a *visible* history of script, such for instance, as stone- and copper-plate inscriptions, there exists a latent history of writing on more perishable materials, like palm leaf and bamboo. Their existence through centuries may be deduced by an analysis of the styles of writing on copper- and stone-plates.

The aim of the present work was not to give a complete, exhaustive record of all scripts of ancient Indonesia, but rather to provide an introduction to the study of early Indonesian scripts, for the work may simultaneously be considered as an example of working procedure. To this end, the author in his appendix *Materials for the Study of Indonesian Palaeography* (pp. 74—79) supplies a large number of good quality photographs — reproduced from other books and magazines. His own photographs (plates I—X) are provided with detailed explanations (pp. 87—96), and aids to further study may be found also in the *Bibliography* (pp. 80—82).

Cornelia Trunkvalter

Vo Nguyen Giap: *Ecrits*. Hanoï, Editions en langues étrangères 1977. 656 pp.

La première partie de la collection comprend des exposés, rapports et allocutions sur plusieurs points importants au sens militaire que l'auteur jugeait nécessaire d'éclaircir dans son traitement du mouvement de résistance vietnamienne contre l'intervention américaine. Le premier exposé de juin 1969 évalue la victoire du peuple vietnamien sur l'offensive de l'armée de l'air et de mer américaine, menée non seulement à partir des bases au Vietnam du Sud et des porte-avions, mais aussi à partir de celles situées en Thaïlande. Bien qu'en ce temps la guerre ne fût pas encore terminée, Vo Nguyen Giap désigne — et à bon droit — les succès vietnamiens en repoussant les attaques aériennes et en surmontant les effets néfastes, comme une victoire de signification stratégique.

La contribution suivante traite des expériences régionales des unités militaires qui tenait tête, à l'arrière-front, à la guerre américaine de destruction. L'auteur souligne l'importance du travail politique et d'organisation pour relever et soutenir leur état de préparation au combat. Certes, il n'entend pas passer sous silence l'équipement moderne et la force de l'adversaire, mais montre comment les unités vietnamiennes pouvaient, en close coopération avec le peuple, les surmonter et les battre.

L'exposé approfondi sur le rôle des grandes villes dans le mouvement de résistance apporte des concepts précieux sur la défense active et passive et examine les fondements de la haute morale et de la résistance de la population. La première partie des *Écrits* est terminée par deux chapitres sur la signification stratégique des unités régionales et par une contribution sur les questions de la guerre maritime, avec une section introductoire contenant à titre d'exemples, les opérations maritimes et riveraines dans l'histoire vietnamienne.

Cependant, le point de gravité de l'œuvre réside dans la deuxième partie où l'auteur s'occupe, au plan théorique, des questions de la guerre de libération nationale au Vietnam, élucide sa ligne de conduite générale et en formule, à partir des expériences de combats, des conclusions stratégiques et tactiques.

Dans cette partie aussi il puise de précieux stimulants dans l'histoire vietnamienne, extraordinairement riche en traditions populaires, révolutionnaires et de libération nationale. L'œuvre éclaircit le concept marxiste de la guerre populaire dans son application aux conditions du Vietnam. D'une signification particulière sont les chapitres consacrées au mode de conduite de la guerre, à l'art militaire et au rôle dirigeant du parti communiste. Les opinions de Vo Nguyen Giap sur ces questions, originellement publiées en 1969, étaient attentivement étudiées aussi à l'étranger, parce qu'elles aident à mieux comprendre les sources des succès vietnamiens de ce temps et aussi ultérieurs, couronnés par la victoire finale et l'unification du pays.

La troisième partie contient une autre étude étendue, traitant de l'armement des masses populaires et de l'édification de l'armée du peuple. Elle avait paru originellement à l'époque avant la signature de l'accord de Paris sur la fin de la guerre au

Vietnam. Les parties d'introduction présentent un exposé des thèses marxistes sur l'organisation militaire du prolétariat dans les contextes historiques de l'Europe et les expériences post-révolutionnaires soviétiques. La relation étroite de l'auteur à l'histoire est évidente aussi en ce qu'il puise des stimulants et des exemples dans l'historiographie vietnamienne classique, et tour d'abord dans le chapitre sur les traditions des forces armées du Vietnam qui remontent loin à l'époque de résistances armées contre les agressions étrangères répétées de la part des seigneurs féodaux chinois. En outre, l'auteur évalue le rôle du parti communiste dans l'armement du peuple, rapporte de nombreux détails sur l'aspect militaire et militaire-politique de la résistance et arrive aux conclusions qui se rattachent non seulement au Vietnam, mais qui sont stimulantes aussi au plan global de la lutte de libération nationale. L'œuvre est un témoignage à l'importance extraordinaire que les dirigeants révolutionnaires vietnamiens attachent au facteur moral et politique et aux principes léninistes de l'édification politique de l'armée.

Les *Écrits* de Vo Nguyen Giap représentent une source irremplaçable et authentique pour l'étude de l'histoire révolutionnaire contemporaine du Vietnam. Leur importance et portée sont d'autant plus hautes que l'auteur avait l'occasion de vérifier et de prouver la validité de ses conclusions théoriques en pratique dans sa fonction de stratégiste des opération décisives dans la guerre victorieuse de la libération nationale.

Ivan Doležal

Anthologie de la littérature vietnamienne. Tome IV. De 1945 à nos jours. Hanoï, Editions en langues étrangères 1977. 717 p.

La Maison des Editions en Langues Etrangères de Hanoï nous présente le quatrième volume de l'Anthologie de la littérature vietnamienne. Il est difficile d'apprécier pleinement la valeur de ce volume qui nous permet de mieux comprendre l'épopée vietnamienne de notre époque.

Ce quatrième tome est organiquement lié au troisième (paru en 1975) et porte sur la période la plus riche de la littérature vietnamienne nouvelle et contemporaine. Il s'agit d'une création littéraire solide, à travers laquelle nous voyons émerger la structure d'une culture nationale originale. L'introduction et les notes ont été écrites par Nguyen Khac Vien et Huu Ngoc et traduites en français par un collectif d'auteurs : Le Van Chat, Huu Ngoc, Pham Huy Thong, Thu Le, Xuan Dieu et Vu Quy Vy avec la collaboration de Mireille Gansel et Françoise Corrèze.

Dans la partie introductoire relativement déployée, les auteurs présentent une explication très érudite, lors même que concise et aisément compréhensible, des conditions et connexions historiques et du développement culturel et idéologique en général de la vie littéraire, avec un exposé sur les auteurs et les œuvres littéraires de la période étudiée. Le lecteur peut prendre connaissance des facteurs principaux qui étaient mis en cause dans la vie littéraire vietnamienne de cette époque. Le livre, en outre de l'introduction déjà citée, est divisé en trois parties, qui par leur délimitation historique, correspondent approximativement aux trois grandes étapes dans le développement de la littérature vietnamienne moderne.

La première partie «La génération des aînés: ceux dont les premières œuvres datent d'avant la Révolution d'Août 1945» contient principalement des extraits de la poésie patriotique de Ho Chi Minh, les poèmes de Tu Mo et Van Dai — l'une des premières femmes de lettres de l'époque moderne. La Révolution d'Août 1945 fut accueillie de façon triomphale par les poètes bien connus avant la guerre comme Xuan Dieu, Che Lan Vien, Luu Trong Lu, Huy Can, Xuan Thuy et Nguyen Huy Tuong. Dans l'œuvre de To Huu une vaste fresque de la résistance nationale et populaire est peinte avec les couleurs les plus variées. To Huu a chanté avec lyrisme la beauté des paysages, les hommes et la nature baignant dans une lumière de l'espérance révolutionnaire.

Comme les poètes, les écrivains prosateurs aussi ont accueilli la Révolution d'Août comme une libération en tant qu'hommes d'art et de culture. Des vétérans comme Ngo Tat To, Nguyen Cong Hoan, Nguyen Hong aux plus jeunes Nam Cao, To Hoai, Nguyen Dinh Thi et Bui Hien, tous tiennent à marquer immédiatement un article de journal, un reportage, les profonds changements qui se sont opérés dans la société qui les entoure, comme en eux-mêmes.

On peut dire que les ouvrages (récits, nouvelles, romans) inspirés part les luttes de la première résistance paraissent plus nombreux que pendant les années de guerre, mais la création littéraire se ressent encore des hésitations idéologiques qui remuent les milieux intellectuels.

La deuxième partie «La deuxième génération: ceux qui ont commencé à écrire après Août 1945. Première Résistance» est dévouée aux personnages littéraires — poètes et prosateurs — dont les efforts ont aidé à bâtir les fondations pour un développement de la littérature patriotique-révolutionnaire. Dans la domaine de la poésie il s'agit avant tout de l'activité littéraire de représentants les plus éminents du mouvement patriotique-révolutionnaire: Hoang Trung Thong, Chinh Huu (au Nord) et Giang Nam, Thanh Hai (au Sud). Le poésie de ces auteurs est une poésie essentiellement angagée parce que elle donne vie aux thèmes sociaux-politiques.

La littérature en prose, plus concrètement que la poésie, reflète le mouvement historique de la société, la vie et les sentiments des hommes au cours de ces années 1960—1975 dominées par la grande lutte menée contre un agresseur puissant et féroce. De nombreuses œuvres prosaïques étaient publiées et plusieurs auteurs se signalant comme des écrivains de talent: Dao Vu, Nguyen Khai, Vu Thi Tuong, Nguyen Ngoc, Nguyen Thi, Anh Duc, Nguyen Sang, Phan Tu et Nguyen Duc Thuan.

Ces auteurs réservent toute leur tendresse, leur affection pour d'autres héros, héroïnes, surtout pour les vieilles femmes qui, à travers des dizaines d'années de résistance, ont acquis un flair extraordinaire quant aux manœuvres ennemies, et un dévouement sans bornes à la révolution.

Outre cela, la première résistance continue à inspirer de nombreux auteurs, l'expérience de ces années s'éclairant d'une lumière nouvelle à mesure qu'on la scrute et que le pays s'engage dans des tâches nouvelles (par exemple Bui Duc Ai, Nguyen Sang, Nguyen Huy Tuong).

La troisième partie intitulée «La troisième génération: ceux de la Deuxième Résistance» embrasse une sélection des travaux de la dernière génération des auteurs qui commençaient à publier des poèmes, nouvelles et contes (par exemple Thu Bon, Le Van Thao, Le Minh Khue, Tran Dang Khoa).

En général, le quatrième tome de l'Anthologie constitue une contribution utile aux connaissances de la littérature vietnamienne dans le monde pour celui qui veut mieux comprendre l'histoire de ce pays.

Le livre est conclu par un Tableau synoptique, un Index des œuvres et un Index des noms de personne.

Ján Múčka

Tac gia van xuoi Viet-nam hien dai (tu sau 1945) (Les prosateurs vietnamiens contemporains) (à partir de 1945). Hanoï, Nha xuat ban Khoa hoc Xa hoi (Editions des Sciences Sociales) 1977. 477 p.

Il n'y a aucun doute que cette publication par une réunion d'auteurs de l'Institut littéraire à Hanoi n'exerce une influence positive sur le développement de l'histoire et de la critique littéraire au Vietnam comme un élément constructif dans la vie littéraire entière de ce pays. Il s'agit ici d'une premier travail scientifique achevé et cohérent sur la production littéraire des écrivains vietnamiens après l'année 1945. Il va sans dire qu'un tel travail n'était pas à même de refermer la production prosaïque tout entière, ni tous les auteurs de cette période. Et en fin de compte, ce n'était même pas l'intention des compilateurs qui remarquent dans leur courte introduction qu'il ne s'agit pas de «l'histoire» de la littérature de cette période, mais d'un exposé scientifique ou d'une analyse de certains problèmes dans la création des représentants principaux de deux générations d'écrivains.

La première partie intitulée «Quelques écrivains actifs déjà avant la Révolution» est consacrée aux travaux d'après la révolution des écrivains bien connus mais dont les commencements appartiennent encore dans la troisième, ou dans la première moitié de la quatrième décade (tels Nguyen Cong Hoan, Nguyen Hong, Nam Cao,

211

To Hoai, Nguyen Tuan, Nguyen Huy Tuong et Bui Hien). Les auteurs des différentes études font une analyse détaillée de leurs écrits d'avant la révolution, suivent les péripéties de leur progrès artistique, confrontent les côtés positifs et négatifs dans leurs travaux, n'évitent pas les questions contestables ni les contradictions de nature idéo-esthétique, exploitent le coup d'œil rétrospectif dans le passé et s'efforcent de donner une évaluation objective au point de vue idéo-esthétique. Ils soulignent le fait que la révolution a donné à cette génération d'écrivains un sens nouveau et un contenu nouveau dans leur création de l'esprit d'un nouvel homme, conditionné par une renaissance intérieure, le menant d'une compréhension individualiste d'un fait vers une conscience de but socialiste.

Dans la deuxième partie du livre «Ecrivains faits durant la résistance anti-française» il s'agit des œuvres d'écrivains éminents, tels Nguyen Van Bong, Nguyen Dinh Thi, Tran Dang, Vo Huy Tam et Thep Moi. Elle reflète les profondes impulsions créatrices provenant d'une conscience révolutionnaire et patriotique très forte. La qualité artistique de leurs œuvres est un résultat de la diversité de leur recherche créatrice. Bien entendu, on ne saurait ignorer les différences qui existent entre les ouvrages individuels quant à la profondeur dans la révélation de la vérité de vie, la plasticité des généralisations artistiques, la mesure et la force en profilant les personnages positifs et négatifs. Aujourd'hui, après tant d'années écoulées, nous évaluons la complexité de l'interprétation artistique et de la généralisation de la vie au Vietam d'alors — une vie se transformant si rapidement et se formant si tumultueusement — comme une recherche hardie, remarquable et créatrice de la part de la jeune et nouvelle littérature vietnamienne.

La troisième partie «Forces nouvelles créatrices pendant l'édification socialiste et dans la lutte pour l'unification de la patrie» examine les œuvres des écrivains plus jeunes: Nguyen Ngoc, Nguyen Khai, Ho Phuong, Huu Mai, Chu Van, Vu Thi Thuong, Nguyen Dich Dung, Nguyen Ngoc Tan et Nguyen Minh Chau. Il s'agit d'une génération d'écrivains qui commence à comprendre le monde intérieur des gens de la société nouvelle, un monde remarquable par une variété extraordinaire non comme un phénomène hétérogène, mais comme un processus uniforme des transformations idéo-sociales. Dans l'ensemble des phénomènes disparates qui caractérisent la littérature vietnamienne de cette époque, on trouve naturellement aussi certains signes ou traits négatifs. C'est tout d'about un certain genre déclamatoire pathétique et une description superflue. Le premier élément se manifeste en ce que l'auteur remplace la révélation des phénomènes et processus du monde réel, par le pathétisme et le didacticisme. Parfois cela mène vers ce qu'on appelle une prose de caractères, qui dans sa forme schématique ne saurait être une contribution permanente dans la littérature.

La quatrième partie «Section de la prose libérée» s'occupe de la production littéraire des écrivains progressifs du Vietnam du Sud, tels Nguyen Thi, Anh Duc, Phan Tu, Nguyen Sang et d'autres. Cette littérature a certains spécificités, elle a débuté dans les années cinquante-soixante de notre siècle et aujourd'hui représente une contribution réelle pour toute la littérature vietnamienne. La thèse que la niveau de la littérature dépend de la connaissance de la vie, s'applique à elle dans tout son étendu. Un fait caractéristique pour la plupart des ouvrages prosaïques venant de la plume de ces écrivains est le dialogue direct avec la réalité.

Une conclusion brève et une mape complète des écrivains et de leurs ouvrages, qui aidera l'orientation et sera donc appréciée par tout expert, complètent le volume.

On peut constater, que le travail du groupe d'auteurs remplit aussi les demandes de l'histoire littéraire qui exige un certain laps de temps avant qu'elle puisse être évaluée, et aussi les demandes de la critique littéraire qui pèse les problèmes vivants et met en action certaines normes et principes tant en relation vers la création littéraire-artistique comme telle, qu'en relation vers la réception sociale de l'œuvre littéraire.

Ján Múčka

Van hoc Cuoc song Nha van (Littérature — Vie — Ecrivain). Hanoï, Nha xuat ban Khoa hoc Xa hoi (Edition des Sciences Sociales) 1978. 555 p.

A l'avenant du mouvement général, tant culturel qu'idéologique, clairement manifeste à l'intérieur de la société vietnamienne socialiste progressive, l'Institut littéraire de Hanoï présente au lecteur une publication prétentieuse, témoignant d'un avancement créatif soutenu dans la théorie et la critique littéraires à base d'une méthodologie marxiste. Il s'agit du premier volume d'un ensemble de travaux littéraires-théoriques, projeté à être réalisé graduellement jusqu'en 1980 et destiné à embrasser tout un complexe de problèmes littéraires-artistiques, philosophiques et idéologiques.

Les chapitres divers de la publication donnent l'impression d'efforts sincers pour créer une théorie littéraire socialiste sur des bases professionnelles et idéologiques solides, comme un des facteurs formatifs de la culture. Accent est mis ici sur le rôle de créer conceptuellement et objectivement les bases théoriques correspondant aux besoins et demandes de la culture contemporaine au sens des critères esthétiques et éthiques du marxisme.

Le volume est divisé en cinq parties, chacune comportant plusieurs chapitres et dont les auteurs sont: Hoang Trinh, Nam Moc, Thanh Duy et Nguyen Cuong.

La première partie intitulée «Littérature et travail, la vie» provient à partir du principe que tout a son origine dans le travail et la recherche de toute cause nous ramène de nouveau vers le travail: Par conséquent, vers le travail, en tant que point de départ, et la littérature (c'est-à-dire, le travail littéraire) comme mode de la réflection de la vie objective réelle. L'auteur de cette section se préoccupe de la solution du rapport «représentation subjective — œuvre littéraire — lecteur — vie», ensuite des questions de rapport entre la littérature et la base sociale, et d'autres formes de la conscience ou du sentiment social (politique, philosophie, science et art). La seconde partie de la «Fonction de la littérature» traite de la place du rôle et de l'importance de la littérature ; la troisième partie, «Caractéristique de la création littéraire» discute le concept de l'image (représentation) littéraire et diverses questions de la langue littéraire comme facteur primaire de la création littéraire. La quatrième partie «Caractère idéologique et artistique de la littérature» traite du problème de l'esprit de parti, de populisme dans la littérature et du caractère national de chaque littérature (d'où le concept de littérature nationale), quant au contenu et à la forme. Les auteurs posent ici tout un spectrum de rapports importants entre l'aspect idéologique et artistique de la création littéraire — tels deux constituants d'un système unique. Enfin, le contenu de la cinquième partie «L'écrivain et la création littéraire» est donné par les problèmes de la communication littéraire dérivant du rapport «écrivain — lecteur» et des questions de la méthode et du talent artistiques. Dans la grande majorité des cas, l'analyse des problèmes ci-dessus se fait à partir d'exemples concrets, ou est démontrée par des œuvres choisies de la littérature vietnamienne.

Comme on peut constater, les auteurs de la publication touchent à un circle très large de questions importantes qui sont si complexes qu'il est tout à fait logique que certains incovénients fussent remarqués pendant une attention concentrée, ayant rapport tout spécialement à une évaluation incomplète des facterus socio-culturels et des déductions qui ne sont pas supportées par une quantité adéquate de matériel scientifique. Cependant, un aspect positif incontestable de ce travail réside en ce que les auteurs ont conscience des fonctions sociales croissantes de la littérature et de l'extension de la sphère de sa réception. L'aspect qualitatif (lors même qu'il ne soit pas toujours logiquement suivi), dont ils se servent dans l'analyse des facteurs de la création littéraire et de sa reproduction sociale, incorpore dans leur travail un élément de conscience idéo-esthétique se manifestant dans une formulation de demandes justifiées envers la production littéraire-artistique. Ces demandes revêtent un caractère légitime en tant que la culture spirituelle d'une société socialiste intègre la littérature dans le système de ses valeurs comme étant elle-même une valeur portant sur la société entière. Il s'en suit alors, qu'il incombe à la théorie et tout particulièrement à la critique littéraire, de formuler une réponse quant à la mesure de l'utilité sociale dans laquelle la littérature remplit ces prétentions.

Des idées nombreuses qui se trouvent dans cette publication il en découle que la théorie et la critique littéraires remplissent dans leur domaine une fonction régulatrice dans le cadre de la politique socialiste culturelle entière. Il importe que dans une évaluation d'une œuvre littéraire concrète, on puisse systématiquement et logiquement appliquer l'unité du critère idéo-esthétique. Cas échéant, il s'agit d'une

214

évaluation pseudo-dialectique, car toute qualité artistique réunit en soi d'une manière formelle aussi les éléments du contenu.

On peut constater que par sa distinction axiologique des valeurs, le présent travail apporte dans le processus littéraire bariolé et progressif, en cours dans la République socialiste vietnamienne, une stabilisation de certaines normes de la culture socialiste générale. Il développe et confirme ceux des principes qui ont commencé à être formés des l'origine de la littérature vietnamienne du réalisme socialiste, comme une conception dans laquelle une fantaisie créative favorise et simultanément vérifie le critère de la véracité idéo-artistique.

La publication du livre «Littérature — Vie — Ecrivain» est incontestablement un placement avantageux et un signe de bonne augure dans le secteur du travail culturel vietnamien, dans le cadre duquel la théorie et la critique littéraires s'efforcent par leurs moyens spécifiques de contribuer à surmonter les contradictions inhérentes à la société et consciemment à créer une continuité de développement dans la culture artistique sociale du Vietnam.

Ján Múčka

Kwon, Hyogmyon: *Basic Chinese-Korean Character Dictionary.* Wiesbaden, Otto Harrassowitz 1978. XXVI + 556 pp.

The age-long cultural influence of China and primarily of written Chinese in Korea and Japan in the past, became strikingly reflected in the writing, vocabulary and partly also in the grammar of these countries. True, in Northern Korea Chinese characters were completely excluded from current use more than a quarter of a century ago and in South Korea, too, the tendency is steadily gaining ground to limit their use solely to a certain type of writings, nevertheless, a knowledge of Chinese characters is indispensable and actual for a deeper study of the Korean language, especially of its vocabulary. This applies in an equal measure also to investigation in the domain of earlier Korean history and in that of literary history.

In many centres of Koreanology, a study of koreanistics is, as a rule, closely associated (as a complementary discipline) to sinology or japanology. This enables students to know the depth of mutual affinities, analogies and influences in the domain of writing, pronunciation, word-formation and grammar among these languages, in particular Chinese on the one hand, and Korean and Japanese, on the other.

Hence, students of and specialists in these disciplines will certainly welcome Hyogmyon Kwon's dictionary precisely because of its many-sided usability. In fact, this work is not the current type of character-explaining dictionary compiled for the needs of students of Korean, but it presents diachronically and synchronically on various levels also the mutual interrelationships (thereby also revealing certain rules) in the pronunciation of these characters in China, Korea and Japan, and in addition, provides examples for the use of characters in words and compounds.

In the *Foreword* (pp. IX—XXVI), the author explains his methodological approach, mode of compilation and final arrangement of the dictionary, and on pp. XV—XVII lists original reference books made use of in its compilation. Wherever possible, he takes support in Korean, Chinese and Japanese reference books, and only in extreme cases turns also to reference books compiled by western scholars.

The dictionary, which was edited by Professor Dr. Bruno Lewin, Professor of Japanese Language and Literature and Korean Language and Literature at the Department of Far Eastern Studies of the Ruhr-University Bochum comprises a total of 2,553 characters in current use, arranged in the classical manner according to 214 radicals (pp. 1—511). This total includes: a) 1,300 characters laid down by the Ministry of Education of the Republic of Korea for common use in 1957 and 1,800 characters contained in Middle and High Schools curricula of South Korea from the year 1972; b) 1,500 characters introduced in the People's Republic of China in 1952 as a basic set, and a further 500 characters added subsequently; c) the standard set of 1,850 characters officially introduced into general use in Japan by the Ordinance from the year 1946.

Of course, identical characters recurring in the above sets are entered in this dictionary only once. The simple system of symbols (chosen by the author) in each basic character clearly indicates to which of the above sets the character belongs. This simultaneously sets apart those characters that are used only in one or two of the three Far Eastern countries. At the same time, the simplified characters are given with the corresponding characters as introduced in Korea in 1963, and in the People's Republic of China in 1964 (*Complete List of Simplified Characters, Jianhuazi zongbiao jianzi*) and also in Japan in 1964 (*Tōyō-kanji-hyō*). Furthermore, the dictionary also gives the so-called vulgar characters or variants of characters.

In each main-entry character, the dictionary also indicates the order and direction of the various stokes in handwriting, so that it is also suitable as a guide book for training technique of writing.

Another item of value is a comparison of the pronunciation of the characters: alongside the Korean way of pronunciation (in the *McCune-Reischauer System* of transcription), also the modern Chinese pronunciation is given with indications of tones (mainly according to *Hanyu-cidian*, Peking 1959 and *Zhongwen-dacidian*, in the transcription of *Hanyu pinyin fangan*, 1957), but also the Middle Chinese pronunciation, based on ancient Chinese of B. Karlgren's *Grammata Serica Recensa*. And in addition, also Japanese pronunciation is given (*kan-on, go-on,* sometimes *kanyō-on* and *tō-in*), based on the rules of *Daijiten,* using the *Hepburn-system* for transcription.

Furthermore, each main-entry character is accompanied by its basic significance in Korean and English, even though, for lack of space, the multi-significance had to be considerably limited. Examples for the use of characters in compounds give the character not only in the first part of any composition but if possible also in the medial and in the final positions. The examples are generally chosen from Korean vocabulary and only if the character is not a common one, are Chinese or Japanese specimens given.

The characters are elegantly hand-written by calligraphers from Seoul and the whole dictionary is printed by phototype.

The dictionary supplement gives: *Index of Pronunciation* (pp. 513—544), where the characters are entered according to the Korean pronunciation in alphabetic order; *Stroke Index* (pp. 545—553), index of characters arranged according to the number of strokes; *Korean Family Names* (p. 554) comprising a list of over 100 Korean family names most commonly in use; *Korean Alphabets (han'gŭl)* (p. 555) and a *List of Radicals.*

Because of the systematic processing, ease of reference, legible print of characters and a multi-purpose usability, this dictionary will certainly become a welcome aid for those who are engaged in Fareastern studies.

I have but two remarks about the dictionary: as the author himself notes on p. XI, some simplified characters may have been involuntarily omitted. A random browsing through the pages revealed such omissions of simplified characters currently employed in China, for instance, in entries under numbers 339, 674, 678, 730 and 910. My second remark also refers to simplified characters. As a matter of fact, students who are not as yet sufficiently familiar with characters and learn to work with contemporary texts in which simplified characters are abundantly used, will not get the full benefit from this dictionary. It evidently needs to be supplemented also with an Index of Simplified Characters, reference being given to the serial number of the main-entry character.

Vladimír Pucek

Korean Studies. Volume 1 and 2. Honolulu, The University Press of Hawaii 1977 and 1978. 284 and 206 pp.

Nowadays we are witnesses to a steadily rising interest in the investigation and learning of Korean culture, both past and present, as well as in the socio-historical processes and contemporary development of Korea. Such circumstances as, e.g.,

division of Korea, the Korean War and efforts of Koreans to unify their country, have also become an impulse for further rapid development of Korean studies throughout the world.

In the post-war years, Korean studies (i.e. a set of disciplines examining Korea in all aspects) have become a new branch at universities and in scientific institutes in many countries. One of these is the Center for Korean Studies at the University of Hawaii which was established in 1972. According to the words of Dae-Sook Suh, Director of the Center, its general goals are: "to enhance faculty quality and performance in Korean studies, to develop comprehensive and balanced academic programs, to stimulate research and publications, to coordinate the resources of the University with those of other institutions of higher learning, and to advance knowledge of Korea. The Center seeks especially to promote interdisciplinary and intercultural approaches to Korean studies." (Introduction in Volume 1.)

Up to now, a number of occasional and colloquium papers of the Center have appeared dealing with linguistics, literature, history, culture, and politology (a complete list is attached at the end of Volume 1). In 1977, the Center began publication of an annual series of *Korean Studies.*

The first two volumes of *Korean Studies* contain seven papers dealing approximately with the same general topics. According to their subjects, Volume 1 comprises the following contributions: two on linguistics, one on history, one on literature, one on music, one on economics, and one on human geography. Volume 2 deals with literary, historical, economic, politologic, and linguistic problems. Both volumes contain reviews and Volume 2 has research notes and a review article.

As regard papers in Volume 1, Chin W. Kim in his article *Rule Ordering in Korean Phonology* (pp. 1—20) discusses the rules that affect sonorants in Korean (especially the liquid, nasals and glides) and investigates their interaction. The purpose of Young-Key Kim-Renaud's paper *Syllable-Boundary Phenomena in Korean* (pp. 243—273) is to examine some problems in Korean phonology, namely neutralization of obstruents, such as the change $h \rightarrow$ dental stop, post-obstruent fortition, and consonant cluster simplification. History is presented by Young I. Lew's *The Reform Efforts and Ideas of Pak Yŏng-hyo, 1894—1895* (pp. 21—61); in his article, the author corrects the conventional view concerning Pak Yŏng-hyo's reform movement which was considered to be only a Japanese affair, with little participation of Korean reformers. Literary contribution *Engineers of the Human Soul: North Korean Literature Today* (pp. 63—110) is written by Marshall R. Pihl; he discusses the north Korean contemporary literature, namely short-story production, brings the analysis of fourteen modern short-story published in Chosŏn munhak (Korean literature) between 1959 and 1973; one of them (*The Son* by Kim Puk-hyang) is given also in an English translation prepared by the author. Byong Won Lee, the author of *Structural Formulae of Melodies in the Two Sacred Buddhist Chant Styles of Korea* (pp. 111—196) examines the archaic style of

Buddhist ritual chant. In his study, *The Korean Kye: Maintaining Human Scale in a Modernizing Society* (pp. 197—222), Gerard F. Kennedy deals with the so-called *kye*, a general class of cooperative economic organization. *Daily Movement Patterns and Communication in Rural Korea* by Forrest R. Pitts (pp. 223—241) is a survey of daily movement and interpersonal contacts made by means of questionnaires in the flat lowlands of Chŏlla Pukto, near the city of Iri.

Volume 2 begins with Chong-un Kim's study *Images of Man in Postwar Korean Fiction* (pp. 1—27); in his survey, the author discusses post-war Korean fiction (meaning south Korean fiction) in terms of the image of man. In *Historiographic Development in South Korea: State and Society from the Mid-Koryŏ to the Mid-Yi Dynasty* (pp. 29—56), Fujiya Kawashima describes some characteristics of South Korean historiography concerning traditional state and society from the mid-Koryŏ to the mid-Yi dynasty. The second article on history, *Trends in Studies of Modern Korean History in South Korea* (pp. 57—65) by Kwang-rin Lee, gives an explanation of trends in the research of modern Korean history. In his article *Foreign Capital and Development Strategy in Korea* (pp. 67—93), Sang Chul Suh examines the role of foreign capital in south Korean economic development. Political problems are discussed in two articles: *The Direction of South Korea's Foreign Policy* (pp. 95—137) by Chae-Jin Lee and *Political Leadership in North Korea: Toward a Conceptual Understanding of Kim Il Sung's Leadership Behavior* (pp. 139—157) by Byung Chul Koh. Chin-Wu Kim analyses in his paper *Linguistics and Language Policies in North Korea* (pp. 159—175) some characteristics in this domain in North Korea since the Second World War.

Both volumes contain papers discussing a wide range of subjects; although focused largely on partial problems, many of them bring fresh approaches and of an especial value is the fact that they furnish us with new stimuli for further research.

Jozef Genzor

Lee, Ki-moon: *Geschichte der koreanischen Sprache* (History of the Korean Language). Wiesbaden, Dr. Ludwig Reichert Verlag 1977. 326 pp.

The book under review is a translation of Ki-moon Lee's (Yi Kimun's) *Kaejŏng Kugŏsa-kaesŏl* carried out by a group of Koreanists in the Section for Korean Language and Culture of the East Asian Department of the Ruhr University, Bochum, under the guidance of Professor Bruno Lewin.

The development of Korean studies has made a significant progress after the Second World War, and especially after 1950. Many new centres for Korean studies were founded in Europe and the USA, where the main emphasis was laid on the study of contemporary Korean, often for utilitarian purposes. However, less attention has been devoted to the history of Korean, except for the most recent period.

Most of the works dealing with the history of Korean have been written in Korean; therefore, this well-arranged and exhaustive volume on the subject in a European language is to be doubly appreciated. There was an urgent need for such a thorough survey because many of the previous works had become obsolete. In this comprehensive work, the author summarizes both the preceding and the contemporary conceptions, as well as his own research on the origin and development of the Korean language and script, from the point of view of modern linguistics.

The book is divided into nine chapters: Introduction (pp. 1—10); The Origin of the Korean Language (pp. 11—30); Rise of the Korean Language (pp. 31—46); Systems of Writing (pp. 47—64); Old Korean (pp. 65—95); Early Middle Korean (pp. 96—118); Late Middle Korean (pp. 119—221); New Korean (pp. 222—267); The Contemporary Korean Language (pp. 268—285).

The concluding chapter contains a description of modern Korean. However, in fact, the author discusses in it only certain tendencies evident in the contemporary use of the language in South Korea. It would have been useful and appropriate had he devoted more attention to the movement for the creation of neologisms based upon original Korean Words. A comparison of these problems with similar tendencies in the Democratic People's Republic of Korea, too, would have been of great interest. (This movement in the DPRK, the so-called *mal tadŭmgi undong,* is now very extensive.) The present reviewer is of the opinion that such comparisons are even necessary, because an inevitable consequence of a non-coordinated purification under conditions of the divided country leads to a greater linguistic divergence between both parts of Korea. After all, the state of division exists practically since 1945 and occupies nearly a half of the period under investigation in Chapter 9, i.e. fully thirty-five years of our century.

Author's Notes (pp. 287—309) are very useful for further study of the problems analysed. Here, one can find extensive data on the literature and the sources, with a commentary. referring to individual chapters of the book. Unfortunately, neither literature nor views of linguists from the Democratic People's Republic of Korea are mentioned here. It would be interesting to compare, as in the case of Chapter 9, their conceptions which in many respects may differ from those of authors whose works are listed in the book (e.g. questions of the origin of Korean, its genealogy etc.).

The book is provided with a detailed Index of Forms (pp. 311—317) and a Subject Index (pp. 318—326). Besides, two maps are added: one on the dialects in Korea (p. XIV) and one on the antiquity of Korea (p. XV).

The transliteration chosen by the author makes it possible to rewrite easily examples in Korean. Names are transcribed in the McCune-Reischauer system. As for Chinese expressions, they are given in their Chinese characters.

The problem of the origin of Korean and its relationships to other languages is of interest to general and comparative linguistics. In this area, as well as in many other questions, definite solutions have not yet been given. Therefore, the reviewed book presenting numerous new impulses and deductions in a lucid way, is a very useful aid not only to Koreanists but also to specialists in the field of general and comparative linguistics.

Jozef Genzor

FitzGerald, Stephen: *China and the World.* Canberra, Australian National University Press 1977. 126 pp.

S. FitzGerald, diplomat and historian who in the seventies was for over three years Australian ambassador to China, on completing his term of office lectured on Chinese foreign policy at the Australian National University. He later revised his series of lectures for publication in book form.

He set about processing his theme primarily as a diplomat investigating the policy of the People's Republic of China (PRC) from the viewpoint of global international relations while simultaneously following the interests of Australian foreign policy. When analysing relations of Chinese policy towards the great powers and regions of importance to it, the author appends also shorter retrospective passages. By means of these excursions involving the entire period since the foundation of PRC, he endeavours to elucidate Peking's changing attitudes on the world arena. In this he did not avoid certain clichés that are often used, although not supported by historical research.

More informative on Chinese foreign policy are those passages that draw support from the author's direct experiences in his contacts with official representatives and members of the diplomatic corps in Peking. S. FitzGerald, however, remarks that he does not intend to make use of all information which he acquired in confidential conversations within the framework of his diplomatic activity. Here he makes public only those data, problems and arguments that are meant to clarify the principal elements in Chinese foreign relations. This also applies to the difficulties encountered in this connection by governments and experts of Western countries.

In the first chapter, the author expounds the motives, theses and development of the Chinese attitude towards world politics, and the next four, he analyses China's relations to the U.S.A., the Soviet Union, Southeast Asia, Japan and Australia. The last — 6th — chapter is concerned with the development of Chinese foreign policy after Mao Tse-tung's death, but considerable attention is also devoted to the role and the ultimate quashing of the extreme political group known as the Gang of Four.

However, in the author's view, this weighty inner-political event did not result in an essential change in foreign policy.

The work lacks a chapter on Sino-Indian relations. This is felt to be a rather serious drawback for relations between these two important Asian powers exert a considerable impact on the situation in Asia and they underwent radical changes from the signing of the famous Five Principles of Peaceful Coexistence up to the armed border conflict in which China occupied part of the disputed territory. This experience fails to lend support to the view (p. 10) that the Chinese leadership is anxious to exercise its influence on other countries not by force, but by the action of the Chinese example.

The author presents an image of Chinese foreign policy with a manifest effort at avoiding polemics or a critical analysis and he touches only marginally on experiences that give support to the discrepancy between official theories and practice, as was manifested, for instance, by the haughty attitude on the part of Peking officials towards representatives of some developing countries (p. 121).

The work also touches on several theoretical aspects and deals with the gradual setting up of the present line in Maoist China's foreign relations, but by its principal content and aims, it remains within the sphere of interests proper to diplomacy and practical politics.

Ivan Doležal

Gibbs, Donald A. — Li, Yun-chen: *A Bibliography of Studies and Translations of Modern Chinese Literature 1918—1942*. Harvard University, East Asian Research Center 1975. 239 pp.

Modern Chinese literature is eliciting an ever-deepening and extending interest on the part of sinologists and students of world literature because of its literary qualities and also as an important means for getting to know twentieth-century China. All those interested in modern Chinese literature of the period 1918—1942 will find their orientation greatly facilitated by the bibliography compiled by Donald A. Gibbs and Yun-chen Li.

The bulk of the Bibliography resides in Parts II, III, and IV. Part II comprises a bibliography of studies of modern Chinese literature divided into General Studies and Studies of modern Chinese literature divided into General Studies and Studies of Fiction, Drama and Poetry. Part III, the most extensive one, is arranged in alphabetic order according to the writers, each entry providing a list of studies on the author and his work, along with a list of translations of his writings into English, arranged according to genres and also alphabetically according to the title in Chinese original. Sinologists will certainly appreciate that the compilers always give also the

Chinese original sources from which the translations had been made. The usefulness of this list to English-reading nonsinologists is manifest. Part IV brings a list of works by unidentified authors. All the entries in the three parts contain complete bibliographic data.

A Bibliography of Studies and Translations of Modern Chinese Literature 1918—1942 lists only translations of Chinese works into English and studies about Chinese literature of that period published in English, French, German, Italian and one also in Hungarian. Studies in Slavonic and other European languages are not included. The compilers in their introduction point to further bibliographic sources — works published particularly in Russian and Japanese, hence in languages in which a large number of important studies on Chinese literature from the period 1918—1942 were published and which have not been included in the present Bibliography.

Besides the Index to the names of authors of studies and translations, the Bibliography carries three Appendices. The first is a list of papers presented at the conference on modern Chinese literature held in Dedham, Mass. in August of 1974 and at the workshop meeting preceding this conference (the majority of these papers were subsequently published in book form in *Modern Chinese Literature in the May Fourth Era*, edited by Merle Goldman, Harvard University Press 1977). Appendix II is a list of works in progress at the time this Bibliography was being compiled and of works whose publication data were unavailable to the compilers. Appendix III contains a list of Chinese sources made use of by the compilers of the Bibliography.

Part I of this work consists of a list of journals, books and collections published in Europe and the United States of America in English, French, German and Italian which formed in fact the basis for Donald A. Gibbs and Yun-chen Li in compiling their Bibliography. As may be expected and as even the authors themselves admit in their Introduction when asking their reading colleagues to send them addenda and corrigenda for a future revised edition, this list of source references is far from complete (e.g. no mention is made of periodicals from Czechoslovak universities though published in Western languages).

To reproach such minor omissions in a work of such magnitude as the present Bibliography attempts to be, might appear to be nit-picking and would certainly be unfair to the authors who have undertaken to compile this important bibliographic aid which every user will appreciate. And in this light, although one could not strictly agree with Ezra F. Vogel when in the Foreword he writes that this is "an exhaustive presentation of all the sources of modern Chinese Literature available in Western languages", yet the authors Donald A. Gibbs and Yun-chen Li are to be commended for their painstaking efforts in producing this praiseworthy and useful work.

Anna Doležalová

223

Gibbs, Donald A.: *Subject and Author Index to Chinese Literature Monthly (1951—1976)*. New Haven, Far East Publications, Yale University 1978. 173 pp.

The Chinese Literature Monthly, a magazine published in English by the Foreign Language Press, Peking, has been a useful aid, since its foundation in 1951, to the English-reading sinological scholars in following up Chinese literature and culture. It kept them briefed up on those cultural events and works that China considered as important, or wished to penetrate into the consciousness of people abroad. Hence, the magazine Chinese Literature Monthly is of importance from several aspects and is intended for professionals as well as for the wider reading public.

Donald A. Gibbs, a co-author of *A Bibliography of Studies and Translations of Modern Chinese Literature 1918—1942*, published by East Asian Research Center, Harvard University 1975, has now published an aid that will be greatly appreciated both by researchers and those interested in contemporary Chinese literature and culture — *Subject and Author Index to Chinese Literature Monthly (1951—1976)*. That there is an urgent need of such works is attested to by the fact that independently of Gibbs's work, an index to the magazine Chinese Literature was edited also in Scandinavia by H. J. Hinrup — *Chinese Literature Index 1951—1976*, London—Malmö 1978.

The Index under review is organized as an integrated subject and author index in an alphabetic order. When reflecting whether to elaborate an author or a title index, Donald A. Gibbs decided, and rightly so, on the first alternative, and the user will certainly appreciate the fact that Gibbs has combined this alphabetic author index with an index of major genres that are furhter subdivided into alphabetically arranged sub-topics. Thus, major genres like Art, Essay, Music, Poetry, Short Story, Theatre and others, are further divided into sub-topics both chronologically according to periods, and also according to subject-matter (e.g. sub-topics of Theatre are Drama Festivals, Foreign Theatre, Local Opera, Modern Opera, Peking Opera, Puppet Theatre, etc.). For the sake of greater lucidity, they are further subdivided according to countries or national minorities.

Donald A. Gibbs's goal has been to make his index cross-listing as complete as possible and in this he has truly succeeded. Such an arrangement of the index facilitates search and information retrieval and generally renders the work effective and time-saving. The user will find each work entered not only according to author, but also in the corresponding major genres and sub-topics and in addition, also under the name of its reviewer, the author of the preface, and the like. And of course, each work is provided with the bibliographic particulars – i.e. number of issue, pages, etc., where the particular work was published in Chinese Literature Monthly.

The Introduction contains detailed directives to the user on the set-up of the *Index*, instructing him about the possibilities of utilizing the system.

It is certainly a metter of regret that Donald A. Gibbs could not carry out his original design to index even the subject matter of short-stories and poems. He gives reasons why it was not possible to include Chinese characters for authors' names at least — a lack of original Chinese sources. This is indeed a drawback; Chinese characters would have been of great value as there is often question of less known authors and titles. Students of Chinese literature and culture will certainly be pleased if the author's hope that it will be possible at a later date to work out a more comprehensive and superior kind of index, comes to be fulfilled. For the time being, every one of us will gratefully reach out for the very useful aid that Donald A. Gibbs has provided through his *Subject and Author Index to Chinese Literary Monthly.*

Anna Doležalová

Revolutionary Literature in China. An Anthology. Selected and Introduced by John Berninghausen and Ted Huters. New York, M. E. Sharpe, Inc. 1976. 103 pp.

This work, first published in the Bulletin of Concerned Asian Scholars, Vol. 8, Nos 1 and 2 in 1976, comprises an Introductory Essay, English translations of eight short stories, a one-act play, seven essays and a Short Annotated Bibliography.

The sixteen works from Chinese literature of the period 1914—1966 included in the anthology were translated by thirteen translators who give an informative introduction to each work with the exception of the short story Debut by Hao Ran. Understandably, a reviewer whose mother tongue is not English can hardly express her opinion on the stylistic qualities of the English translation (some comments were made relating to this point when the translations were still in manuscript form, by Howard Goldblatt in Modern Chinese Literature Newsletter, Vol. 2, No. 1, Spring 1976), but she may at least observe in this case that the translations are correct as regards the subject-matter.

The compilers of the anthology selected five essays of basic importance written in the period 1921—1932, by renowned authors — Guo Mo-ruo, Cheng Fang-wu, Mao Dun and Qu Qui-bai. In addition there are also two short articles by Ye Sheng-tao and Zheng Zhen-duo as examples of a sharp condemnation of the literary style represented by the first short story in the anthology, viz. Zhou Shou-juan's We Shall Meet Again (the present reviewer would assign it to the commercial type of writing of the genre known as Butterfly Literature, while the translator Perry Link designates it as an example of popular urban fiction of the 'teens). The compilers then proceed in their selection in a chronological order of the stories — On the Bridge, by Ye Sheng-tao; A Day, by Ding Ling; In Front of the Pawnshop, by Mao Dun; Hatred, by Zhang Tian-yi, a one-act play Man and Wife Learn to Read, by Ma Ke; the stories Silence, by Qin Zhao-yang; The Guest, by Zhou Li-bo and Debut, by Hao Ran, reffered to above.

Of course, it is the intrinsic right of compilers of any anthology to make their selection according to their discretion and taste. It is possible to cast doubt on the choice of the particular writers and works, yet in practice this is superfluous in the case of every major cross-section of literature. The book under review may be said to make accessible to the English-reading public a number of interesting works from modern Chinese literature which, doubtless, is a praiseworthy and meritorious effort regardless of the fact whether readers and particularly experts on the subject will endorse the compilers' claim, as expressed in the title, that there is question of specimens of revolutionary literature.

John Berninghausen and Ted Huter in their interesting Introductory Essay endeavoured to bring closer to their readers the problems involved in Chinese literature of our century, concretely, of the type they call revolutionary literature. They warn that in dealing with revolutionary literature in China we should keep in mind firstly, that revolutionary as well as non-revolutionary literature is an outgrowth of traditional Chinese literature and is related to modern Chinese society, and secondly, that revolutionary literature reflects specific Chinese revolutionary changes that are related to modern experiences and revolutionary struggles of other societies in this century.

So far so good. But the fundamental issue resides in what they concretely consider and especially what they do not consider to be revolutionary literature (e.g. in China after the year 1949). Before going on to specify four stages in the development of revolutionary literature in China, they put forward the following — in this reviewer's opinion very vague — definition: "Revolutionary literature originates in the effective and evocative verbal expression of social reality crafted in literary form by people living in an unjust society." After this definition, which is meant to embrace revolutionary literature generally, hence, is not specifically aimed at Chinese conditions, the authors explain the expression "unjust society" in terms that in turn beg the question whether, according to their judgment, there exists another than an unjust society — since they write about "systemic injustices existing in societies at any stage of development".

In the first developmental stage, they differentiate very clearly revolutionary from non-revolutionary literature by the conscious expression of the unhappiness, suffering or exploitation as a consequence of the way in which society is organized and not as a fatalistic component of "human condition". They see another differentiating criterion in the expression that alleviation of social injustices by a fundamental restructuring of unjust society is both possible and desirable. The second stage of revolutionary literature in China was reached, in the authors' view, after the formation of the League of Leftwing Writers and they consider as the best revolutionary works to be those by authors who perceived severe contradictions in society and who endeavoured to transform their independent vision into a work of art. The third stage is limited to the period of the War of Resistance Against the

Japanese. The authors specify it by a closer contact of writers with the common people in mobilizing their patriotism, as a consequence of which revolutionary literature is recast in popular forms. This literature simultaneously serves the purposes of propaganda and becomes more didactic. The authors consider the period of post-liberation China as the fourth stage and in it they analyse problems of literary creation, the negative and positive specific traits and tendencies that in their view are most important. After the year 1965, they see a hope of professional writers being able to continue developing revolutionary literature to a higher level, uniquely in Hao Ran's work. At the same time they realize that the potential impact of China's choice resides in its accent on a growing participation of ordinary people in the creation and appreciation of literature and in its search to de-professionalize literary production.

The introductory essay is written with a solid knowledge of the issues and brings numerous deep insights. However, the characterization of the development of Chinese revolutionary literature into four stages betrays a lack of a uniform criterion — the authors' considerations belong to different qualitative planes and their scrutiny of the various stages are not from the same visual angle, so that their modes of characterizing these stages methodically differ. As has been implied earlier in this review, it is not always clear what the authors consider as specific traits of revolutionary literature in the individual periods which distinguish it, say, from progressive, or socially committed literature. However, these remarks, perhaps maximalist or rather perfectionist in nature, are not meant to detract in any way from the interesting and instructive value of this stimulative introductory essay.

The anthology is supplemented with a Short Annotated Bibliography into which the authors included works that they evidently consider to be relevant and representative. But the annotations of some of the books published in Czechoslovakia contain remarks unrelated to the purpose of the book and unchecked by the compilers. A brief characteristic of the various contributors is also provided.

Anna Doležalová

Sudby kultury KNR (1949—1974) (The Fate of Culture of PRC (1949—1974)). Ed. by Krivtsov, V. A., Markova, S. D. and Sorokin, V. F. Moscow, Nauka 1978. 381 pp.

The book under review was written by a team of the Institute of Far Eastern Studies of the USSR Academy of Sciences, headed by V. F. Sorokin. This six-member team is made up of foremost Soviet sinologists who are authors of several monographs and numerous studies and articles on problems of cultural policy in the

People's Republic of China, as also on questions of Chinese literature, literary criticism, theatre, film and creative arts. The Fate of Culture of PRC is the first publication systematically to follow up the principal aspects in the development of PRC's policy in the domain of literature and art as well as in that of literature, theatre, film and creative arts during the first 25 years since the foundation of PRC.

The book, divided into seven chapters, comprises two principal parts.

The first of these presents a chronological analysis of the principal traits in the development of PRC's cultural policy. An evaluation is given of all the important and relevant political campaigns, literary and artistic discussions, polemics, important conferences and directives of the managers of cultural life in PRC. Considerable attention is devoted to the development of forms and methods of enforcement and implementation of the various requirements and exigencies, notions and under-takings of the leadership in the field of culture. The authors analyse in detail the theoretical and practical divergences and contradictions in the cultural policy of PRC with regard to Leninist cultural policy pursued in the socialist countries. They follow these issues from the standpoint of theoretical postulates and their reflection in literary and artistic practice, setting them within the broad context of Mao Tse-tung's views on literature and art, into the context of Chinese traditions, the situation in Chinese literary and artistic production and the overall trends of the political evolution in PRC during the period 1949—1974. This part of the book is chronologically divided into three chapters: For a Socialist Way of Development of Culture — 1949—1956 (by V. F. Sorokin), From "Hundred Flowers" to the "Cultural Revolution" — 1956—1965 (by S. D. Markova), and "Cultural Revolution and Its Consequences" — 1965—1974 (by A. N. Zhelokhovtsev). Quite a number of works have appeared in sinologic literature dealing with problems or time sectors of the cultural policy of PRC. A considerable part of these were written by Soviet sinologists and were published in Russian. However, the book under review provides the most complex view of these problems. The principal value of this first part does not reside mainly in its uncovering new, unknown facts (although it makes a contribution also in this respect), but primarily in its complex and systematic way of processing and its consistent Marxist evaluation of all the aspects, trends an events of the cultural life in PRC during the period under study.

The second part of the book consists of four chapters devoted respectively to literature (by V. F. Sorokin and S. A. Toroptsev), theatre (by I. V. Gayda), film (by S. A. Toroptsev) and creative arts (by V. L. Sychov, i.e. N. E. Annenkov). These chapters present an adequate analysis of the respective fields of artistic creation and the policy of Chinese leadership applied to these artistic genres. At the same time they apply and concretize the basic tendencies analysed in the first part of the book. Using concrete material, the authors document the consequences of the cultural policy of PRC, the responses and reactions provoked by the various tendencies in literary and artistic authors, the interventions they caused in their creative and human destiny, as well as the gradual lowering of the standard of literary and artistic output that followed the first years of their promising development.

In both parts of the book the authors follow closely the development of Soviet-Chinese cultural relations, their concrete manifestations and their reflection in Chinese culture within the appropriate domains. They document the changes in the evaluation and manner of accepting Soviet culture and its theory, seen in broader and deeper relations than in previous sinologic literature. From this point of view, too, this book brings new concrete concepts and theoretical evaluations. In this, as well as in further problem circuits, e.g. in analysing cultural campaigns, directives, theoretical discussions, Mao Tse-tung's attitudes and those of the leaders of cultural life, and their application in creative practice, the authors search and find well-founded answers to questions relating to the roots and causes of the various changes in the cultural policy of PRC; in this they take as their bases the whole complex of political, cultural, literary and artistic aspects.

All the authors worked with a wealth of original sources, Chinese materials — books and journals — and the appended bibliography comprising 282 entries, includes also relevant publications and periodicals in Russian and western languages. The Foreword introduces the reader into the problems to be discussed, while the Conclusion summarizes the principal theoretical results arrived at in the study and presents also a concise appraisal of the situation and the perspectives opening to Chinese culture following Mao Tse-tung's death. The Foreword and the Conclusion have been written by the chief of the author team V. F. Sorokin. The use of this valuable and very instructive book would have been greatly facilitated if an index of names had been appended. It is well known that a considerable number of Chinese literary and dramatic works dating from the period of PRC has been translated into Russian, and the Russian-reading public would certainly have welcomed the inclusion in the book of a bibliography of such Russian translations.

This book is without doubt an important contribution to an investigation of the development of culture in PRC as part of a political development in the country. Its second part presents a relatively concise, but an adequate overview of a twenty-five-year development of literature, theatre, film and creative arts in PRC. The subject of the cultural life of PRC during the years 1949—1974 is systematically processed in all its complexity and in concrete theoretical and artistic expressions. The book contains weighty judgements and much information, often as yet unpublished, of interest to scholars, and by its mode of treatment, it is accessible to those interested in cultural-political, literary and artistic aspects of evolution in PRC.

Anna Doležalová

229

Franke, Herbert (Ed.): *Sung Biographies*. Part 1—3. Wiesbaden, Franz Steiner Verlag 1976. 1271 pp.
Franke, Herbert (Ed.): *Sung Biographies*. Part 4. Painters, Wiesbaden, Franz Steiner Verlag 1976. 157 pp.

After the *Eminent Chinese of the Ch'ing Period*, edited by A. W. Hummel, and the *Dictionary of Ming Biography*, edited by L. C. Goodrich and Fang Chaoying, this is the third dictionary devoted to the great, or at least the remarkable personalities of Chinese history from the period of a single dynasty in old China.

As stated in the *Editor's Note*, this represents the result of part of the work on the Sung Project originated by the late Professor E. Balázs. If the first two "dictionaries" were fairly alike in their pattern, then the one under review differs considerably, due primarily to the different conditions under which the project had to be realized. While the former two volumes originated in the American sinological community and were associated with the name and efforts of Fang Chaoying as one of the principal collaborators and editors, the latter saw the light of the day among German scholars and, it appears, in a less favourable financial and especially linguistic situation. While the dictionaries dealing with the last two dynasties are written in English, *Sung Biographies* are trilingual (English, German, French). The numerous biographies written by Japanese scholars could only rarely be translated into competent English.

The biographies in the dictionary under review, in contrast to those in the preceding ones, are of an uneven standard; some are sketchy, like many short articles by Japanese scholars, while some are the result of original research and painstaking work, like the solid contributions by the late D. R. Jonker on the poet Lu Yu (pp. 691—704), Lü Pen-chung (pp. 729—735) and Yang Wan-li (pp. 1238—1245).

Probably due to considerable editorial difficulties as regards the biographical section of the Sung Project, the biography of Chao K'uang-yin (917—975), the founder of the Sung dynasty, or that of the great historian Ssu-ma Kuang (1019—1086), have not been included. As a student of Chinese literature I should like that the biographies of at least such prominent Chinese poets as Yen Shu (991—1055), Ch'en Shih-tao (1053—1101) and Hsin Ch'i-chi (1140—1207) be included.

The editor's remark that this book should be named "Draft Sung Biographies" ought to be taken as an expression of modesty. Probably more care should have been taken to set up and maintain some sort of uniformity. Perhaps also the aid from the *Deutsche Forschungsgemeinschaft* for four years was inadequate as regards the time span. Projects of this type are often more exacting than would appear at first sight and from time to time require a certain upgrading or correction if they are to meet their objective. International scientific projects have come to be systemic institutions and if they are to be successful, they must be able to cope with certain factors that obstruct their work. The Sung Biographical Project seems to have suffered from certain drawbacks in the domain of coordination, particularly as regards the methodology of research and a sense of proportion in processing of the various biographies. Otherwise, one can hardly account for the fact that G. C. Hatch has devoted over 15 pages to Su Hsün (1009—1066) and 69 to Su Shih (Su Tung-p'o) (1037—1101), while C. Shirokauer's biography of Chao Shih-chao consists of a little more than two lines and that of Chao Shan-chien not the one whole page.

The book is intended to all those interested in the most diverse aspects of Chinese history, literature, culture and art of the Sung dynasty and will serve them as a useful source of reference.

Marián Gálik

Stryk, Lucien — Takashi, Ikemoto: *The Penguin Book of Zen Poetry.* London, Allen Lane 1977. 160 pp.

This is the largest and most comprehensive collection of Zen poetry that has appeared so far in English and the book has a double aim: one is to acquaint the reader with the almost 1500-year old tradition of Ch'an (Zen) poetry from the T'ang dynasty in China to the present day in Japan, the other to open the way to a better understanding of the Zen ideas and its fruits in the realm of poetry and arts.

We shall deal in a somewhat more circumstantial way with the first of these aims, which is also the subject of the rather comprehensive *Introduction* written by Ikemoto Takashi, an introductor of Zen literature to the West and a collaborator with the American poet and critic Lucien Stryk on some books like *Afterimages: Zen Poems of Shinkichi Takahashi, Zen Poems of China: The Crane's Bill,* and others. The *Introduction* points to the evolution of Zen poetry up to its present state in Japan in Shinkichi Takahashi's poems, but it is rather a pity that no mention is made of any other Zen poets in contemporary Japan.

When writing that part of the *Introduction* which deals with T'ang poetry, Ikemoto Takashi seems to have forgotten that he was not writing for Japanese, but for Western readers and made no effort whatever to provide original Chinese equivalents for his Sino-Japanese names. It might perhaps be all the same to a European or an American reader whether Baso is in reality Ma-tsu (died 788) or Daie-Soko is Ta-hui Ts'ung-k'ao (1089—1163), or Joshu is Chao-chou Ts'ung-shen (778—897), or Mumon-Ekai is Wu-men Hui-k'ai (1182—1260). But it will certainly surprise him to find out that the famous Chinese poet Su Tung-p'o (Su Shih) (1036—1101) is here "masked" as layman Sotoba. This resembles the dilemma of a modern reader who in a text by a Japanese author and intended for the Western public, cannot for the life of him see why Mō Takutō should signify Mao Tse-tung, or Shō Kaiseki should stand for Chiang Kai-shek. Even though the use of Sino-Japanese names and terms has its tradition in the domain of Zen literature, this is hardly admissible when Chinese poets are mentioned.

Chinese poems translated or analysed in the book under review deal either with the so-called enlightenment (*sambodhi, wu, satori*) which allegedly "is not a state of mere quietude, it is not tranquilization, it is an inner experience which has a noetic quality; there must be a certain awakening from relative field of consciousness, a certain turning-away from the ordinary form of experience which characterized our everyday life" (Suzuki, D. T.: *Essays in Zen Buddhism. Second Series.* London, Rider and Co. 1970, p. 24), or with death which is the final point behind life full of pain and suffering. As regards the first statement, it should be noted that "noetic quality" has a negative sign, for enlightenment "is not a conclusion reached by reasoning, and defies all intellectual determination" (ibid., p. 31). Only snobs or Zen experts may pretend or really enjoy lines like; "Searching Him took /My strength./ One night I bent /My pointing finger-/ Never such a moon." This poem points to the connection with *kung-an* (public case) No. 3 from *Wu-men kuan* by Wu-men Hui-k'ai, but the latter involved only a pointing finger, not the moon. Perhaps by his bent finger the poet intended to express the idea that mystic enlightenment is as difficult to achieve as to reach the moon, or that a knowledge of truth (which in Zen-Buddhism is logically unknowable) is important, nonetheless, efforts at achieving this knowledge hardly require that the moon be exchanged for the finger or the other way round.

Poems of greater artistic value and also more comprehensible are those devoted to death. Thus, Ta-hui Ts'ung-k'ao, one of the foremost authorities for the concept of enlightenment and one Suzuki's most important sources in this question, wrote: "Life's as we/ Find it — death too./ A parting poem?/ Why insist?" The poem was evidently an answer to his pupils' pressings. Another master Yu-ching (Tendo-Nyo-jo) (1163—1228) who was a Chinese teacher of Dōgen (1200—1253), one of the two great Japanese pioneers of Zen Buddhism, wrote shortly before his death: "Sixty-six years/ Piling sins,/ I leap into hell-/ Above life and death."

It was only in Japan that Zen-Buddhism achieved an unusual impact on national life and culture. Eisai (1141—1215), the first of the two great Japanese pioneers, went so far as to preach that Zen might help "in protecting the country" or propagated tea-drinking as being "the most wonderful medium for nourishing one's health" because in it lies "the secret of long life" (De Bary, Wm. Th. (Ed.): *The Buddhist Tradition in India, China and Japan.* New York, Columbia University Press 1969, p. 366). In Japan, Zen Buddhism affected a wider sphere of culture than in China. This was due also to the support given to this teaching by the Tokugawa rulers from 1603 to 1867. The Department of Foreign Affairs was managed by Zen monks and they also led foreign trade delegations, as they were experts on China. Chinese impact in the domain of art and literature could always be direct and new, at that time modern impulses could always be introduced and enforced. Zen impact in Japanese literature was greater than in Chinese literature. As is well known, the impact of Ch'an or even Buddhism *in toto* never altered nor even affected the formal aspect of Chinese poetry: it only poured new ideas into old vessels. In Japan, the eminent poet Basho (1644—1694) was the initiator of and the greatest writer in the *haiku* form. He was a Zennist although he did not believe in *Dhyana-dharma* completely; he did not search for supernatural enlightenment, although he did learn from the conciseness, suggestion and paradoxical devices of Zen experience and style. In his *haiku:* "Old Pond,/ leap-splash-/ a frog", one cannot look for the enlightenment, but only for the atmosphere of surprise, the impression of the ephemeral, for impermanence (*aware*) and perhaps also for something unpronounced though written, profound and subtle (*yūgen*). Similar traits may be found in the haiku by other Japanese authors, e.g. that of Kikaku (1661—1707): "Above the boat,/ bellies/ of wild geese." Or that of Issa (1763—1827): "I am leaving-/ now you can make love/ my flies." Or that of Lady Sute-jo (1633—1698): "Woman –/ how hot the skin/ she covers."

As regards the second aim of the book, it should be observed that Zen poetry may be viewed as a certain source of inspiration and creative instruction, as shown by the poems of Gary Snyder, William Carlos Williams or even Denise Levertov and also by studies on similar topic by Kanaseki Hisao, *Haiku and Modern American Poetry,* East-West Review (Kyoto), 3, 1967—68, 3, pp. 223—241, then Lucien Stryk, *Zen Buddhism and Modern American Poetry,* Yearbook of Comparative and General Literature (Bloomington), 15, 1966, pp. 186—191, or N. Fuwa, *The Concept of Short Poetry: William Carlos Williams and Matsuo Basho.* M. A. thesis (Bloomington 1967). For the *haiku* translations see excellent study by Etiemble *Sur quelques adaptations et imitations du haiku* in his *Essais de littérature (vraiment) générale,* Paris, Gallimard 1975, pp. 147—167. One remark is probably necessary: the values of this poetry should be so transformed that they be aesthetic and otherwise effective also in a new environment.

Marián Gálik

Wu-men Hui-k'ai: *Wu-men kuan. Zutritt nur durch die Wand.* Aus dem Chinesischen übersetzt von Walter Liebenthal. Heidelberg, Verlag Lambert Schneider 1977. 142 S.

Als 91-jähriger gab Professor Walter Liebenthal (1886) die in der Reihenfolge sechste Übersetzung des klassischen Werkes des chinesischen Ch'an-Buddhismus:

Wu-men kuan vom Mönch Hui-k'ai (1182—1260) heraus. Wir denken dabei an die Übersetzungen ins Englische und ins Deutsche. Mehrere Übersetzungen dieses Werkes in einer nur wenig mehr als fünfzigjährigen Geschichte (die erste Übersetzung ins Deutsche erschien im Jahre 1925) beweist bestimmt dessen Beliebtheit unter den Lesern.

Meister Hui-k'ai redete in *kung-an* (japanisch *kōan*), was Liebenthal als „Aufgaben" übersetzt, gut wäre jedoch auch die Übersetzung als „Geschichten". Den Stoff dazu entnahm Hui-k'ai verschiedenen „Sammlungen" älterer Meister oder den „buddhistischen Legenden" (S. 19). Diese *kung-an* sind von Hui-k'ai immer kommentiert. Der Kommentar überschreitet manchmal den Umfang der eigentlichen „Geschichte" um das Vielfache (z.B. im Falle der ersten, *Der Hund des Chao-chou* betitelten Geschichte geht es etwa um das Zwanzigfache). Dem Kommentar folgt immer der dichterische Text, der eine Antwort auf den Text der *kung-an* darstellt.

Wenn ich diese Rezension schreibe, schreibe ich sie als Andersgläubiger (*wai-tao*), mit dem Unterschied, daß ich genau das Gegenteil jenes bin, der im *kung-an* Nr. 32 Buddha fragte, ob die Frage nach der Buddhaschaft ohne oder mit Worten gestellt werden soll. Budha erwiderte ihm nicht, der Mann jedoch erreichte eine Erleuchtung.

Die Geschichten vom *Zutritt nur durch die Wand* sind von exegetischen Charakter, wenn auch deren Kompilator behauptet, daß „Verständnis durch Worte suchen" dasselbe sei, als „mit dem Stock nach dem Mond zu schlagen, den Schuh zu kratzen, wenn der Fuss juckt" (S. 40). An ähnliche Behauptungen haben wir uns in der Geschichte der chinesischen Philosophie gewöhnt. Interessant an ihnen ist die Tatsache, dass nachdem sie ausgesprochen wurden, sich niemand genau daran hält. Hätte sich Lao-tzu an sein Maximum gehalten und ohne Worte belehrt, hätte er niemals das meist übersetzte chinesische Buch geschrieben. Warum hat Hui-k'ai überhaupt geschrieben, wenn er überzeugt war, daß „ein Verständnis durch die Worte" unmöglich sei?

An Professor Liebenthals Übersetzung ist sympatisch, daß er zumindest bei der Übersetzung von Hui-k'ais Werk nicht versuchte ein Missionär des Dhyana-Buddhismus zu sein. Da jedoch das rezensierte Buch, im Milieu in dem es entstand und für die Zuhörerschaft, der es bestimmt war, keinen rein philologischen und literarischen Charakter haben sollte, enthält es auch eine religionistische Auslegung. Bei dieser, ähnlich dem Meister Hui-k'ai, versuchte auch er sich kurz zu fassen, denn wenn auch „jedes Wort zu viel ist", kein Wort „zu wenig gewesen wäre" (S. 138).

Als „Anhänger fremder Lehre" glaube ich nicht an die Erleuchtung (*wu, satori*). Hinter diesem mystischen Wort verbirgt sich etwas wie ein Bemühen Schwerverständliches zu begreifen, z.B. deswegen, weil es unlogisch, sinnlos oder auch unausgesprochen ist, wie in der oben erwähnten Geschichte Nr. 32. Bewegt sich eine Fahne, dann muß es unter normalen Umständen z.B. der Wind sein, der sie bewegt hat. Mit *citta,* was nach Liebenthal in diesem Falle Schicksal (S. 99), nach H. Dumoulin, *Wu-men kuan. Der Pass ohne Tor,* Tokyo, Sophia University 1953, S. 43, das Bewußtsein bedeutet, hat das nichts gemeinsames. Oder aber es hat, dann jedoch müssen wir anerkennen, daß „die Wirklichkeit über alle Erklärungen hinausliegt, daß es ebenso richtig wäre zu sagen, Fahne, Wind und Bewußtsein bewegen sich, wie zu sagen, sie bewegen sich nicht" (Dumoulin, S. 42). Ist jedoch die Wahrheit als Übereinkunft zwischen der Aussage und der Wirklichkeit definiert, wie können über eine Wirklichkeit zwei völlig gegensätzliche Aussagen gemacht werden?

Den einzelnen Verfassern der Ch'an Geschichten (meist Paradoxe) ging es nicht um diese Übereinkunft, da sie weder an Logik, noch an Vernunft glaubten. Die in der Struktur eines jeden *kung-an* verankerten Prämissen sollten der mystischen Erleuchtung dienen, welche in dem aus dieser Geschichte und deren Unverständlichkeit hervorgehendem Erlebnis war. Dabei wurde eine und dieselbe Prämisse in der Ch'an Lehre (wenn das überhaupt eine Lehre ist) verschiedentlich erklärt. Laut Geschichte Nr. 30 z.B. ist (der Buddha) *citta, (Citta)* ist der Buddha (*Chi hsin chi Fo*), aber laut Nr. 33 ist *Citta* nicht der Buddha (*Fei hsin fei Fo*). Für manchen mag Professor Liebenthals Kommentar ausreichend sein: „Alles ist Buddha. Darum ist es sinnlos, etwas über ihn aussagen" (S. 102). Mir reicht das nicht. Schon deshalb, weil *citta* lediglich ein unbedeutender Teil von allem ist. Erfahren wir aus der Geschichte Nr. 21, daß Buddha (indem er alles ist) auch ein Arschwisch (genauer ein zugeschnittenes Holz, das wie unser Toilettenpapier gebraucht wurde, S. 82) ist, wissen wir den Witz und die Aufrichtigkeit der Buddha-dharma Anhänger und der Boddhidharma Nachfolger zu schätzen. Fraglich bleibt bloß, inwieweit dies zur Erkenntnis der Buddhaschaft oder zum oben charakterisierten Erlebnis führt. Wenn jedoch im Ch'an (Zen) „die letzte Wirklichkeit" (Dumoulin) „über Affirmation und Negation hinauslegt", sind unsere logisch determinierten Überlegungen sowieso nutzlos.

Hui-k'ais Werk gehört wirklich zum Schatz der Weltliteratur und von dieser Sicht aus muss auch die Arbeit des Übersetzers sowie die Bereitwilligkeit des Herausgebers, es den Lesern in Form eines schönen Buches zugänglich zu machen, positiv bewertet werden.

Marián Gálik

Doctoral Dissertations on China, 1971—1975. A Bibliography of Studies in Western Languages. Compiled and Edited by Frank Joseph Shulman. Seattle and London, University of Washington Press 1978. 329 pp.

This is a supplement to *Doctoral Dissertations on China: A Bibliography of Studies in Western Languages, 1945—1970,* compiled and edited by Leonard H. D.

Gordon and Frank J. Shulman, Seattle and London, University of Washington Press 1972, 317 pp. It is presumed that similar publications will appear at five-year intervals. The first volume lists a total of 2,208 doctoral dissertations dealing with China and completed in Europe, America and Australia between 1945—1970, and the second annotates 1,573 of those completed between 1971—1975.

The book under review provides a picture of an unprecedented upsurge of Chinese studies among young scholars during the first half of the seventies. Compared with the 25 years of the postwar period, this represents a 300-percent increase in output and interest.

This development is evident also in the various fields of sinological research. For instance, as regards relations of China and Chinese cultural influence abroad, the first bibliography contains 61 works from the period 1945—1970 and the second one exactly as many for the five years 1971—1975. If during the postwar quarter-century six doctoral dissertations were submitted from the domain of relationships between China and the German linguistic circuit, the number was eight during the first half of the seventies (of these, three were devoted to the work of the German writer and poet Hermann Hesse). Somewhat less striking, although still considerable is the difference also in the study of cultural relations between China and France, where the respective figures are ten and seven for the two very unequal periods in question.

An essentially greater attention than ever before was devoted during 1971—1975 to China in the domain of international economic and political relations since 1949. While the number of studies elaborated during the first period amounted to 163, the second period, five times shorter counted 126.

A corresponding increase of interest is also noticeable in the study of Chinese literature of the 19th and 20th century. Here, too, doctoral theses written up to 1970 numbered 54, and those worked out during the period 1971—1975 counted 25. The author who attracted the greatest interest on the part of young adepts of sinological scholarship was Lu Hsün. Again, the numbers of works written about his life and works in the first and the second periods were eleven and five, respectively. Mao Tun attracted attention only during the first postwar period (three studies), Yeh Sheng-t'ao only in the second one (two studies), Lao She had three works devoted to him in the first and one in the second period. Chinese literature after the year 1949 was dealt with in two dissertations during the first, and in six during the second of these periods.

The rise in interest proved colossal as regards study of mass communications and journalism. Only a single dissertation from this domain was defended in 1970 (a French one), while the number rose to ten during 1971—1975.

Among subjects of doctoral dissertations of the first half of the seventies, we find the names of prominent Chinese politicans, philosophers and men of letters who until then had not appeared as prospective for these works. If we refer to the 20th century, then during the period 1971—1975 we find as subjects of doctoral dissertations for the first time the names of Liang Sou-ming (born 1893) twice, Chang Chün-mai (1887—1966), Chiang Pai-li (1882—1938), Liao Chung-k'ai (1878—1925), Teng Yen-ta (1868—1940), Fung Yu-lan (born 1895), Lin Shu (1852—1924), Feng Chih (born 1905), Hsiao Hung (1911—1942) and Tsou T'ao-fen (1894—1944) who had until then stood outside the interest of doctoral candidates. Interest declined in Ts'ai Yüan-p'ei (1868—1940) whose life and works were dealt with in five doctoral dissertations during the first period and in only one in the second period. This also applies to Liang Ch'i-ch'ao (1873—1929) — with eight works devoted to him in the first, and only two in the second period. Among the great, or at least noteworthy foreign personages insofar as they had some relation to China, pride of place goes to the American poet Ezra Pound with six dissertations, then follows Hermann Hesse referred to above, the German economist Max Weber and the French poet Paul Claudel with three dissertations. The works of G. W. F. Hegel, B. Brecht and the American poet Kenneth Rexroth in their relation with Chinese philosophy and literature, were always processed in two dissertations each.

As regards the study of imperial China and republican China up to the year 1949, the greatest number of dissertations were written from the domain of history (a total of 411), but the greatest popularity was enjoyed by Chinese issues after the year 1949 including economics (100 dissertations), international economic and political relations (126 dissertations), politics and government (165 dissertations) and education (86 dissertations).

The reader will feel probably disappointed at not finding there dissertations written in the U.S.S.R., for which their authors received the "candidate status" (kandidat nauk) or the "doctoral status" (doktor nauk). All the more so, as adequate up-to-date information was easily available in the journal Narody Azii i Afriki (Peoples of Asia and Africa), Nos 1,4 (1972), 1,4 (1973), 1,4 (1974), 1,4 (1975) and 1,4 (1976).

Of the 35 known dissertations, ten are given below for which their authors were conferred the "doctoral status". These are such works as by their extent and significance surpass those submitted for the Ph. D. in the West. They are the following: L. E. Cherkassky: Novaya kitaiskaya poeziya (20-e—30-e gody) (Modern Chinese Poetry of the 1920s and 1930s); L. M. Gudoshnikov: Evolyutsiya gosudarstvennogo stroya Kitaiskoi Narodnoi Respubliki (Evolution of the State Apparatus of the People's Republic of China); G. Ya. Smolin: Antifeodalnoe vosstanie v Kitae vtoroi poloviny X — pervoi chetverti XII v. (The Anti-Feudal Uprising in China from the Second Half of the Tenth up to the First Quarter of the Twelfth Century) — all from the year 1971. — M. V. Vorobyov: Chzhurcheni i gosudarstvo Tszin (X v — 1234 g) (The Jurchens and the Chin Empire — Tenth Century to 1234) — from the year 1972. — E. L. Serebryakov: Lu Yu (1125—1210). Zhizn i tvorchestvo (Lu Yu, 1125—1210. His Life and Works);

A. I. Shifman: Lev Tolstoi i Vostok (Leo Tolstoy and the Orient) — both from the year 1973. — A. S. Stepanov: Leninskaya politika mira na Dalnem Vostoke (1920—1922 gg.) (Leninist Policy of Peace in the Far East in the Years 1920—1922); V. S. Starikov; Sovremennaya materialnaya kultura kitaitsev v Manchzhurii, eë istoriya i razvitie (Contemporary Material Culture of the Chinese in Manchuria: its History and Development); L. S. Vasiliev: Nekotorye problemy drevneishei istorii Kitaya (genesis tsivilizatsii v basseine Khuankhe — formirovanie materialnoi kultury etnosa) (Some Problems of Ancient History of China: the Genesis of Civilization in the Huang-ho Valley — the Growth of the Material Culture of the Ethnos) — all from the year 1974. — L. S. Kyusadzhyan: Problema maoizma v sovremennom antikommunizme (The Problem of Maoism in Contemporary Anti-Communism) — from the year 1975.

The present reviewer likewise misses adequate data from Italy which is here represented by only two universities from the Vatican City, but no mention is made of the sinological centres in Rome, Venice and Naples. As is evident from the reviewer's conversations with Italian colleagues, they would welcome if their dissertations were to appear in future volumes of doctoral dissertations on China.

Marián Gálik

Rickett, Adele Austin (Ed.): *Chinese Approaches to Literature from Confucius to Liang Ch'i-ch'ao.* Princeton, New Jersey, Princeton University Press 1978. 267 pp.

The book under review contains something over one half of the papers presented at a conference on old Chinese literary criticism held in St. Croix, Virgin Islands, in December 1970 under the chairmanship of Professor Herbert Franke.

This selection, made available after a lapse of more than seven years, brings works less sophisticated technically and more easily comprehensible also to the reading public at large. Some of them had already been published also outside this selection, and the omission of any reference in the *Preface* to the titles of the various essays and the place where they appeared is felt to be a drawback. This would certainly be of interest to many students of old Chinese literary criticism. To the present reviewer only one of these contributions is known, namely Dr. Helmut Martin's study *A Transitional Concept of Chinese Literature 1897—1917. Liang Ch'i-ch'ao on Poetry-Reform, Historical Drama and the Political Novel,* Oriens Extremus, 20, 1973, 2, pp. 175—217.

The editor of the book, Professor A. A. Rickett in her *Introduction* underscores the significance of the Ch'an-Buddhist belief in the "branch-hanging antelope" (*ling-yang kua-chiao*) and of the image or "sign" based on that belief, consisting in an assertion that the "essence of poetry (and of good literature in general, M. G.) lies not in the words (the traces or tracks), but in what lies beyond the words" (P. 3). The same might be said of Chinese literary criticism. The antelope's horns, the meanings of the critical concepts will for long absorb investigator's attention and will prove a hard nut to crack.

The title of the book truthfully corresponds to its content. The book really starts with Confucius and ends with Liang Ch'i-ch'ao.

Donald Holzman in his paper *Confucius and Ancient Chinese Literary Criticism* endeavours to analyse the views of the great Sage on questions relating to literature and comes to the conclusion that he "has paid little or no attention to the true meaning of poetry" and "has ruthlessly extracted (from it, M. G.) a moral lesson at any price" (p. 33). Confucius considered even the most representative work of literature of that time, the anthology *Shih-ching (The Book of Poetry)* to be an educational handbook, a treasure-house of knowledge, a model for stylistics, and it seems, also for social and diplomatic life. Literature merely served as a means to an end which was a successful administration of state affairs. The existence of literature had a justification solely insofar as it helped resolve moral and political problems of the times.

David Pollard, one of the few Europeans following the complex ways, metamorphoses and occasionally perhaps also the peripeteia of Chinese terms (ideas), studies in his essay the concept of *ch'i*, originally employed in Chinese philosophical works and, from about the beginning of the 3rd century A. D., a part of Chinese literary criticism. As a rule, he draws support for it from the works of Kuo Shao-yü and Hsü Fu-kuan, from the philosopher Kuan-tzu (died 645 B. C.) up to the well-known statesman and man of letters Tseng Kuo-fan (1811—1872). The initial meaning of "vapor", "breath" became, in the course of further evolution, a semantic expression for vitality in the domain of nature and for creativity in literature.

Yu-shih Chen (Diana Yu-shih Mei) is the author of the essay entitled *The Literary Theory and Practice of Ou-yang Hsiu*. This essay takes contact with her extensive study *Han Yü as a Ku-wen Stylist,* Tsing Hua Journal of Chinese Studies, n.s., VII, 1968, 1, pp. 143—208, originally submitted as Ph.D. dissertation, Yale University 1967. Mrs. Yu-shih Chen had evidently for aim to set up a critical picture of the literary criticism of the most prominent adherents of the *ku-wen* movement, as attested to also by her other quite remarkable essay on Su Shih (Su Tung-p'o) (1036—1101), published in Monumenta Serica, XXXI, 1974—1975, pp. 375—392, similar to the one under review. In this essay, Mrs. Yu-shih Chen points to such terms as *hsin* (objective validity), *chien* (simplicity), *ch'ang* (universality) and particularly to the idea of *tzu-jan* (nature) that, according to Ou-yang Hsiu, "connect literature and the external world" and "underlines all his (i.e. Ou-yang's, M. G.) other ideas about reality and truth, whether in literature or in life" (pp. 73—74).

While Yu-shih Chen was interested in the literary criticism of the T'ang and Sung periods, A. A. Rickett, absorbed principally by Wang Kuo-wei's (1877—1927) *Jen-chien tz'u-hua* which she translated and published in Hong Kong in 1977, concentrated her attention on the Sung period — one of the most important sources of Wang Kuo-wei's criticism. In this case it is Huang T'ing-chien (1045—1105) and in particular his formula *to-t'ai huan-ku* (evolving from the embryo and changing the bone) pointing to the process of creativity making use of imitation in traditional Chinese poetry.

Mr. Siu-kit Wong contributed to the collection with his study of two very important "matching terms" — and highly recurrent, too — in the history of old Chinese literary criticism: *ch'ing* which usually, though not always, means feelings or emotional experiences, and *ching,* usually translated as scene or scenery. Although Dr. Wong devoted more attention and effort to the concept of *ch'ing* than any other student of Chinese literary criticism, he does not endeavour here more exactly to define the meaningful elements of this "sign" and in his view the fluidity of Chinese critical language seems to be "the first problem to grapple with in the study of Chinese literary criticism; semantic studies should be useful by *defining* the fluidity" (p. 129).

The Ch'ang-chou School of Tz'u Criticism by Chia-ying Yeh Chao is a very erudite study and simultaneously a valuable contribution to the history of Chinese literary criticism of the 18th and 19th centuries. And as it lays stress on the theoretical aspects of this topic (particularly in the domain of allegory) it also represents a contribution in the field of Chinese traditional poetry.

John C. Y. Wang's study on the Chih-yen-chai's Commentary on the *Dream of the Red Chamber,* and C. T. Hsia's important essay on Yen Fu and Liang Ch'i-ch'ao as advocates of new fiction, are of a different design than the other studies in the collection devoted to questions of poetry. The contribution of the former lies principally in the classification of literary and critical procedures of the authors of Chih-yen-chai's Commentary, while the latter will be of interest by its notes on the as yet unprocessed materials referring to Yen Fu (1853—1921) and on the section called *Lun yu-hsüeh* (On Juvenile Education) from *Pien-fa t'ung-i* (A Comprehensive Proposal for Government reforms) by Liang Ch'i-ch'ao (1873—1929) which speaks of the need to create new fiction and gives a high appreciation of the educational value of old Chinese novels, like *Water Margin, Three Kingdoms* or *Dream of the Red Chamber.* It should be observed that this last part is dealt with in even greater detail the study by Dr. Martin referred to above, op. cit., pp. 178—189.

Marián Gálik

Dudbridge, Glen: *The Legend of Miao-shan.* London, Oxford University 1978.
128 pp.

Dr. Glen Dudbridge entered the world of the sinological scholarship some years ago with his work *The Hsi-yu chi. A Study of the Antecedents of the Sixteenth-Century Chinese Novel,* Cambridge 1970, and he now offers this new book to interested readers and critics.

In it the author paints a rather detailed portrait of one of the figures in the Chinese demotic Pantheon — Miao-shan (Kuan-yin), king Miao-chuang-yen's daughter. First, we are made to follow the birth of the legend and its old versions up to 1500, an interesting feature being its connection with the early *pao-chüan* tradition. As expressed in this book "the term 'pao-chüan' covers a corpus of popular texts written largely in a characteristic mixture of prose with verse for chanting or singing" (p. 44). We find the story of Miao-shan in *Hsiang-shan pao-chüan* in its different editions.

The most interesting and probably also of the greatest value is that part interpretating Miao Shan's story in the sixteenth and seventeenth century. This is related to Dudbridge's study and specialised erudition. In his exposition of a short novel *Nan-hai Kuan-yin ch'üan-chuan,* probably from the late sixteenth century, the author of the book under review utilized his researches in the domain of *Hsi-yu chi,* since one of the editors of both *Nan-hai* and *Hsi-yu chi* in 100 chapters was the same man named Chu Ting-ch'en. He also makes an analysis of the plays *Hsiang-shan chi* and *Hai-ch'ao yin* written on the theme of Miao-shan, further of *pao-chüan* called *Kuan-yin chi-tu pen-yüan chen-ching* from the seventeenth century, and on the basis of the latter, also of the teaching of the Hsien-t'ien ta-tao (Great Way of Former Heaven), one of the religious sects in South China and South-East Asia, usually connected with women and their interests.

The last two parts of the book are concerned with a structural treatment of the setting of the story and its message for the readers as a charter for female celibacy and a supreme act of filial piety.

The Notes and the List of Works Cited will certainly prove useful to investigators in the field of *pao-chüan* and Chinese popular literature.

Marián Gálik

Eight Chinese Plays from the Thirteenth Century to the Present. Translated with an Introduction by William Dolby. London, Paul Elek 1978. 164 pp.

After the pioneering work *A History of Chinese Drama,* published in 1976, the first of its kind in any Western language, impressive by its extent and valuable contribution, Dr. Dolby of Edinburgh, Scotland, presents the professional reading community with eight as yet untranslated plays (or parts thereof) from the late thirteenth or early fourteenth century up to the mid-1950s.

This selection, made judiciously and with taste, opens with a brief *yüan-pen* attributed to Liu T'an-ch'ing and entitled *The Battling Doctors* and continues with further plays of which the one by Shih Chün-pao (1192—1276) called *Ch'iu Hu Tries to Seduce His Own Wife (Yüan tsa-chü)* will certainly appeal to the reader.

To us elderly readers of Dolby's selection and sinologists, who in the late fifties or early sixties had the opportunity of admiring the refined art of Peking Opera and its uncrowned king Mei Lan-fang (1894—1961), the latter's version of the play *Hegemon Kings Says Farewell to His Queen (Pa-wang pieh chi)* may be particularly appealing. Dr. Dolby's translation brings to mind Tu Chin-fang's splendid performance of the beautiful Yü, wife of the legendary Hsiang Yü (232—202 B.C.). And above all, that unforgettable moment when this woman, holding a red lantern in hand, leaves her tent in expectation of the decisive battle in which her husband and she herself will depart from the scene of Chinese history, speaks of all similar senseless battles of the past, and of those who fell in them: "What did they fight for all those past heroes of mighty mettle, when all they won was their bones lying chill on the field of battle?"

Persisting interest in the Chinese dramatic heritage as such is attested to also by the last translation in the book under review *Indentifying Footprints in the Snow*, *ch'uan-chü*, Szechwanese drama.

The so-called Cultural Revolution in the second half of the sixties put an end to the development of Peking Opera and generally also to the traditional drama in the People's Republic of China.

The book under review is preceded by the author's *Introduction* and is supplemented with *Notes* indispensable for a more adequate understanding of the translated plays.

Marián Gálik

Münke, Wolfgang: *Die klassische chinesische Mythologie*. Stuttgart, Ernst Klett Verlag 1976. 338 pp.

Das besprochene Buch ist das dritte aus der Reihe „Wörterbuch der Mythologie" und folgt nach Band I: *Götter und Mythen im Vorderen Orient,* und Band II: *Götter und Mythen im Alten Europa.* Wolfgang Münke, vissenschaftlicher Mitarbeiter der Staatsbibliothek Preussischer Kulturbesitz, früher in Marburg/Lahn, jetzt in West-Berlin, arbeitete an diesem Buch fast zwanzig Jahre. Es ist eine forscherische Tat, die an die Arbeit der großen Sinologen der Vergangenheit wie M. Granet, G. Haloun, H. Maspero, bzw. andere, sowie an das Werk der Nestoren der gegenwärtigen Sinologie B. Karlgren oder W. Eberhard anknüpft. Dem Leser fällt sofort auf, daß Münke vor allem die Primärquellen dem Studium zu unterziehen versucht. Gegen die Sekundärliteratur ist er oft mißtrauisch und bedient sich ihrer lediglich in solchen Fällen, wo sie ihm helfen kann bestimmte forscherische Aspekte zu klären, bei denen die kargen und sich oft widersprechenden Angaben der Primärquellen nicht ausreichen.

Ein solches Vertrauen in die eigenen Kräfte muß gewiß positiv bewertet werden, auch wenn andererseits nicht zu vergessen ist, dass auch die Sekundärliteratur manchmal nützlicher sein kann, wie es auf den ersten Blick erscheinen mag. Wir denken dabei an bestimmte Werke hochgebildeter chinesischer Forscher, auch wenn es nicht gerade solche waren, die sich speziell mit der Mythologie befaßt hätten, jedoch große Kenntnisse besaßen, und es ist möglich, dass die Ergebnisse ihrer Forschung auch für den gegenwärtigen Forscher von Nutzen sein könnten. Es sind dies Werke, denen Herr Münke seine Aufmerksamkeit nicht widmete (oder zu denen er keinen Zutritt fand), wie z.B. *Shen-hua tsa-lun* (Verschiedene Forschungen über die Mythologie) von Mao Tun aus dem Jahre 1929, wo sich auch eine umfangreiche Studie über die chinesische Mythologie, S. 1—73, befindet, oder das zweiteilige Booklet desselben Autors, das ebenfalls im Jahre 1929 unter dem Pseudonym Hsüan Chu erschien und *Chung-kuo shen-hua yen-chiu ABC* (Eine Einführung ins Studium der chinesische Mythologie) betitelt wurde. Mao Tun war seinerzeit unter anderem auch ein strenger Kritiker des, soweit es uns bekannt ist, einzigen Vorgängers Münkes E.T.C. Werner, des Autors von *A Dictionary of Chinese Mythology*. Mao Tun kannte dieses Werk von Werner aus dem Jahre 1932 nicht, er wurde jedoch eingehend mit Werners über 400 Seiten umfassenden Buch bekannt *Myths and Legends of China*, das Hyman Kublin als den „forerunner" des bekannten Wörterbuchs von Werner bezeichnete. Der, aus der anthropologisch orientierten Konzeption des schottischen Wissenschaftlers und Literaten Andrew Lang (1844—1912), die in der zweiteiligen Arbeit, *Myths, Literature and Religion* aus dem Jahre 1887 ihren Ausdruck gefunden hat, hervorgehende Mao Tun versuchte „verschiedene Stoffe der chinesischen Mythologie zu bewerten und zu analysieren" (*Chung-kuo shen-hua yen-chiu ABC*, Band 2, S. 97). Bei dieser Gelegenheit, jedoch noch eingehender, unterwarf Mao Tun im Buch *Shen-hua tsa-lun*, in der Studie *Chung-kuo shen-hua yen-chiu* (Das Studium der chinesischen Mythologie) einer Kritik Werners allzu breiten Zutritt zur Frage der Mythologie und die unkritische Auswahl im Bereich der Materiale. Als Hauptquelle der chinesischen Mythen diente Werner der Roman *Feng-shen yen-i*, ein Werk, das in die Ming-Epoche eingereiht wird; weitere wichtige Quellen waren die Bücher *Li-tai shen-hsien t'ung-chien*, *Shen-hsien lieh-chuan* und *Sou-shen chi*. Mao Tun zweifelt daran, ob diese Werke, die vorwiegend von „Geistern und Unsterblichen" sprechen, als chinesische Mythen betrachtet werden können (ebenda, S. 69). Nichteinmal in der dem Werk *A Dictionary of Chinese Mythology* beigefügten *Bibliography* führt Werner so wichtige Primärquellen an, wie es *Ch'u-tz'u, Mu t'ien-tzu chuan, Lieh-tzu, Huai-nan-tzu* oder *Shu-i chi* waren, die für Mao Tun die bedeutendsten Nachschlagewerke darstellten, ebenso wie für Münke, bloß fügt letzterer noch auch andere historische, philologische und philosophische Werke hinzu.

Während für Werner die Mythologie noch eine Art von „polytheology and demonology", und das Wörterbuch, das er schuf, etwas wie ein Who's Who of the Chinese Otherworld war, versucht Münke an die Gründlichkeit der alten deutschen philologisch orientierten Geistesgeschichte anzuknüpfen. Indes für Werner das Studium dessen, was er Mythologie nannte, eher einem allgemeinen und relativ ästhetisch orientierten Begreifen des chinesischen Lebens nicht nur der Vergangenheit, sondern auch der Gegenwart dienen sollte, will Münke richtig zu einer wissenschaftlichen Bewertung der einzelnen Komponente der chinesischen Mythologie mit all den schwierigen Problemen, die zu lösen sind, gelangen. Es genügt ein einzelnes Stichwort, z. B. *Hsi Wang-mu* (Westkönigsmutter) in beiden Wörterbüchern zu vergleichen, um die sehr unterschiedlichen Zutritte zu sehen, den einen literarisch-ästhetisierenden, den zweiten historisch-philologischen, von denen letzterer natürlich der wissenschaftlich adäquaterer und wirkungsvollerer ist.

Einzelne mythologische Termini sind im rezensierten Buch oft umfangreiche Studien, so z. B. ist den Termini *Hou T'u* und *She* 27 Seiten, dem Terminus *Yü* 14, dem Terminus *Yao* 6 Seiten gewidmet. Andere sind relativ kurz, z. B. *P'an-ku* oder Kuhhirt und Weberin (*Niu-lang und Chih-nü*) haben nichteinmal den Umfang von einer Seite.

Die relativ umfangreiche *Einführung in eine chinesische Mythologie* kann man schwer als einen positiven Beitrag zum Studium der chinesischen Mythologie betrachten. Sie ist eher eine lange Reihe von Anmerkungen, Bemerkungen, manchmal recht chaotisch oder impressionistisch aneinandergereiht, die vielleicht bei der Ausarbeitung einzelner Stichwörter (es sind ihrer im Buch über 80) helfen konnten, für den Leser können sie eher eine „Irreführung" bedeuten, als das, wozu sie ursprünglich hätten dienen sollen.

Bei den einzelnen zitierten Primärquellen hätten auch die chinesischen Ausgaben, und bei den einzelnen Zitationen dieser Werke auch die Paginierung angeführt werden können.

Es wäre gut, wenn das rezensierte Buch bei seiner eventuellen weiteren Ausgabe um neue Termini bereichert werden könnte.

Marián Gálik

Shneider, M. E.: *Russkaya klassika v Kitae* (Russian Classics in China). Moscow, Nauka 1978. 271 pp.

Following a series of studies written in the second half of the 1960s and the first half of the 1970s dealing with questions of reception and influence of Russian classics of the nineteenth and the beginning of the twentieth century in China, the well-known Soviet sinologist M. E. Shneider, from the Institute of Oriental Studies in Moscow, has now published the book under review, well-grounded and well-balanced collection of his own views, linked to the research of his Soviet colleagues and foreign researchers in the domain of Sino-Russian literary relations from Pushkin to Gorky.

Six giants of Russian literature are here introduced to interested readers: A. S. Pushkin, F. M. Dostoyevsky, A. N. Ostrovsky, A. P. Chekhov, L. A. Andreyev and A. M. Gorky. To the justified query of the reader as to why other great figures of Russian literature are not included in his list, M. E. Shneider has a ready reply. In his view, "the existence of relatively thorough studies on the fate of the works of L. Tolstoy, Turgenev and Gogol in China excludes for the time being and urgent necessity of these themes being further processed" (p. 13). Soviet readers have at their disposal the extensive work by A. I. Shifman, *Lev Tolstoy i Vostok* (Leo Tolstoy and the Orient) which includes a chapter about Tolstoy in China, and V. V. Petrov's book, *Lu Sin, Ocherk zhizni i tvorchestva* (Lu Hsün, An Outline of his Life and Work) which also speaks about Gogol. The latter is dealt with in further Soviet studies (p. 13), and recently also in papers by foreign sinologists, as evident from Goldman, M. (Ed.), *Modern Chinese Literature in the May Fourth Era*, Cambridge, Harvard University Press 1977. Nonetheless, I cannot help the impression that Gogol deserves greater attention. And this applies in a like measure also to the work and impact of I. S. Turgenev.

In the 1920s and 1930s, Turgenev seems to have been the most translated author, alongside Gogol, in China (cf. p. 34). Turgenev was a favourite author of Lu Hsün (p. 169), Yü Ta-fu (p. 10), but also of Kuo Mo-jo (not mentioned in this connection in the book) whose reading of Turgenev's *Virgin Soil (Nov)* made him aware "of the similarity between Turgenev's superfluous heroes and Chinese literary men..." (Leo Ou-fan Lee, *The Romantic Generation of Modern Chinese Writers*, Cambridge, Harvard University Press 1973, p. 192). Turgenev made an impression on the writer and poet Ho Ch'i-fang, as evident from B. McDougall's book, *Paths in Dreams. Selected Prose and Poetry of Ho Ch'i-fang*, St. Lucia, University of Queensland Press 1976, pp. 63, 91, 226, 228—230. One who wrote relatively often about Turgenev was Mao Tun. Some of the latter's short pieces reminded Ah Ying (Ch'ien Hsing-ts'un) of Turgenev's poems in prose as is implied in *Yeh hang chi*

245

(Night-Boats), Shanghai 1935, p. 43. Mao Tun in his article *T'an wo-ti yen-chiu* (On My Research) from his collection *Yin-hsiang, kan-hsiang, hui-i* (Impressions, Feelings and Reflections), 2nd ed., Shanghai 1937, p. 79, did admit that from Russian literature he had read much from Tolstoy, Chekhov, Gorky and contemporary Soviet authors, but little from Turgenev and he did not like to read him. Nevertheless, his notes about Turgenev played their role in the history of Sino-Russian literary relations, and one of his articles, for instance, *Tu-ko-nu-fu-ti "Fu yü tzu"* (Turgenev's "Fathers and Sons") has remained until now unknown to literary history. It is to be found in the book *Han-i Hsi-yang wen-hsüeh ming-chu* (Great Works of Western Literature Translated into Chinese), Shanghai 1935, pp. 177—185. This particular book is an abundant source of bibliographic information on translated works and provides an analysis of some of them. A bibliographic rarity as regards Turgenev is Kao T'ao's *"Kui-tsu chih chia" ch'ien chi* (Foreword to "A House of Gentle-folk"), published in a rather obscure magazine Mo-so (Gropings), 1, March 1928, 3, pp. 43—45. This novel had been translated into Chinese in 1927 and appeared in Commercial Press in 1928 in the series Wen-hsüeh yen-chiu hui ts'ung-shu (The Series of the Literary Association).

The bibliographic and factural knowledge of materials of Mr. Shneider and his colleagues is impressive. A total of 937 entries comprising especially translations of Russian writers into Chinese, literature dealing with the reception and influence of Russian literature in China, further, those works that affected this reception and influence, and finally the most diverse journals and newspapers in which this became manifest or where Sino-Russian literary relations were elucidated in some manner, all this is evidence of the author's responsible approach and painstaking efforts to include everything substantial to his subject or that might throw light on the given topic.

However, as even seemingly well surveyed literary regions in China still conceal many "blank spots", it might not be out of place if, within the limits of this review, a point were to made of additional materials, besides those mentioned above, relating to Russian writers dealt with in Shneider's book.

It may prove profitable in future to take note of the views expressed by Cheng Chen-to in his book *Wen-hsüeh ta-kang* (The Outline of Literature), vol. 4, Shanghai 1927, pp. 315—376, which might be seen as an attempt at discussing the history of the nineteenth century Russian literature within the context of other important literatures of Europe, the U.S.A., Japan and Chinese literature itself. A certain source for a knowledge of Mao Tun's relation to the nineteenth century Russian literature is also the work, not included in the book under review, *Hsi-yang wen-hsüeh t'ung-lun* (An Outline of Western Literature), 2nd ed., Shanghai 1933 (1st ed. 1930).

Ah Ying, often mentioned in Shneider's work, is the author of the article *Ch'ing-tao* (Robber in Love), written in November 1927 following his reading of

Pushkin's story *Dubrovsky,* translated into Chinese by Chao Ch'eng-chih and published in the collection *P'u-ssu-chin hsiao-shuo chi* (A Collection of Pushkin's Stories), Shanghai 1924. It brings out Pushkin's reception by the revolutionary intelligentsia of that time, particularly the members of the Sun Society (T'ai-yang she). Dubrovsky from Pushkin's story of the same name, Carl from Schiller's *The Robbers,* and even Kriemhild from *Nibelungenlied* were to young Ah Ying literary paragons, and it would seem, also objects of socio-political admiration. Cf. Ch'ien Hsing-ts'un: *Li-ti wen-i* (Literature of Power), 2nd ed., Shanghai 1929, pp. 53—60 and 112—121.

Chung Mi, referred to on p. 66, was the pseudonym of Chou Tso-jen whose article *San ko wen-hsüeh-chia-ti chi-nien* (Remembrance of Three Writers) is accessible in his book *T'an lung chi* (On Dragon), Shanghai 1927, pp. 17—23. It partly refers to Dostoyevsky. Dostoyevsky is also dealt with in the article by the Japanese author Nakayama Shōzaburō entitled Dostoyevsky and Turgenev and published in Chinese translation in Fang Chi-sheng (tr.), *Wen-hsüeh-chia-ti ku-shih* (The Stories on Men of Letters), Shanghai 1936, pp. 77—83. Another article by the same author in the same book is about Chekhov. And since Chekhov has been mentioned, it might be noted that Mao Tun translated Bunin's Reminiscences of Anton Chekhov into Chinese and published them in the book *Hui-i, shu-chien, tsa-chi* (Reminiscences, Letters and Sketches), Ch'ung-ch'ing 1944, pp. 77—125.

For those who might like to have an idea of the proportion of accessible or known materials existing in the U.S.S.R. and Peking Library, largest in China, dealing with the analysed Russian classics, it may be noted that Shneider mentions 25 book translations from Pushkin (not including poetry), and in July 1953, Peking Library, possessed 40 various translations (including poetry). Shneider further mentions 57 translations from Chekhov and Peking Library listed 68 in 1954; likewise, Shneider refers to 41 translations from Dostoyevsky, while Peking Library had 35 in 1956. Cf. Feng Ping-wen, *Ch'üan-kuo t'u-shu-kuan shu-mu hui-pien* (A Bibliography of Bibliographies Compiled by Chinese Libraries), Peking 1958, No. 1725, 1745 and 1734.

Along the methodological line, Shneider's book takes contact with the achievements of Soviet Marxist comparative literary scholarship, studies problems of reception and influence of Russian literature in China on the basis of genetic-contact relations and typological affinities. Shneider's most original and scholarly most noteworthy contributions are those relating to L. Andreyev and A. Ostrovsky.

In the field of sinological scholarship, this book represents the first attempt at a wide-ranging application of Marxist comparatistics in the research of Sino-Russian literary relations. It constitutes a methodological base and a material repository to all those who will pursue this study in the future.

Marián Gálik

247

Bischoff, Friedrich A.: *Interpreting the Fu. A Study in Chinese Literary Rhetoric.* Münchener Ostasiatische Studien, Band 13, herausgegeben von Wolfgang Bauer und Herbert Franke. Wiesbaden, Franz Steiner Verlag 1976. XVII + 466 pp.

The study of this most difficult and refined kind of Chinese poetry is evidently flourishing now, especially in the USA. Burton Watson published in 1971 the slender volume *Chinese Rhyme-prose. Poems in the Fu Form from the Han and Sixth Dynasties Periods* (Columbia), which includes one *fu* by each of thirteen poets, with a minimum of annotation and an appendix on the early critical statements on the *fu* form. David R. Knechtges dealt essentially with four *fu* by a Han philosopher: *The Han Rhapsody. A Study of the Fu of Yang Hsiung (53 B.C.—A.D. 18)*, Cambridge 1976.

The two above-mentioned books differ not only in subject and method, but also in the terminology chosen for the object of their effort: *fu* is translated both as rhyme-prose or rhapsody; the use of the latter word was criticized by F. Bischoff. He does not try to translate the word *fu*, but even turns it into an English word when using, instead of e.g. "writing of the fu", the neologism "fuing".

In the Table of Contents hidden away on p. XVII, we do not discover which authors of the *fu* are represented in Bischoff's selection of seven *fu*; his analysis of them is due to a decade of his readings with his students. Bischoff has translated, and in a most minute way has even explained, all the historical, literary and even linguistic problems of the following *fu*, most of which have been translated several times into other languages: Li Pi (lived from 722—789), "The Chess Fu" (*Ch'i fu*); Po Chü-i, "Examination Fu" (*Hsing-hsi hsiang chin-yüan fu*); T'ang T'ai-tsung, "The Little Pond" (*Hsiao-ch'ih fu*) from the year 625, and Hsü Ching-tsung, "Reply to the Fu on the Little Pond" (*Hsiao-ch'ih ying-chao*); Su Shih, "The Red Cliff" (*Ch'ih-pi fu*); and Ou-yang Hsiu, "The Autumn Sound (*Ch'iu-sheng fu*). There follow, in the form of an Appendix and Addendum, Han Yü's, Miscellanea, The Dragon and the Clouds, The Good Physician, Mr. Told, "The 'Thousand Li' Horse" and Unicorn (pp. 385—416).

The volume also includes a list of Rhetorical and Miscellaneous Terms, derived mostly from Greek and Latin and used abundantly in the text, as well as a List of Quoted Books and Articles, but no index which would at least partially introduce the reader to the immense wealth of facts and ideas.

F. A. Bischoff, a specialist in T'ang studies who is of Austrian origin and who is presently attached to the University of Indiana, has concentrated almost all his efforts on an explanation of almost every Chinese character (called *kanji* by the author) and however welcome his short introductory study may be, it cannot provide a systematic treatment of the subject. The main value of this book consists in its showing how complicated it is to appreciate and understand this kind of scholarly poetry.

A book-length study on the *fu* genre is still lacking.

Marina Čarnogurská

Furth, Charlotte: *The Limits of Change. Essays on Conservative Alternatives in Republican China.* Cambridge, Harvard University Press 1976. X + 426 pp.

The title "Limits of Change" is more adequate to the nature of the eleven essays (plus two introductory ones of a more general nature) than the subtitle "conservative alternatives" which presumes that we do possess a criterion for what was conservative at such a complicated period as the first decades of the 20th century have undoubtedly been (not only Republican China is dealt with in the book). It immediately comes into mind that we would also need another criterion — what is antithetic to it: progress, innovation, alternation, modification. In view of the well-known Chinese inclination towards tradition, the notion of a willingness to change is better suited to the description of personalities and processes in the said period.

If the first introductory essay by Benjamin I. Schwartz is really general in nature (*Notes on Conservatism in General and in China in Particular*), the second one by Ch. Furth, *Culture and Politics in Modern Chinese Conservatism* brings numerous ideas to be found elaborated in her study on Chang Ping-lin — *The Sage as Rebel: The Inner World of Chang Ping-lin.*[1]

The other essays are grouped into four parts: national essence, political modernization against revolutionary politics, the new Confucianism of the post May Fourth era, modern historicism and the limits of change, respectively. In other words: old and new historicism, politics and Confucianism. Among the important personalities dealt with in the essays are: Liu Shih-p'ei, Liang Chi and Liang Shu-ming, the Hung-hsien Emperor, i.e. Yüan Shih-k'ai, Hsiung Shih-li, Mou Tsung-san, T'ao Hsi-sheng and Chou Tso-jen; for some unknown reason, the biographical data are mostly omitted. There are no other conservatives described in the book, like Ch'ien Mu, K'ang Yu-wei or Fung Yu-lan, to name only a few.

The scope of the book is rather ambitious, since complicated issues from the Manchu, Republican and People's Republic period are being studied, the last one of course mostly indirectly. We may also agree with the choice of central issues,

---

[1] When reading those essays the reviewer was rather disappointed by the absence of what had been promised by the editor in the Preface on p. VII, viz. "the elimination of male oriented language" ... "according to the guidelines drawn up by the Los Angeles Westside Women's Committee".

although quite important fields, like literature or art, have been left aside. It is right that philosophy or thought have been privileged because of their having played a great role, even though originating within a very narrow group of intellectuals.

The first notion of Chinese nationalism during the late Ch'ing period was *kuo-ts'ui* (from Japanese *kokusui*) — "national essence" or "national excellence". It is studied here in the broad context of the new intelligentsia by L. A. Schneider who convincingly shows that its partisans, originally proud defenders of national heritage, lost their influence about 1920 since they were found somewhat "aristocratic" just in this regard. Martin Bernal presents a case study on the same issue in Liu Shih-p'ei's early development until 1907. We are confronted i.a. by the strange fact that the adherents of the "national essence" found considerable interest in Terrien de Lacouperie's theories that much in China's historical development was due to the influence from the ancient Near East. This is all the more surprising since we know that the Frenchman has been educated in Chinese Classics.

There was not much consistency in the ideas and development of the *kuo-ts'ui* movement. We may appreciate the difficult task of Ch. Furth when explaining the Legalist-Taoist outlook of the Confucian Chang Ping-lin, with a flavour of racialism. Only one thing is clear, viz. that Chang was a conservative and therefore belongs into the book under review.

Lin Yü-sheng describes the suicide of Liang Chi (1918) as "an ambitious case of moral conservatism", while Guy Allito studies the life and activities of his better known son Liang Shu-ming (or Liang Sou-ming). Both the conservatives were trying to preserve the traditional moral values which the son attempted to put into practice in small rural territories following "the Mencian assumption that the people of other areas would, 'with their necks stretched out, rush like a torrent' to follow the lead of the virtue" (p. 233).

The third part of the book dealing with politics, is rather short. E. P. Young denotes the president and emperor Yüan Shih-k'ai as "a modernizing conservative" because his was the effort to redefine elements out of the Chinese past, as well as the experiences of other countries and use them in order to move China gradually into the modern world. It is worth while to read how Yüan and the monarchists tried to reestablish the monarchy under the pretext of guaranteeing the constitution. Under the rather general title *The Kuomintang in the 1930s* L. A. Eastman deals with what might properly be called incipient fascism (Eastman is right when criticizing the "less precise" term of conservatism in the beginning of his study), viz. the Blue Shirts, the CC clique, Chiang Kai-shek's New Life Movement, etc. It is meanwhile difficult to agree with Eastman's conclusion that "conservatism — in the sense of a conscious desire to maintain the status quo — was rare during the Nanking period" (p. 209).

The new and much more refined Confucianism after the fall of the imperial one is not given much attention at the present time, because it is believed to be rather obsolete and without any influence outside a small group of interested. Tu Wei-ming in his welcome study on Hsiung Shih-li's quest for authentic existence, is evidently of a different opinion which he, however, defines very cautiously: "Indeed, it is not inconceivable that some contemporary intellectuals find in Confucianism not a fixity of past wisdom, but a reservoir of humanistic insights, meaningful to their own existence and relevant to their perceptions of the vital issues of the modern world" (p. 243). Hsiung Shih-li (1885—1968)[2] is undoubtedly a telling example for the author's thesis: a man with a few students only, who did not write much, is shown to have had a lasting influence simply as a Neo-Confucianist. The same attitude is openly shown by Hao Chang in the last essay of the fourth part of the book: *New Confucianism and the Intellectual Crisis of Contemporary China.*

It is, however, not the contemporary China which brings us to the end of the book; we still have to return to the thirties. Arif Dirlik presents the reader with perhaps the most important study of the volume: T'ao Hsi-sheng: *The Social Limits of Change.* T'ao, during the years 1926—1928, "was not a defender of traditional values...but one of the first major Chinese Marxist historians, an advocate of revolutionary change" (p. 305). This is really a revealing study on a retrograde evolution which fits the frame of the volume. Finally, there is another conductive study by David E. Pollard, *Chou Tso-jen: A Scholar who Withdrew.* Nevertheless, such a contradictory personality can hardly be understood if only a part of his life is studied, especially the less important one.

It seems futile to examine according to the different definitions of conservatism whether one or another of the personalities dealt with in the present volume corresponds with the scheme. It is much more important to see that a great amount of indispensable information and insight has been offered by the contributors, all of U.S.A. universities. A historian would probably be thankful for a greater amount of factual information, he would prefer biographies to essays in which most of the authors follow, willy-nilly, the general leitmotiv. Less initiated readers may wonder if Chang Ping-lin and Chang T'ai-yen, Liang Shu-ming or Liang Sou-ming are one and the same person; they will have to find out for themselves which of the three forms of writing the name of Lacouperie is the right one. The rather frequent misprints could have been easily eliminated through a more careful proof-reading.

All in all, the volume brings much of what we need to know for a better understanding of our century.

Josef Fass

---

[2] Liu Shu-hsien, for some reason not quoted by Tu Wei-ming, studied also the ideas of Hsiung Shih-li (and Mou Tsung-san): *The Contemporary Development of a Neo-Confucian Epistemology.* Inquiry, *14,* 1971, Nos 1—2, pp. 14—40. Liu asserts on p. 38, note 3 that Hsiung was born already in 1883, not in 1885.

David, Kenneth (Ed.): *The New Wind. Changing Identities in South Asia.* The Hague—Paris, Mouton Publishers 1977. 537 pp.

The present book, devoted to socio-anthropological problems of the Indian subcontinent, has come into existence thanks to the efforts of eighteen scholars, but especially to those of Kenneth David, its editor and also the author of an insightful Introduction and an Epilogue (explaining broadly what is meant by "changing identities"). It consists of seventeen papers, contributions to the IXth International Congress of Anthropological and Ethnological Sciences, Symposium on Changing Identities in South Asia. In the words of the general editor Sol Tax, the volume exemplifies the method of analysis used by a new generation of social anthropologists in which a basic problem (in this case continuity and change) is informed by a central concept (social identity) and by a methodological conflict (empiricist vs. intellectualist vs. materialist) (p. V).

The essays included in the volume are of different quality as to the method, range of theory and levels of analysis. They represent the views of Western as well as Eastern scholars, the majority of authors being from South Asia. Their approaches to the problem, i.e. the study of changing identities in South Asia are different. Some of them stem mainly from traditional questions (religion, caste) and, highlighting as yet understressed features of structures, use more traditional methods. They discuss the previously existing structure of identities in term of homologies between diverse features in the levels of ideology, norms, and behaviour. Some of them stress repetitive processes of positional and ideological changes throughout South Asian history. The papers of this type are included in Part I named *The Standing and the Moving,* and they are as follows: *The Rise of Social Anthropology in India (1774—1972): A Historical Appraisal* by L. P. Vidyarthi; *Indian Civilization: New Images of the Past for a Developing Nation* by S. C. Malik; *Defied Men and Humanized Gods: Some Folk Bases of Hindu Theology* by A. Aiyappan; *Prestations and Prayers: Two Homologous Systems in Northern India* by R. S. Khare; *Power in Hindu Ideology and Practice* by Susan Wadley; *Gods, Kings, and the Caste System in India* by L. K. Mahapatra; *Hierarchy and Equivalence in Jaffna, North Sri Lanka: Normative Codes as Mediator* by Kenneth David; *Toward an Ethnosociology of South Asian Caste Systems* by McKim Marriott and Ronald Inden; *Method and Theory in the Sociology of Louis Dumont: A Reply* by Owen M. Lynch; *Flexibility in Central Indian Kinship and Residence* by Doranne Jacobson.

Papers included in Part II, named *The Moving and the Standing,* treat of the emerging identities in South Asia such as agricultural labour unions, revitalized tribal identities, ethnic identity, identity choice as the central problem in situating caste, etc. They present differently interpreted continuities and transformations of the previous structure, and the approaches used, though divergent, are progressive and new as to theory and methodology.

The paper *Role Analysis and Social Change: With Special Reference to India*, by M. S. A. Rao, reviews briefly structural and interactional development of role theory and then deals with the role analysis in relation to social and economic change and development in India.

Joan P. Mencher, in her essay *Agricultural Labor Unions: Socioeconomic and Political Considerations*, discusses the background of labour union activities in different parts of Kerala, and the reasons of their divergent development there. She employs a dialectal model which postulates change as a process of transformation through resolution of conflicts.

The paper *Caste Elements Among the Muslims of Bihar*, by Zeyauddin Ahmad, focuses on ways through which the Muslim society borrowed caste elements, and on the extent to which a Hindu caste system has been evolved to the Muslim community. It also illuminates the reasons, political, economic, religious, and others, for the weakening impact of Hinduism on Muslims with the passage of time.

The two interesting papers on the Santals follow, i.e. *Ecological Adaptation to Technology — Ritual Conflict and Leadership Change: The Santal Experience*, by Sikant Mahapatra, and *The Santalization of the Santals*, by Mohan K. Gautam. The former deals with the evolution of political democracy in a Santal tribal community, which has given rise to two contradictory patterns of leadership within the community, and with the impact of political democracy on the solidarity-emulation conflict.

Mohan K. Gautam shows to what extent and how the Santals' cultural borrowing and modernity have influenced the Santal traditions and ideals. He discusses the ongoing process of Santalization of the Santals which is reflected in their relations and identity.

The aim of Mahadev L. Apte's contribution *Region, Religion, and Language: Parameters of Identity in the Process of Acculturation* is "to describe briefly an extended culture contact situation resulting from the migration of one community to a different linguistic region and to analyze the ethnic identity problems faced by its members" (p. 383). The author looks for the primary parameters of identity of a Marathi-speaking community in Tamilnadu. He comes to the conclusion that language, although serving as the main criterion distinguishing this community from the dominant population, plays but a secondary role in creating the consciousness of identity, the primary role being ascribed to caste, religion, and region.

The last essay included in the present volume, *Identity, Choice and Caste Ideology in Contemporary South India* by Steve Barnett, is based on the study of recent changes in a South Indian caste. It shows how changes in caste ideology allowed and shaped the other ideological developments of class, cultural nationalism, etc. Identity and identity choice are considered here the central forms of ideological struggle in South Asia, the central problem in situating caste today.

Part III brings the recordings of the discussion of one of the Congress sessions.

This is an excellent book collecting the papers by many renowned scholars who used different theoretical and methodological approaches in their study of identity changes in South Asia, enabling the reader to compare and judge for himself which approach is the best suited to explain the problem.

The book may be considered an important contribution to anthropological studies on South Asia.

Anna Rácová

Türk Dünyası El Kitabı (Handbook of the Turkic World). Ankara, Türk Kültürü Araştırma Enstitüsü 1976. VIII + 1452 pp., map.

This work on the Turkic World, the first to appear in Turkey, was published on the occasion of the 50th anniversary of the founding of the republic, by a group of scholars associated with the Türk Kültür Araştırma Enstitüsü (Institute for Research of the Turkish Culture). The preparation of the work took long to complete and during that time also its concept became altered, as may be seen from its contents. The policy adopted by the Editorial Board not to include contributions with explicative notes but only with references at the end of each paper, was not strictly adhered to either, although the violations here might be said to be to the benefit of the topic dealt with.

Despite the protracted preparation lasting several years, the editors failed to process all the cultural expressions of Turkish nations, a fact admitted in their introduction. The domains left unprocessed include those of music, sport, the military art, history of science, and even those of ethnography and folklore — a rather surprising omission, smacking of temerity. On the other hand, topics and problems dealt with in the section on the foundations of Turkish culture, are again taken up in that on Turkish history, and certain concepts from the historical section about contemporary Turkey are to be met with in both the first and the fifth chapters. Such overlappings betray a lack of a well thought-out, consistent design and cast a reflection on the editorial work.

The book is made up of five principal sections: I. Geography of Turkic countries; II. Foundations of Turkic Culture; III. Turkic History; IV. Modern Turkic World; V. Contemporary Problems of the Turkic World.

It is not easy to express a judicious opinion on this large complex of investigated problems. As already observed, not all the contributions are elaborated in the same manner. Part of them are of a scientific standard, some present their subject-matter in a popularized-scientific manner, while some, unfortunately achieve but a propaganda level. And this makes the reliability and applicability of the data questionable.

254

As might be expected, the most reliable to the reader will be data concerning modern problems of the Turkish republic. As regards earlier history, literature, economics, this issue is less relevant. But in the case of data concerning the Turks or Turkic peoples outside the Turkish territory, the data have often to be taken very critically, one reason being that many of them are based on pure estimates.

This is closely related to other aspects of the data, viz. their complex and actual nature. Due to the protracted preparation of the book, ranging over ten years and more, the earlier papers fail not only to mention the latest concepts, but also to list the more recent bibliographic references. For example, Ahmed Temir, in the section On Kipchak Literature (p. 503) only "expects" the publication of materials written in Kipchak language from Kamenets-Podolskii, which appeared as far back as 1967 (*Dokumenty na polovetskom yazyke XVI v. Sudebnye akty kamenets-podolskoi armyanskoi obshchiny*), prepared by T. I. Hrunin. Moscow 1967. Naturally, the edition of a further monument of this language (E. Schütz: *An Armeno-Kipchak Chronicle of the Polish-Turkish Wars in 1620—1621*. Budapest 1968) was unknown to him. This is only one case in point. Several such examples could be cited, particularly as regards foreign literature. This is closely related to errors in foreign-language (non-Turkish texts), especially in bibliographic data.

The above remarks concern for the most part, the technical aspects of the book which, in a case like this, is an important though not the principal issue. This handbook, intended for Turkish readers, will fulfil its aim as the first, or perhaps primary information on various questions of the past and the present of the Turkic World.

Vojtech Kopčan

Vaughan, D. M.: *Europe and the Turk. A Pattern of Alliances 1350—1700.* Reprint.New York, AMS Press 1976. viii + 305 pp.

This work, by now a classic of European historiography on relations between Europe and the Ottoman empire at the time of its rise, appeared in an unaltered edition thanks to AMS Press, New York. It certainly was a happy decision to reprint this valuable book which, by the quantity of the material collected and its successful interpretation terminates a long stage of research into the relations of the European continent towards the Ottoman empire, primarily in the field of political history.

As intimated in the preface, the authoress herself is aware that a new wave is rising in the investigation of the history of the Ottoman empire. Recent studies of source documents from Turkish, but also European archives have yielded a spate of notes and concepts from the economic and social history of the Ottoman empire and have

considerably altered the traditional Christian image of the Turk as the "deadly enemy of Christendom". World turkology and historiography on the Ottoman empire, in numerous books and partial studies has brought out correlations also in the domain of political history. It would be of interest to confront or rather complement Vaughan's book with these novel concepts, but that would require undue space and ultimately would only show that in many respects, particularly as regards European aspects, the book is still a good guide in the history of European-Ottoman relations. It might be substantially supplemented only on issues to which recent investigations have devoted enhanced attention, such for instance, as the question of *devshirme,* the attitude of Renaissance Europe towards the Turks, the relation between protestantism and the Ottoman empire, and that to the European eastern allies, etc.

The division of the book into six chapters, viz. I. The Failure of Europe to Repel the Turk; II. The Early Ottoman Empire as a Naval Power and Economic Force; III. The Ottoman Empire and the European Balance of Power; IV. The Turk and the Counter-Reformation; V. Europe and other Enemies of the Turk; VI. The Last Turkish Aggressions and their Results, is also well balanced as regards the extent of individual chapters. One might perhaps reproach the authoress with the fact that of three European anti-Ottoman fronts — the Mediterranean, the Danubian and East European, eventually the Caucasian — she devotes attention mostly to the Mediterranean one. Similarly in her response to Ottoman expansion she has in view primarily Western, less so Central and Eastern Europe.

Vojtech Kopčan

Sugar, Peter F.: *Southeastern Europe under Ottoman Rule 1354—1804.* Seattle and London, University of Washington Press 1977. xiii + 365 pp. A History of East Central Europe, Vol. V.

This, the fifth volume in the series of monographs on *A History of East Central Europe,* published by the University of Washington, comes from the pen of one of the professors at this university, Peter F. Sugar known rather as an expert on the history of Austria-Hungary. The author has this to say about his aims: "It was my intention to present a chronologically organized series of descriptive pictures that in their totality depict life in Southeastern Europe under Ottoman Rule." And this also determines the structure of his book which is divided into five principal parts including thirteen chapters: I. The Ottomans; II. Life in the European "Core" Provinces of the Ottoman Empire, 1413—1574; III. The Vassal and Tribute-Paying

States; IV. Life in the European "Core" Provinces of the Ottoman Empire, 1574—1804; V. General Considerations. As auxiliary material, the book has several appendices which give a list of Ottoman sultans, grand viziers, rulers and princes of the Balkan countries, chronological tables, glossaries of geographical terms and foreign (Ottoman) expressions, and an index.

The author takes note of the manner of incorporation of Balkan States and parts of conquered Hungary into the system of the Ottoman State, of the characteristic marks of Ottoman State organization, social structure of the Ottoman empire, and finally also the effects of Turkish domination on the development of nations of South-eastern Europe.

In the first part, Sugar underlines two fundamental elements in the formation of the Ottoman State — one Islamic, the other Turkish. The entire Ottoman social organization with the sultan at its head, was made to stand on these — including further influences — as the base. Theoretically, the sultan was an absolute ruler who governed his empire through the intermediary of the ruling class (the author calls them Professional Ottomans). Professional Ottomans were reminiscent of European feudal nobility, but in contrast to this, they had no legal rights, although tradition gave them extensive power. In practice, they could stem from any stratum of the Ottoman society if they met certain conditions; on the other hand, they were absolutely powerless against the sultan who could dismiss them at any time, or have them executed. When it happened that a certain group of Professional Ottomans acquired an unduly great influence, the sultan chose these people from a different environment (in the 15th century, he used the janissaries against a clan aristocracy, etc.) in order to ensure his political supremacy. All the political and administrative functions were in the hands of this class which was divided into higher and lower grades within the parallel functional organizations. In a sense, the Ottoman Empire had a functional administrative structure whose offices were manned by specially trained bureaucrats of various ranks who were simply the temporary executors of political decisions that remained the exclusive right of the ruler. This administrative-political functionalism had a considerable influence on the creation of the Ottoman social pyramid, divided horizontally into strata of "social classes", and vertically into Muslims and *millets*. The top of this pyramid was occupied by the sultan, below him came the Professional Ottomans and the rest was the *reaya* which by its work, supported the State and the ruling top. The position of the various groups in the *reaya* (here belonged merchants and tradesmen, whether Muslim or Christian and all the farming population regardless of denomination) depended on the importance their employment had for the central power, and this became reflected also in their position in the social structure. Each socio-professional group was strictly regulated and its members had certain duties and rights.

As the author remarks — "viewed from the administrative-political angle, the

Ottoman Empire was organized into horizontal layers of social classes in accordance with their professional activities. The duties and rights of each class reflected the degree of importance that the government attached to its economic activities".

Vertically, the population was divided into muslims and *millets* (religious community) of the Orthodox, the Armenians, and the Jews. These were parallel organizations, and each was independent within the limits of its own competence. The purpose of the *millet* system — according to Sugar — was simply to create a secondary imperial administrative and primary legal structure for the *zimmi*.

This horizontal and vertical division of the society formed some sort of a network. Each individual belonged to one of the meshes of such a net and within it he was able to move relatively freely. A horizontal movement from one *millet* into another could take place through conversion, but far more complicated was movement within the framework of one *millet*, for it disrupted the social structure. This permitted the Ottomans effectively to deal within the complex religious-ethnic and linguistic environment of Southeastern Europe. This structure was considered unchangeable, especially while it fulfilled its mission. Its great weakness, however was that it overlooked the basic traits of human nature and social life. In an endeavour to ensure the functioning of these socio-economic units, the Ottomans, after having liquidated the former ruling strata, set up a new class of local leaders who did not represent any new nobility, but who later stood at the head of movements for an independence of their nations.

In addition to the so-called "Core" provinces, Sugar also deals with Vassal and Tribute-Paying States in southeastern Europe. In his view, Dubrovnik was the only vassal territory that profited from Ottoman protection. In the case of Transylvania, its relative independence was helped to be maintained by the Habsburg-Ottoman rivalry. The worst off were the Danubian princedoms of Walachia and Moldavia which paid a high price for their political semi-independence and cultural autonomy.

Sugar devotes considerable attention to the question of Ottoman legacy left to Southeastern Europe. The author is not of the opinion that Ottoman domination was the only cause of the backwardness of Balkan nations. In his view, one cannot speak of Ottoman backwardness up to the end of the 18th century. Differences between the Balkans and parts of the rest of Europe became more apparent only in the 19th century.

The most interesting change brought into Southeastern Europe was, according to Sugar, the large demographic transformation of the area, the consequences of which still determine the relationship of its people to each other. Mass migrations northwards of Serbs, Roumanians, Albanians and partly also of Greeks provoked by Ottoman aggressions created a complex ethnical situation in many places of the Balkans and this may be considered to be part of Ottoman legacy.

But a far more complicated issue is that of the consequences of Ottoman domination in agriculture and in the economy of these lands. Since the beginning of

258

Ottoman domination in Southeastern Europe right up to the 18th century, no major change took place in agricultural production. In Hungary — the territory between the Danube and the Tisza — the Ottoman aggression coincided temporarily with a large-scale soil erosion which had far-reaching consequences for this region. As to the devastation of large parts of Hungary by the Ottomans, the author puts the blame rather on the Hungarian nobility that brought about the situation in the first quarter of the 16th century.

As to the Balkan countries, Sugar states that "nor can it be argued that Ottoman rule produced technological backwardness in the agricultural sector of the economy". Even though farming implements were primitive, they did not differ from those used by cultivators elsewhere in Europe. A more explicit lagging behind already in the Ottoman era was manifest in manufactures and in transportation, especially in maritime transport. Here, however, in the author's view not only Ottoman incompetence or unwillingness to change the traditional, mediaeval mode of production in Guild corporations was to blame, but also competition of foreign, primarily European goods and the policies of European powers who succeeded in enforcing their will in the economic sphere. In this respect, the Ottoman legacy had a very adverse effect on the broad masses of populations of these regions.

Sugar considers as very harmful the sequelae in the political sphere. Balkan politicians and statesmen of the 19th and early 20th century, famous for their "laziness, egoism and venality" proved to have been the most disturbing consequence of the Ottoman legacy. The conditions of the last years of Ottoman rule, when venal and egoistic violators of the law just blossomed amidst a stupid bureaucracy, served as a model to the first generations of Balkan politicians who took their place.

Sugar's book points to the author's remarkable ability systematically to array a considerable quantity of data from Balkan and Ottoman history and to set up, in many points an original conception of the development of Southeastern Europe under Ottoman rule. On the other hand, however, he seems to have in many cases subordinated his choice of facts and data to his functionalistic conception.

Vojtech Kopčan

A t s ı z, B.: *Das Osmanische Reich um die Mitte des 17. Jahrhunderts. Nach den Chroniken des Vecîhî (1637—1660) und des Mehmed Halifa (1633—1660).* München, Dr. Dr. R. Trofenik 1977. CXXXIII + 144 + 123 + 108 S. Beiträge zur Kenntnis Südosteuropas und des Nahen Orients, XXI. Band.

Die osmanischen Chroniken gehören zu den Grundquellen für die politische Geschichte des Osmanischen Reiches. Hinsichtlich der Bedeutung der Chroniken von Vecîhî und Mehmed Halife für das zweite Drittel des 17. Jahrhunderts entschloss sich der Autor die Handschrift von Vecîhîs Werk aus Leiden (Cod. 894 Warn.) und die Handschrift *Târîh-i Gılmânî* von Mehmed Halife aus Wien (H. O. 82) als Faksimile zugänglich zu machen. Beide Chroniken sollen als Grundlage zur Bearbeitung der politischen Geschichte des Osmanischen Reiches in der Mitte des 17. Jahrhunderts dienen.

In einer kurzen Einleitung (S. VI—XV) bringt Atsız die Übersicht der bedeutendsten politischen Ereignisse im Osmanischen Reich der Jahre 1633 bis 1660, sowie eine Übersicht der regierenden Sultane und Großwesire (nach *Hadikat ül-vüzera*).

Einen wesentlichen Teil des Buches bildet die Übersicht der bedeutendsten Quellen und Literatur zu diesem Zeitabschnitt. Die osmanischen Quellen sind natürlich am gründlichsten bearbeitet. Durch Vergleiche osmanischer Chroniken versuchte der Autor ihre wechselseitige Abhängigkeit, insbesondere die Verwendung der Werke Vecîhîs und Mehmed Halifes festzustellen. Wir führen die wichtigsten Ergebnisse des Autors an. Peçevîs Werk war nich Vecîhîs Quelle. Beim Vergleich von Karaçelebizâdes und Vecîhîs Werken kommt der Autor zum Schluß daß „Vecîhî Karaçelebizâde benützt hat. Es ist jedoch nicht auszuschließen, daß beide Chronisten eine gemeinsame Quelle zur Verfügung hatten, die mir unbekannt ist". Im Fall von Müneccımbaşı bewies Atsız, daß dieser osmanische Geschichtsschreiber Vecîhîs Werk kannte und verwendete. Solakzâdes und Vecîhîs Beziehung formuliert der Autor nicht konkret, er beweist jedoch, daß Solakzâde Kâtip Çelebis Werk *Takvîm üt-tevârîh* verwendet hat.

Die Beziehung des Werkes von Kâtip Çelebi zu Vecîhî bewertet der Autor so, daß die beiden Zeitgenossen ihre Werke gegenseitig nicht benützt haben. Was spätere Geschichtsschreiber wie Silahdar Mehmed Ağa, Na'îmâ, Abdî Pascha und Defterdar Mehmed Pascha betrifft, haben diese so von Vecîhîs als auch von Mehmed Halifes Werk geschöpft.

Die persischen Quellen zu diesem Zeitabschnitt der Geschichte des Osmanischen Reiches führt der Autor sehr kurz aus dem Werk C. A. Storeys an, arabische Quellen ebenfalls. Ausführlicher befaßt sich der Autor mit armenischen Quellen und führt auch deren Inhalt an.

In europäischen Sprachen verfaßte Quellen führt er lediglich in bibliographischen Angaben an und es muß gesagt werden, daß diese bei weitem nicht vollständig sind. Wir möchten nur Werke wie *Ortelius redivivus, Theatrum Europaeum, Calendar of State Papers,* herausgegebene und nicht herausgegebene Berichte von habsburgischen Gesandten usw. erwähnen. Ähnliche Vorwürfe könnten wir auch dem relativ umfangreichen und annotierten Literaturverzeichnis gegenüber äußern.

Der nächste Teil des Buches ist Vecîhîs Leben und Werk gewidmet (S. CVI—CXXI); hier werden die Ergebnisse der älteren Literatur über das Leben und Werk des Autors ergänzt und richtiggestellt, und eine Übersicht über die

260

Handschriften seines historischen Werkes und Position des Werkes zwischen den beiden offiziellen Chroniken — Na'îmâ und Râşid, gebracht.

Wesentlich kürzer spricht der Autor vom Leben und Werk Mehmed Halifes (S. CXXII—CXXVIII). Er informiert über die Handschriften des Werkes und polemisiert mit B. Kütükoğlu. Im Abschluß dieses Teiles des Buches vergleicht er beide Chroniken von der sprachlichen Seite her.

Einen bedeutenden Teil des Buches (S. 1—144) stellt der Inhalt beider Chroniken dar, in dem der Autor in kürzerer oder umfangreicherer Form über den Inhalt der einzelnen Seiten informiert. Uns scheint diese Art der Bearbeitung beider Chroniken nicht die idealste zu sein. Unserer Meinung nach würde der Benützer des Buches, schon auch zum Vergleich beider Texte, aus einem wohl durchdachten Index von Namen und geographischen Bezeichnungen, sowie einem Sach- und Inhaltsregister größeren Nutzen ziehen.

Aus nicht identifizierten Namen und Ortsbezeichnungen: S. 93 Kel Yanoş — Kemény János; S. 94—95 STL — Sibiu, ung. Szeben, dt. Hermannstadt; S. 95 Bocay — Bocşa, heute Pecica im Banat.

Die Faksimile der Leidener Handschrift von Vecîhîs Werk (Cod. 894 Warn.), sowie der Wiener Handschrift von *Tarih-i Gılmânî* (H. O.,82) bieten die Möglichkeit beide Werke für die historische Arbeit viel mehr wie bisher zu nützen.

Trotz der hier angeführten Einwände bringt das rezensierte Buch von Atsız wertvollen Stoff zur Kenntnis der politischen Geschichte des Osmanischen Reiches im zweiten Drittel des 17. Jahrhunderts.

Vojtech Kopčan

Gökbilgin, M. Tayyib: *Osmanlı Müesseseleri, Teşkilâtı ve Medeniyeti Tarihine Genel Bakış* (General View on the Ottoman Institutions, Organizations and History of the Civilization). İstanbul, Edebiyat Fakültesi Matbaası 1977. 194 pp. İstanbul Universitesi Edebiyat Fakültesi Yayınları, No. 2272.

Right at the start it may be said that the title promises more than the book eventually supplies. Essentially, these are university lectures which Prof. Gökbilgin delivered in the more recent period to his students on a very interesting though not adequately researched topic. Naturally, this does not involve a systematic exposition of all the institutions and organizations in the Ottoman empire from its beginning until the time it ceased to exist, but only some selected chapters from the more interesting and important periods in the development of the Ottoman State. The book deals with these questions in the initial period of the Ottoman empire, and then in the 16th century. Hence, this is not a systematic presentation since a very important link is missing in this chain, namely the period of Sultan Mehmed II.

The introduction brings general comments on the institutions and their basic division with emphasis being laid on the significance of ancient Turkish institutions for the Ottoman State — of course alongside Islamic ones.

The exposition of the institutions form the times of Osman I, the founder of the Ottoman dynasty, is based on preserved Ottoman sources, which, unfortunately, come for the most part from a later period. For instance, when dealing with the function *çavuş* which the sources mention as coming from the times of Osman I's reign, it should have been noted that it is an ancient Turkish title and shown how it was used in Ottoman times. And it would certainly have been useful to discuss at some length also the influence of Byzantine institutions, even though this subject has long been given attention in professional literature.

The development of the Ottoman princedom during the reign of the next ruler Orhan I brought in further institutions, among which mention should be made of the vizierate, the sultan's privy council — the *divan,* and the creation of military organizations.

Under the reign of Murad I, the office of *kazasker* was established and a sultan's close relation (brother, son) ceased to be the highest commander of the army; this post was filled by a stranger. When speaking about the levy or tax on war prisoners claimed by the sultan i.e. 1/5 of the price (or every 5th prisoner), Gökbilgin wrongly refers to this levy *pendjik* as *ispendje,* a difference made clear recently by H. İnalcık (*Osmanlılar'da raiyyet rüsûmu.* In: Belleten, *23,* 1959, p. 602. See also D. Bojanić-Lukač: *De la nature et de l'origine de l'ispendje.* In: WZKM, *68,* 1976, pp. 9—30).

In view of the character of the book, the polemics with the Bulgarian historian A. K. Burmov appears to be too extensive, if not overdone, for Burmov presented his paper *Les problèmes de la conquête de la péninsule des Balkans par les Turks* as far back as 1960 at an International congress of historians in Stockholm.

In the subsequent sections the author deals with prominent Ottoman commanders in Rumelia (i.e. Albania, Macedonia and Thrace) with the complex situation in the Ottoman empire following the defeat of Bayezid I by Tamerlane near Ankara in 1402, and with the ensuing civil war. Undoubtedly, the author's design not to omit the problem of the most significant social or socio-religious movement Şeyh Bedreddin at the beginning of the 15th century, was correct, but his appraisal ought to have been supplemented with the most recent results of a marxist research, primarily those embodied in the works by E. Werner and N. Filipović. Reflections on Murad II's Period (1421—1451) are concerned rather with the political history and the principal problems which this ruler had to face than with the subject-matter indicated in the title.

The second part of the book is devoted to Ottoman institutions and organizations in the 16th century, hence, the important period of Mehmed II's reign is skipped over, although a series of weighty measures were enacted during this time, dealing precisely with institutions, political and military organizations. The author notes that the dynamics of development in the Ottoman society continued during this century at the rate as in the preceding one, and even increased in certain aspects; military and political power achieved its peak, decrees and regulations were complemented, institutions and organizations were given their definitive forms. Gökbilgin devotes special attention to the Caliphate which, after the conquest of Egypt by Selim I in 1517, passed on to Ottoman sultans.

The closing section called the Period of Sultan Suleyman The Magnificent, is made up of a few shorter chapters dealing with Ottoman campaigns during this period, of State dignitaries, the tax system and manners of distribution of State income, the questions of *devşirme* and of provisioning Istanbul.

Valuable material is to be found in the supplements where the author publishes 17 documents from the 16th century included in the cadi records of Bursa and dealing with various Ottoman institutions.

Despite a certain lack of a systematic treatment, the book brings numerous interesting insights and concepts.

Vojtech Kopčan

Frank, G.: *Die Herrscher der Osmanen. Aufstieg und Untergang eines Weltreiches.* Wien — Düsseldorf, Econ Verlag 1977. 347 S.

In seiner Edition Packende Kulturgeschichte gab der Econ Verlag einige hervorragende Bücher heraus, die die Kultur und das Leben mehrerer ins Vergessen geratener Völker der ganzen Welt einem breiteren Leserkreis zugänglich machten. Franks Buch ist dem Staat, oder genauer seinen Herrschern, den osmanischen Sultanen gewidmet, für deren Leben und Taten sich Europa mehr als ein halbes Jahrtausend interessiert hat. Man kann also kaum sagen, daß es ein neues Thema wäre und genausowenig kann von einem Mangel an Stoffen zu diesen Fragen die Rede sein. Es steht jedoch fest, daß der Zutritt, den der Autor zur osmanischen Geschichte wählte, in der Gegenwart eher selten ist, wenn auch vor einigen Jahren ein Buch ähnlicher Art im Englischen von N. Barber erschienen ist.

Das Buch Die Herrscher der Osmanen handelt vom Leben und Herrschen aller 36 Sultane dieser Dynastie, deren Regierungszeit in fünf Zeitabschnitte eingeteilt wird: 1. Die Gründung des Osmanischen Reiches (1299—1412); 2. Das Große Serail (1413—1566); 3. Der Staat verliert an Macht (1566—1703); 4. Die Jahre des Verfalls (1703—1839); 5. Der Zusammenbruch (1839—1922).

Den einleitenden Teilen, die dem Einzug der türkischen Völker in die islamische Geschichte, einer Übersicht der Entwicklung des Osmanischen Reiches und einer

Analyse des Wortes Sultan gewidmet sind, folgen mehrseitige Medaillons über die einzelnen Sultane samt deren Abbildungen. Hier erwarten den Leser größere oder kleinere Enttäuschungen. In der Mehrzahl der Fälle übernahm der Autor die Charakteristiken der Sultane aus den älteren Geschichten des Osmanischen Reiches, ob es sich nun um J. von Hammer, J. W. Zinkeisen, N. Jorge, die Enzyklopädie des Islam handelt, oder in besseren Fällen aus monographischen Bearbeitungen des Lebenswandels der einzelnen Sultane stammt. In den kurzen Porträts widmet er sich der politischen Geschichte, den Hauptereignissen während der Regierungszeit der jeweiligen Sultane, den Intrigen, aber auch derer kulturellen Tätigkeit.

Abgesehen von den inhaltlichen Mängeln und den zahlreichen Fehlern in der Chronologie, in der Bewertung der Begebenheiten usw., deren Aufzählung mehrere Seiten einnehmen würde, wirkt die uneinheitliche Transkription der türkischen und islamischen Namen und geographischen Bezeichnungen des Autors sehr störend. Obwohl das Deutsche bereits seit mehreren Jahrzehnten über ein akzeptiertes Transkriptionssystem verfügt, das zumindest in wissenschaftlichen Publikationen verwendet wird, finden wir in Franks Buch alle möglichen Transkriptionsarten islamischer aber auch slawischer Namen, je nach der Quelle, aus der der Autor die Angaben übernahm. Und so begegnen wir auf einer Seite der Transkription Čirmen und Tchendereli Khalil (S. 46), zwei Seiten weiter finden wir Plochnik, Lazar Gresljanowitsch, Milosch Obilitsch und Čekirge. Ähnliche Fälle ließen sich noch mehr anführen. Schließlich beweist die Erklärung des Authors Schreibweise der Namen im Anhang lediglich seine eigene Unsicherheit in diesen Fragen.

Im Anhang finden wir weiter eine Liste der osmanischen Sultane mit Angaben über deren Regierungszeit, osmanische Berufsbezeichnungen und Ämter, eine Zeittafel (mit einigen Fehlern und den nicht immer repräsentativsten Daten), ein Literaturverzeichnis (die Auswahl der Literatur ist zufällig, z.B. bei Selim III. fehlt das Buch St. J. Shaw: *Between Old and New. The Ottoman Empire under Sultan Selim III, 1789—1807.* Cambridge 1971, bei den Herrschern des 19. Jahrhunderts die Bücher von B. Lewis und R. H. Davison).

Das Buch hat ein Personen-, Sach- und Ortsregister.

Im Hinblick auf die angeführten Mängel kann man das Buch G. Frank's nur schwer als ein erfolgreiches Werk betrachten.

Vojtech Kopčan

Teply, K.: *Die kaiserliche Großbotschaft an Sultan Murad IV. im Jahre 1628. Des Freiherrn Hans Ludwig von Kuefsteins Fahrt zur Hohen Pforte.* Wien, Verlag A. Schendl 1976. 151 S. 12 farbige Tafeln.

Hinsichtlich der langjähringen Kämpfe des österreichischen Kaiserreichs mit den osmanischen Türken bewahren die österreichischen Museen und Bibliotheken eine bedeutende Anzahl bemerkenswerter Denkmäler an diesen einstigen Erzfeind auf. Außer Handschriften und musealer Exemplare ist dies auch eine relativ große Anzahl von Werken der bildenden Kunst, unter denen Abbildungen aus dem Leben der osmanischen Gesellschaft, die im Cod. 8615 und 8626 erfaßt und in der Nationalbibliothek Wien hinterlegt sind, besondere Aufmerksamkeit verdienen. Zu jenen Werken, die kürzlich zugänglich gemacht wurden, gehört auch die Kollektion von Bildern, die das Museum der Stadt Perchtoldsdorf aus dem Besitz der Familie Kuefstein gewonnen hat. Elf Gouachemalereien, die den Verlauf der Botschaft von Hans Ludwig von Kuefstein zur Hohen Pforte festhalten und ein Ölgemälde, das ebenfalls diese Begebenheit betrifft werden — auf eine eindrucksvolle Weise von K. Teply bearbeitet — einem weiteren Interessentenkreis im rezensierten Buch präsentiert.

Zur Bearbeitung dieses Bildermaterials wurde der Herausgeber anscheinend durch die reichhaltige Dokumentation, die durch diese Botschaft erhalten blieb, angeregt. Ausser der Hauptrelation blieb auch das Tagebuch des Botschafters nebst weiterem diplomatischen Material erhalten. Anhand dieser erhaltenen Dokumente vermittelte K. Teply nicht nur eine plastische Darstellung des Verlaufs der Botschaft, der Persönlichkeit von Botschafter Hans Ludwig von Kuefstein, sondern identifizierte auch den Maler jener Bilder, Franz Hörmann, und verfaßte mit Hilfe weiterer zeitgenössischer Nachrichten vertraute Auslegungen zu den einzelnen Abbildungen.

Neben der einleitenden Ölmalerei, die den Aufbruch der Großbotschaft aus Wien darstellt, erfassen die Gouachebilder folgende Szenen: die Audienz beim Statthalter von Ofen; das Han von Harmanli und ein türkisches Begräbnis; den Einzug der Großbotschaft in Konstantinopel; den feierlichen Empfang für den Großbotschafter im Diwan — nach K. Teply — stellt das Blatt eine Szene aus der Abschiedsaudienz dar; die Audienz des kaiserlichen Großbotschafters; den At Meydani-Platz; den Tanz der Mevlevî-Derwische; die Bestrafung der Schuldigen im Osmanischen Reich; Unterhaltungen türkischer Frauen — nach K. Teply „sehr wahrscheinlich gestaltete der Maler die Szene nach Bildern, wie sie in Istanbul massenhaft zum Verkauf an Fremde hergestellt wurden"; einen türkischen Hochzeitszug; türkische Reiterspiele.

Es ist interessant, daß mehrere Erscheinungen aus dem Leben der osmanischen Gesellschaft beinahe alle europäische Maler interessierten, z. B. der Strafvollzug (siehe Cod. 8626), Reiterspiele oder *cirid* (Cod. 8615), türkische Frauen, Derwische, Begräbnisse (siehe beide Wiener Kodizes, sowie Life in Istanbul 1588. Ed. by S. Skilliter. Oxford 1977 und weitere Abbildungen).

Im Anhang finden wir auch eine Übersicht benützter Quellen, der Literatur, die Belege und ein Register.

Das Buch kann als eine wervolle Bereicherung des ikonographischen Materials

europäischer Herkunft über das Leben der osmanischen Gesellschaft in der ersten Hälfte des 17. Jahrhunderts betrachtet werden. Die mustergültige Bearbeitung ist hoch zu schätzen.

Vojtech Kopčan

Shaw, Stanford J.—Shaw, Ezel K.: *History of the Ottoman Empire and Modern Turkey.* Volume II: *Reform, Revolution and Republic. The Rise of Modern Turkey, 1808—1975.* Cambridge—London—New York—Melbourne, Cambridge University Press 1977. xxvi + 518 pp.

This second volume of the History of the Ottoman Empire and Modern Turkey follows closely on the publication of the first one (1976) — its co-author being Ezel Kural Shaw. During the period followed in the present volume, Turkey has passed through momentous changes in the political, military, economic and cultural life and this by way of reforms, the revolution of the Young Turks, a national liberation movement, up to an independent, national stateshood.

Serious efforts at reforming the Ottoman empire appeared already towards the end of the 18th century, under Selim III, but for diverse reasons they were unsuccessful. A truly new era of reforms in the empire was ushered in only with the reign of Mahmut II (1808—1839), particularly after he had succeeded in destroying the Janissaries (1826) and further inner opponents. His reign is the subject of the first chapter. The Beginnings of Modern Ottoman Reforms: The Era of Mahmut II, 1808—1839. The reforms set up during his reign concerned the central government and the government of the provinces, the army — where reforms were especially urgent — the organization of urban administration and education.

The authors devote considerable attention to *Tanzimat* (1839—1876) when the efforts at reforms were crowned with the first great successes, and to the principal personalities of this period: Mustafa Reshid Pasha, Ali Pasha and Fuad Pasha who in their various functions (as grand viziers, foreign ministers or ambassadors) were greatly responsible for the reforms. Similarly, the authors deal in great detail with the forms and content of reforms in the domain of State, military, administrative policies and further public functions, with fundamental changes in legislature and the tax system, in the production sphere, and finally also in culture and education. The principal problems encountered in foreign policy of the empire and their impact on developments at home are dealt with in concise sub-chapters.

The authors call their third chapter Culmination of the Tranzimat: The Reign of Abdulhamit II, 1876—1909. During this period the reforms were being implemented and Europeanization of the empire produced under complex foreign and

266

inner political conditions. A brief constitutional period, the military defeat by Russia (1877—1878), the Congress of Berlin, problems with national minorities — these are the principal events at the beginning of this period. However, yet further events proved unfavourable to the Ottoman empire: it lost one territory after another and nationality difficulties within the empire went on increasing. The authors go on to analyse in detail the policy of Abdulhamit's autocratic government and its organs. In the section devoted to modernization, they show how the Ottoman empire endeavoured to deal with financial problems which were a prerequisite of success for any further programme of reform. They bring evidence that Abdulhamit's financial reforms proved instrumental in increasing national income and lowering state expenditure in numerous items. Among the positive aspects of Abdulhamit's government, we may include construction of railways, roads, improvement and extension of post office and telegraph services, improvement in the state of agriculture and forest protection. This period is also marked by an incontestable development of industry and an increased volume of foreign trade, although this proved to have been at the expense of the Ottoman empire and in favour of its European partners. In the closing section of this chapter the authors take up some aspects of the Ottoman society, providing data from Ottoman live statistics on the composition of the population, conditions in towns, urban administration, development in the army in education, with attention being given also to cultural development which was strongly hindered by the Sultan's censorship.

Abdulhamit's absolutism became the cradle of the Young Turk Movement which strove to save the desintegrating empire for other reasons and by other means than advocated by past ideology.

This period of the government by the Young Turks, 1908—1918, is the subject of the fourth chapter. In the authors' view, this period "depended, accelerated and polarized the major views that had been gathering momentum in the Ottoman empire during the nineteenth century: Ottomanism and nationalism, liberalism and conservatism, Islamism and Turkism, democracy and autocracy, centralisation and decentralisation — all to the point where the empire might well have blown up had this not been accomplished by the events of World War I" (p. 273).

The Young Turk Revolution which on its crest brought such figures to the head of the Ottoman empire as Cemal Bey, Talat Bey and Cavit Bey — notorious from the declining days of the empire — likewise failed to resolve the key problems of the State. The government was faced with weighty problems of inner policy and the ensuing wars for Tripolis, and then with the Balkan States, revealed fully the inner weakness. A notable and a new factor for the subsequent emergence of the Turkish nation was the birth of Turkish nationalism. Insofar as modernization was concerned, this became most strikingly manifest in the domain of militarism where a major role was played by German experts, or as they are commonly known today, military advisers.

The authors present the Empire's joining in the First World War and its course briefly and according to the various fronts until the final defeat of the Central Powers in 1918. The close of the chapter is concerned with the occupation of the Ottoman empire by the Allies and with the peace conferences, particularly the treaty of Sèvres which confirmed the definite dissolution of the empire.

The Turkish War for Independence, 1918—1923 is the title of the fifth chapter which investigates the national liberation movement of the Turkish nation under the leadership of Mustafa Kemal against imperialist powers. The authors indicate the sources of strength in the fight for national liberation, its principal events and stages, the wars with the Greeks and the Armenians, right up to the abolition of the sultanate and the proclamation of the republic.

The last chapter, The Turkish Republic, 1923—1975, brings an overview of political events in the form of brief entries, analyses the ideological bases of Turkish republicanism and its economic development.

The Appendix lists the names of Ottoman Grand Viziers and Prime Ministers for the period 1939—1922, of the presidents of the Turkish republic and its premiers. The book is supplemented with an abundant bibliography to the History of the Ottoman Empire and Modern Turkey, 1808—1975 and an extensive Index.

The book constitutes a fine summary of the last phase of the history of the Ottoman empire and the fortunes of modern Turkish republic.

Vojtech Kopčan

Tursun Bey: Tarih-i Ebü'l-Feth (History of the Conqueror). Hazırlayan Mertol Tulum. İstanbul, Baha Matbaası 1977. XXXII, 272 pp., map. İstanbul Fetih Cemiyeti, 74.

Of late, a revived interest may be noted in the work of the Ottoman historian from the 15th century (deals with the period 1442—1488), Tursun Bey.[1] Some years ago, this work appeared under the title *Fatih'in Tarihi*, adjusted into modern Turkish, in the series of historical studies edited by the newspaper Tercüman (1001 Temel Eser, No. 21). And at the time the work under review was published, preparatory work was in progress on a further edition with an English translation.[2]

---

[1] This work was first published on the basis of three manuscripts Revan No. 1097 and 1098, Aya Sofya No. 3032 by Mehmed Arif as a supplement to Tarih-i Osmanı Encümeni Mecmuası, Istanbul 1330 H.

[2] *Tursun Beg: The History of Mehmed the Conqueror,* Text in Facsimile with English Translation, Glossary, Notes and Index by H. İnalcık and R. Murphey. Chicago 1978.

The editor Mertol Tulum wrote two short introductory chapters to the work. In the first, titled Tursun Bey's Life, he speaks of the author's life, origin and official career on the basis of the latter's data. In the second chapter, he deals with the work: its origin, content, manuscripts, language and style.

The editor's remarks should be supplemented with notes from a more recent study by H. İnalcık: *Tursun Beg, Historian of Mehmed the Conqueror's Time*.[3] When studying the Cadi Records of Bursa, İnalcık traced the name of the historian's father and further details about his family. Tursun Bey's father was Hamza Bey, a son of Firuz Bey — the founder of a family that played an important role in the history of the Ottoman empire during the period 1380—1480. Hamza Bey was sancakbey of Tekke and later beylerbey of Anatolia. İnalcık also makes more precise the date of Tursun Bey's birth — after the year 1426 (Tulum places it between the years 1422 and 1427). İnalcık succeeded in tracing further details pertaining to the historian's person in the Cadi Records of Bursa, but mainly such as related to his family. Nevertheless, he did not succeed in ascertaining the date of Tursun Bey's death.

When analysing *Tarih-i Ebü'l-Feth*, İnalcık observes that Tursun Bey lacks a sense of objectivity in his relation to certain personages, e.g. the grand vizier Mahmud Pasha, and endeavoured to curry favour with them.

In the introduction, Tulum notes that the work originated in the years 1490—1495 and served as the most important source to the subsequent historian Kemalpashazade. The reason why so few historians made use of Tursun Bey's work is to be ascribed, according to İnalcık, to the style of the work, the author having used high-flown literary language.

Tulum's edition is based on four manuscripts and in addition, makes use, besides the three already used by Mehmed Arif — i.e. Aya Sofya Kütüphanesi, No. 3032 and Topkapı Sarayı Kütüphanesi, Revan No. 1097 and No. 1098 — also of the ms from the same library, Hazine No. 1470.

Editorially, the text (pp. 3—215) has been carefully prepared in Latin transcriptions of references to the Koran, Hadis or proverbs, occurring in the text in Arabic, given in footnotes. Editorial notes relating to manuscript variability are inserted after the text (pp. 217—226).

An index of names, geographical and historical terms greatly facilitates orientation. In order to make the work accessible to a wider circle of readers, the editor appended a relatively extensive glossary of Ottoman expressions (pp. 238—272) with explanations in modern Turkish. The book also has a map with geographical terms mentioned in the History of the Conqueror.

This edition of Tursun Bey's work by Mertol Tulum will certainly satisfy a wide circle of readers interested in the history of Sultan Mehmed II's reign.

Vojtech Kopčan

---

[3] In: Wiener Zeitschrift für die Kunde des Morgenlandes 69, 1977, pp. 55—71.

Hazai, Gy.: *Kurze Einführung in das Studium der türkischen Sprache.* Budapest, Akadémiai Kiadó 1978. 190 S.

Der große Aufschwung der turkologischen Forschung in den letzten Jahrzehnten (für den Zeitraum der vergangenen fünf Jahre wird dies gut durch die von A. Tietze sowie dem Autor dieses Buches zusammengestellte periodische Bibliographie — *Turkologischer Anzeiger 1—4* — dokumentiert) und die großen qualitativen Veränderungen waren ein ausreichender Grund die Fragen der türkischen Sprachwissenschaft zusammenzufassen, vornehmlich deshalb, weil die letzte Zusammenfassung dieser Problematik das Buch *Philologiae Turcicae fundamenta* (Wiesbaden 1959) darstellt. Es ist wichtig zu bemerken, daß in diesem Buch „Die türkische Sprache, nicht nur wie sie in ihren Produkten jahrhundertelang erscheint, steht, sondern auch als Kommunikationssystem einer Sprachgemeinschaft mit allen ihren Forschungsdimensionen, die heute in der Untersuchungen bekannt sind". Der Autor versuchte dabei die Probleme möglichst im Hinblick auf die allgemeine Sprachwissenschaft, auf die Erweiterung ihres Forschungszieles und methodischen Repertoirs, darzustellen.

Was den zeitlichen Umfang betrifft, widmet das Buch Aufmerksamkeit vor allem dem gegenwärtigen Stand der Forschung (seit 1959), berücksichtigt jedoch natürlich auch die Ergebnisse älterer Forschungen. Mit Rücksicht auf die lange Herstellungszeit umfaßt Hazais Buch nur die Produktion bis 1974 und lediglich in einigen Fällen auch die späterer Jahre (1975—1976).

Die *Kurze Einführung in das Studium der Türkischen Sprache* ist in fünf Kapitel eingeteilt: Einleitung: 1. Die Geschichte der türkischen Sprache; 2. Die Gegenwart der türkischen Sprache; 3. Dialektologie; 4. Bibliographischer Anhang.

Der einleitende Teil befaßt sich mit der oft diskutierten Frage der Terminologie, der Übersicht der bisherigen Forschungen, den Fragen der Bibliographie und der Handbücher.

Im umfangreichsten, der Geschichte der türkischen Sprache gewidmeten Kapitel behandelt der Autor nicht nur die Fragen der Entwicklung der türkischen Sprache, der Periodisierung, die grammatischen und lexikalen Veränderungen, sondern lenkt auch sein Augenmerk auf die Problematik der Quellen zu diesen Fragen. Besonders wertvoll sind Hazais Anregungen für eine weitere Erforschung der Quellen zur Geschichte der türkischen Sprache, zweifelsohne auch deshalb, da diese aus den reichen Erfahrungen des Autors hervorgehen, der gerade in jenen Fragen einen keineswegs geringen Beitrag zur Turkologie leistete. Lehrreich sind ebenfalls die Überblicke von Ansichten über die Schaffung der türkischen Literatursprache und über die Entwicklung der Veränderungen in der Sprachstruktur. Hazai macht namentlich auf die Fragen der Periodisierung des Türkischen aufmerksam und fordert bei der Lösung dieser Problematik theoretische Klarheit und methodische Konsequenz. Die letzten zwei Teile dieses Kapitels sind der Frage des Wortschatzes im Türkischen, sowie den Einflüssen des Türkischen auf andere Sprachen gewidmet. An dieser Stelle möchten wir hinzufügen, daß es auch Arbeiten über türkische Wörter im Slowakischen, bzw. Tschechischen gibt, so z.B. J. Blaşkoviç: Çek dilinde türkçe kelimeler. In: I. Türk Dil Kurumu okunan bilimsel bildiriler. Ankara 1960, S. 87—112, V. Blanár: Otázka lexikálnych turcizmov v slovenčine. In: Jazykovedný časopis, 13, 1962, S. 76—87 und M. Odran: Tjurkskije leksičeskije elementy v slovackom jazyke. Baku 1969 (Kandidatendissertation).

Das zweite, dem gegenwärtigen Türkischen gewidmete Kapitel befaßt sich in seinem ersten Teil mit der Analyse bedeutenderer Arbeiten, die im erforschten Zeitraum entstanden sind. Es geht um die Phonologie des Türkischen von Lees, um Swifts *A Reference Grammar of Modern Turkish,* um die mißlungene Applikation der Transformationstheorie auf das Türkische von Meskill, um die Bücher von Johanson (*Aspekt im Türkischen*) und Hřebíček (*Turkish Grammar as a Graph*). Im Teil über die Morphologie und die Syntax analysiert der Autor die Ergebnisse der sowjetischen Turkologie, die zum Erforschen des Türkischen in diesen Umkreisen der Grammatik bedeutend beigetragen hat. Des weiteren beachtet Hazai die Probleme der türkischen Lexikographie, die Sprachreform und andere thematische Fragen (Semantik, Stilistik usw.).

Das verhältnismäßig kurze dritte Kapitel befaßt sich mit der Dialektologie, ihren bisherigen Resultaten und Perspektiven. Selbständige Teile sind den anatolischen und balkanischen Mundarten des Türkischen, sowie der historischen Dialektologie gewidmet.

Der Bibliographische Anhang bringt in alphabetischer Reihenfolge eine ausgewählte Bibliographie aus den Jahren 1959—1974 mit bedeutenderen Anfügungen für die Jahre 1975—1976.

Hazais Buch ist eine gelungene Einführung ins Studium der türkischen Sprache. Zu seinem unzweifelbaren Positiva kann angeführt werden, daß es von Sprachbarrieren nicht eingeschränkt wird, und daß es an die pertraktierten Fragen objektiv und kritisch herantritt. Wir sind der Ansicht, daß das Buch, bei seinen Neuauflagen um die neueste Produktion ständig ergänzt, für lange Jahre ein Standardwerk bleiben kann.

Vojtech Kopčan

Menemencioğlu, Nermin (Ed.), in collaboration with Fahir İz: *The Penguin Book of Turkish Verse.* Bungay (England), Penguin Books 1978. 416 pp.

Poetry has always been an essential of Turkish cultural life. It dominated classical art literature through the centuries and is important and popular even in modern times.

This English anthology is perhaps the most comprehensive selection of Turkish verse ever published in translation. It covers from pre-Ottoman times (about 1300) up until 1975. It displays Turkish poetry in all its variety and genres. It offers samples of pre-classical and classical divan poetry, of the popular mystics and poets, of those poets who broke with tradition in the last century and introduced a new, West-oriented literature, and of modern poetry in its colourful aspects, trends and orientations. Considering the difficulties inherent in selecting a sample representing such a long and rich poetic heritage, the editors did very well, indeed.

The brief sketches of these poets' lives and art included in the contents at the beginning of the book represent a useful concise reference of Turkish poets. The Introduction includes historical essays on the Ottoman Period 1300—1850 by Fahir İz and on Modern Turkish Poetry 1850—1975 by N. Menemencioğlu. The first outlines the general characteristics and development of the classical and popular poetry, while the second provides a survey of the subsequent developments and a discussion of the work of individual poets in relation to the general trends in the culture and society. Though brief, these introductory articles are illuminating and together with the biographical sketches provide a useful introduction to and understanding of Turkish poetry.

We find in this book two contrasting methods of rendering poetry into another language. John R. Walsh, the translator of the divan poetry (and a few of the verses of the popular and transitional poets), preserves almost perfectly the form of the original while retaining its spirit. His results are a pleasure to read and most remarkable considering the difficulty of such a task.

On the other hand, those who translated most of the popular poetry and the works of the later periods (the latter from about 1850) choose to translate more freely. This method seems more appropriate when dealing with most of the modern poetry. With respect to the popular and some of the earlier poets and those modern ones who adopted the prosody of the popular folk literature, the original forms and rhyme schemes have in most cases been replaced by simpler ones or not rhyming verses (though some efforts to retain original form have met with varying degrees of success). The method of free translation has been used traditionally in translating to English.

From this reviewer's viewpoint, the approach exemplified by J. R. Walsh is preferable in presenting the poetry with its original unity of form and content in its context of artistic complexity, especially when it concerns traditional poetry belonging to a culture so different from the European.

Most of the translations in this anthology are by N. Menemencioğlu. Other translators besides her and Walsh are Talât S. Halman, Bernard Lewis, Murat Nemet-Nejat, Feyyaz Kayacan, Taner Baybars, Richard McKane, David Silk, Hilary Sumner-Boyd, Mina Urgan and Larry V. Clark. The translations are generally of high quality, especially considering that the method of translator-philologist and translator-poet collaboration does not appear to have been used.

The section of divan poetry was selected for translation mostly from Fahir İz's work *Eski Türk Edebiyatında Nazım*, I, Istanbul 1966. Many of the modern poems included in this book were gathered from various earlier published English translations.

This anthology successfully presents Turkish poetry, past and present, to interested Western readers, and Turkologists will find it useful as well.

Jitka Zamrazilová-Weltmanová

Ergün, Mehmet: *Bir sinemacı ve anlatıcı olarak Yılmaz Güney* (Yılmaz Güney als Filmemacher und Erzähler). Istanbul, Doğrultu Yayınları 1978. 320 S.

Die, der Persönlichkeit des namhaften türkischen Künstlers Yılmaz Güney gewidmete Publikation ist das zweite monographische Werk des jungen Kritikers Mehmet Ergün. Konnten wir beim Rezensieren von Ergüns erster Monographie — sie erschien unter dem Titel Bekir Yıldız' Realität in unserer Erzählung (*Hikâyemizde Bekir Yıldız Gerçeği*. Istanbul, a Yayınları 1975. 147 S. Unsere Rezension wurde in Asian and African Studies, *13*, 1977, S. 268—270 veröffentlicht) — mit dem allzu subjektiven Zutritt des Autors zum Schaffen des zeitgenössischen türkischen Prosaikers nicht übereinstimmen, ist es uns hingegen diesmal möglich mit Befriedigung zu konstatieren, daß des Autors Ansichten über die Arbeit von Yılmaz Güney als Filmregisseur, Drehbuchautor, Schauspieler und Prosaiker durch Objektivität und Kritizität gekennzeichnet ist.

Die Monographie besteht aus sechs Teilen. Der erste Teil (S. 15—41) stellt eine theoretische Einleitung in die Problematik des Filmschaffens dar. Den Autor weist auf die außerordentliche Bedeutung der Kinematographie vom Aspekt derer Ausnützung im Klassenkampf hin. Dies gilt vor allem für die Entwicklungsländer, wo das materielle und kulturelle Niveau der breiten Bevölkerungsmassen sehr niedrig ist, und wo gerade der Film mit seiner Zugänglichkeit Voraussetzungen dazu schaft, von den hegemonischen Kräften für ihre Ziele ausgenützt zu werden. Der positive Einfluß von Werken der Filmkunst mit einem revolutionären Inhalt auf die breiten Massen stellt andererseits wieder eine konkrete Drohung für jene Kräfte dar, und daher sind die Schöpfer solcher Filme Verfolgungen ausgesetzt. Abschließend klassifiziert Mehmet Ergün im ersten Teil der Publikation jene Probleme, mit denen sich engagierte Filmemacher in der Türkei auseinanderzusetzen haben.

Nach einer kurzen Charakteristik der einzelnen Entwicklungsphasen der türki-

273

schen Kinematographie bewertet Mehmet Ergün im zweiten Teil der Publikation (S. 43—79) den Beitrag von Yılmaz Güney als einen der Spitzendarsteller ihrer fortschrittlicher Strömung. Der Autor erforscht die Etappen, die Yılmaz Güneys Filmkunst durchgemacht hatte, bevor sie wegweisend für die türkische Kinematographie wurde.

Güneys Auffassung der Kunst ist der dritte Teil der Publikation (S. 81—112) gewidmet. Mehmet Ergün unterwirft seiner Kritik zwischen dem Künstler und dem revolutionären Kampf, sowie zwischen Kunst und Politik. Er findet Unklarheiten und Widersprüche in Güneys Ansichten. Eine erhöhte Aufmerksamkeit widmet Mehmet Ergün in diesem, sowie in den beiden letzten Teilen der Monographie der Widerspiegelung der Realität im Prosa- und Filmschaffen von Yılmaz Güney. Er gelangt zur Ansicht, daß es Yılmaz Güney am vielseitigsten gelungen ist die Realität zu erfassen im Roman *Boynu Bükük Öldüler* (1971, Sie starben gedemütigt), der mit Recht als ein kritisch-realistisches Werk bezeichnet werden kann.

Mit der Persönlichkeit Yılmaz Güneys als eines Filmemachers befaßt sich der vierte Teil der Monographie (S. 113—245). Ergün analysiert hier einige der wichtigsten Filme aus Güneys letzter Schaffensperiode. Die größte Aufmerksamkeit widmet er den Filmen *Arkadaş* (1974, Der Freund) und *Endişe* (1974, Die Unrast), bei denen er vor allem die Tatsache schätzt, daß die in den Filmen gestalteten Personen sich im Einklang mit der abgebildeten Realität entwickeln und dem Vorhaben des Künstlers entsprechen. Ergün hebt auch Güneys Fähigkeit hervor naturalistische Szenen und Details zu meiden. Ein weiteres Positivum von Güneys Filmschaffen sieht der Author dem Monographie in des Künstlers Auffassung der Einzelperson als einer Einheit des gesellschaftlichen Ganzen, was in der türkischen Kinematographie eine völlig neue Erscheinung ist. Im Film *Endişe* wird sogar ein ganzes Volkskollektiv zum Helden. Das bisjetzt letzte Filmwerk, zu dem Yılmaz Güney das Drehbuch schrieb, den Streifen *Bir Gün Mutlaka* (1975, Eines Tages sicher), unterzieht Mehmet Ergün der Kritik wegen dessen elitärer Auffassung des revolutionären Kampfes, gleichzeitig jedoch schätzt er ihn als den ersten Versuch um ein Werk mit politischem Inhalt in den türkischen Kinematographie. Als Abschluß dieses Teiles der Publikation faßt der Autor den Beitrag des Schauspielers, Drehbuchautors und Regisseurs Yılmaz Güney für die türkische Kinematographie zusammen. Er sieht dessen Beitrag vornehmlich darin, daß Güney einen wahrhaftigen „Volkstyp" des Filmhelden, der sich gegen sein Schicksal auflehnt, geschaffen hat, und daß er die ersten Schritte zur Darstellung der geschichtlichen Realität mit derer klassenbedingten Grundlage getan hat.

Im abschließenden Teil der Monographie (S. 247—315) bewertet Mehmet Ergün Yılmaz Güneys prosaisches Schaffen, das er in drei Zeitabschnitte unterteilt. Für den ersten Zeitabschnitt, in den Güneys erzählerisches Werk der Jahre 1956—1957 fällt, ist die Flucht des Autors vor der Wirklichkeit, dessen Zuneigung zum Existentialismus charakteristisch. Ergün zufolge sind die in den Erzählungen jener Zeit dargestellten Handlungen verschleiert, deren Inhalt undeutlich. Die Gestalten der Erzählungen sind jenen Gedanken, die der Autor durch sie ausdrücken will, angepaßt, und Ergün charakterisiert sie als bloße Schatten lebendiger Menschen. In den letzten Erzählungen der ersten Periode von Güneys prosaischem Schaffen kann eine Abweichung von den existentialistischen Ideen beobachtet werden, der junge Autor stagniert jedoch, was die formale Seite betrifft.

Sehr positiv bewertet Mehmet Ergün das einzige, in die zweite Entwicklungsperiode von Güneys literarischem Schaffen fallende Werk, den Roman *Boynu Bükük Öldüler,* der in den Jahren 1961—62 entstanden ist. Den wichtigsten Beitrag sieht er in des Autors Bemühung um ein Erfassen der Tendenzen zu Änderungen in der sozialen Struktur, die auch auf das halbfeudale Land dringen. Als ungenügend jedoch erscheint ihm die Lösung der Problematik des Widerstandes durch individuelles Auflehnen der einzelnen Gestalten.

Der Autor der Monographie charakterisiert die dritte Periode des prosaischen Schaffens Yılmaz Güneys als eine teilweise Rückkehr zu seinen frühen Erzählungen. Er stellt fest, daß Güney — bemüht dem Leser eine bestimmte, vom Autor in der Einleitung zum Werk von vornherein proklamierte Idee vorzulegen — das Dargestellte dieser seiner Absicht unterwirft, wobei es ihm nicht gelingt, eine Einheit zwischen Idee und dem Dargestellten zu erreichen. Für Güney gewinnt an Wichtigkeit lediglich das, was er sagen will, und so widmet er keine ausreichende Aufmerksamkeit dem, wie es zu sagen sei, was Ergün der Tatsache zuschreibt, daß sich der Künstler allzusehr auf seine Popularität verläßt. Als vollständigstes Werk der letzten Periode hält Mehmet Ergün das Prosawerk *Sanık* (1975, Der Beschuldigte). Er weist hier auf die positive Einwirkung der szenarischen Arbeit des Autors auf dessen schöpferische Methode hin.

Mehmet Ergün beanstandet bei Yılmaz Güney, daß dessen letzten prosaischen Werke, die, in den Einleitungen dieser Werke gesteckten Absichten nicht erfüllen, er selbst jedoch begeht bei seiner Arbeit dieselbe Inkonsequenz. Erfuhren wir doch in der Einleitung zur rezensierten Monographie (S. 5—14) vom Wunsch des Autors Yılmaz Güney als „gesellschaftliche Erscheinung" zu erfassen, können wir abschließend feststellen, daß es leider nur beim Wunsch geblieben ist. Die Monographie zeigt Yılmaz Güney zwar als einen vielseitigen, mit großer Perspektive sich entwickelnden Künstler, den gesamtgesellschaftlichen Bereich seines Werkes berührt sie jedoch nur am Rande, sie bringt ihn in keinerlei Zusammenhang mit der politisch-sozialen Situation im Lande.

Xénia Celnarová

Elçin, Şükrü: *Halk edebiyatı araştırmaları* (Research of Folk Literature). Ankara, Dsi Basım Ve Foto-filim İşletme Müdürlüğü Matbaası 1977. V + 367 pp.

The book is a compilation of forty-three chronologically arranged scientific papers which the foremost Turkish folklorist Prof. Dr. Şükrü Elçin published in professional journals or read at congresses and seminars during the period 1959—1977.

Ş. Elçin introduces this selection of his works with a study in which he reflects on the term folk literature (pp. 1—16) and on its application within Turkish context. He disagrees with Fuad Köprülü's opinion that work which does not point to a concrete author, cannot be considered as literature. Similarly as the outstanding expert on Turkish folklore Pertev Naili Boratav, Ş. Elçin, too, under folk literature understands also anonymous works, including such genres as folk songs, proverbs, riddles.

Practically one half of the discourses included in this publication is devoted to problems relating to folk poets (the author makes use of such terms as *aşik, saz şâiri, ozan*). Alongside new data on the life and work of less known folk poets from the 15th—20th centuries, we meet here also with such prominent representatives of Turkish folklore as are Köroğlu and Karaca Oğlan (this poet's name is more commonly given in sources as Karacaoğlan). In the article titled Saz Şâirlerimizden Koroğlu Hakkında (pp. 177—181, About Koroglu, One of Our Saz Poets) the author deals with the moot question of the existence of two folk poets of the same name. Ş. Elçin is of the same professional opinion as Saddedin Nüzhet Ergun, Cahit Öztelli and Hasan Eren, that the poet Köroğlu of whom he speaks in the first and fifth part of his work *Seyâhatnâme* (Book of Travels), the voyager Evliyâ Çelebi cannot be identified with Köroğlu, a participant in the Celâlî uprising in the 16th century. In contrast to C. Öztelli's view that Köroğlu, a member of the janissary corps lived in the second half of the 16th and the beginning of the 17th century, Ş. Elçin assumes this poet-soldier to have lived towards the end of the 16th and the first half of the 17th century. This difference of views is also apparent from the fact that Ş. Elçin does not transcribe the poet's name in accordance with the above folklorists as "Kuroğlu", but adheres to the form "Koroğlu".

The polemics with Cahit Öztelli's opinion is carried on also in the study Halk Edebiyatımızda Kaynaklar Meselesi ve XVInci Asır Ozanı Karaca Oğlan (pp. 297—324, The Question of Sources in Our Folk Literature and the 16th Century Folk Poet Karaca Oğlan). Already Saddedin Nüzhet Ergun and Fuat Köprülü admitted the existence of several folk poets who used the pseudonym Karaca Oğlan. Ş. Elçin thinks it wrong to ascribe all the poems in the last four verses of which their author calls himself Karaca Oğlan to one of the most prominent personalities of 17th century folk poetry, as does C. Öztelli. The author cites sources that go to prove that a different poet named Karaca Oğlan lived and made poems in the 16th century. His poetry leads to surmise that he was a member of the *Bektaşi* order. The study brings specimens from this author's work representing twenty-four poems transcribed from manuscript records.

A valuable contribution to a knowledge of the history of folk literature is Elçin's study on *aşık* Seyit Osman (pp. 234—266) who lived and worked in the 19th century in Southeastern Anatolia. The author values highly this poet's language, free from Arab and Persian loanwords, and his realistic portraying of the life of the nomad tribe Avşar from which the poet descended.

Of extraordinary significance to a knowledge of Turkish folk culture are manuscript collections of folk poetry coming from the pens of the folk poets themselves, of narrators, soldiers, mullahs, scribes. Such a manuscript collection *cönk* represents an anthology from the works of the compiler's contemporaries. The problems concerning manuscript anthology of folk poetry are represented in the book under review, both in general (pp. 7—18), and also concretely through an informative section on the manuscript record of the work of Turkish poets staying in Algeria towards the end of the 17th and beginning of the 18th century which Ş. Elçin found at Oxford in 1972 (pp. 229—231).

In folk literature of Turkish nations, the horse held an equally significant position as it had in their nomad way of life. In myths, epos and legends of these nations, horses of a supranatural origin and endowed with miraculous properties had become equal partners with epic heroes. Elçin's study Atların Doğuşları İle İlgili Efsaneler (pp. 47—51, Legends Relating to Horses' Origin) brings evidence that in certain regions of Anatolia the faith in a horse's supranatural origin persists to this day. Another valuable study is that dealing with the horse's function as a gift in the history and folk epic of the Turks (pp. 56—62).

Şükrü Elçin devotes attention not only to folk epic works linked by their origin to the countryside, but also to urban folklore as evident from the comprehensive study Kitabî, Mensur, Realist İstanbul Halk Hikâyeleri (pp. 105—136, Book, Prosaic Istanbul Folk Stories). Here, the author presents a thorough analysis of six anonymous stories relating to the reign of sultan Murad IV. (1623—1640), and points out the harmonic coexistence of realistic and imaginative elements in the plot of these stories. He notes that stories are typical examples of prosaic creations by folk narrators — *meddahs* — handed down orally. However, as a consequence of the fact that editors of their lithographic or printed versions failed to preserve their original language, style and partly also narrative elements, these works lost some of their pristine originality.

In addition to the studies and papers referred to above, the publication under review brings also interesting contributions dealing with such items as Turkish folk epos (pp. 30—38, 90—99, 103—104), riddles (pp. 63—72), proverbs (pp. 137—150, 165—176) and further domains of folklore. It may therefore be considered to be a valuable contribution to a knowledge of the cultural heritage of the Turkish nation.

Xénia Celnarová

Scherner, Bernd: *Arabische und neupersische Lehnwörter im Tschuwaschischen.* Versuch einer Chronologie ihrer Lautveränderungen. Wiesbaden, Franz Steiner Verlag GMBH 1977. XXX + 231 S. (= Akademie der Wissenschaften und der Literatur. Veröffentlichungen der Orientalischen Kommission. Band XXIX).

Wie es wohl bekannt ist, kommt dem Tschuwaschischen in den historisch-vergleichenden turkologischen Forschungen eine besondere Stellung, in den altaistischen Untersuchungen sogar eine Schlüsselposition zu. So ist es verständlich, daß nicht nur die Erhellung der Außenbeziehungen dieses wichtigen türkischen Idioms, sondern auch seiner inneren Geschichte eine wichtige Aufgabe für die Sprachforscher bildet.

Die Beantwortung der Fragen der tschuwaschischen Lautgeschichte stößt jedoch auf nicht wenige Schwierigkeiten. Das ergibt sich vor allem daraus, daß die Geschichte des Tschuwaschischen — wie das auch bei vielen anderen Turksprachen der Fall ist — durch Schriftdenkmälern mangelhaft dokumentiert ist. Aus diesem Grunde nehmen die Lehnwortstudien in der Erforschung des Tschuwaschischen einen besonderen Platz ein. Von der Erhellung der oft komplizierten Lehn- und Dialektbeziehungen des Tschuwaschischen erhofft man, den Hauptstrom der sprachlichen Ereignisse von den Nebenströmen zu trennen bzw. deren Chronologie zu klären.

Das vorliegende Buch wurde einer wichtigen Lehnwortschicht des Tschuwaschischen, nämlich den arabisch-neupersischen Bestandteilen, gewidmet. Diese Lehnwörter sind höchstwahrscheinlich erst nach dem 8. Jahrhundert in mehreren Etappen und durch Kanäle in die Sprache eingedrungen. Die Klärung der Einzelheiten um diese Lehnwortschicht kann so einen nicht unbedeutenden Beitrag zur tschuwaschischen Lautgeschichte liefern.

Scherners Buch gliedert sich wie folgt: Vorwort; Abkürzungen; Anmerkungen zu den čuv. und tat. Quellen; Zitierweise; Zur Transkription (pp. V—XXX). I. Einführung (pp. 1—8). II. Veränderungen einiger gtü. Laute im Čuv. (pp. 9—24). III. Die arabischen und neupersischen Laute im Čuv. (pp. 25—97). IV. Ar. np.-čuv. Etymologien (pp. 98—183). V. Indices (pp. 185—231).

Die Arbeit zeigt eindeutig, daß Scherners Versuch, die arabisch-neupersische Lehnwortschicht systematisch zu analysieren, einen wichtigen Fortschritt in die Richtung der Lösung der Probleme bedeutet. Der Verfasser präsentiert ein gut durchsiebtes Material, das er vielseitig analysiert. Er bietet eine sorgfältige Darstellung der Probleme, auf die er — im Rahmen der gegebenen Möglichkeiten — eine adäquate Antwort zu geben versucht. Daß die offen gebliebenen Fragen manchmal überwiegen, liegt in der Natur der Sache: all das spiegelt den aktuellen Forschungsstand wider.

Scherners Buch ist ein begrüßenswerter Beitrag zur tschuwaschischen Lautgeschichte, der die Diskussion um die strittigen und ungelöst gelassenen Fragen anspornen und sich auf diese Weise auf die tschuwaschischen Sprachforschungen weiterhin sehr positiv auswirken wird.

Georg Hazai

Wirtschaftsgeschichte des Vorderen Orients in islamischer Zeit. Teil 1. (Economic History of the Near East in Islamic Period. Part I.) Leiden—Köln, E. J. Brill 1977. 405 pp. Handbuch der Orientalistik, Hrsg. von B. Spuler. Erster Abteilung VI. Band, 6. Abschnitt, Teil 1.

This first part of the Economic History of the Near East in Islamic times includes thirteen studies dealing with the sources, general and specific issues in the economic history of this region.

The question of sources is treated of by B. Lewis, one of the leading personalities in contemporary Islamic research. In his contribution "Sources for the Economic History of the Middle East" (pp. 1—17), previously published in "Studies in the Economic History of the Middle East", ed. by M. A. Cook. London 1970, he points to the lack of sources for an economic history of Islamic countries. According to the availability and quality of documentary sources he divides the history of the Middle East since the rise of Islam into three periods: Early, Middle and Late. The Late Period which in the greater part of the territory begins in the 19th century, is characterized by a wealth of sources, while in the other two periods — as in most civilized regions — the number of sources declines as research is pushed further back into the past. In addition to Islamic sources, Lewis takes note also of such as are the result of the activity of foreigners or minorities in the Islamic world (principally of Jews and Armenians). Similarly, he does not confine himself uniquely to diplomatic materials, but has recourse also to numismatic and epigraphic elements, and then to the area of such an importance to the Islamic world, the literary domain (poetry and belles lettres), and to administrative and military manuals, etc.

M. Rodinson investigates the influence of Islamic religious conditions on the economic life (Les conditions religieuses islamiques de la vie économique, pp. 18—30). The author takes note of the koranic reglementation of the economic life of the country, the influence of koranic ethics on the approach to the economic activities and later of the ideological attitude of Islam towards the economic life.

The next study is concerned with general questions of economic history — The Organization of Labour (pp. 31—52) and comes from the pen of G. Baer. In the first part the author deals with the organization of the trades and manufacture in the Middle Ages. As one of the foremost experts on this question, he investigates in great detail the organizations and functions of Islamic Guilds during the Ottoman period and in the closing section he devotes attention to Modern Trade Unions in the Near East and Northern Africa.

The function of slavery in Islamic society is taken up by H. Müller (Sklaven, pp. 53—83), who rightly notes in his introduction that slavery at every period was conditioned by economic factors. He follows up the development of the question of slavery, the manners of acquiring slaves in the Islamic world, the types of slaves, the attitude of Islamic law towards slavery. He notes in detail the import of slaves and the principal regions from which they had been imported, and their utilization.

A. S. Ehrenkreutz studies the origins of Islamic financial system and its development in the Omayyad and Abbasid caliphates in his contribution Money (pp. 84—97).

The well-known expert on questions of market prices in the Near East, E. Ashtor, studies the prices of cereals, bread, meat, sugar, spices and further commodities during the course of the 10th to 15th centuries in his paper The Development of Prices in the Medieval Near East (pp. 98—115). He notes that grain prices were a reliable indicator of the general economic development (p. 103). His data on the prices of spices on Egyptian and Syrian markets may be of interest also to historians of European economic history. In his conclusion, Asthor summarizes his results in his statement "we would once more draw attention to the fall of prices of agricultural products which began at the end of the tenth century in Iraq and a hundred years later in Egypt. Further, there emerges from our findings the rise of wages, both nominal and real ones, during the same period. So the situation of the Near Eastern workers was in the later Middle Ages much better than in the times of the Abbasid and Fatimid caliphs" (p. 114).

B. Spuler's study Die wirtschaftlichen Entwicklungen des iranischen Raumes und Mittelasien im Mittelalter (pp. 116—159) is of an encyclopaedic nature, in which the author provides first-hand information on the land-tilling population, its taxation, on agricultural production, catte rearing, land holding and its distribution, and natural resources. Next, Spuler is concerned with the role of cities in the economic life of Iran and Central Asia, the organization of Guilds and their production, commerce and ensurance of trade connections, with the content and extent of foreign and home trade, taxes and social distribution of the population.

Several of the issues brought up by B. Spuler's article are investigated in greater detail by A. K. S. Lambton in her Aspects of Agricultural Organization and Agrarian History in Persia (pp. 160—187). Lambton makes use of both the structural and the historical approach to problems of Iranian agriculture. Her insights into the interactions between agriculture, dependent on irrigation, and politics, are of great interest.

A similar topic, but relating to Egypt, is dealt with by Richard S. Cooper in Agriculture in Egypt, 640—1800 (pp. 188—204). Cooper takes note, in the first place, of natural factors that affected Egyptian agriculture, and then technological factors — agricultural implements, manner of artificial irrigation, agricultural practices and finally political and economic factors. In this section, he follows up the role of the State in managing agriculture and irrigation, questions of land-holding and political stability, capital and labour. The author holds that the decline in Egyptian agriculture form the 11th century was caused by a failure to maintain the irrigation system or invest in agricultural improvements, and failure to retain a productive labour force on the land.

B. Rosenberg devoted attention to the economic development of Maghreb since the arrival of the Arabs until the end of the colonial period (L'histoire économique du Maghreb, pp. 205—238). In his study, the author takes note of the economic characteristic of the various regions of the Maghreb and follows up the basic trends of its development.

The economic life of Muslim Spain is studied by R. Arié (La vie économique de l'Espagne musulmane, pp. 239—254), who gradually follows up the development of economics in towns through agriculture, commerce, overland and maritime routes.

On the basis of contemporary Arab treatises on agriculture (al-ʿAwwām, Abu-l-Khayr and others), Lucie Bolens makes an analysis of economic procedures in Muslim Spain (L'agriculture hispano-arabe au Moyen âge, pp. 255—275).

The most extensive contribution to this collective work Matériaux pour l'histoire de l'agriculture en Irak: *al-filaha n-nabatiyya* by T. Fahd (pp. 276—377) consists of an analysis of an ancient compilation translated in the 10th century into Arabic by Ibn Wahshiyya under the title *Al-Filaha n-nabatiyya* (Nabatian Agriculture). The author presents a rather detailed content of this work according to the various chapters and in conclusion compares it with similar ancient and Islamic studies.

Work with the book is greatly facilitated by carefully prepared indexes of persons, names of localities, technical terms and maps.

This first volume of an Economic History of the Near East in the Islamic Period constitutes a valuable contribution to several issues relating to the economic development of countries ranging from Persia up to Muslim Spain. However, the work would have certainly profited by a general introduction or conclusion which would have summed up the results achieved by the various investigators. Such a summary is to be provided only by the second volume.

Vojtech Kopčan

281

Ashtor, Eli: *A Social and Economic History of the Near East in the Middle Ages.* London, William Collins Sons and Co. Ltd. 1976. 384 pp.

In the present publication Professor Ashtor gives a succinct summary of his considerable knowledge of the social and economic conditions in the Near East in the Middle Ages. His book is primarily concerned with the period from the origins of Islam (beginning of 7th cent.) up to the occupation of Arab countries by Ottoman Turks (16th cent.) and here again, the author devotes particular attention to the economic and social development of the central Islamic countries: Syria, Iraq and Egypt.

Even a cursory perusal of this publication makes it clear that the author has made use of numerous original sources and secondary literature, that he is knowledgeable of the nature of Byzantine feudalism and of course, of the economic and political development of Mediaeval Europe. Another priority that stood him in good stead here is his thorough formal training in economics and sociology. These circumstances and Ashtor's ability to view the political, economic or social aspects of historical development within their mutual relations, impart an extraordinary significance to this publication. And besides, this is the first book of its type from the domain of the history of Islamic countries.

At first sight, many things in the economic development of the Islamic world appear to be simple: Arab conquerors, who for the most part were nomads, occupied the ancient Near East in the 7th century and practically destroyed agricultural cultures in the valleys of the Euphrates, the Tigris and the Nile rivers. This disruptive intervention into the economy of the Middle East countries based primarily on agrarian production was not caused so much by the incursion itself of the soldiery as rather by a mass migration of nomads from the Arabian Peninsula who refused to settle down; they drove their flocks and herds to graze across cultivated regions which they devastated, and made raids on the sedentary population, as a result of which farmers ran into towns and the abandoned land turned into steppe and desert.

Right in the first century of Islamic era, a governing military oligarchy was formed from the Arab conquerors, that lived and grew rich from war booty and taxes levied on the conquered population. But already in the early Abbasid State (from mid-eighth cent.), a multinationality merchant and artisan stratum began to prosper; the complex governing bureaucratic apparatus came to be infiltrated, alongside the Arabs, also by nationals of other countries — Persians, Syrians, Copts, Greeks. The first centuries of the Abbasid rule and also the initial era of the disintegration of the caliphate were marked by an enormous economic progress of the Islam world. Prof. Ashtor elucidates the causes of this prosperity which, however, in a class-antagonistic society was often disturbed by frequent social unrest and uprisings.

The author pays particular attention to economic conditions then prevailing in Iraq and Iran under the rule of the Buyids and the Seldjukids, and in Egypt under the

Tulunids and the Fatimids. He takes note of the new progress in agriculture (particularly as regards cultivation of essential crops: wheat, rye, barley, oil, dates, etc.) and follows up the extension of commerce, the crafts and their specialization. In this connection he rightly underlines the importance of payments in ready-money and the development of banking. Mediaeval Islamic rulers disposed of relatively adequate quantities of gold (they imported it from Western Sudan), and their own stability was directly proportional to the quality of the gold coins which they minted. However, payment in kind went on alongside that in money: farmers paid their taxes directly in farm produce.

The book under review devotes considerable attention to the Islamic tax system in general, and naturally enough also to the forms in which it was applied in the various Islamic countries. The Arabs, as is generally known, initially left the soil in the conquered countries, in the hands of the native inhabitants. As time went on, however, relations regarding possessions (land tenure — the rise of latifundiae, etc.) became very complicated, and the tax system became adapted to the altered ownership conditions. Prof. Ashtor rightly notes that the majority of Islamic states maintained considerable mercenary armies paid from taxes.

An important part of the book are numerous statistical data which the author collected from original sources. Although data of Mediaeval Islamic historians and geographers must be taken with a certain reserve, yet many of the figures, such for instance, as those relating to tax revenues in the various countries, prices of certain farm products, textiles, etc., are very instructive.

In our view, this publications is an excellent and reliable aid not only to students of Islamic history, but even to historians as such, for mediaeval history of Islamic countries, if it is to be comprehensive, cannot be interpreted without taking into account the prevailing economic and social factors.

Ján Pauliny

Bidwell, Robin: *Travellers in Arabia*. London, The Hamlyn Publishing Group Limited 1976. 224 pp.

Bidwell's publication represents, after a certain lapse of time, a serious attempt at making accessible to the English reader the process of discovering Arabia. The topic itself, treated of here in a popular form, is attractive, but not an easy one. For since the mid-18th century, Arabia was visited by numerous travellers each of whom discovered "something".

Bidwell in his exposition endeavoured to proceed chronologically. He leaves out reports by ancient travellers, geographers and cartographers and begins with modern discoverers of Arabia — the Italian Ludovici di Varthema (visited Arabia in 1502) and the Englishman Joseph Pitts (travelled in Arabia in the second half of the 17th cent.). He reconstructs the principal features of their travels, recalls certain characteristic episodes and cites extracts from their diaries, concluding with an evaluation of the contribution of their travels.

Bidwell adopts a similar procedure in portraying the lives of subsequent travellers, i.e. Carsten Niebuhr (travelled in Arabia in 1761—1767), Johann Ludwig Burckhardt (in Arabia in 1809—1817), Richard F. Burton (visited Mecca and Medina in 1853), W. G. Palgrave (travelled in Northern Arabia in 1862), C. M. Doughty (travelled through northwest Arabia in the years 1875—1878) and Henry St John B. Philby who lived for many years in Arabia until his death in 1960. Bidwell reserved considerable space in his book to these personalities and underscored their share in discovering Arabia also by processing their biographies in separate chapters. By this he evidently meant to gratify the taste of English readers (he may even have been led to it by his own personal interest), for with the exception of C. Niebuhr, all the above travellers were either from Great Britain, or in British service (e.g. J. L. Burckhardt). This particular circumstance might in itself be overlooked as of no consequence (after all, it is up to the author to decide which personage he will bring into the limelight), if top-rank travellers were not thereby assigned to the sidelines; such are, e.g. the Spaniard Domingo Badia y Leblich (who, under the name of Ali Bey, was the first European to visit Mecca in 1807), or the outstanding German Ulrich Jasper Seetzen who, after remarkable travels through Syria, Palestine and Hejaz, finally met a tragic end in the late summer of 1810 in Yemen.

After Niebuhr, Burckhardt, Burton, Palgrave, Doughty and Philby, Bidwell writes about further travellers in chapters which he heads according to the geographical division of Arabia as follows: *Travellers in the Hejaz* (pp. 116—137); *Travellers in Eastern and Northern Arabia* (pp. 138—161); *Travellers in South-west Arabia* (pp. 162—191); *Travellers in Oman* (pp. 192—219). In these chapters Bidwell has included numerous travellers (see his Index to the book) thus making proof of his considerable knowledge of the topic.

No special emphasis is laid in the book on motivation behind these travels of discovery (business, political, or scientific incentives); the reader, however, becomes all the more acquainted with the travellers' traits of character. The author examines their impressions, makes frequent quotations from their travelogues, and besides their personal courage, he especially appreciates their sense of objectiveness in judging the natives.

Bidwell's book is very lively in its own way. This is partly due to the fact that the author himself has extensively travelled through Arabia, knows its inhabitants, is familiar with their customs, and also with the climatic conditions prevailing in this desert region. As might be expected, Bidwell is well informed also on the new, contemporary development, both political and social, taking place in Arabia.

And finally, a point should also be made of the representative graphic design of the book under review, the abundant black-and-white and colour illustrations with appropriate explicative texts, all of which goes to make of it a very attractive reading.

Ján Pauliny

Ibn Ishāq: *Das Leben des Propheten.* Aus dem Arabischen übertragen und bearbeitet von Gernot Rotter. Tübingen und Basel, Horst Erdmann Verlag 1976. 287 S. (Bibliothek arabischer Klassiker, Band 1).

Ausgewählte Teile aus der Biographie des Muḥammad von Ibn Ishāq bilden den ersten Band der vom Verlag Horst Erdmann in Tübingen begonnenen Serie *Bibliothek arabischer Klassiker.* Das Ziel dieser Serie wird es sein dem deutschsprachigen Leser einige bedeutende Werke der arabischen mittelalterlichen Literatur zugänglich zu machen. Die Ausdehnung dieser Literatur sowie ihre Eigenständigkeit macht die Aufgabe keineswegs leicht.

Gernot Rotter, Ibn Ishāqs Übersetzer standen etwa 1400 Seiten arabischen Textes mit Anmerkungen (nach der Kairoer Ausgabe aus dem Jahre 1955 gerechnet) zur Verfügung, aus denen er ungefähr ein Neuntel ausgewählt, übersetzt und adaptiert hat. Wer den Text von der Sīra kennt, der weiß, daß es recht schwierig ist eine gute Auswahl aus diesem Buch zu treffen. Wichtige Ereignisse aus dem Leben Muḥammads werden nämlich im Buch oft von einer Vielzahl unwesentlicher und vom heutigen Standpunkt aus gesehen bedeutungsloser Angaben überdeckt. Außerdem ist die Art in der arabische Geschichtsschreiber historische Begebenheiten widergeben (indem sie die Auslegung in eine Menge kleiner narrativer Einheiten atomisieren) für den Europäer fast unverständlich.

Auch trotz dieser Schwierigkeiten ist Rotter die Auswahl geglückt. Der Leser wird in der Übersetzung mit der Persönlichkeit und den Lebensgeschicken des Propheten Muḥammad auf jene Weise bekannt gemacht, wie sie von der ältesten islamischen Geschichtsschreibung interpretiert werden.

Gernot Rotter hat den arabischen Text nicht nur ausgewählt und übersetzt, sondern ihn auch gewissermaßen adaptiert. Er ließ ganze Überlieferungen aus den einzelnen Kapiteln (wenn wir die Gliederung des Textes in Kapitel laut der ägyptischen Ausgabe akzeptieren) weg, und übertrug die abrupte arabische Erzählweise in ein verständliches, glattes Deutsch. Im Zusammenhang mit einer solchen Adaptation ergibt sich die Frage, inwieweit der adaptierte Text den Charakter und das Spezifikum des Originals treu widergibt. Und eine weitere Frage: gewinnt der Leser nicht wirklich einen verzerrten Anblick auf die älteste arabische Prosaliteratur? Sollen wir auch über Details reden, es ist z. B. nicht klar, warum der

Übersetzer Zitate aus dem Koran in Majuskeln und die Überliefererketten wieder in Petit setzen ließ, obwohl beide einen integrierenden Bestandteil der arabischen Vorlage bilden.

Unserer Meinung nach gibt es in Europa bislang wenig Leserübersetzungen aus der arabischen klassischen Literatur. Diese Tatsache wird von vielen Faktoren verursacht. Als Schwierigstes erscheint jedoch, sich zu entscheiden was und wie übersetzt werden soll.

Ján Pauliny

Khoury, Raif Georges (Hrsg.): *Asad ibn Mūsā, Kitāb al-Zuhd.* Wiesbaden, Otto Harrassowitz 1976. 124 S.

Das rezensierte Buch stellt eine Neuauflage des kleinen arabischen eschatologischen Werkes Kitāb al-Zuhd, das Asad ibn Mūsā (750—827) zugeschrieben wird, dar.

Den Text dieser Sammlung edierte zum ersten Mal Rudolf Leszynsky (Heidelberg, 1909) nach der Handschrift Berlin 1553 (dat. 665 A. H.). Der Ausgabe fügte Leszynsky die Übersetzung sowie kurze Einführungen hinzu. Leszynsky reihte in die Übersetzung das einleitende Kapitel, in dem sich Angaben über die einzelnen Gewährsmänner befinden, nicht ein und ließ aus der Übersetzung auch die Isnāde zu den einzelnen Überlieferungen weg. Seine deutsche Übersetzung des edierten Textes weckt nach außen hin also gar nicht den Eindruck, daß wir es mit einem Ḥadītbuch zu tun haben. Weder in der Einleitung, noch in den Anmerkungen schenkte Leszynsky irgendeine Beachtung der Identifizierung der Gewährsmänner, welche die Asad ibn Mūsā zugeschriebenen Überlieferungen erhalten haben. Ebensowenig bezog er irgendeinen Standpunkt zu den einzelnen Überliefererketten. Anscheinend gab er sich damit zufrieden, daß die Sammlung Asad ibn Mūsā zugeschrieben wird und leitete davon mechanisch ab, sie enthalte islamische eschatologische Vorstellungen aus dem 3. Jahrhundert der Hiǧra.

Die Bedeutung der Neuauflage liegt vor allem darin, daß R. G. Khoury hauptsächlich alle biographischen Angaben über Asad ibn Mūsā (s. *Vie et personnalité*, S. 21 sqq.) ergänzte und dessen Beziehung zum Ḥadīt und zur ältesten islamischen narrativen Literatur (s. *Activité littéraire*, S. 31 sqq.) erforschte. In diesem Zusammenhang ist vor allem der Teil von Khourys in französischer Sprache verfaßten einleitenden Studie wichtig, wo vom Titel und dem Inhalt des Werkes Kitāb al-Zuhd (S. 39 sqq.) die Rede ist. Der Titel dieses Kleinwerkes hat bereits Leszynsky überrascht, da es hinsichtlich seines Inhalts einen etwas ungewohnten Namen trägt. Khoury beweist, daß dieses Werk ursprünglich nicht so geheißen hat.

Weiter ist es wahrscheinlich, daß das, was davon erhalten blieb, lediglich einen Teil dessen darstellt.

Außer der Berliner Handschrift (nach dieser edierte Leszynsky) benützte Khoury bei der Neuauflage auch die zweite Kopie dieses Werkes, und zwar die Handschrift Damašq, al-Ẓāhiriyya (Zah. mağ. 100/1). Seine Ausgabe enthält den möglichst vollkommenen Text (einschließlich aller certificats de lecture, samāᶜ), wobei im kritischen Apparat nicht nur auf Varianten, sondern auch auf Fehler in Leszynskys Ausgabe aufmerksam gemacht wird. Dem Buch schloß Khoury Indizes zur französischen Einleitung sowie zur arabischen Edition an.

Ján Pauliny

Corriente, F.: *A Grammatical Sketch of the Spanish Arabic Dialect Bundle.* With a Prologue by Emilio García Gómez. Madrid, Instituto Hispano-Arabe de Cultura 1977. XVI + 196 pp.

Despite the considerable linguistic and cultural importance of mediaeval Spanish Arabic, Corriente's monograph is the first systematic description of the latter. Another important feature of the present study stems from the fact that it has been written by applying modern linguistic methods to an extensive body of documentary material. The author approaches Spanish Arabic as a dialect bundle despite the fact that common traits clearly prevail over local ones.

The Hispano-Arabic dialect cluster resulted from an interference of Romance substratum with Arabic dialects brought to Spain when the Muslim political domination had been established in the eighth century. Spanish Arabic belongs to the Western group of dialects, as shown by the isogloss delimitating the occurrence of the /nv—/ and /nv —— ū/ morphemes for the first persons of the imperfective verbs. In phonology, Spanish Arabic is marked by the preservation of the interdentals and, above all, by the substitution of stress for the vowel quantity. In morphology, it displays the internal passive as well as some other less conspicuous features. In syntax and lexicon, a Hispano-Arabic core cannot satisfactorily be defined in terms of data available so far.

The book is divided into the following parts: Phonology (pp. 22—73), Morphology (pp. 74—120), Syntax (pp. 121—150), Lexicon (pp. 151—153) and Texts in Phonemic Transcription (pp. 154—158). The book is closed by seven indices (pp. 159—196) as follows: (1) Spanish Arabic items, (2) Other Arabic dialects, (3) Mozarabic, (4) Other Hispanic Romance languages, (5) Other languages, (6) Toponyms and personal names (from Romance sources), and (7) Glossary of some grammatical terms. Further, the book has a prologue in Spanish, by E. G. Gómez (Prólogo, pp. IX—XVI), a Spanish and an English preface by the author (Prefacio, pp. 1—5; Preface, pp. 6—9), Abbreviations (pp. 10—11), Symbols (p. 12), and an extensive Bibliography (pp. 13—21).

Despite the great number of carefully collected data which are, moreover, classified by means of sound linguistic criteria in all vital parts of the monograph, we cannot fully agree with the author in his general conclusions, notably that 'the modern dialects are not the offsprings of ClAr (= Classical Arabic) nor, as a whole, of any post-Islamic koine, but are rather the result of the evolution of OA (= Old Arabic) stock and of the interference of foreign elements in a given sociolinguistic contour' (p. 8). Nevertheless, the evidence gathered by some other scholars in favour of a post-Classical basis of modern dialects, irrespective of wheather called Arabic koine in the sense given to this term by C. A. Ferguson (*The Arabic Koine,* in: Language, *35,* 1959, pp. 616—30), or Middle Arabic (see e.g. Joshua Blau, *The Emergence and Linguistic Background of Judaeo-Arabic. A Study of the Origin of Middle Arabic.* Oxford, The Clarendon Press 1965, etc.), — seems to be more conclusive. And even if admitting — in the case of the tribal, to a considerable extent homogeneous, Bedouin migrations to Ifrīqiyā and, further on, to the Iberian Peninsula — some aspects of a tribal and dialectal continuity, these can hardly be presented in this straightforward and immediate form.

Further, it is almost generally accepted that there is no convincing reason to approach modern Arabic dialects as an undifferentiated whole, especially after the stimulating study of Ferguson and the extensive documentary evidence provided by Blau (see above). "In contrast to the urban Middle Arabic dialects," Blau writes, "which arose as far back as the beginning of the Islamic era, the Bedouin dialects at first preserved their main features unchanged. Many Bedouin dialects were, it is true, affected by migrations which had brought different tribes into contact with each other and sometimes caused intermingling. Yet even these Bedouin dialects maintained a structure that was, on the whole, synthetic, thus remaining akin to Classical Arabic, as against the more analytical urban dialects. Consequently, the linguistic picture after the conquests is characterized by a clear dichotomy between analytical urban vernaculars and synthetic Classical Arabic and Bedouin dialects" (Blau, op. cit., p. 8).

In dealing with the Spanish Arabic dual ending /-ay/, as occurring instead of the expected /-ayn/, the author rightly attributes this phenomenon to a 'peculiar morphemic distribution' rather than to a phonemic change (p. 41). Nevertheless, we cannot accept the author's treatment of the elision of /n/, in cases like ᶜaybaqar (from the syntactic ᶜayn baqar) "prunes", in terms of an analogical development stimulated by the above described morphemic distribution associated with the dual. It seems far more likely that the phenomenon (of course, the elision cannot be specifically related to /n/) is stimulated by a word-formational process of a *naḥt*-type root shortening in

288

cases like ᶜaybaqar (ᶜayn baqar),[1] ḥabqurr (ḥabb qurr), ᶜabšamī (from the underlying ᶜAbd Šams),[2] etc.

Nor can we fully agree with the author's definition of 'i̯ᶜrāb: "case and mood morphemes with the shape of vowels attached to the end of nouns and verbs (characteristic of OA and ClAr)" (viz. Glossary of some grammatical terms, p. 196). As evident, the 'i̯ᶜrāb endings include, besides pure vocalic elements, both mixed vocalic-and-consonantal suffixes (viz external plurals, dual, the so-called xamsat 'afᶜāl endings, etc.), as well as zero-vowels (jazm of the jussive). The symbolic value of the Arabic term ḥarakāt al-'i̯ᶜrāb, as co-occurring with terms like ᶜalāmat al-'i̯ᶜrāb, ẓawāhir al-'i̯ᶜrāb, 'awāxir al-kalām lil-'i̯ᶜrāb,[3] can hardly be transferred into English.

These few remarks are, of course, not intended to cast any shadow over this pioneering work, its over-all reliability, methodological freshness and its extensive documentary evidence. The book will be of interest not only to the Arabic dialectologists and linguists but, to a considerable extent, to all those for whom a better knowledge of Spanish Arabic is but a way leading to a more thorough understanding of mediaeval literatures and cultures in Iberian peninsula, greatly stimulated by the impact of the Arab cultural supremacy.

Ladislav Drozdík

Chrestomathie der modernen arabischen Prosaliteratur (Readings in Modern Arabic Prose). Bearbeitet und herausgegeben von Manfred Fleischhammer und Wiebke Walther. Leipzig, VEB Verlag Enzyklopädie 1978. 277 pp.

After R. Brünnow — A. Fischer's *Arabische Chrestomathie aus Prosaschriftstellern*, Berlin 1928 (and subsequent editions), which proved to be a highly efficient tool for acquiring a basic reading competence in Classical Arabic, the German-speaking students of Arabic have now at their disposal another excellent chrestomathy. It contains expertly selected samples of modern Arabic prose,

---

[1] Brockelmann, C.: *Grundriß der vergleichenden Grammatik der semitischen Sprachen*. I. Bd. Berlin, Verlag von Reuter und Reichard 1908, pp. 65 and 481.

[2] Fleish, H.: *L'arabe classique. Esquisse d'une structure linguistique*. Beyrouth, nouvelle éd., revue et augmentée. Dar El-Machreq Editeurs 1968, pp. 161—2.

[3] For ᶜalamāt and ẓawāhir al-'i̯ᶜrāb see e.g. the Arabic version of Fück, J.: ᶜArabīya. *Untersuchungen zur arabischen Sprach- und Stilgeschichte*. Berlin, Akademie-Verlag 1950 (translated into Arabic by Dr. ᶜAbdalḥalīm an-Najjār, *al-ᶜArabiyya. Dirāsāt fīl-luġa wal-lahajāt wal-'asālīb*. al-Qāhira, Maṭbaᶜat Dār al-kutub al-ᶜarabī 1951), pp. 3—4. For the term 'awāxir al-kalām lil-'i̯ᶜrāb, see the Egyptian edition of al-Xwārizmī's *Mafātīḥ al-ᶜulūm*, al-Qāhira, ᶜUṯmān Xalīl 1930, p. 29, etc.

covering approximately the last five decades of our century. The domain of modern Arabic prose literature is conceived, by the editors, liberally enough as to include a great variety of text which reflect the most outstanding political, cultural and ideological processes recently taking place in the Arab world. The reader consists of two distinct parts: fiction texts (Belletristische Texte, pp. 15—134), and non-fiction texts (Nichtbelletristische Texte, pp. 135—277). Every author included is shortly introduced by relevant bio- and bibliographical data and, furthermore, all texts are carefully annotated.

The main goal of the present reader is to improve the proficiency of students in Modern Written Arabic by means of an extensive reading, to make them acquainted with the most recent changes and innovations of the language, and to introduce them to modern Arabic fiction as well as to the most representative aspects of the 20th century cultural and political milieu.

In considering the editorial meritoriousness of a relatively extensive textual body, like the present one, it is of course always easy to disagree with the editors about the disputable question of priority and preference, about whom or what to include in particular rather than someone or something else, etc. What really matters, hewever, is the whole of the textual corpus and its ability to fulfil the general purpose of the work. When viewed from this angle, one may hardly find any other anthology of modern Arabic prose which would offer more plastic and up-to-date picture of the Arab political and cultural scene than the present work.

The reader is of interest from a linguistic point of view, too. The texts reveal all the main lexical and stylistic developments observable in the 20th century Arabic. The texts are presented without simplification and pre-digestion, and their understanding presupposes two years of a previous college-level instruction in Arabic, as a minimum requirement.

The annotation of texts bears witness to a high scholarly niveau, pedagogical skill, and thorough care and attention. Nevertheless, with regard to the prevailing usage in Modern Written Arabic, it would have perhaps been more suitable to suggest a 'less classicized' reading in *kullu mri'in* (viz. *kullu mri'in wa-ḥāǧatuhū* "jedem nach seinen Begehren oder seiner Bedürftigkeit", p. 127, note 7), notably *kullu mra'in* which, after all, co-occurred with the former as early as in Classical Arabic as a free alternation. The voweling of *imbaryālī* "imperialistisch" (p. 240, note 29) or *imbaryāliyya* "Imperialismus" (p. 254, note 13) instead of/besides *imbiryālī*, *imbiryāliyya* "Imperialismus" (e.g. Schregle, p. 605), *imbariyāliyya* (new Baranov, p. 43), etc. reflects but a low degree of lexicographical codification in the linguistic domain of Modern Written Arabic.

The reader will be of invaluable help to students of Arabic at the intermediate and advanced levels of instruction.

Ladislav Drozdík

Fenech, E.: *Contemporary Journalistic Maltese.* An Analytical and Comparative Study. Leiden, E. J. Brill 1978. XVIII + 251 pp.

Although a number of Maltese grammars and lexicons have already been written in the 18th and earlier centuries,[1] it is not until the beginning of the nineteenth century that Maltese was given a more systematic attention on the part of grammarians, lexicographers and schoolmasters. The first book which had a real impact on the study of Maltese was the *Taghrif Fuq il-Kitba Maltija* (System of the Maltese Writing), published by the *Ghaqda tal-Kittieba tal-Malti* (Society of Maltese Authors) only in 1924. After this date, a number of valuable descriptive and normative works, by A. Cremona, J. Aquilina, and other scholars, followed in rapid succession.

Maltese developed for many centuries quite independently of any noticable normative work. This fact is clearly felt in all spheres of cummunication in which this language happens to be used, and in particular, in the present-day journalistic usage.

The present research is based on the three existing Maltese dailies, namely *L-Orrizont* (The Horizon), *In-Nazzjon Taghna* (Our Nation), and *Il-Hajja* (The Life). The total of their issues, as published in August 1973 (78 issues, with a total number of words exceeding 5,000,000), has been subjected to the analysis. The study was supplemented by questionnaires, private correspondence and personal interviews. Since the study is quite specifically concerned with the genuine journalistic Maltese, all articles and poems which have been published in the literary page of these newspapers, were excluded therefrom.

The book consists of an Introduction (pp. 1—15) and six chapters: (1) Phonology and Orthography (pp. 16—38), (2) Morphology (pp. 39—60), (3) Syntax (pp. 61—79), (4) Lexical and Phraseological Aspects (pp. 80—145), (5) Style (pp. 148—208) and (6) Conclusions (pp. 211—227). Further, two appendices are added: The Segmental Phonemes of Standard Maltese (pp. 228—233) and The Language of Older Maltese Newspapers (pp. 234—243). Finally, a Bibliography (pp. 244—246) and an Analytical Index (pp. 247—251) conclude the study.

In general, the method of research adopted includes the following procedures: Relevant phonological features of spoken Maltese are examined and their impact on the spelling of the journalistic language is established. Then, morphological and

---

[1] Some of the most important pioneer works on Maltese: Agius de Soldanis, G. F.: *Damma tal Kliem Kartaginis mscerred fel fom tal Maltin u Ghaucin* (Lexicon of the Carthaginian Language as used by the Inhabitants of Malta and Gozo), 1750. 4 vols, in manuscript form preserved at the Royal Malta Library.

———, *Nuova Scuola di Grammatica per agevolmente apprendere la lingua Punica-Maltese.* Roma 1750.

Vassalli, M. A.: *Alfabet Mālti Mfysser byl Mālti u bit-Talyān — Alfabeto Maltese spiegato in Lingua Maltese ed Italiano.* Roma 1790.

———, *Mylsen Phoenico-Punicum Sive Grammatica Melitensis.* Romae 1791, etc.

syntactic peculiarities of the newspaper language are analysed. Considerable attention is paid to the lexicon and phraseology, in particular to various types of neologisms, especially those obtained by way of loan translation or direct lexical borrowings based on phonemic transfer. Stylistic aspects of journalistic Maltese are given due attention as well. Whenever necessary, the author refers in grammatical matters to E. F. Sutcliffe's *Grammar of the Maltese Language* (3rd Impression, Malta 1960) and A. Cremona's *Taghlim Fuq il-Kitba Maltija* (9th Edition, Malta 1968).

The linguistic evidence adduced in the monograph clearly demonstrates that journalistic Maltese is branded by a number of characteristic features in which it differs from both literary and spoken Maltese. The book is a valuable contribution to the study of journalistic Maltese in general. The method of investigation, followed in the present research will, no doubt, provoke similar studies in other languages and possibly in different domains of their application, too.

Ladislav Drozdík

Davidson, Basil: *Africa in Modern History (The Search for a New Society)*. London, Allen Lane 1978. 431 pp.

Few writers have done more to analyse and explain the history and culture of Africa than Basil Davidson and few by their long and intimate experience are better qualified to do so. The book under review is a history of modern Africa by way of the development of African political ideas and practice. It is divided into six parts and since only the last one deals with the post-independence period, those interested in problems of contemporary Africa might feel at first a bit disappointed. Yet after reading the whole book they will probably change their minds for then it can be more clearly seen how present-day history of Africa organically flows from the old, and that it would otherwise be inexplicable.

The book deals with approximately the last one hundred years of African history during which Africans moved into the modern world and in the last decades have fully become a part of it. This was shown in a singular manner in 1974 when the utterly 'undeveloped' peoples of the Portuguese colonies brought down a dictatorship in Europe which the European people in question had failed to overcome during nearly half a century of protest.

In the first two chapters the author deals with the situation in Africa on the eve of European conquest at the end of the nineteenth century. Here he offers a good description of the pre-colonial and 'pre-nationalist' African community which was slowly developing as Africa's own civilization and which was turned into chaos by the ignorant, high-handed approach of the new European masters. Modernization of African society was necessary but it should not have come in such a ruthless, destructive form.

From the economic point of view, the nineteenth century in Africa certainly was (save for the last two decades) a period of growth. The pre-colonial economies proved capable of large and continuous expansion within purely indigenous structures where the external factors worked only as stimuli. The author expresses his belief that nineteenth-century Africa was moving towards a large, although slow and diffused reorganization and that it was the European expansion late in the nineteenth century that stopped this growth on its best way to systemic change.

The third and fourth chapters of B. Davidson's book are devoted to the period 1890—1939 and deal with the characterization of the colonial model and the African responses to its imposition. The author begins with an examination of the reasons that led to the sudden scramble for Africa. He points out that these reasons were often more political and strategic than economic, as seen from the fact that although the imperialist countries' national interests had in the second half of the nineteenth century become more and more identified with colonial possession, later they often discovered that they needed no new territories at all. In another part of the third chapter the author offers an explanation for the problem of African participation in the invading campaigns. He points out that although Africa 'before nationalism' had no psychological barriers against recruitment of men from one ethnic group to fight against those of another, few of the Africans were real volunteers. Many were made to join by coercion, or corruption of their chiefs or lineage headmen and thus simply passed from one form of bondage to another.

When examining colonial doctrines the author shows that while the Europeans spoke of progress and trusteeship for the benefit of Africans, reality was quite different. Forced labour, land expropriation and destruction of the existing African trading enterprise took place wherever there was any prospect of economic interest or gain. And where there was none, the 'just and human' indirect rule could be widely promoted. The author is very critical also when examining the system of forced labour imposed in most of the regions, no matter how laboriously Africans might produce within their own non-cash economies. Colonial attitudes took it for granted that they worked only when the Europeans employed them. Otherwise, they were held to be 'idle' and 'refusing civilization'. Here the cruelty of forced labour or 'contract work', its more or less disguised modification, is compared to that of slavery.

In another part of his profound analysis of the colonial system before the Second World War B. Davidson explains how Africa was affected by the great slump and the period of colonial protectionism that followed.

The fourth chapter which deals with African responses to colonial rule up to the

Second World War shows that the protests varied both in quantity and quality. And again the ignorant European attitude is exposed to the author's criticism — the trouble with the Africans was not that they had lost land, cattle and freedom; it was simply, as was often portentously explained, that they were unable to adjust to the 'psychological strains' of modern life. In another example fears of 'communism' that the colonial administration tended to see in any kind of radicalism are revealed to be ridiculous since one could hardly speak of a class nature of the protest at that time.

The whole examination of the problem of African responses to colonial penetration and rule is characterized by the author's search for sources and development of nationalism in various kinds of African protest. At the end he arrives at the conclusion that African nationalism has been born in the most classical form: by reaction to a foreign but dominant nationalism.

The drive for nationhood i.e., the problems of the period from 1940 to about 1960 are examined in the next chapter. The new role of Africa in the post-war politics is explained and innovations of the modern technological world are shown as factors that quickened the already rapid course of events. Among internal factors the role of the multitude's social needs is shown as being of increasing importance. The story of the march into political independence in British West Africa, in French Africa, in 'settlers' colonies' and in 'the lesser empires' respectively, is presented in the second part of this chapter.

Although the coming of independence could in those days seem a climactic moment dividing the past from an altogether different future, the biggest problems were yet to be solved. The price for political independence of the imported model soon proved to be a high one. This is, roughly speaking, what the last chapter of the book deals with. The given model had soon failed to work and a number of states embarked on the search for a model based on local realities. While the future of capitalism in Africa is seen as the future of the imported model, the author stresses that scientific socialism (of the new republics of the mid-1970s) cannot be labelled as another imported model, because in this case '...the methodology of revolution had put down independent roots into the realities of Africa's search for a new community and acquired indigenous content as well as form' (p. 376).

Most valuable are B. Davidson's remarks on nation building in the independent states. One must agree that a real nation can only be built on the basis of social needs, since they cut through every ethnic or regional dispute; that is, by building it upwards from the bottom and not downwards from the top. And this trend, as the reviewer sees it in agreement with the author's opinion, is likely to command the future.

In spite of a few misprints (e.g. FRELIMO began its armed struggle in 1964, not 1974 (p. 351) and some others less misleading), the book provides a valuable historical analysis of the problems Africa faces today.

Ján Voderadský

Gugler, Josef—Flanagan, William G.: *Urbanization and Social Change in West Africa*. Cambridge—London—New York—Melbourne, Cambridge University Press 1978. xvii + 237 pp.

This is the second book in the series Urbanization in Developing Countries and is devoted to a study of problems in a region that has experienced the most rapid rate of urban population growth in the world between 1950 and 1970 (although the level of urbanization in West Africa remains rather low when compared with that of other countries). The process of rapid urbanization has been going on in spite of a lack of commensurate industrial growth and the widespread unemployment indicates that West African cities have outstripped their economic foundations, whereas their primary functions continue to be administration and commerce.

Urbanization in West Africa is characterized by glaring disproportions. The cities boast of modern buildings and facilities occupied and utilizied by national and expatriate elites, but they also contain overcrowded tenements and shacks erected without any control on the part of public authorities. Many projects have been designed in attempts to solve the housing problem, but they have remained out of reach for the biggest part of those in need — the low income groups. The rate of urbanization has been so rapid since the Second World War and the consequences of this explosive growth are such that there is every reason to view the process as overurbanization.

J. Gugler and W. G. Flanagan have divided their book into nine chapters. They begin with a historical sketch of the problem pointing out that urban patterns have long been established in several parts of West Africa, a feature that distinguishes the region from much of the remainder of Subsaharan Africa. Having shown the particularities of West African urban centres, the authors come to the criticism of the 'Western ethnocentrism' of the established definitions of the city derived from one historical experience. They show that the examples from West Africa (e.g. the character of Yoruba cities) serve to broaden our experience in the forms a city organization may take.

Pre-colonial towns did not survive as such, but were transformed with the increasing European contact and control. The present pattern and conditions of urbanization in West Africa owe much to the colonial past. The most dense concentration of towns is to be found in the southern coastal parts, and the capital city of every West African country that touches the sea is located on the coast. The authors show that as a consequence of their location on the geographic periphery of the new states, the capitals of West Africa have acquired a regional rather than a national political character and they stand as symbols of faction rather than national unity.

The third chapter of the book presents a study of rural-urban migration. The relationship between economic and noneconomic factors is examined and the authors come to the conclusion that the rate of rural-urban migration has to be seen as the result of the aggregate of economic, social and political conditions.

Many of the urban residents of West Africa maintain strong ties with the rural area which they consider to be their real home. Motivations in this urban-rural relationship are profoundly studied in the fourth chapter. The authors stress the reciprocity of the relation: while the urban dweller enjoys the social security provided by the solidarity of his native village, he is, on the other hand, urged to keep alive his attachment to it. The man who has not returned to his home for some time may be visited by a delegation from the village who entreat him to return; many high-income earners spend most of their vacations in their home village in spite of the evident discomfort; they are expected to invest money, energy and advocacy on behalf of the rural area etc. When examining the prospects of the urban-rural ties, various factors that may in future influence it negatively (the second-generation urbanites show to have loosened their ties with rural areas, ...) or positively (rural development reduces the gap the urbanite has to bridge in order to reintegrate himself with the village, ...) are taken into consideration.

The following chapter deals with the problem of social relationship in the urban setting. Since most of the migrants associate with men from the same village or ethnic group, the role of the urban-based small ethnic unions is discussed here. They do not limit their activity to the provision of enjoyment in the company of those of like mind, and the authors show how unions can at times deal effectively with problems confronting the immigrant. He is helped when in need or trouble, but on the other hand, he is subjected to the authority of the union. Although ethnic unions may at times be referred to as voluntary associations, they are usually quite indispensable to the immigrant's survival in town.

The role of large-scale ethnic organizations aiming to lobby for their rural interests is analysed in the following part of the chapter. It is recalled that ethnic groups in West Africa do not constitute social classes and they are more accurately thought of as a vertical than a horizontal cross section of society.

In the next chapter an interpretation of change is offered by identifying three analytically distinct realms of it: historical, situational and biographic change.

Chapters seven and eight discuss the functions of the extended family nowadays (showing that urbanization has not affected them in West Africa as much as in other parts of the world) and the changes in the position of women. Urban wives, most of them engaged in market trade, are described as being often economically quite independent of their husbands and an example of Dakar women who have actually turned their husbands into salaried employees is added.

The last chapter of the book deals with social stratification and it is seen here as a three-tier structure of elite, urban employed and rural masses. In the part on the elite, the authors state that besides senior civil servants and politicians a third elite group, that of the officer corps of the army, came to be recognized after the military takeovers in the mid-1960s. The reviewer is of the opinion that as far as the structure of the elite is concerned, the army officers need not be referred to as a separate group since they actually just penetrated into the elite group of the politicians and thus acquired their elite status.

In some parts (chapters one and nine), the authors tried to embrace too broad a range of problems (e.g. political history of the first African states, criticism of the slave trade, consideration on what precipitated the scramble for Africa in the nineteenth century, the position of independent African states in world politics, the impact of military rule on civil administration,...) without clearly relating them to the problem of urbanization they have chosen to study. In spite of this, their book is a valuable contribution to the study of one of the most urgent problems Africa has to deal with today.

Ján Voderadský

Mondjannagni, Alfred Comlan: *Campagnes et Villes au Sud de la République Populaire du Bénin* (Villages and Towns in the South of the People's Republic of Benin). Paris, Mouton 1977. 615 pp., 60 maps, 42 figures, 47 tables and 28 photos.

This book is a very detailed study written by an African on a part of his native country and the amount of information presented in this synthetic regional study is impressive indeed. The southern part of the Republic of Benin is defined as being geographically quite distinct from its central or northern regions, as well as from the southern parts of the neighbouring countries such as Nigeria, Togo or Ghana. Although, when examining the factors that characterize the region under study the author shows that it is rather homogeneous, he does not forget to stress its immense diversity.

The book is divided into three chapters. The first one begins with a geographical description of the physical features of the country, while its second part is devoted to a general characterization of the population. Most interesting here is the examination of the origins of Adja and Yoruba, the two main ethnic groups.

The second chapter deals with the organization of the traditional rural life. Its economic bases, taxation, the techniques of agricultural production, as well as some nonagricultural rural activities are discussed here. A detailed examination of the origins, structure and significance of rural markets in the socio-economic organization of the region is well documented by photographs and maps. When studying the urban organization, the author comes to the conclusion that there are three generations of towns, where the colonially developed administrative and commercial centres are only the last of them.

The third chapter examines in various ways the economic, political and cultural relations between villages and towns. Attempts by the government to reorganize them are submitted to a critical analysis.

The book is abundantly provided with helpful maps, figures, tables and an extensive bibliography. It will prove of great value to anyone studying Benin as well as to all students of rural and urban life in African countries.

Ján Voderadský

Arnold, Guy: *Modern Nigeria*. London, Longman 1977. xiii + 192 pp.

This book by G. Arnold, a journalist and freelance writer who specializes in African affairs, is a comprehensive survey of Nigeria's recent past. It provides a background for interpreting the future development of the fastest growing nation in Africa.

The author begins with a short historical sketch, up to the early 1970s, when he starts to examine Nigeria in more detail. He characterizes the regime of general Gowon focusing on its failures, giving thus the reasons for the military coup that toppled it in 1975. G. Arnold approves of the change-over stating that the new regime of General Mohammed came at the right time, when everyone was ready for a change. The mid-1970s in Nigeria are seen here as a period of transition from the post-colonial era of reliance upon the old metropolitan power, to a more independent and powerful position when the country could provide decisive leadership for the continent as a whole. In the author's opinion, Nigeria might also be able to give the OAU the sort of backing that would begin to make that body an effective organization in world terms. A most disturbing feature of independent Nigeria's political development is found to be the absence of any clear ideological orientation. This need for orientation appears all the more important in a society which has such obvious extremes of wealth and poverty, as present-day Nigeria. As Chief Obafemi Awolowo (one of the country's prominent figures) put it in 1973: 'A situation such as we now have, under which the good things of life are assured to a small minority of Nigerians and almost totally denied to the vast majority of our countrymen, is pregnant with impredictable dangers for all of us, if allowed to continue for much longer' (p. 19).

In another part of his book G. Arnold shows how oil has rapidly changed the whole economic, political and social life of Nigeria, since it became the mainstay of its economy. Although the country has achieved rapid economic growth, it has gained little economic development and it remains to be an economic mixture of prosperity and backwardness. When examining the influence of the oil boom on Nigerian

298

politics, the author points out that it can be seen as a factor uniting the nation since it gave the Federal Government an effective economic weapon of control over the states.

Another important consequence of the oil boom — the giant Nigerian Third Development Plan (1975—1980), the biggest and most ambitious ever launched by an African country, its basic strategy being to raise Nigeria to the ranks of developed countries — is discussed in a separate chapter. In another part of the book the author stresses that despite oil, agriculture (employing about 70 % of the labour force) is the basis of life in Nigeria and the economy is and must remain based upon it.

In a survey of Nigeria's foreign policy, G. Arnold shows its growing radical influence in Africa as well as in the world. Nigeria became one of the first African states to recognize MPLA as the government of Angola and took a strong line in its support. It also plays an increasingly important role in South African affairs. In spite of the fears of some smaller African states, Nigeria is becoming a power in Africa.

Other chapters, not mentioned in this review, deal with education and manpower, labour, transport and communications, corruption, neocolonialism and the press. The book is provided with thirty black-and-white photographs, eight appendices and an index of names and terms. It is of great value to anyone interested in contemporary Nigeria, of which it gives a brief but rather complex picture.

Ján Voderadský

The Cambridge History of Africa. Volume 2. *From ca 500 B.C. to A.D. 1050.* Edited by J. D. Fage. Cambridge, Cambridge University Press 1978. vii + 840 pp., 67 figures, 38 plates, bibl.

Volume 2 of *The Cambridge History of Africa* deals with the beginnings of history and is thus a natural sequence to Volume 1 on the prehistory of this continent. Faced with a task to review a volume covering such an enormous space and time, one can do hardly more than to list its contents and comment on its wider conceptual framework.

Difficult as it is to mark out periods of African history which are equally valid for all parts of the continent, due to the extremely wide variations and differences in the degrees of social and material development among African peoples, some sort of unity in this volume could be distinguished. A major element in this volume that gives it an African-centred unity is that this period saw "the beginning of history" in virtually every part of Africa, the only two exceptions being Egypt with an older tradition of history and the extreme south-west of the continent — a very recent participant in history. The period covered saw the introduction and spread of the use of iron and iron-working throughout the African continent where, as Professor Fage put it in his Introduction, "the adoption of iron-working could well have been more significant than it was in some other parts of the world", it was "an important factor helping to consolidate earlier socio-economic achievements and providing a platform from which further, wider and ever-accelerating advances might be made" (p. 2). It seems that in much of Africa there was a minimal time gap between the introduction of iron-working and the growth and expansion of agriculture. Over the larger part of sub-Saharan Africa, both the introduction of iron-working and the introduction of agriculture seems to have been due to the expansion of Bantu-speaking Africans.

Still, during the very long period of history covered here, from about the middle of the first millennium B.C. to about the beginning of the second millennium A.D., the wide variations in the degrees of social and material development to be found among African peoples were even accentuated, since Africa north of the Sahara and partly also the eastern littoral were brought into closer touch with developments in the Near East and the Fertile Crescent, than the rest of the African continent lying to the south of it. For the whole of the period covered by this volume, Africa north of the Sahara participated in the major civilizations derived from the Near Eastern tradition and its Mediterranean and Red Sea offshoots. During this period the three great monotheistic religions — Judaism, Christianity and Islam, coming from the Semitic world, were carried into North Africa and, as Chapters 7 and 9 on Christianity in Mediterranean Africa and Christian Nubia or Chapters 8, 10 and 11 on the great period of African Islam show, became firmly entrenched there. Sub-Saharan Africa did not immediately share in the culminating advances of human social evolution to the north and northeast.

A by-product of this is a relative scarcity of evidence, of any kind, for the larger part of the continent lying south of the Sahara. For lands south of the desert, historical evidence first begins to become available only about the beginning of the second millennium A.D. An imbalance of historical source materials for the period resulted in the uneven geographic distribution of the regional chapters. Of the ten specifically regional chapters, only two are devoted directly and wholly to sub-Saharan Africa. The rest deal with North Africa, the Nile Valley and Ethiopia. Thus Chapter 2 by R. C. C. Law deals with North Africa in the period of Phoenician and Greek colonization, ca 800 to 323 B.C., Chapter 3 by the same author with North Africa in the Hellenistic and Roman periods, 323 B.C. to A.D. 305. P. L. Shinnie in Chapter 4 discusses the Nilotic Sudan and Ethiopia, ca 660 B.C. to ca A.D. 600. W. H. C. Frend writes about the Christian period in Mediterranean Africa, ca A.D. 200 to 700. Michael Brett tells the story of the Arab conquest and the rise of Islam in North Africa in Chapter 8 and in Chapter 10 surveys the Fatimid revolution (861—973) and its aftermath in North Africa. Then comes once again P. L. Shinnie with Christian Nubia in Chapter 9 and in Chapter 11 Nehemia Levtzion gives an account of the Sahara and the Sudan from the Arab conquest of the Maghrib to the rise of the Almoravids.

Thus, the only two chapters dealing wholly and directly with sub-Saharan Africa are Chapter 5 Trans-Saharan contacts and the Iron Age in West Africa and Chapter 6 by Ronald Oliver and Brian M. Fagan on the emergence of Bantu Africa. Raymond Mauny, in Chapter 5, is at his best in dealing with the early exploring voyages, on which he is an authority, and in general in the combination for this period of archaeological data and fragmentary documentary evidence. Positive is his attempt to include both opposing standpoints in matters of controversy. As it is clear from Chapter 5, North African civilization failed to make headway south of the desert, still sub-Saharan Africa was not altogether cut off from the momentous developments in world civilization. Iron-working was one momentous step from the Stone Age into history. In Africa south of the Sahara it seems that men have gone straight from the Stone Age to the use of iron as their first metal. But an emergence of a wholly African civilization had to wait until Sudanic cultivators south of the Sahara had found and developed new crops on which agriculture might be based. With agriculture and with iron technology the foundations were laid on which an African civilization was developed and then, as is shown in Chapter 6 based on currently available, unevenly spread, archaeological evidence, quickly spread over almost all the rest of sub-Saharan Africa by the expansion of the Bantu-speaking people. The theory of Bantu expansion elaborated here by two distinguished scholars, one a historian, the other an archaeologist, combines the virtues of the two disciplines. Based on inadequate evidence it, however, remains in a constant flux, subject to much argument and speculation and in need of re-evaluation in the light of new discoveries.

The principal problems of this synthesis with its broad generalizations, brought up to date by recent excavations and current research, are discussed with an impressive array of references and notes enclosed largely in the bibliographical-analytical essays, a bibliography, and an index, which will greatly facilitate the work of specialists, scholars and students, without overburdering the text. It deals with a period for which archaeological evidence is still of major importance though, from the time of Herodotus who was writing about 430 B.C., the historical evidence begins to become available for the whole of the continent north of the Sahara. For the rest of Africa, a major problem is one of documentation. Despite the expansion of African historical and archaeological studies in the present state of research into the iron age in Africa, the absence or the difficulty of discovering effective documentation given the prevailing level of research techniques and the uneven distribution of evidence, makes it by no means easy to interpret developments in the world's largest tropical land mass. Much depends on the historical perspective.

The authors draw with real understanding on the whole range of available sources and produce a synthesis in which external forces are seen interacting with autochtho-

301

nous historical developments. North Africans are seen as active and positive proponents of Phoenician, Greek, Roman and Arab influences and of the great religions and cultures of Judaism, Christianity and Islam. They adapted them to their own needs and purposes and contributed to their development.

The last but not least, in Chapter 1, appropriately entitled The legacy of prehistory: an essay on the background to the individuality of African cultures, Professor J. Desmond Clark, the editor of Volume 1 of the series, provided the fruits of the latest archaeological discoveries to sketch a picture of the emergence of man and of his biological and cultural evolution in Africa.

The present volume, as the preceding three, lives up to the tradition of Cambridge histories, traditionally regarded as setting a very high standard of scholarship. It is a very good work of reference which should be appreciated by all potential readers.

Viera Pawliková

The Cambridge History of Africa. General Editors J. D. Fage and Ronald Oliver. Volume 3. *From ca 1050 to ca 1600.* Edited by Ronald Oliver. Cambridge, Cambridge University Press 1977. xiii + 803 pp., maps, bibl.

Volume 3 of the multi-volume *Cambridge History of Africa* is actually also the third one published in a series of eight (after the volumes 4 and 5), launched as early as 1966 under the joint expert editorship of Professors Ronald Oliver and J. D. Fage and to be completed by the end of the 1970s. In accordance with the overall plan, each of the eight volumes is edited by a distinguished volume editor under the supervision and guidance of the general editors. The *Cambridge History* convention of multi-authorship in multi-volume historical publishing has also been followed in this important Cambridge venture to cover the history of the African continent from its very origins to the present day. The very scope and significance of this Cambridge project, together with the projected Unesco *General History of Africa* also planned in eight volumes, should definitely lead to the destruction of the "Dark Continent" image of Africa.

The opening and the closing dates of the present volume are the fall of Ghana and the great conquests of the Almoravids to the north and south of the western Sahara at one end, and at the other end, the period is roughly marked by the fall of Songhay and the Moroccan conquest of the Niger bend "which destroyed the political unity of the western Sudan established during more than three centuries of strong rule by successive dynasties of Mali and Songhay" (p. i). This periodization works best so far

302

as West Africa is concerned — for obvious reasons there is as yet no generally accepted scheme of periodization equally valid for Africa as a whole and, for example, the cut-off dates of the Unesco History are not the same — yet this periodization can be applied for most regions where the crucial developments marking roughly the opening and closing dates of the period were singled out. The five and a half centuries covered in this volume coincide with the transition of Iron Age cultures from their early experimental stages into mature ones characterized by complex, many-tiered political systems and elaborated long-distance trade.

In North-Eastern Africa, this period saw Egypt as the seat of an independent, sovereign power, controlled in turn by the Fatimids, then by the Ayyubids and finally by the Mamluks, and witnessed the religious and cultural consolidation throughout the northern half of Africa accompanied by the penetration and entrenchment of Islam and the parallel spread of Arabic as the language of theology and higher learning.

In the sub-Saharan Sudan, this period was rather one of penetration which saw Islam "established as a potent factor in the political and trading systems of most of the major states" (p. 2). In sub-Saharan Africa, wherever Muslim clerics, scribes and merchants, regarded as men of cosmopolitan outlook and respected for their knowledge and various worldly skills, settled, the nuclei for future expansion of Islam were established.

In East Africa, where Christian Ethiopia successfully blocked Islamic expansion inland into the Ethiopian highlands, during this period Islam spread on the narrow strip of the palm-fringed coastline and on the off-shore islands south of the Juba, reaching as far as the Zambezi.

Throughout this period, East African hinterland, the part of West Africa lying to the south of Hausaland and the whole of Africa south of the Equator, were beyond the range of Islamic influence and the main themes of historical development were internal ones until the opening by the Portuguese of the Atlantic sea-routes and of the sea-borne trade during the last century or so of the period covered in this volume. The advent of the major external influences in the shape of the Ottomans and voyaging Europeans during the sixteenth century were the crucial factors that mark the end of the period. As the editor warns us, the relatively thin and uneven nature of the surviving evidence makes the discernment of the main internal themes of historical development very difficult. Archaeology, though as yet little developed, due more to lack of research than to lack of evidence, is the best potential source of evidence for most of the period and most areas.

Nevertheless, certain broad themes can and have been discerned and traced in this symposium, such as the specific developments in state formation in the country of the Jukun, the Nupe, the Yoruba and the Edo or the theory of Bantu expansion — the successful southward progress and settlement of much of eastern, central and

303

southern Africa by Bantu food-producers — during which the interaction of pastoralism and agriculture and the spread of new farming as well as iron-using and iron-smelting techniques were aiding in the development of political and social changes.

All this is summed up in a succinct introduction by Professor Oliver, suggesting something of the basic set-up, the themes examined and the way in which historical reconstruction is presented. Then nine regional essays follow. After I. Hrbek's readable, competent discussion of Egypt, Nubia and the Eastern Deserts, there follow Tadesse Tamrat's account of Ethiopia, the Red Sea and the Horn, and Neville Chittick's survey of the East Coast, Madagascar and the Indian Ocean. H. J. Fischer and Nehemia Levtzion jointly cover the Sudan and Maghrib. Then J. D. Fage takes on with a discussion of Upper and Lower Guinea, David Birmingham deals with Central Africa from Cameroon to the Zambezi, and together with Shula Marks covers Southern Africa, and Ronald Oliver, with the East African interior, brings the story to its close.

There are some thirty-two pages of analytical bibliographical essays and forty-six pages of detailed bibliographies for the more interested and inquisitive readers. As many as twenty beautifully done maps are also excellent aids.

The Cambridge History of Africa is a good standard work of reference and, until the Unesco *General History* appears, also the best and most comprehensive available. It might be expected, if only because of the composition of the Committee responsible for its preparation and drafting, that the nature of the approach adopted in the *General History of Africa* commissioned by Unesco, the interpretation offered there, the presentation of facts and even the facts themselves may differ from what is offered here. The Unesco History may, perhaps, better reflect the present-day controversies, different methodological and ideological approaches and intellectual trends in the analysis, interpretation and reconstruction of the historical development of Africa. Also it may not be built around exactly identical concerns and interests as the *Cambridge History is*. All this may sound premature judgement, but the Unesco History, composed of a larger number of more specialized shorter chapters, seems to pay greater attention to certain aspects and factors neglected here, e.g. a deeper theoretical analysis of African political, economic and social structures during the period, and also seems to do more to bind the different chapters together in an attempt to characterize the historical development of Africa over the period.

As regards the *Cambridge History of Africa,* one criterion — that of good scholarship has been certainly met ; it is and will remain a standard reference for this period of African history and a fitting competitor and complement to the long awaited *General History of Africa* commissioned by Unesco.

Viera Pawliková

Lipschutz, Mark R.—Rasmussen, R. Kent: *Dictionary of African Historical Biography*. London, Heinemann Educational Books Ltd. 1978. 292 pp., 2 maps.

The rapid development of African historical studies since 1960s have made the study of African history perhaps the most vital and stimulating of all the areas of African studies. This expansion which has led to an enormous increase in African publishing has also made it increasingly difficult, if virtually no longer possible, to keep up with the results of the most recent historical research over the whole continent, even for an Africanist. Hence, the importance of practical reference books designed for the needs of students starting in African studies who need a quick and easy access to large body of information as well as all those who are interested but cannot often have ready access to the copious results of African historical scholarship and the enormous mass of new historical data.

This volume, originally conceived by Dr Rasmussen some ten years ago to fill in the gap in straightforward reference tools for the field of sub-Saharan African history, has been designed to serve the practical needs of both students and teachers of African history and help to make the whole mass of historical data that they face easier to manage. The approach adopted here is biographical, its serviceability to the understanding of broader historical themes having been fully demonstrated by a series of African Historical Biographies edited by Professor Obaro Ikime and published by Heinemann, a biographical series on a smaller scale published by the East African Publishing House and some separate biographies of great Africans.[1] Though not intended as a definitive biographical dictionary of African history, it contains fairly rich biographical material, in all roughly 800 biographical sketches of historical figures alphabetically arranged in dictionary form, complemented with lists of rulers, explanations of titles and similar material related directly to individual personalities. Since the primary criterion for choosing each name has been its prominence in the general literature, to the extent that academically favoured geographical regions of Africa predominate, and the bibliographical citations which

---

[1] Historical Biographies seem in vogue in African studies today. Thirteen have been planned or have already appeared in the series edited by Professor Obaro Ikime and published by Heinemann, and I understand there are some more to come.

Biographical studies of great African leaders which have been published in Africa in the series Uganda's, Kenya's and Tanzania's Famous Men, are devoted to outstanding Africans of the 19th century most of whom revealed outstanding skills in diplomacy and war to prevent European conquest, such as e.g. *Nabongo Mumia of the Baluyia* by John Osogo, *Mutesa of Uganda* by M. S. M. Kiwanuka or *Omukama Chwa II. Kabarega* by A. R. Dunbar. Other biographies include Enoch Rukare's *Nuwa Mbaguta*, John Rowe's *Kabaga Mwanga* and *Sir Apolo Kaggwa* and Michael Twaddle's *Semei Kakungulu*. See also Iliffe, J.: *Modern Tanzanians. A Volume of Biographies*. Nairobi, East African Publishing House 1973 and King, K. — Salim, A.: *Kenya Historical Biographies*. Nairobi, E.A.P.H. 1972.

follow each of the roughly 800 entries are keyed to the complete references in the bibliography at the end of the book, this *Dictionary of African Historical Biography* can also serve as a springboard to specialized studies of certain historical themes. Thus, this volume besides being a handbook to the best available specialized sources, reflects some of the main trends, approaches and biases of the African historical research and writing of the 1960s and early 1970s with its interest in famous African leaders and African responses to European colonialism. The emphasis is therefore placed on the nineteenth century and historical figures then prominent make the bulk of the volume. The year 1960 is used as a cut-off date and the figures who became prominent only after that year are not included.

The compilers were well aware of the chronological as well as geographical imbalance and have attempted to tilt at least the latter by incorporating some presently little-known African historical figures from academically less popular and investigated geographical regions of Africa or by mentioning some such names in the index of supplementary information. It indicates where information can be found on such figures who do not have their own entries, e.g. Reuben Um Nyobe, Ouezzin Coulibaly or Ahmad al-Mansur, and lists alternative names and variant spellings.

Subject Guide to Entries, divided into fifteen categories, is meant to indicate the breadth of material covered in the book and facilitate the identification of individuals representative of important historical themes. This subject index does not, however, list all the entries contained in the Dictionary. Most categories are further subdivided into three broad geographical regions — Western, Eastern and Southern Africa.

For the sake of convenience under the heading of Imperialism /V/ African responses, African leaders are divided into collaborators with Europeans and resisters to the imposition of colonial rule. It has been argued many times that such strict categorization is highly arbitrary and this attempt at categorization simply proves this. One is surprised to find Moshweshwe (or Moshoeshoe, as his name is sometimes spelt) among collaborators, considering that the existence of the now independent Lesotho totally encircled by the Republic of South Africa is a legacy of remarkable political, diplomatic and military skills of this African leader. Lobengula is missing altogether, even though some other African leaders figure in two or even three categories, namely Samori, Moshweshwe or the famous female ruler Nzinga. Strangely enough, this same Nzinga, Queen of Ndongo and Matamba in present-day Angola, correctly incorporated into the category of female rulers of Southern Africa, though she could be as well identified as an early resister to European (Portuguese) conquest, also figures among Western African migratory state leaders together with Samori Touré, Agyen Kokobo, Dogbagrigenu and 'Umar ibn Idris.

Information on Africans of course prevails, but quite a number of non-Africans whose careers had a strong bearing on African history, are also included.

Historical Dictionaries, though of varying informative value, do meet a real need and recent years have seen a boom in their publication.[2] The dangers and pitfalls that beset them are enormous but, in this particular case, the two compilers have admirably managed to avoid them and provided us with a sound and reliable work of reference, certainly the fruit of years of meticulous labour. It is a most welcome addition to the all too small a corpus of straightforward practical reference books on African history, a ready and quick reference source for all those prominent persons (and events) in Africa's history about whom a person already familiar with in broad contours may wish to refresh his memory, or about whom a person not already acquainted with can pick up enough factual information and biographical details to satisfy a limited need or to furnish him with leads from which he can track down further information.

Viera Pawliková

Steinhart, Edward I.: *Conflict and Collaboration. The Kingdoms of Western Uganda, 1890—1907.* Princeton, New Jersey, Princeton University Press 1977. 311 pp.

As the title implies, the book is intended as a contribution to the long-standing argument over the response of African peoples to the imposition of colonial rule. Since the announcement, some fifteen years ago, of the theme of African resistance and protest as a major concern of African historians, an extensive research has been conducted in this field with some noteworthy results. Achievements of East African historiography in research of early anti-colonial resistance and protest movements have been connected with the nationalist interpretation of the Dar es Salaam school. Though the approach adopted by this historical school has not overlooked the possibility that Africans were willing to employ multiple strategy and in fact were continually reassessing their options in the light of changing political realities, it nevertheless concentrated on the important movements of resistance and rebellion and the treatment of defection, submission and collaboration as aspects of these rebellions has been minimized.

The study of collaboration is, no doubt, politically sensitive. Simultaneously there has appeared a dangerous tendency to a semantic obfuscation which has led some historians to strip collaboration in the African context of its overtones of opportunism, moral corruption and political self-seeking, to ignore the genuine reasons for collaboration and to camouflage the activities of African agents of the Europeans in

---

[2] A series of African Historical Dictionaries has been published jointly by Metuchen, N. J. and Scarecrow Press, London, each volume to cover a different African country. The twelfth volume in the series, published in 1977, was on Sierra Leone, others are to follow.

positive, often laudatory, terms by portraying them as astute accomodators, modernizers or innovators. Collaborating Baganda chiefs, among others, have been treated in this fashion and have been described variously as revolutionaries or loyalists in the high places, who helped to carry through the process of adaptation of Western culture and technology and of the transformation of Buganda into a modern state.[1]

The views strictly contrasting resistance to collaboration and resisting societies to collaborating ones have been successfully challenged and in a number of studies of the drama of colonial penetration and African reaction to it it has been argued that resistance to and collaboration with the European colonizers were not diametrically opposed but were part of a single experiment by the peoples concerned to come to terms with the new situation. Any study of resistance should also include collaboration and neutrality which are the situational counterparts of resistance at any point of time.

Dr Steinhart has been known for his critique of the prevailing interpretation of early African resistance to colonial penetration and control, identified with work of Dr Terence Ranger and the so-called Dar es Salaam historical school. He has expounded his views in a number of provocative articles touching upon the interpretative apparatus of the nationalist school and the nationalist interpretation of protest with "its misinterpretation of anti-colonial manifestations as nationalist or proto-nationalist in sentiment and its disregard of other sources of anti-colonial feeling and ideology" and with its "tendency to ignore or misrepresent responses to colonial intrusion which do not conform to the themes of resistance and protest".[2] Refuting the nationalist interpretation of protest and the interpretative apparatus of the nationalist school, he has offered a counter interpretation based on a non-nationalist, anti-colonial, revolutionary, anti-foreign, and anti-authoritarian sentiment, which is held to be better suited to explain the popular and persistent bases of African protest and the implications of resistance and protest for later social and political movements.

Quite naturally, the study under review can thus be seen as a final elaboration of Dr Steinhart's previous ideas on collaboration and resistance placed within a broader class analysis. As is briefly stated in the Preface, this study of collaboration and

------

[1] Low, D. A.: *Conversion, Revolution and the New Régime in Buganda, 1860—1900*. In *Buganda in Modern History*. Berkeley—Los Angeles, University of California Press 1971, pp. 13—54; Wright, Michael: *Buganda in the Heroic Age*. Nairobi, Oxford University Press 1971.

[2] Steinhart, Edward I.: *The Nyangire Rebellion in Bunyoro, 1907: Anti-Colonial Resistance and Nationalism*. In: Asian and African Studies (Bratislava), *12*, 1976, p. 45 and 46 respectively. See also Steinhart, E. I.: *Primary Collaboration in Ankole*. University of East Africa Social Science Council Conference, 1968—1969, History Papers (Kampala, Makerere Institute of Social Research, n.d.), pp. 191—197 and Steinhart, Edward I.: *Resistance and Nationalism: A Critique of the Ranger Hypothesis* (unpublished).

conflict is intended as an attempt to gain insight into the characters and policies of African political élites who chose actively to cooperate with the arrival of European, in this case, British, imperialism. The means by which powerful external forces were accommodated to the domestic political scene by the leaders of the local African polity is the process called collaboration. Collaboration, in this interpretation, means an active policy of cooperation and compromise, not submission, defeat, or resignation. In the author's definition, "in an African context, freed from the derogatory connotations and nuances of moral corruption assumed by the term in the wake of the European experience of Quisling and Petain, collaboration can be understood as one option among several open to African leadership in the situation of crisis and conflict engendered by the scramble for African territory and the colonization of the continent by the European powers" (p. viii).

Having arrived at this particular definition of the concept of collaboration, collaboration is used as a tool for analysis of varying policies in response to the advent of colonial rule among the political élites of the three kingdoms of Western Uganda — Bunyoro, Ankole and Toro which ultimately culminated by 1901 in the establishment of regimes of collaboration in all the three kingdoms. The overwhelming military and technological superiority of the invading imperialist forces plus the African leadership inability to arouse and sustain popular support from the commoners coupled with the defection, submission and eventual active collaboration of the most important chiefs ultimately undermined the military resistance and allowed for the establishment of a regime of collaboration.

An outline of the nineteenth-century historical background on the eve of imperial penetration is given together with an analysis of the social and political structure of the three related lacustrine societies, since "the class structure of lacustrine society and the political schisms and divisions within these three states are the keys to understanding how regimes of collaboration came to be established" (p. 209). "Although the personalities and characters of the leading protagonists of the contending policies of resistance and collaboration cannot be minimized, the social and economic structures in which they operated were crucial to the determination of the responses to colonialism that they adopted" (ibid.).

Despite the pronounced resolve to distinguish class differences as a factor in determining whether an individual would resist or collaborate, the author's concerns are with the ruling class and the critical choices facing African political leadership rather than with peasants and their refusals to submit to colonial domination. A comparative method known as "controlled comparison" which was developed in ethnographic and sociological research was adapted to this historical research project and, by this comparative method, the responses to colonial impact and the establishment of colonial domination in the three kingdoms of Western Uganda were used to fill out a theory of colonial collaboration. The focus adopted here certainly allows a better understanding of the collaborators and the politics of collaboration than of African attempts to prevent colonial domination. Indeed, less space has been devoted in the volume to the study of resistance and its failure is seen as a failure of political leadership to raise popular support and a significant movement among the populace and as a function of the success of an alternative strategy by the African political leadership. The development of the collaborationist theme has enabled the author to view particular instances of African resistance, such as e.g. the Nyangire rebellion of 1907 in Bunyoro, from a perspective very different from that of a nationalist historian of the 1960s, namely the interpretation advanced by Professor Godfrey Uzoigwe.[3] For him, "in general, each of the three regimes of collaboration involved not just the creation of a collaborative mechanism in the form of a recognized and rewarded hierarchy of appointed chiefs; it also involved a continual renegotiation of the terms and conditions of chiefly cooperation. This renegotiation, often accompanied by conflict, might well be deemed 'resistance' by those inclined to emphasize the heroic elements in African behavior. Whatever the label, the process was one of constant maneuver for political advantage: a politics of collaboration" (p. 258).

Based on all kinds of available factual material, vernacular as well as English-language sources, on the original researches carried out in the field and in the archives, *Conflict and Collaboration* is a competent, well-written and readable, provocative and thought-provoking attempt at the development of a new African historical perspective on the much-debated theme of African response to the imposition of colonial rule. In this respect, *Conflict and Collaboration* raises a number of very interesting questions for future research. A book of this quality is a fruitful source of knowledge and of scholarly argument and polemics. Its strength lies in the very careful collation of traditions and of documentary evidence, the fruit of a number of years work, of which nearly half were spent in Uganda. It sheds new light on subtler ingredients in motivations, intentions and initiatives of collaborating African political leadership in the process of the establishment and functioning of the regimes of collaboration in the three kingdoms of Western Uganda, though sometimes perhaps to the detriment of other aspects of the complex phenomena, neglecting somehow other options open to the African populace — the spirit of unrest, discontent, of constant resistance and defiance which operated beneath the narrow circle of collaborating chiefly establishment and manifested itself in varied forms of

---

[3] See Uzoigwe, G. N.: *The Kyanyangire, 1907: Passive Revolt against British Overrule.* In: Ogot, B. A. (Ed.): *War and Society in Africa.* Ten Studies. London, Frank Cass 1972, pp. 179—214, which quotes Ranger's and A. B. Davidson's ideas as inspiration. Also in Uzoigwe, G. N.: *Revolution and Revolt in Bunyoro-Kitara.* Two Studies. (Makerere History Papers No. 2.) Kampala, Longman of Uganda 1970.

African refusals to submit to colonialism. Or could it be, as Professor Ranger once argued, that our Western colleagues really have a better grasp of collaborators?[4]

Viera Pawliková

Wauthier, Claude: *The Literature and Thought of Modern Africa.* Second English Edition. Preface by Tchicaya U Tam'si. London, Heinemann Educational Books 1978. 415 pp.

The virtues of this enlarged second English language edition of a highly successful survey of writing by African intellectuals, originally published in French in 1964 by Editions du Seuil as *L'Afrique des Africains: Inventaire de la Négritude,* are many. It is equally interesting and rewarding to readers without any knowledge of African writing over the past three or more decades as it is to specialists on African literatures.

The great merit of the original book was its success in examining the developing literacies, literatures and thought of sub-Saharan Africa in their political and intellectual context and in indicating the immense potentialities of African literary studies, the numerous facets and openings waiting anxiously to be explored. In this regard this has been perhaps the most competent work yet published on modern African literatures and thought which has had an influential effect on the study of African literatures. The author has admirably succeeded in seeing the Africa of the Africans, this vast and complex domain, in its manifold political, economic, sociological and cultural dimensions and in blending myriads of essential facts into the main structure of the book, to draw a well-balanced and solidly grounded picture of African cultural revival. To understand more fully the whole process of Africa's emancipation in the study of the African cultural renaissance, the author has not limited himself to its purely literary manifestations, but developing literatures of sub-Saharan Africa have been examined in the more general context of the whole African cultural revival alongside works by other African intellectuals — politicians, historians, ethnologists, economists, jurists and theologians, who have all played a role in the awakening of Africa.

---

[4] "... to my mind Russian scholars have assessed the significance of African resistance to colonial rule in a more accurate fashion than their Western colleagues. The former have a better understanding of the 'resisters'; the latter have a better grasp of the 'collaborators'. But if we are fully to understand the nature of African reactions to colonial rule, we must take account of collaboration and resistance alike." See Ranger, T. O.: *African Reactions to the Imposition of Colonial Rule in East and Central Africa.* In: *Colonialism in Africa 1870—1960.* Volume 1 The History and Politics of Colonialism 1870—1914. Edited by L. H. Gann and Peter Duignan. Cambridge, Cambridge University Press 1969, pp. 303—304.

This approach has resulted in an original study of the modern trend of nationalist thought as expressed in the languages of the former colonial powers, from its beginnings in anti-slavery pamphlets of the eighteenth century to the new wave of African intellectuals of the after independence period.

Chronologically, the original study was limited in time to cover the period from the beginning of the Second World War to May 1963, the date when a summit conference of the thirty-two independent African states which founded the Organization of African Unity took place in Addis Abeba. This date was considered the closing point for the main substance of the book, though the text was up-dated to early 1966 in respect to major political events. Works of over 150 authors were examined in the three parts of the original study: Return to Origins, Revolt and The New Africa. To this new edition, the author has now added a long, roughly seventy-page long postscript, quite appropriately entitled After Independence, touching upon the problems of the last decade and a half in Africa, that have seen a prodigious growth of modern African literatures in European languages. These years, while seeing a lot of political upheavals on the African continent causing a whole plethora of good and bad prognostications, have at the same time given a great impetus to the African literatures and have been to the African intelligentsia and writers a major source of inspiration and reflection. But while the writers of the independent African countries have been facing the problems of the New Africa and its newly-won freedom and their writing often reflects their growing disillusionment with the ups and downs of African independence, South African literature, more often than not written from exile, is still concerned with the task of liberating South Africa; it is a cry against the oppressive nature of the blackman's existence in the Republic of South Africa, Zimbabwe and, not so long ago, also in the former Portuguese territories of Angola and Mozambique. Defining the role of the intellectual as a writer, teacher, spokesman and liberator, this study settles and examines the role of the black intellectual as a "spiritual guide to a political revolution in Africa", his obligation to vouch for the national liberation, which is seen "first and foremost an act of culture". One characteristic common to most African writing has thus been its political commitment and continuing protest.

A crucial question for originating African literatures has been, no doubt, that of language. "The language destiny of Africa" is quite correctly touched upon here, since the problem of a national language as an authentic means of national expression has proved one of great concern to African intellectuals. African intelligentsia have, however, attached great importance not only to the problem of keeping the languages of the colonialists as official languages after independence, of equal importance have been their attachment to the rehabilitation of all that seemed of value in African social institutions, their effort to recover the precious ingredients of African culture, the creative traditions and challenges of their societies, and to shed new light on African history.

312

The study deals with a variety of topics. The inclusion of West Indian and Caribbean work plus the modest excursions into the American Negro writing and occasional forays into the works of the pioneers of the African intelligentsia, such as ex-slaves Ignatius Sancho or Olaudah Equiano, known as Gustavus Vassa, or a pioneer West African nationalist and political philosopher James Africanus B. Horton, gives an introductory survey of how modern African literatures began to develop. A discussion of négritude, its origins and development, revals the divergent views held by African writers on its authenticity and examines the recent offensive against the concept. Its main preoccupations are, however, with social, political, economic and cultural problems of Africa and how they impinge on the works of African authors. It tries to suggest something of African intellectuals' response to the traditions and challenges of their societies and the world in prose, poetry, drama, political works and pamphlets, ethnological, economic, linguistic and historical studies, something of their way of feeling towards the realities of existence, of perceiving their environment, its problems and destinies. It asks some key questions. Some of its analyses and judgements on different aspects of the awakening of Africa and on the reactions of cultivated Africans to colonialism, racism, foreign domination and the complexities of the newly-won independence, make one aware of new problems and nuances.

The style of the study is extremely lively. Brilliant insights and truths are conveyed behind often provocative labels which he displays throughout the book.

One can go on mentioning the specific beauties and virtues of this work but, it is doubtful whether by so doing, one can add significantly to the general impression that it is a well-written book which owes a good deal of its effect to the author's irresistible enthusiasm, sense of interest and sympathy for the subject and felicity of language. The study is equally important to those who have followed the progress and development of modern African literatures from its very beginnings as to an unenlightened reader; it provides stimulating ideas and positive suggestions for further thought.

Viera Pawliková

BOOKS RECEIVED

Ashtor, Eli: *A Social and Economic History of the Near East in the Middle Ages*. London, William Collins Sons and Co. Ltd. 1976. 384 pp.

Atsız, B.: *Das Osmanische Reich um die Mitte des 17. Jahrhunderts. Nach den Chroniken des Vecîhî (1637—1660) und des Mehmed Halifa (1633—1660)*. München, Dr. Dr. R. Trofenik 1977. CXXXIII + 144 + 123 + 108 pp. Beiträge zur Kenntnis Südosteuropas und des Nahen Orients, XXI. Band.

Bidwell, Robin: *Travellers in Arabia*. London, The Hamlyn Publishing Group Limited 1976. 224 pp.

Binswanger, K.: *Untersuchungen zum Status der Nichtmuslime im Osmanischen Reich des 16. Jahrhunderts*. Mit einer Neudefinition des Begriffes "Ḍimma". München, Dr. Dr. Rudolf Trofenik 1977. 418 pp.

The Cambridge History of Africa. Volume 2. *From ca 500 B.C. to A.D. 1050*. Edited by J. D. Fage. Cambridge, Cambridge University Press 1978. xvii + 840 pp., 67 figures, 38 plates.

Casparis de, J. G.: *Indonesian Palaeography. A History of Writing in Indonesia from the Beginning to C. A.D. 1500*. Handbuch der Orientalistik, Dritte Abteilung, Vierter Band, Erste Lieferung. Leiden/Köln, E. J. Brill 1975. 96 pp., 10 plates.

Chrestomathie der modernen arabischen Prosaliteratur. Bearbeitet und herausgegeben von Manfred Fleischhammer und Wiebke Walther. Leipzig, VEB Verlag Enzyklopädie 1978. 277 pp.

Cvetkova, Bistra A.: *Les institutions ottomanes en Europe*. Wiesbaden, F. Steiner Verlag 1978. 134 pp.

Davidson, Basil: *Africa in Modern History. The Search for a New Society*. London, Allen Lane 1978. 431 pp.

Dudbridge, Glen: *The Legend of Miao-shan*. London, Oxford University 1978. 128 pp.

Eight Chinese Plays from the Thirteenth Century to the Present. Translated with an Introduction by William Dolby. London, Paul Elek 1978. 164 pp.

Elçin, Şükrü: *Halk adebiyatı araştırmaları*. Ankara, Dsi Basım Ve Foto-filim İşletme Müdürlüğü Matbaası 1977. V + 367 pp.

Fenech, Edward: *Contemporary Journalistic Maltese. An Analytical and Comparative Study*. Leiden, E. J. Brill 1978. XVIII + 251 pp.

Frank, Gerd: *Die Herrscher der Osmanen. Aufstieg und Untergang eines Weltreiches*. Wien—Düsseldorf, Econ Verlag 1977. 347 pp.

Der fromme Sultan Bayezid. Die Geschichte seiner Herrschaft (1481—1512) nach den altosmanischen Chroniken des Oruç und des Anonymus Hanivaldanus. Übersetzt, eingeleitet und erklärt von Richard F. Kreutel. Graz—Wien—Köln, Styria Verlag 1978. 311 pp.

Gibbs, Donald A.: *Subject and Author Index to Chinese Literature Monthly (1951—1976)*. New Haven, Far East Publications, Yale University 1978. 173 pp.

Gibbs, Donald A.—Li, Yun-chen: *A Bibliography of Studies and Translations of Modern Chinese Literature 1918—1942*. Harvard University, East Asian Research Center 1975. 239 pp.

Gökbilgin, M. Tayyib: *Osmanlı Müesseseleri, Teşkilâtı ve Medeniyeti Tarihine Genel Bakış*. İstanbul, Edebiyat Fakültesi Matbaası 1977. 194 pp. İstanbul Universitesi Edebiyat Fakültesi Yayınları, No. 2272.

Graaf de, H. J.—Kennedy, J.—Scott, W. H.: *Geschichte*. Handbuch der Orientalistik, Dritte Abteilung, Erster Band, Zweite Lieferung. Leiden—Köln, E. J. Brill 1977. VII + 247 pp., map.

Gugler, Josef—Flanagan, William G.: *Urbanization and Social Change in West Africa*. Cambridge —London—New York—Melbourne, Cambridge University Press 1978. xvii + 237 pp.

Hana, Corinna: *Sun Yat Sen's Parteiorgan Chien-She (1919—1920)*. Münchener Ostasiatische Studien. Band 14. Wiesbaden, Franz Steiner Verlag 1978. 430 pp.

Hazai, György: *Kurze Einführung in das Studium der türkischen Sprache*. Budapest, Akadémiai Kiadó 1978. 190 pp.

314

Hinrup, Hans J.: *An Index to "Chinese Literature" 1951—1976*. London, Curzon Press 1978. 231 pp.

Ibn Isḥāq: *Das Leben des Propheten*. Aus dem Arabischen übertragen und bearbeitet von Cernot Rotter. Tübingen—Basel, Horst Erdmann Verlag 1976. 287 pp. (Bibliothek arabischer Klassiker, Band 1.)

Khoury, Raif Georges (Ed.): *Asad ibn Mūsā, Kitāb al-Zuhd*. Wiesbaden, Otto Harrassowitz 1976. 124 pp.

Korean Studies. Volume 2. The Center for Korean Studies. Honolulu, The University Press of Hawaii 1978. 206 pp.

Krüger, Eberhard: *Zum Verhältnis von Autor und Werk bei dem modernpersischen Erzähler Ṣādeq Hedáyat*. Islamkundliche Untersuchungen, Band 42. Freiburg, Klaus Schwarz Verlag 1977. 158 pp.

Kwon, Hyogmyon: *Basic Chinese-Korean Character Dictionary*. Wiesbaden, Otto Harrassowitz Verlag 1978. XXVI + 556 pp.

Lean, Geoffrey: *Rich World, Poor World*. London, George Allen and Unwin 1978. 352 pp.

Lee, Ki-moon: *Geschichte der koreanischen Sprache*. Deutsche Übersetzung von Bruno Lewin. Wiesbaden, Dr. Ludwig Reichert Verlag 1977. 326 pp.

Lipschutz, Mark L.—Rasmussen R. Kent: *Dictionary of African Historical Biography*. London, Heinemann Educational Books Ltd. 1978. 292 pp., 2 maps.

Majer, H. G.: *Vorstudien zur Geschichte der İlmiye im Osmanischen Reich*. I. Zu Uşakizâde, seiner Familie und seinem Zeyl-i Şakayık. München, Dr. Dr. Rudolf Trofenik 1978. IV + 347 pp.

Münke, Wolfgang: *Die klassische chinesische Mythologie*. Stuttgart, Ernst Klett Verlag 1976. 338 pp.

Pidgin and Creole Linguistics. Edited by Albert Valdman. Bloomington—London, Indiana University Press 1977. 399 pp.

Revolutionary Literature in China. An Anthology. Selected and Introduced by John Berninghausen and Ted Huters. New York, M. E. Sharpe, Inc. 1976. 103 pp.

Rickett, Adele Austin (Ed.): *Chinese Approaches to Literature from Confucius to Liang Ch'i-ch'ao*. Princeton, New Jersey, Princeton University Press 1978. 267 pp.

Ronan, Colin A.: *The Shorter Science and Civilisation in China*. Volume 1. Cambridge, Cambridge University Press 1978. 326 pp.

Steinhart, Edward I.: *Conflict and Collaboration. The Kingdoms of Western Uganda, 1890—1907*. Princeton, New Jersey, Princeton University Press 1977. 311 pp., bibl., maps.

Sugar, Peter F.: *Southeastern Europe under Ottoman Rule 1354—1804*. Seattle and London, University of Washington Press 1977. xiii + 365 pp. A History of East Central Europe, Vol. V.

Teply, Karl: *Die kaiserliche Großbotschaft an Sultan Murad IV. im Jahre 1628. Des Freiherrn Hans Ludwig von Kuefsteins Fahrt zur Hohen Pforte*. Wien, Verlag A. Schendl 1976. 151 pp., 12 tables.

Türk Dünyası El Kitabı. Ankara, Türk Kültürü Araştırma Enstitüsü 1976. VIII + 1452 pp., map.

Turkologischer Anzeiger 3. Wien, Orientalisches Institut 1977. 217 pp.

Tursun Bey: *Tarih-i Ebü'l-Feth*. Hazırlayan Mertol Tulum. Istanbul, Baha Matbaası 1977. XXXII + 272 pp., map. Istanbul Fetih Cemiyeti, 74.

Utas, Bo: *A Persian Sufi Poem: Vocabulary and Terminology* (Concordance frequency word-list, statistical survey, Arabic loan-words and Sufi-religious terminology in Tarīq ut-tahqīq). Scandinavian Institute of Asian Studies Monograph Series, No. 36. London—Malmö, Curzon Press Ltd 1978. 214 pp + 53 ar.

Vaughan, Dorothy M.: *Europe and the Turk. A Pattern of Alliances 1350—1700*. Reprint. New York, AMS Press 1976. viii + 305 pp.

Wauthier, Claude: *The Literature and Thought of Modern Africa*. Second English Edition. Preface by Tchicaya U Tam'si. London, Heinemann Educational Books 1978. 415 pp.

Wirtschaftsgeschichte des Vorderen Orients in islamischer Zeit. Teil 1. Leiden—Köln, E. J. Brill 1977. 405 pp. Handbuch der Orientalistik, Hrsg. von B. Spuler. Erste Abteilung, VI. Band, 6. Abschnitt, Teil 1.

315